Reducing Inequality for Shared Growth in China

Reducing Inequality for Shared Growth in China

Strategy and Policy Options for Guangdong Province

THE WORLD BANK
Washington, D.C.

ISBN: 978-0-8213-8484-8
eISBN: 978-0-8213-8501-2
DOI: 10.1596/978-0-8213-8484-8

Library of Congress Cataloging-in-Publication Data

Reducing inequality for shared growth in China : strategy and policy options for Guangdong province.
    p. cm.
  Includes bibliographical references and index.
  ISBN 978-0-8213-8484-8 — ISBN 978-0-8213-8501-2 (electronic)
  1. Guangdong Sheng (China)—Social conditions—21st century. 2. Guangdong Sheng (China)—Social policy. 3. Guangdong Sheng (China)—Social planning. 4. City planning—China—Guangdong Sheng. 5. Education—China—Guangdong Sheng. 6. Social change—China—Guangdong Sheng. 7. Guangdong Sheng (China)—Politics and government—21st century. I. World Bank.
  HN740.G83R43 2010
  307.3'4095127—dc22

                                                                    2010030042

Cover photo: Panorama Media Limited
Cover design: Naylor Design, Washington, DC

Contents

Boxes

Map

Figures

Tables

Foreword

To narrow the gap between the rich and the poor and to achieve common prosperity have been a noble dream of human society for millennia; they are also a part of the pursuit of equality and justice in various cultures and societies. More than two thousand years ago, *The Book of Rites*, a Confucian classic, already described a society of "grand unity," which contained basic thoughts about fairness, sharing, and social harmony. Today, the gap between the rich and the poor is a problem faced not only by Guangdong Province or China, but also by many developing and industrial countries. Indeed, it is a long-term challenge of human society. Therefore, narrowing this gap in Guangdong will not only contribute to Guangdong's own scientific and harmonious development, but also offer an opportunity to explore and experiment with innovative ideas and practices, which will provide lessons and experiences for other provinces of China and other countries of the world.

At the end of 2007, not long after I came to work in Guangdong, World Bank President Robert Zoellick and I reached an agreement on a joint study on reducing the urban-rural disparity in Guangdong. Over the past year or so, the World Bank gave this study very high priority, expedited the process, and devoted extraordinary efforts to make it a success. More than 20 experts in various fields were selected to participate on the

World Bank team, and more than 10 field missions were conducted to gather data and information on the urban-rural disparity and to provide high-quality analysis and advisory services to Guangdong based on empirical evidence. Similarly, the CPC Guangdong Provincial Committee and the Provincial Government also attached great importance to this collaboration with the World Bank. Excellent support and collaboration were provided; many government agencies and experts in related fields from the province participated in this joint study. In short, this project has had unprecedented high-level, broad-ranging, and innovative international cooperation. Juan José Daboub, former World Bank Managing Director, considered this one of the most successful World Bank knowledge collaborations in China, and Guangdong one of World Bank's best partners.

The joint effort by the two sides has now borne fruit that is represented by high-quality research. Based on rich international experiences and a unique international perspective, the report provides in-depth analysis of the urban-rural disparity in Guangdong, as well as major challenges and opportunities to address these challenges. Based on these analyses, the report puts forward an innovative "three-pillar" strategic framework: eliminating absolute poverty, reducing inequality of opportunities, and containing inequality of outcomes. The report also makes a series of policy recommendations concerning the relocation of industries and labor, developing rural financial service, reforming the rural land system, and improving basic education and medical services in rural areas. These recommendations are constructive and forward looking, reflecting the rich experience of the World Bank in reducing poverty and narrowing urban-rural disparities.

Since the beginning of reform three decades ago, the Guangdong Provincial Party Committee and the Provincial Government have made poverty reduction a priority. Measures and programs have been implemented, such as those reducing poverty through human capital development, through partnerships between the more developed regions and less developed regions, through production-oriented poverty alleviation measures, and through the establishment of the minimum living allowance system. As a result, the percentage of the population living in poverty has been falling, the standard of living of poor people has seen continuous improvement, and the basic living conditions as well the conditions for economic activities in rural areas are improving gradually. Between 2001 and 2007, the number of people living in poverty in the province dropped from 4.11 million to 3.16 million, a significant accomplishment.

However, we are also keenly aware that—as a result of multiple constraints such as geographic location, natural endowment, economic foundation, history, culture, and institutions—considerable imbalance still exists in Guangdong's social and economic development. This imbalance is reflected most acutely by the growing development and income disparities among different regions within the province, between urban and rural areas, and between different population groups. Reducing these disparities has become a major challenge that must be addressed earnestly to implement the scientific development concept in the province.

Guangdong is at a critical juncture in its transition to a trajectory of scientific development. In response to the changing domestic and international situations, the Provincial Party Committee and the Provincial Government are vigorously implementing a coordinated regional development strategy and striving to narrow the urban-rural disparity and build a harmonious society. The publication of the resulting report from the World Bank–Guangdong joint research project will not only record the hard work and wisdom of both sides, but also certainly provide significant guidance and inspiration to Guangdong's effort in reducing urban-rural disparities. Many comments and suggestions in the report are very pertinent and insightful. Taking into consideration the reality of Guangdong, I believe that the future poverty reduction work in the province should be pushed forward with a focus on the following four areas:

- First, we need to treat the development-oriented poverty reduction strategy characterized by "household-level planning and individual level responsibility" as a major social and economic development strategy. To help people in need is a fine tradition of the Chinese people, and development-oriented poverty reduction is an important measure to reduce the number of people living in poverty. We are preparing to implement the development-oriented poverty reduction strategy characterized by household-level planning and individual-level responsibility, and a special meeting will be held to make related arrangements and give instructions. This strategy takes a "one-on-one assistance" approach. Specifically, it will match the 3,409 poor villages and 700,000 poor households (per capita annual income below 1,500 yuan) in the less developed regions of Guangdong with entities in the more developed Pearl River Delta region; government agencies at the provincial, municipal, and county levels; public service units; as well as enterprises with resources and willingness to participate. A tailored development strategy will be designed for each poor village, and a specific method will be developed for every household. The goal is to fundamentally change the situation of the poor villages and lift the poor households out of poverty within three years. Such an approach can allocate resources in government agencies, public service units, and enterprises more directly and accurately; reduce resource waste; and improve targeting for poverty eradication. This innovative approach for poverty reduction is conducive for mobilizing resources from all sectors of the society, increasing income of the poor households, improving the general environment for development of the poor villages, and guiding all social sectors toward the goal of common prosperity.

- Second, we need to give high priority to the "dual transfer" of industry and labor. The urban-rural income gap is, to a great extent, due to the inequality in employment opportunities for urban and rural residents. The dual transfer of industry and labor aims at achieving a more efficient allocation of resources and further integration of urban and rural development, which will lead to a higher level of equality of opportunities and help narrow the urban-rural income gap. At the same time, we also recognize that the industries and labor are elements of the market economy and their movements and relocations are governed by intrinsic rules of the market. Therefore, when promoting the dual transfer, we will follow the principle of "government guidance and market-led operation" and obey the fundamental rules of the market. We shall optimize the spatial allocation of resources by speeding up the industrial transfer; achieve regional integration in the Pearl River Delta; and enhance the spillover effect from the Pearl River Delta to the East and West Wings, and the mountainous region. We shall strengthen vocational training for rural laborers and improve their ability to be employed in nonfarming jobs. In this way, more rural residents can participate in the industrialization and urbanization process and benefit from the overall economic development.

- Third, we need to deepen reforms in income distribution. Sound and fair income distribution is an important part of the institutional design for reducing inequality in opportunities and containing inequality in outcomes. Efficiency and fairness need to be properly balanced in both primary distribution and secondary distribution of income, and secondary distribution should pay more attention to fairness and let taxation and public finance play a greater role in narrowing disparities between rural and urban areas and between rich and poor people. More efforts should be made to increase the income of low-income people, raise the proportion of middle-income people, effectively adjust excessively high income, and prohibit illegal income. In this way, a more reasonable and orderly income distribution structure will be formed.

- Fourth, we need to push for equalization of basic public services between urban and rural areas. Equalization in basic public services is an issue of social justice as well as an important means for containing inequality in outcomes. Difference in individual incomes is an unavoidable reality, but more equality in people's access to basic public services can greatly reduce the gap between the rich and the poor. Priority should be given to education: we shall strive for more balanced development in compulsory education between urban and rural areas. We also need to speed up efforts to create a basic health care system covering both urban and rural residents and to make sure that farmers have access to basic health services. We need to establish an integrated social security system covering both urban and rural residents and continuously expand coverage and increase the level of protection. Moreover, we need to improve housing conditions for rural residents and improve rural infrastructure to create better living conditions as well as a better environment for economic activities. In summary, our goal is to ensure that "students have good education, workers have fair incomes, the sick receive medical care, the old are taken care of, and all people have reasonable housing." In fact, while discussing with the World Bank this research project on urban-rural disparities, we also initiated the planning for achieving equalization of public service between urban and rural areas by 2020—which will contribute to the narrowing of urban-rural disparities.

I believe that, through efforts in the above areas, significant progress will be accomplished in reducing urban-rural disparities and promoting balanced regional development in Guangdong in a few years. By that time, we will invite the World Bank experts back to Guangdong to evaluate our work and give further guidance.

Reducing urban-rural disparities is an arduous long-term task that requires persistent efforts from various parties concerned. This cooperation between Guangdong and the World Bank marks a very good beginning. I look forward to more and deeper exchanges and cooperation in a broader range of areas in the future, and to continuously exploring new modalities of collaboration. These efforts will undoubtedly make new contributions to the poverty reduction undertaking in Guangdong.

Wang Yang
Member of the Political Bureau, Communist Party of China
CPC Central Committee
Secretary of the CPC Guangdong Province

Foreword

This book is a product of the World Bank's advisory services to the Guangdong Provincial Government. The work was initiated when the President of the World Bank, Robert Zoellick, visited Guangdong in December 2007. During the visit, Party Secretary Wang Yang of Guangdong province highlighted the increasing challenge of inequality and regional disparity of economic growth, and they welcomed the analytical and technical support of the World Bank in understanding the issues and recommending a way forward. I am very pleased to see that, benefiting from the excellent collaboration and support from the Policy Research Office of the CPC Guangdong Provincial Committee and the Guangdong Provincial Department of Finance, the World Bank team was able to propose a framework to approach this complex set of issues and to offer specific policy recommendations. I was honored to present the Vice Presidential Unit Team Award to the task teams in early 2010. It was the first time that we presented such an award to our counterpart teams.

After three decades of impressive economic growth and poverty reduction, China now faces the challenge of ensuring that its strong growth is shared more broadly and equally among its population. The economic downturn caused by the global crisis in late 2008 may have forced a focus on short-term actions to stimulate the economy and maintain growth;

however, it is important to recognize that longer-term issues, such as unbalanced growth, will determine the vitality of the economy and the cohesion of society.

Despite being China's leading growth powerhouse, Guangdong province—like other provinces—faces major challenges in tackling inequality, and the World Bank team examined these along three dimensions: absolute poverty, inequality of opportunity, and inequality of outcomes. *Absolute poverty*, which deprives individuals of the minimum means for basic living, remains a significant concern in rural Guangdong. *Inequality of opportunity*, which denies individuals the same opportunities to pursue their life goals, is also widespread, as evidenced by disparities in access to education and health services. *Inequality of outcomes*, which is reflected in disparities among households and individuals in terms of income and wealth, has risen to an alarming level. Some inequality of outcomes is inevitable and even good for efficiency and growth—particularly when inequality of income reflects uneven performance among individuals. However, inequality of outcomes can become harmful to growth when it is too high and generates substantial inequality of opportunity and distortion in market and public institutions, threatening social stability.

The Guangdong authorities have recognized the urgent need to address these development challenges, and this joint exercise of the World Bank and Guangdong teams aims to inform the province's overall strategy for fostering more pro-poor, equitable growth. For such a strategy to work in practice, it must be founded on evidence-based analyses that take into consideration Guangdong's particular situation, as well as lessons from other countries and regions around the world. This study is designed to provide such analyses, focusing on key areas that were jointly identified by the Guangdong authorities and the World Bank study team.

The study proposed a three-pillared strategy to address inequalities in Guangdong province.

- First, the government could assume the responsibility of eliminating absolute poverty through its social assistance program. The minimum living allowance (*Dibao*) system could be expanded to better address the needs of poor and vulnerable people in Guangdong. The system can be implemented with more fiscal inputs, better defined financing responsibilities, improved targeting mechanisms, and more transparent governance approaches.

- Second, the government could help boost rural income by ensuring more equal opportunities: promoting rural labor transfer to nonfarming jobs, improving investment climate in less developed regions, deepening rural finance reform, and providing better protection of the land rights of the rural population.
- Third, the government could help invest in people by ensuring more equal provision of services in basic education, skills development, and health care. Further reform of the intergovernmental fiscal system is essential to the success of these efforts.

Inequality is clearly related to spatial imbalance of growth, and more balanced growth is desirable. However, two centuries of economic development have shown that spatial disparities in income and production are inevitable. In fact, while the concentration of economic activities in the Pearl River Delta region of Guangdong is a key factor behind the regional and urban-rural disparities within the province, it has come with the gains of an agglomeration economy—an important source of productivity growth. Because economic growth cannot be expected to spread evenly across space, Guangdong will need to reduce inequality and promote development on the basis of spatially unbalanced growth.

Building on its impressive growth record, the Chinese government has highlighted the need and its determination to pursue a more sustainable and balanced growth, as well as a harmonious development process in which natural wealth is preserved, human capital is valued, and the benefit of growth is broadly shared by its citizens. Consistent with this national strategy, the Guangdong government outlined its priorities in facilitating the integration of urban and rural economies, reducing disparity, and promoting equality in social service provision. As the pioneer of reforms in China for three decades, Guangdong is well-positioned to take on these new challenges and implement a comprehensive approach to development. Guangdong's success in fostering shared growth will not only position the province as a leader in China's new phase of development, but also provide a valuable example to other countries grappling with similar challenges.

The World Bank is committed to supporting our client countries to achieve their long-term development goals. We are honored to be associated with Guangdong's endeavor in translating its vision and strategy into a coherent policy framework and concrete actions. This joint program has been one of our most successful knowledge collaborations with China. It will prove to be a valuable experience as the World Bank continues to explore ways to strengthen our knowledge partnership with China.

James W. Adams
Regional Vice President
East Asia and Pacific Region
The World Bank

Acknowledgments

This book is the result of a study that was carried out in 2008–09 by a World Bank team led by Xiaoqing Yu (Social Protection Sector Manager, Lead Economist) and Chunlin Zhang (Lead Private Sector Development Specialist). Members of the team included Arvil Van Adams (consultant), Gaurav Datt (Senior Economist), Emanuela Di Gropello (Senior Human Development Economist), Yang Du (consultant), John Langenbrunner (Lead Health Economist), Guo Li (Senior Agricultural Economist), Tao Su (Team Assistant), Minna Hahn Tong (consultant), Dewen Wang (consultant), Jun Wang (Lead Financial Sector Specialist), Lihong Wang (Project Officer, IFC), Meiyan Wang (consultant), Liping Xiao (Education Specialist), Lansong Zhang (Operations Analyst), Shuo Zhang (Health Specialist), and Luan Zhao (consultant).

This study was conducted under the overall guidance from David Dollar (former China Country Director), Emmanuel Jimenez (Human Development Sector Director, East Asia and Pacific Region), and Hsiao-Yun Elaine Sun (Operations Manager, China Department). Bert Hofman (Country Director, the Philippines), Shahid Yusuf (Adviser, World Bank Institute), and Min Tang (Deputy Secretary General, China Development Research Foundation) were peer reviewers. The team also benefited from advice and support from many other colleagues, including Tunc Tahsin

Uyanik (Sector Manager, Financial and Private Sector Development, East Asia and Pacific Region), Fang Cai (Director General, Chinese Academy of Social Sciences), Louis Kuijs (Senior Economist), Nancy Cooke (China Country Program Coordinator), Shaohua Chen (Senior Statistician), and Yue Qu (consultant).

The World Bank team enjoyed an excellent partnership with its counterparts in Guangdong province. Many institutions and individuals made valuable contributions to this work. The team wishes to express its particular appreciation for the collaboration of the two leading counterparts of the study—Policy Research Office of the Communist Party of China (CPC) Guangdong Provincial Committee, and the Provincial Department of Finance. Throughout the process of the study, they provided guidance, insights, and strong support to the World Bank team. They helped organize the field visits, technical meetings, and workshops. They facilitated the interaction of the World Bank team with many provincial departments, municipalities, firms, schools, clinics, employment offices, banks, residents, and service providers. They supported the sharing of information, access to critical data, and discussion of preliminary findings. The World Bank team owes a special debt of gratitude to the following individuals for their leadership and generous efforts: Liu Kun (former Director General of the Provincial Department of Finance, now Vice Governor), Mo Zhen, Wei Haifeng, Lin Ying (Policy Research Office), Li Shuyuan, Lin Hua, Zeng Xiaohong, and Liu Jie (Provincial Department of Finance).

This World Bank study was carried out as part of an overall Guangdong–World Bank joint analytical program, in which parallel studies in related areas were organized by six Guangdong research teams. The Bank team would like to express its thanks to the six Guangdong teams for their generosity with their time and knowledge: Policy Research Office of the CPC Guangdong Provincial Committee, Guangdong Provincial Development Research Centre, Guangdong Provincial Academy of Social Sciences, Provincial Academy of Urban-Rural Planning and Design, South China Agriculture University, and Sun Yat-Sen University.

The team also wishes to thank the Office of the Publisher at the World Bank for its assistance in the publication of this work. Mary Fisk was the production editor, and Patricia Katayama was the acquisition editor. Limei Sun (Program Assistant) provided excellent support to the team throughout the editorial process.

Abbreviations

ABC	Agriculture Bank of China
BOC	Bank of China
BOCOM	Bank of Communications
BRI	Bank Rakyat Indonesia
CBRC	China Banking Regulatory Commission
CBT	competency-based training
CCB	Chinese Construction Bank
CFGR	comprehensive fiscal growth rate
CPC	Communist Party of China
CPI	consumer price index
CULS	China Urban Labor Surveys
FAR	floor area ratio
FCE	free compulsory education
FGT	Foster-Greer-Thorbecke curve
FI	financial institution
GDP	gross domestic product
GER	gross enrollment rate
GMI	guaranteed minimum income
GNI	gross national income
ICA	Investment Climate Assessment

ICBC	Industrial and Commercial Bank of China
ICP	International Comparison Program
LAS	land administration system
LURC	land use right certificate
L/D	loan-to-deposit ratio
MA	Medical Assistance or Medical Aid (scheme or system)
MOF	Ministry of Finance
MSEs	micro- and small enterprises
NCD	noncontagious disease
NER	net enrollment rate
NPL	nonperforming loan
NRCMS	New Rural Cooperative Medical Scheme
O&M	operation and maintenance
OECD	Organisation for Economic Co-operation and Development
OOP	out-of-pocket
PBB	performance-based budgeting
PBC	People's Bank of China
PISA	Programme for International Student Assessment
PPP	purchasing power parity
PPS	probability proportionate to size sampling
PRD	Pearl River Delta
PSB	Postal Savings Bank
RCB	rural commercial bank
RCC	rural credit cooperative
RCCU	rural credit cooperative union
RCU	rural cooperative union
RFI	rural financial institution
SCB	state-owned commercial bank
SENAI	National Industrial Training Service
SENCE	National Service of Training and Employment
SETA	Sector Education and Training Authority
SME	small and medium enterprise
SOE	state-owned enterprise
TDR	transferable development right
TEOS	two exemptions, one subsidy
THC	township health center
TIC	trust and investment company
TIMSS	Trends in International Mathematics and Science Study

UCC	urban credit cooperative
UEBMI	Urban Employee Basic Medical Insurance
URBMI	Urban Resident Basic Medical Insurance
URI	Urban Residency Insurance
VTB	village and township bank

Overview

China has just commemorated the 30th anniversary of the launch of its reform and opening up. The three decades since 1978 have been marked with an impressive performance of economic growth and poverty reduction that is unprecedented in human history. Going forward, however, China faces the serious challenge of ensuring that its strong growth is shared more broadly and equally among the population to continue reducing poverty and to contain and reverse the trend of rising inequality. Addressing this challenge is a key component of the strategy to pursue more balanced urban-rural development and a higher degree of social harmony, which has been promoted strongly by the national leadership since 2002.

As China's leading growth powerhouse and a pioneer of reform and opening up for three decades, Guangdong province is now facing the same challenge and has the opportunity to lead the nation again in paving the way for pro-poor and more equitable growth, setting an example for other provinces to follow. The recent global economic downturn significantly complicates the challenges faced by Guangdong. In response to immediate concerns, the government may be focusing on short-term measures to sustain growth. Meanwhile, maintaining long-term

This overview was prepared by Chunlin Zhang and Xiaoqing Yu.

competitiveness and more balanced development requires that the government continue to tackle a series of long-term issues in a timely and sensible manner. Indeed, the sharp economic slowdown that China has experienced since late 2008 has its roots in domestic imbalances, which are characterized by an overreliance on investments and exports rather than domestic consumption for growth. The weakening support of domestic consumption for growth is clearly linked to the rising income inequality. In this sense, the global crisis has only highlighted the need for attention to this longer-term challenge.

To this end, the provincial authorities need to develop an overall strategy for reducing inequality. For the strategy to work in practice, it must be founded on evidence-based analyses that adequately take into consideration Guangdong's particular situation and lessons from other countries and regions around the world. This World Bank study is designed to provide such analysis. The study has resulted in eight chapters and one policy note (Zhang 2009) on a series of subjects jointly identified by the Guangdong authorities and the World Bank study team.

Although inequality is often discussed in terms of income, this study adopts a broader concept. It defines inequality as having three dimensions: absolute poverty, inequality in opportunity, and inequality in outcomes. Absolute poverty is a state in which individuals are deprived of the minimum means for basic living. It is an extreme form of inequality. Inequality in opportunity occurs when individuals do not have the same chances to pursue their life goals due to predetermined circumstances beyond their control (for example, gender, race, place of birth, family situation). Inequality in outcomes refers to disparity among households and individuals in terms of income and wealth.

This overview summarizes the key findings of the eight chapters and one policy note. It is organized as follows. The first section provides a background of Guangdong, while the second describes the current situation of inequality in the province. Next is a discussion of the potential impacts of the transfer of industrial activities ("industrial transfer") in mitigating regional disparity, followed by the recommendation of a three-pillar strategy for Guangdong. The fifth section focuses on the elimination of absolute poverty through the minimum living allowance (*Dibao*) system, and the sixth turns to policy actions needed to increase opportunities for the rural population by moving them to jobs, increasing their access to finance, and ensuring that their land rights are better protected. The seventh section further assesses Guangdong's options for investing in people through more equitable service delivery in compulsory education, skill development, and health care, with the aim of enhancing the capacity of the poor to seize and utilize opportunities. The last section concludes this overview.

Background of Guangdong Province

Guangdong, a province of over 93 million residents, is located on the southern coast of China (see map O.1). It consists of 21 municipalities, which are commonly divided into four regions: the Pearl River Delta (PRD) region (9 municipalities), the northern mountainous area (5 municipalities), and the eastern wing (4 municipalities) and western wing (3 municipalities) of the PRD.[1]

Over the past three decades, Guangdong has maintained an annual average growth rate in gross domestic product (GDP) of 13.7 percent. It is now one of the most developed provinces in China, accounting for over 11 percent of China's 2007 GDP, the highest among all the provinces.

Map O.1   The Four Regions of Guangdong Province

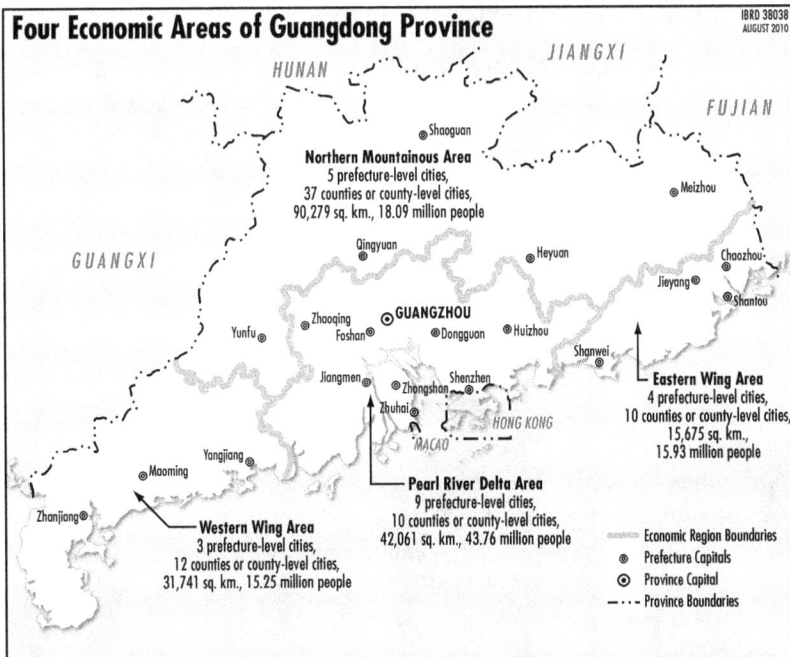

Four Economic Areas of Guangdong Province

IBRD 38038
AUGUST 2010

Source: Guangdong Urban Rural Planning Academy.

Taking Guangdong province as an economy, it would be ranked as the fourteenth-largest economy in the world in terms of purchasing power parity (PPP) (Green 2008).

Guangdong's economy has been highly industrialized and urbanized. In 2007, secondary and tertiary industries accounted for 51.3 percent and 43.3 percent, respectively, of its provincial GDP (Guangdong Provincial Bureau of Statistics 2009, table 3-4) and 63.1 percent of the residents lived in urban areas (Guangdong Provincial Bureau of Statistics 2009, table 4-6). The province is also well established as the leading export province of China. Over 30 percent of China's exports in 2007 were from Guangdong province (Guangdong Provincial Bureau of Statistics 2009, table 17-12). The ratio of exports to GDP in Guangdong was 90.3 percent in 2007, the highest among Chinese provinces. The export-oriented industries have been supported by an influx of migrant workers from inland provinces. Guangdong had about 26 million migrant workers in the province around 2007, compared to its total labor force of 54 million (Xing and Mi 2008; Guangdong Provincial Bureau of Statistics 2009).

The Challenge of Inequality in Guangdong

Historical achievements notwithstanding, Guangdong is facing a serious challenge of inequality. In assessing the current situation, this study found that absolute poverty remains a significant concern in rural Guangdong, inequality in opportunity is widespread, and income inequality has risen to an alarming level.

Absolute Poverty

What is the current poverty situation in Guangdong? Before answering this question, a number of measurement issues must be clarified. First, when measuring poverty, per capita income and per capita consumption are the most commonly used welfare measurements. Generally speaking, income is regarded as a (partial) measure of welfare opportunity and consumption is a measure of welfare achievement. While both measurements have their justifications and limitations, consumption is usually considered a more stable measurement, especially when income reporting can be misleading (World Bank 2009, 188). This study considers both income poverty and consumption poverty.

Second, an appropriate poverty line needs to be defined. A range of poverty lines has been used in China.[2] The official poverty line (785 yuan per person per year for 2007, or $0.57 per person in 2005 PPP dollars) does not seem appropriate for Guangdong. The official poverty line for China is one of the lowest in the world—19.0 percent lower than the one used in the Lao People's Democratic Republic, 20.4 percent lower than Vietnam, and 55.3 percent lower than Mongolia (Ravallion, Chen, and Sangraula 2008). Of course, a lower poverty line does not have to lead to less satisfactory performance in poverty reduction. However, it does affect the information that feeds into the government's decision-making process. As a highly dynamic economy with a high aspiration that growth be broadly shared, it may be appropriate for Guangdong to set the poverty line with a view toward catching up with developed economies in this regard. With this in mind, this analysis uses the $2 per day poverty line (in PPP)[3] to estimate the poverty situation and analyze the profile of the poor. This poverty line was equivalent to 2,263 yuan per year for rural Guangdong and 3,195 yuan per year for urban Guangdong in 2007. The rural line was about 42.4 percent of the mean rural per capita income, while the urban line represented 20.2 percent of the mean urban per capita income in Guangdong in 2007.

Third, measuring poverty requires an appropriate data set. This study uses provincial household survey data covering 2,560 rural households and 1,600 urban households for the years 2005 and 2007.[4] The sample includes migrants who had lived in Guangdong for more than six months at the time of the survey. It represents the Guangdong subset of the national household survey sample and was collected by the provincial Bureau of Statistics following principles and procedures designed by the National Bureau of Statistics. While the sample at the provincial level is limited in size to analyze the implication of particular policy measures, it is sufficiently representative for the purpose of this study. Going forward, the provincial government is strongly advised to strengthen its capacity for poverty and inequality monitoring by improving the content and size of its household surveys and using the monitoring results systematically.

Using the $2 per day poverty line and the data set described above, chapter 1 in this volume concludes that, in rural Guangdong, 10.3 percent of the residents lived in income poverty and 18.6 percent in consumption poverty in 2007. In urban areas, residents whose income or consumption in 2007 fell below $2 per day accounted for over 1 percent of the population. There is a high degree of consistency between the findings in Guangdong and those at the national level that absolute poverty is a rural phenomenon.

Who are the poor in Guangdong? Analysis of the data for 2007 suggests the following:

- *Most of the poor live in the eastern and western regions.* Two-thirds of those who lived in consumption poverty in 2007 were found in the eastern and western regions. The rest were almost equally split between the PRD region and the northern region, with 16.2 percent and 17.5 percent, respectively. The high percentage of poor residing in the PRD region is worth noting, given the region's very high level of wealth and income.

- *Poverty is more pervasive among larger families.* In 2007, 45 percent of the rural income poor were in families consisting of one couple with three or more children, and another 34 percent lived in families comprising three generations.

- *Most of the rural poor are less educated.* In 2007, 85 percent of the rural income poor who were 16 years of age or above did not have a high school or higher education. Moreover, compared with those who had a high school education, those who were illiterate were 1.72 times more likely to be poor. By the same token, primary school graduates were 96 percent more likely to be poor and junior secondary school graduates were 19 percent more likely to be poor.

- *Most of the income poor are able to work.* In 2007, 88 percent of the poor were from households in which no members had lost the ability to work. However, the data also show that the loss of working ability doubled the probability of being poor.

Inequality in Opportunity

Inequality in opportunity is often related to inadequate investment in people and an uneven playing field. First, opportunity becomes unequal when individuals have unequal access to basic social services. A child can be doomed to have a higher probability of poor health and a lower probability of getting a high school education or vocational training than others just because he or she was born to a family that lives in a rural area and is financially poorer than others. Second, individuals with similar health, educational attainment, and skills may end up with unequal opportunities due to unfair competition in the market. For example, they may face discrimination in employment due to their gender, household registration (*hukou*), family background, or other factors. Similarly, their access to land, capital, infrastructure, and other means of production may be unequal due to factors beyond their control. Chapters 6 and 8 assess the situations of education and health care. Their findings suggest that inequality in opportunity is a widespread problem in Guangdong.

Education. Although Guangdong has made tremendous strides in implementing the new free compulsory education (FCE) scheme, educational challenges remain very acute in rural areas. Although disparities with urban areas have been decreasing, they remain significant for completion of primary education and access to junior secondary education and highly significant for completion of and access to senior secondary education and above. Noticeable gaps can also be seen among households of different income quintiles and among geographic areas of different GDP per capita, with the largest gap appearing between the very wealthiest and the others. Finally, although gaps in educational quality cannot be fully appreciated without comparable assessment of learning outcomes, gaps in completion rates and other intermediate outcomes, such as provision of books and infrastructure quality per student, also indicate major quality gaps.

While there may be several reasons for the persistent outcome gaps, gaps in spending per student and a still too-limited effect of the FCE scheme are certainly parts of the explanation. The evidence shows that, despite increased spending in rural and disadvantaged areas, gaps in compulsory education spending per student widened between urban and rural and between advantaged and disadvantaged areas during 2004–07. In other words, spending increased faster in urban and wealthy areas. The problem is the small relative size of the FCE scheme, in which the main subsidy that replaced miscellaneous school fees does not even reach the level of the fees collected in 2004 in rural areas. The problem is compounded by the different local fiscal capacities and lack of sufficient financial prioritization of rural areas within each geographic area (county, city, district). The increasing gaps in spending are worrisome, as they make it difficult to close the quality gap and educational attainment gap, particularly in junior secondary education. Urgent action is therefore needed to start reducing these gaps while providing adequate incentives for more effective use and management of education spending. Guangdong has room both to increase public compulsory education spending and to improve further the way this spending is used, allocated, and managed, to a large extent by building on the new FCE scheme.

Health care. Inequality in the health sector represents another major challenge for Guangdong. Significant evidence indicates that the health care services provided to the poor and economically disadvantaged are much less adequate than for others, since the distribution of health care services remains highly dependent on that of income and wealth.

In terms of health outcomes, chapter 8 points to significant regional disparities in infant mortality. The worst-performing municipality has an infant mortality rate three times higher than the best-performing one, and the infant mortality rate of the PRD region is much lower than those of other regions. Of the nine municipalities with infant mortality rates higher than the provincial average in 2007, seven were non-PRD municipalities. Similar disparities can be seen in mortality rates for children under five years of age.

Inequality is also evident in the utilization of health services. For example, according to official data, in seven of the nine PRD municipalities, nearly 100 percent of pregnant women deliver their babies in hospitals. Nine of the 10 municipalities with hospital delivery rates below the provincial average in 2007 were non-PRD ones.[5] In these municipalities, 10–20 percent of pregnant women still had their babies delivered outside the hospital setting.

A greater disparity can be observed in the utilization of outpatient and inpatient services. In all non-PRD municipalities, the number of outpatient visits per person was below the provincial average in 2007. Similarly, all but one of the non-PRD municipalities fell below the provincial average in terms of number of hospitalizations per person in 2007. The municipality with the highest volume (Dongguan in both cases) had a volume six times higher for outpatient services than Jieyang (the municipality with the lowest volume for outpatient services), and five times higher for inpatient services than Qingyuan (the municipality with the lowest volume for inpatient services).

These differences in utilization are clearly not a result of better health among people in poorer regions. Rather, data and anecdotal evidence suggest that they are most likely a result of financial constraints. For example, in 2006, 18 of the 21 municipalities had per capita government health spending below the provincial average. All but one of the non-PRD cities and four of the PRD cities reported per capita government health spending of less than 41 yuan, compared with the provincial average of 78 yuan and the highest level (in Shenzhen) of 247 yuan. In terms of private spending, the 2007 Guangdong household survey data show that, on average, health spending of an urban resident was 2.5 times more than that of a rural resident. Even among rural residents, the poorest 20 percent spent only 96 yuan on average, while the richest 20 percent spent 3.5 times more than that, at 450 yuan on average.

The high share of out-of-pocket expenditure in total health expenditure is also a cause for concern. This share stood at 45.1 percent in 2006, significantly higher than the average of 36.3 percent for upper-middle-income countries in 2002 (Gottret and Schieber 2006). This issue deserves special attention from the provincial government, because when the income distribution is significantly unequal, the high share of out-of-pocket expenditure in total health expenditure implies a high share of the population that finds health care services unaffordable and is thus left out.

Indeed, the relationship between health needs and available municipality resources for health is clearly disproportionate, as suggested by figure 8.13 in chapter 8. Roughly speaking, the 21 municipalities can be divided into three groups. The first group of five PRD municipalities (Guangzhou, Huizhou, Shenzhen, Zhongshan, and Zhuhai) has higher per capita spending on health (higher than the 71 yuan of Zhongshan) and lower infant mortality rates (lower than the 0.476 percent of Guangzhou). The second group comprises two municipalities (Heyuan and Shantou) with low spending and low infant mortality rates. All of the remaining 14 municipalities fall into a third group characterized by higher infant mortality rates and low government spending on health. Their levels of per capita government spending on health are all lower than 71 yuan, and their infant mortality rates are all higher than the 4.76 percent of Guangzhou.

Inequality in Income

Analysis of the provincial household survey data set provides insights into the current situation of income inequality in Guangdong province. For Guangdong overall, the Gini coefficient—a measure of the extent to which a particular income distribution diverges from an absolutely equal distribution—stands at 0.394 for 2007, after adjustments for cost-of-living differences between rural and urban areas. This level is lower than the levels for China overall and for countries such as the Russian Federation (0.399), Thailand (0.420), and the United States (0.408), but it is higher than for many other developing countries, such as India (0.368), Indonesia (0.343), and Vietnam (0.344).

What are the sources of this inequality? As elsewhere in China, urban-rural disparity is one of the key sources of overall income inequality. Chapter 1 shows that in 2007, based on the Theil index of inequality, which is useful for its decomposability, income disparity between urban and rural households accounted for 23.4 percent of Guangdong's overall inequality.

Table O.1   Decomposition of Income Inequality in Guangdong Province, 2007

Components	Theil index	% of total
Total	0.282	100.0
Inequality among rural households of the PRD region	0.049	17.4
Inequality among urban households of the PRD region	0.062	22.0
Inequality among rural households of the non-PRD region	0.044	15.5
Inequality among urban households of the non-PRD region	0.024	8.4
Inequality between rural households of the PRD and non-PRD regions	0.016	5.8
Inequality between urban households of the PRD and non-PRD regions	0.021	7.5
Inequality between rural and urban households of the province	0.066	23.4

Source: Guangdong Bureau of Statistics 2007.

What explains the remaining 76.6 percent? The huge gap between the PRD and non-PRD regions in economic development might point to regional disparity (table O.1). However, the data show that inequality within the PRD region itself contributed most to the observed overall inequality. Twenty-two percent of the overall inequality came from inequality among urban households in the PRD region, and inequality among rural households in the PRD added another 17.4 percent. Within-PRD inequality thus explains 39.4 percent of the provincial total. In contrast, inequality between the PRD and non-PRD regions only contributed 13.1 percent (5.7 percent for rural households and 7.4 percent for urban households) of the total. Therefore, in addition to the well-documented factor of urban-rural disparity, regional disparity is a significant source of inequality, but inequality within the PRD region has been much more significant to overall inequality in Guangdong province.

Reducing Inequality with Spatially Unbalanced Growth

Inequality in Guangdong province has geographical roots.[6] The natural geography of the province is such that the PRD region is endowed with significant advantages over other regions. The PRD region has also enjoyed proximity to, and historical ties with, Hong Kong, China, and Macao, China, and through them, the rest of the world. As a result, Guangdong's economic growth has been highly unbalanced in a spatial sense. Economic activities are concentrated in the PRD region, where per capita GDP is much higher and the growth rate much faster than those of the lagging regions. This imbalance has obviously contributed to urban-rural disparity and regional disparity in household income, which are both sources of inequality and rural poverty. Therefore, if the spatial distribution of economic growth could be made more balanced—for example, through the transfer of industrial activities ("industrial transfer")—from the PRD to lagging regions, then reducing inequality would be easier and faster.

The Trend of Industrial Deconcentration from the PRD and the "Pull" Forces

Having examined available data on the evolution of the spatial pattern of Guangdong industry during 1998–2007, Zhang (2009) found that deconcentration from the PRD did take place in recent years, but only on a minor scale relative to the size of Guangdong's industry. Its strength is far from what would be needed to reduce regional disparities in industrial development significantly. The most significant sign of the deconcentration movement is the strong catch-up of two cities close to the PRD, namely Heyuan and Qingyuan. However, more detailed analysis suggests that the rise of the two cities can be attributed only partially to the deconcentration of a few industries (for example, nonferrous metallurgy and mining, as well as nonmetal mining products) from the PRD. Overall, a clear trend of transfer of labor-intensive industries from the PRD to other regions of Guangdong does not seem to have emerged.

Why has the trend of deconcentration been so weak, despite government promotion since 2005? One plausible explanation is that PRD firms had only weak incentives to move out, and more new firms still preferred to establish themselves in the PRD region because of the existence of some "pull" forces—that is, economic forces that reward firms for locating in the PRD region. It appears that the power of the "push" forces in the PRD region—forces that strengthen incentives for firms to move out of the PRD region—has been neutralized significantly by the pull forces. The most important pull force to Guangdong is agglomeration economy, which rewards the geographical concentration of firms. In particular, concentration of industrial activities in the PRD region enables firms there to reap significant gains in productivity. The second pull force is a favorable investment climate, in which the PRD region has a clear advantage over other regions.

A key implication of the existence of the pull forces is that geographical concentration of industrial activity can, contrary to common perception, be both desirable and inevitable. It is one of the underlying reasons urbanization boosts productivity. Indeed, as the *World Development Report 2009* (World Bank 2008) has found, economic growth is seldom balanced, and efforts to spread it prematurely will jeopardize progress. Two centuries of economic development show that spatial disparities in income and production are inevitable. A generation of economic research confirms this; there is no good reason to expect economic growth to spread smoothly across space.

Shifting the Policy Focus to Improvement of the Investment Climate

The available evidence on industry in Guangdong suggests only a moderate trend of deconcentration from the PRD region. Industrial transfer from the PRD to other regions will certainly continue, but given the market force of an agglomeration economy, its scale is unlikely to be large enough to alter significantly the spatial concentration of growth in the PRD region. This trend implies a tougher challenge for the Guangdong provincial government: it must reduce inequality on the basis of spatially unbalanced growth.

How to achieve such a reduction, then? One option for Guangdong is to allow the full play of an agglomeration economy in shaping economic geography and shift the focus of policy efforts to improving the investment climate of lagging regions. More comparable investment climates between lagging regions and the PRD region would not only reduce the potential cost of relocation of a firm from the PRD to a lagging region, but would also encourage private business creation and expansion in the lagging region.

Reducing Inequality: A Three-Pillar Strategy

Given the limited potential to make economic growth more even among regions, what strategy should the Guangdong provincial government adopt to reduce inequality? This study recommends a three-pillared strategy: eliminating absolute poverty, reducing inequality in opportunity, and containing inequality in outcome.

Eliminating Absolute Poverty

Absolute poverty is in fundamental conflict with the social values of most societies and certainly with those of China. Ensuring that individuals are free of absolute poverty is the responsibility of the government. Public interventions are needed to protect the livelihoods of society's neediest members and should be executed in the most transparent and efficient manner. Therefore, one of the most important policy objectives for Guangdong province is to eliminate absolute poverty in a limited period of time. Particularly given the province's leading role in China's development and reform, it is only appropriate that high priority be placed on this policy objective. The financial and administrative strength of the province rules out any question regarding the attainability of this goal.

Reducing Inequality of Opportunity

Inequality of opportunity conflicts with the value of fairness in most societies. Moreover, it hurts economic efficiency and long-term growth. Institutions and policies that promote a level playing field—where all members of the society have similar chances to become socially active, politically influential, and economically productive—contribute to sustainable growth and development for two sets of reasons. First, there are many market failures in developing countries, notably in the markets for credit, insurance, land, and human capital. While correcting market failure is the ideal response, when this is not feasible or far too costly, some forms of redistribution—of access to services, assets, or political influence—can increase economic efficiency. Second, high levels of economic and political inequality tend to lead to economic institutions and social arrangements that systematically favor the interests of those individuals and groups with more influence. Both middle and poorer groups of the population end up with talent that is left unexploited. Society as a whole is then likely to be more inefficient and to miss out on opportunities for innovation and investment (World Bank 2005).

Therefore, the appropriate policy objective with regard to inequality of opportunity is to reduce it as much as possible. Public policy and resources need to be focused on ensuring that members of society have similar chances to be economically productive and socially active regardless of their predetermined circumstances. In the case of Guangdong, two main sets of interventions are most important and relevant. First, public policies should promote more equal access to education, health services, and basic social protection. Second, public and market institutions should be oriented toward providing a level playing field for individuals.

Containing Inequality in Outcomes

The nature of inequality in outcomes measured in terms of income and wealth is more complicated. Some inequality in outcome is "good" for efficiency and growth, so government policy should not pursue a completely equal distribution of income and wealth, particularly when inequality in income reflects uneven performance among individuals. Matching reward with performance is the foundation of market-based incentives and has been an essential element of China's successful reforms. Urban-rural inequality in outcomes can also be good when it is caused by robust productivity growth in the urban sector, implying that the gap will narrow at some point as urbanization and productivity growth continue.

However, inequality of outcomes can also be "bad," making a case for some government intervention. Even when inequality reflects unevenness of performance among individuals, it can become harmful to growth when it generates substantial inequality in opportunity and distortion in market and public institutions in such a way as to threaten social coherence and stability. Not all income inequality reflects performance gaps; a great deal of inequality in outcomes may reflect unequal opportunity, an uneven playing field, or a society's failure to prevent theft—not the usual criminal act of theft, but the theft of public property and the abuse of public power through corruption.

The most appropriate government policy toward inequality in income and wealth, therefore, is to contain it to a socially acceptable level with minimum cost in terms of efficiency. What, then, is an acceptable level of inequality in income for Guangdong province? How much of the existing income inequality observed in chapter 1 is "good"? These questions require another study on the extent to which the existing income inequality reflects performance gaps. This study focuses more on the elimination of absolute poverty and the reduction of inequality of opportunity, which will both contribute to a more equal distribution of income and wealth.

The Role of the Intergovernmental Fiscal System

A key source of inequality is regional disparity in growth. As argued earlier, since concentration of economic activities is inevitable, the challenge is to reduce inequality on the basis of spatially unbalanced growth. To succeed in coping with this challenge, the role of the intergovernmental fiscal system is of fundamental significance. Without intergovernmental transfer, the spatially unbalanced growth and regional disparity in income distribution will be fully translated into regional disparity in access to key social services, such as education and health care, which inevitably results in inequality in opportunity. The transfer of government revenue from richer regions to poorer regions inevitably weakens incentives for revenue generation. However, a well-designed intergovernmental transfer system has the potential to achieve the optimal balance between equity and incentives. As suggested by the problems with financing of education and health care services mentioned above, reform of the intergovernmental fiscal system remains an area where a major breakthrough is needed for Guangdong to implement the three-pillar strategy proposed here.

Eliminating Absolute Poverty through the *Dibao* System

As in the rest of China, the minimum living allowance (*Dibao*) program is the main policy instrument for the Guangdong government to address absolute poverty for rural and urban residents. The program is designed to provide direct transfers to households whose average net per capita incomes are below a locally defined threshold of minimum living standard.

Despite the impressive progress made by Guangdong in sustaining and expanding its rural *Dibao* program, a review of implementation experience indicates that the program has yet to achieve its objectives. The key issues hindering the achievement of objectives include level of program coverage, amount of fiscal input, design of some key policy features, and administration of the program.

Building on over a decade of experience with *Dibao*, and given the province's fiscal strength, Guangdong is in a position to lift the poor out of absolute poverty by expanding and improving the *Dibao* program. It will require determination in setting priorities, improvements in policy design to enhance efficiency, and strengthening of safety-net institutions to ensure that the program is well governed.

Expanding Program Coverage by Protecting Adequate Fiscal Input

Coverage of the rural *Dibao* program is low compared to the levels of poverty in Guangdong. Results from the 2007 rural household survey show that the program reached less than 5 percent of poor rural households, measured against a poverty line of $2 per day. The limited coverage was especially apparent in the eastern and western areas of the province, which had income- and consumption-based poverty rates of 20 percent and 36 percent, respectively, compared to a program coverage rate of only 2.7 percent. The data also point to continued imbalances across different regions of Guangdong: Although the eastern and western areas accounted for over 60 percent of the province's poor, the 2.7 percent coverage rate was lower than those of the other two regions.

One main reason for the low breadth (coverage) and depth (level of protection) of the program is the inadequacy of the fiscal input to it. Currently, financing responsibility is shared between the provincial and local governments, with a significant redistributive element. However, data suggest that the number of beneficiaries in different parts of Guangdong is strongly correlated to the sufficiency of local funds for the *Dibao* program.

A rather remarkable contradiction can be observed between the policy statement and the program reality, and, indeed, in that sense, the program in Guangdong is not markedly different from that in the rest of China. While the program is designed as an entitlement program with the stated principle "all who are eligible shall receive benefit," in reality, the depth and breadth of the program are not driven by basic needs but are largely determined by local fiscal capacity.

Moving forward, Guangdong needs to increase program coverage by (1) setting the level of minimum allowance based on a clearly defined approach (for example, basic consumption basket); (2) budgeting the total level of fiscal input required based on needs; and (3) rationalizing financing responsibilities among different levels of government. The principle of cost sharing is sound, but it may be necessary to introduce provincial funding more biased in favor of the poorest regions and ensure that budget allocations at the local level are ring-fenced.

Improving Policy Design to Raise Program Efficiency

Although rural *Dibao* is still in the early takeoff phase at the national level, Guangdong has already experimented with the program for over a decade. Drawing from the experience of urban *Dibao*, which follows the same program design philosophy, a range of policy and program design issues that need to be addressed for the program to function properly and meet its stated objectives can be identified. Four issues and the recommended solutions are highlighted here.

The eligibility threshold. Despite the use of the term "minimum living allowance," the *Dibao* thresholds are apparently not set or adjusted according to any scientific measure of the minimum living requirement. Instead, they often depend on historical levels and fiscal capacity. The thresholds are also not associated with any particular poverty line, making it very difficult to measure how well the program is achieving its goals.

The actual levels of *Dibao* thresholds used in Guangdong appear to be too low, particularly compared to poverty standards that are arguably more appropriate for the province. In 2007, the monthly threshold for rural *Dibao* was below 100 yuan in 28 percent of counties (cities) and between 101 and 150 yuan in 54 percent of counties (cities, districts).

These levels are quite low compared to a higher poverty threshold equivalent to $2 per day (or 189 yuan), which may be more suitable for Guangdong, given its level of development.

Chapter 2, on rural *Dibao*, recommends that Guangdong (1) adopt a much more scientific and systematic approach to setting and adjusting the poverty lines; (2) align the *Dibao* eligibility threshold with the poverty line; and (3) consider, as the program is developed further, introducing an equivalence scale that takes into account household size in determining thresholds.

Benefit structure. *Dibao* is designed as a classic guaranteed minimum income (GMI) program, which is common among countries in the Organisation for Economic Co-operation and Development (OECD).[7] According to such a design, households are expected to receive benefits equal to the difference between the *Dibao* threshold and their actual per capita income, multiplied by the number of household members. Although this is conceptually clean and well justified, the difficulty in determining the actual income of families—especially for rural households—makes it virtually impossible not to overshoot or undershoot and makes performance evaluation impossible.

Given the nature of income and the difficulty of fully recording household income, chapter 2 recommends that the Guangdong authorities consider adopting a much simpler benefit structure. The benefit structure could have two to three flat benefit levels and grant benefits to eligible households depending on where their income roughly stands. It would be a more honest and realistic approach, more feasible administratively, and, in fact, what has largely been in place. Addressing such inconsistencies between policy design and implementation is important to ensure the credibility of the program.

Targeting mechanism. *Dibao* in China uses a combination of income and asset testing and community participation for targeting and determining household eligibility. Households apply, their names are posted openly for community feedback, and then the authorities review and selectively verify. Besides income and assets, major sources of consumption needs such as chronic disease are also taken into consideration.

While such a combination of means testing is a sensible approach conceptually, it gives grassroots authorities significant discretionary power in determining eligibility. Proper checks and balances have not been put into place, and marginalized groups may not receive fair treatment. As the program expands, this type of highly discretionary approach may leave it vulnerable to abuse and criticism.

Considering the difficulty in verifying household income, chapter 2 recommends that the Guangdong authorities consider piloting a proxy means-testing mechanism. Proxy means tests basically require statistical analysis of data from detailed household surveys to identify the key determining and easily observable factors of poverty. They use a formula and relative weights to generate a score for applicant households based on easily observable characteristics, such as location and quality of dwelling, ownership of durable goods, demographic structure of the household, and the education and possibly occupations of adult members. Eligibility is determined by comparing the household's score against a predetermined cutoff. Proxy means tests are useful for reducing discretion and ensuring greater transparency and fairness. They are also appropriate for addressing chronic poverty, which accounts for a significant share of the poor.

Strengthening Program Administration and Governance

The rural *Dibao* program in Guangdong suffers from lack of resources for administrative capacity. Much of the program administration has been pushed down to the lowest level (community or village), which is not even a level of government. The ratio of beneficiary households to staff is very high, making it impossible to verify eligibility, handle grievances, ensure proper financial management, or monitor the program.

As Guangdong moves away from relying on self-reported income and explores new targeting methods such as proxy means testing, the information requirements will be enormous. Chapter 2 highlights the need for Guangdong to invest in its safety-net institutions by establishing sound processes and systems for targeting, making payments, and preventing and detecting error, fraud, and corruption. Investments are also needed in monitoring and evaluation to measure program success. A well-developed management information system and full staffing are needed for the *Dibao* program at every level.

Boosting Rural Income by Giving People Opportunities

Most rural poor people can improve their incomes and their lives if they have access to better opportunities. Opportunities that are broadly related to the three factors of production—labor, capital, and land—are particularly important. First, rural poor people will be able to share the fruits of urban productivity growth if they have equal access to urban off-farm jobs. Second, they will be able to help themselves better if they have equal access to finance. Third, they will be able to improve their well-being if public and market institutions provide better protection of their rights over land.

Helping People Move to Jobs

The fundamental cause of urban-rural income inequality in a developing economy is often development itself. When an economy develops, its urban sector enjoys higher productivity and faster growth than the rural sector, leading to a gap in incomes between rural and urban households. The basic approach to closing this gap is to help rural labor move to urban jobs, allowing the rural population to share urban income in a productivity-enhancing manner.

This approach seems very appropriate for Guangdong for several reasons. First, as will be discussed in chapter 1, 88 percent of the rural poor are from households in which no working-age members have lost the ability to work. Second, wage income already accounted for 56.9 percent of net income for rural households in Guangdong in 2007, compared to 38.6 percent for China overall, 52.5 percent for Jiangsu province, and 48.5 percent for Zhejiang province. Third, industrialization and urbanization in the PRD region have created a huge number of urban jobs. Moving more of Guangdong's rural labor to urban jobs in the PRD region and beyond is therefore a natural approach for reducing urban-rural income inequality.

While transferring rural labor to off-farm—and in most cases urban—jobs will ultimately help improve rural income and reduce inequality, analysis is needed to understand the profile of the farmers, and to identify the appropriate policy actions required. This implies two main questions: First, how many rural laborers remain in Guangdong who are not needed for agricultural activities, and what are their characteristics? Second, what are the main barriers that prevent Guangdong's labor market from being highly mobile, and how can such barriers be removed to facilitate the transfers?

The size of transferable rural labor of Guangdong. If government policies for labor transfer need to focus on laborers who are "transferable," the first step is to determine the size of Guangdong's pool of transferable labor. An analysis of the rural household survey data collected by the Guangdong provincial Bureau of Statistics (see chapter 1 for data description) suggests that about 60 percent of the province's rural labor force may already be transferred in the sense that their working time is devoted to off-farm activities, which include local off-farm activities (35 percent) and migrant off-farm work (25 percent). This does not imply, however, that the remaining 40 percent can all be transferred. A more in-depth analysis of the profile of the remaining labor is needed.

The most frequently used methodology for measuring the size of transferable labor is to estimate the difference between the total rural labor force and the total labor demand for agriculture. However, this methodology is flawed because the labor allocation to agriculture is determined not only by agricultural productivity, but also by many other factors, such as prices of agricultural outputs and job opportunities in the nonagricultural sector. Furthermore, the estimation is often based on aggregated data that do not capture the variations caused by individual characteristics.

Chapter 3 uses a different methodology. It first analyzes the profile of transferred rural labor using the rural household survey data. After obtaining an understanding of the key determinants of migration decisions and outcomes, the study estimates the probability of transfer among rural workers in various age groups and obtains the total number of transferable rural labor. Employing this methodology, chapter 3 concludes that out of the 11.67 million nontransferred rural laborers in Guangdong province in 2007, 4.35 million, or 37.3 percent, are transferable. This pool includes 1.54 million, or 13.2 percent, who could potentially be transferred to migrant jobs, and 2.8 million, or 24 percent, who would do better with local off-farm activities.

Policy interventions to facilitate labor transfer.   What is required to bring the 4.35 million rural workers to migrant or local off-farm jobs? This is the central question that must be answered before the necessary government policies can be formulated.

The first is to facilitate migration. It is important to recognize that the share of transferable rural workers who could migrate to urban labor markets can be influenced by government actions to a certain extent. Using the rural household survey data, chapter 3 identifies four important determinants of a rural worker's decision to move to a migrant job: age, gender, years of schooling, and whether he or she has preschool children. Young male rural workers are more likely to migrate to nonlocal off-farm jobs. Rural workers with longer years of schooling are more likely to take migrant jobs, but having preschool children can significantly lower their probability of moving to migrant jobs. None of these findings is surprising. Government actions could help address some of the key factors that influence migration decisions. In particular, two sets of actions may be effective: (1) enhancing rural education and vocational training to prepare rural labor better for urban employment opportunities, and (2) providing better social services (such as child care, education, and health services) to rural migrant children in the urban areas.

However, these measures may not be sufficient. In the past, on the demand side, the dynamic PRD region created millions of urban jobs for migrant farmers; on the supply side, there were probably 1.5 million rural Guangdong farmers who had the potential to take those migrant jobs. For some reason, demand and supply failed to meet. While the 1.5 million rural Guangdong workers stayed in their home areas, millions of jobs in the PRD region were filled by migrant workers from outside Guangdong. Because of lack of data on these non-Guangdong migrant workers, further investigation of the cause of this phenomenon is not possible. However, the phenomenon does underscore that the effectiveness of government policies designed to promote rural labor transfer to migrant jobs will be seriously compromised if the root causes of the problem are not identified correctly. Further study of this issue is strongly recommended.

There is also a range of policy issues that would affect the migration decisions and actions of not only rural labor from Guangdong, but also those from the rest of China. Whether these issues can be addressed successfully affects the well-being of rural migrants as well as the competitiveness of the Guangdong economy. Chapter 3 highlights in particular four issues that Guangdong needs to tackle further and that it is well positioned to do. They include (1) the restricted access to social services and protections dictated by the residency requirements (*hukou*); (2) the labor regulations that, on the one hand, may imply serious restrictions on the employers' hiring and firing decisions and, on the other hand, cannot ensure basic rights of the migrant workers and the bargaining power they need to acquire; and (3) the limited coverage of social insurance programs.

The second policy intervention is to create off-farm jobs in rural areas. While much attention has been rightly given to the need to facilitate rural-urban migration over the past few years, the creation of local off-farm jobs in rural areas should be a policy priority. In the context of Guangdong, since nearly two-thirds of remaining transferable rural labor would be better off with local off-farm activities, opportunities that are far away may not help them move to more productive jobs and better income. For fostering the development of off-farm activities, a wide range of policies, including tax, land, and rural finance, are highly relevant. It should also be emphasized that the most effective way of maximizing local off-farm job creation is to improve the local investment climate to facilitate business creation and expansion, as discussed in the section on reducing inequality with spatially unbalanced growth above.

Making Finance Work for Rural Households and MSEs

Financial sector development can play a crucial role in reducing inequality in many ways. One area in which it can have a direct impact—and in which the Guangdong provincial government could potentially make a significant difference—is access to finance for rural households and micro- and small enterprises (MSEs).

The inadequacy of financial services for rural households and MSEs.
Rural households and MSEs are often victims of unequal access to finance. Chapter 4 finds that Guangdong is no exception, and that the province even lags considerably behind the national average and other coastal provinces in terms of access to finance for rural households and MSEs. According to China Banking Regulatory Commission (CBRC) statistics, only 13.6 percent of rural households in Guangdong had borrowed from formal financial institutions in 2007, compared to 13.5 percent in Zhejiang, 17.3 percent in Jiangsu, 23.4 percent in Shandong, 36.7 percent in Fujian, and a national average of 34.6 percent.

Moreover, it seems not the case that Guangdong rural households are less bankable than the national average or their counterparts in other provinces. The provincial household survey data indicate that the percentage of rural households with outstanding debt to informal moneylenders in 2007 was 4.6 times that of rural households with outstanding loans to formal financial institutions.

MSEs did not fare any better; in 2007, only about 5.0 percent of Guangdong's small businesses had ever borrowed from banks, compared to 7.5 percent nationally, 5.5 percent in Jiangsu, 8.2 percent in Fujian, 10.2 percent in Zhejiang, and 11.2 percent in Shandong.

Access to credit is not the only area in which rural households and MSEs are underserved. Like urban dwellers, rural households and MSEs have diverse demands for financial services, such as savings deposits, payments, remittances, insurance, and leasing. However, the 2002 household survey data indicate that only 34.8 percent of farming households in the lowest income quartile had savings deposit accounts (46.5 percent in the next-lowest income quartile, and 63.2 percent in the third-lowest income quartile). The percentage of all rural households in Guangdong with saving accounts stood at 53 percent, significantly lower than the

national average (62 percent) and the percentages of comparable provinces (72 percent in Jiangsu, 76 percent in Fujian, 81 percent in Shandong,
and 90 percent in Zhejiang). Of those households in the lowest income
quartile that did not have savings deposits in banks, average cash holdings were as high as 5,425 yuan at the end of the year (7,759 yuan for
the second-lowest income quartile).

The inability of financial institutions to serve. What is lacking in
Guangdong in general—and in rural areas, in particular—is not savings, but
the ability of financial institutions to turn savings into productive loans. At
the end of 2007, the combined loan-to-deposit (L/D) ratio of financial
institutions in Guangdong, including branches of state-owned commercial
banks (SCBs), stood at 58 percent, indicating that they were able to lend
out slightly more than half of what they had collected in deposits. This
compared poorly with comparable provinces and the national average. The
L/D ratio for rural financial institutions was even lower at 32 percent,
which was less than half of that in the comparator provinces.

The L/D ratio is a meaningful indicator of effectiveness of intermediation, because if the actual ratio is lower than the prudential threshold by
a wide margin, there is reason to believe that an undue amount of the savings has either gone to investment in fixed-income financial instruments,
such as government securities and bonds issued by policy banks, or has
flown to other parts of the country through the intrabank funds transfer
systems. If it is not a surprise that the national banks were the channels
of outflow, the roles played by the rural credit cooperatives (RCCs)
should be, as they were touted as the mainstay of rural finance.

While a large portion of funds flows out of Guangdong, those that find
their way into lending in Guangdong have had a lower rate of repayment
than elsewhere in China. Despite faster than average economic growth
and spectacular urban prosperity in Guangdong, loan portfolio quality has
been notoriously bad in the past many years. As of the end of 2007, the
combined nonperforming loan (NPL) ratio of all financial institutions in
Guangdong stood at 9.3 percent, higher than those of the comparator
provinces and the national average. Among them, the Agriculture Bank of
China (ABC) and the RCCs exhibited even poorer loan quality. Measured
by the risk-based loan classification criteria, the ABC's nonperforming loan
ratios were as high as 26.5 percent, while the RCCs' were 19.8 percent.

Actions the provincial government could take. Suffice it to point out
that there is little the Guangdong government can do to influence the

decisions of the financial institutions directly. What it can do, though, is to make conditions more conducive for the financial institutions that would scale up their operations in Guangdong of their own volition. There are several areas where the Guangdong government can take immediate action, keeping in mind their impacts and implications for the medium and long terms.

First, launch a pilot of village-level, member-based financial cooperatives in selected rural and mountainous areas. The pilot should help fill the void of basic financial services, deposits, and loans for rural households that have been denied access due to the withdrawal of SCB presence since 1998 and the diminishing role of RCCs as they are being restructured into joint-stock rural commercial banks and becoming increasingly urban. Several experiments with such financial cooperatives are already taking place in China, notably those promoted by the Leading Office for Poverty Alleviation and Development of the State Council and the Agriculture Department of the Ministry of Finance in Henan and Sichuan, with World Bank support. For the cooperatives to be successful, care should be taken to preserve the autonomy and initiative of members and to avoid willful interference by government officials at all levels. The provincial government should set up an auditing unit to protect the interests of members through periodic audits as a public service to the newly established financial cooperatives.

Second, revise policies and guidelines to promote microcredit companies under the overall sponsorship of the People's Bank of China (PBC) and the CBRC. It is critical that the provincial policies avoid the mistakes of provinces that chose to set thresholds even higher than those stipulated by the PBC and the CBRC. The systemic risks posed by such microcredit companies are minimal, as they do not take public deposits. Artificially constraining their ability to formulate and borrow will cause a systemic risk because few, if any, such companies can even hope to be sustainable. The Guangdong provincial government should take a broader perspective and a pragmatic approach to promoting microcredit companies. The microcredit companies should be established not only at county level but also at township level. To foster competition and provide a level playing field, Guangdong should consider allowing multiple microcredit companies to be set up in all counties, with lower thresholds of paid-up capital and relaxed restrictions on their funding limits and geographic expansion. It should be understood that microcredit companies require economies of scale to achieve meaningful outreach and commercial sustainability.

Third, redesign fiscal incentive programs to promote access to finance by rural households and MSEs, with a special focus on the reduction of transaction costs, the introduction of innovative products and instruments such as microleasing and factoring (or reverse factoring), and branchless banking models. The intended beneficiaries of fiscal subsidies should be well defined, and the enhancement of their welfare should be subject to monitoring and evaluation. Giving monetary rewards to foreign and Chinese financial institutions to attract them to Guangdong should be reconsidered, since doing so wastes public resources and hampers the healthy development of the financial sector. If the Guangdong government wishes to stimulate the credit supply to rural households and MSEs, it can replace the volume of loans with the number of loans as a basis for award. Awards based on volume of loans actually encourage banks to lend to large borrowers at the expense of MSEs. Such subsidies or tax treatments should not be institution-specific—that is, they should be awarded without discrimination among financial institutions. Any financial service providers wishing to serve the rural and MSE borrowers should have equal access to the fiscal stimulus. The government should not resort to interest rate subsidy but to nondistortive policy actions that help bring down transaction costs. In addition, in certain geographic locations with extremely adverse natural conditions, it makes economic sense to move the people out of such locations rather than forcing the rural financial institutions (RFIs) to set up or maintain outlets without commercial prospects or social benefits.

The Guangdong government may also wish to reconsider the policies encouraging the proliferation of government-owned credit guarantee companies and policy-oriented reguarantee companies. The role of such credit guarantee companies is dubious at best, as they may add to transaction costs without raising overall credit supply. The wide spread of credit guarantee schemes tends to perpetuate moral hazard in the credit market and erode the fragile credit culture, without bringing about the intended addition of credit.

Fourth, restructure the Financial Working Office (Jinrongban) *to balance its roles and functions* as an owner and regulator of local financial institutions and markets. The increasing responsibilities of the provincial government in maintaining local financial stability and providing access to finance justify the addition of regulatory and supervisory functions. The CBRC does not have enough capacity to oversee the numerous local financial institutions, which are rising in number as the experiments with new types of financial institutions continue. In the meantime, the provincial government does not have an explicit regulatory and supervisory function. The result-ing vacuum not only creates uncertainty and opportunities for regulatory arbitrage, but it also leaves potential risks unattended. Guangdong will be a pioneer in charting new waters for the next generation of financial reform if it takes the initiative in this important area.

Fifth, plan a thorough study of the issues and problems surrounding the RCCs to explore a real pilot for restructuring, one aimed at making the RCCs truly resilient financial institutions with good governance and sound control systems. The RCCs should be freed from their ambiguous roles and become real commercial financial institutions without the label of "serving *sannong*"—that is, agriculture, farmers, and rural communities. Local governments and the CBRC should make a commitment not to interfere with the internal operations of post-restructuring rural coopera-tive unions (RCUs) and rural commercial banks. The shareholders, direc-tors, and management should be allowed to execute their responsibilities fully under the new governance framework. In exchange for granting RCUs this much-needed autonomy, the regulatory authorities should be decisive and prompt in closing down failing RCUs and should announce their policy in this regard in advance to make it a credible deterrent to mismanagement. It would also be wise for the government to take a sober-minded approach to the creation of government-dominated finan-cial holding companies by amalgamating the existing RFIs and financial institutions run by local government or state-owned enterprises. Such top-down conglomeration rarely works unless fundamental changes are introduced in governance and incentives. The recommended pilot on village-level financial cooperatives could be combined with the pilot on dealing with insolvent RCCs, as the two are complementary.

Reforming Land Policies for Better Rights Protection and a Healthier Development Pattern

Although industrialization and urbanization contribute to rising gaps in urban-rural productivity and income, they also raise the demand for—and hence the potential value of—rural land, which is an important source of rural income. Data show that income from farming activities still accounts for almost 60 percent of farmers' per capita income in today's rural China. Protecting farmers' rights over land is therefore critical to reducing urban-rural income inequality. Adequate protection can not only help boost rural income but also generate a market signal that reflects the true social cost of land, helping the urban sector develop on a land-efficient path.

Many national and provincial policies aim to protect farmers' rights over land and improve land use efficiency in the economy. Guangdong province could lead the nation in land policy reform by doing more in this regard and being more innovative. Three specific reforms could be considered, as described below.

Establishing a land registration system and granting land rights certificates. Farmers in rural China generally do not enjoy a high degree of land tenure security, and the situation in Guangdong is no exception. Some local governments have continued to support or at least allow community-level land readjustments, using different justifications. Frequent land readjustments, even on a small scale, will weaken farmers' perception of land tenure security, and a low degree of tenure security will negatively affect farmers' long-term investment and production behavior on the land. Land readjustments at the community level will also create rent-seeking opportunities for local elites. In light of these negative impacts, the Rural Land Contracting Law of 2003 basically prohibited land readjustment, and this legislative intention was reinforced in the Property Rights Law of 2007. Extending farmers' land leases from a 30-year term to an open-ended one, as announced by the Communist Party of China (CPC) Central Committee in mid-October 2008, sent the clearest and strongest signal of the central government's determination to grant farmers a higher degree of land tenure security.

Tenure security is also crucial for healthy development of the land market in both rural and urban areas, in terms of protecting land rights as well as reducing land conflicts. Guangdong has enjoyed an increasingly active rural land market since the 1990s. However, an emerging phenomenon is that farmers' interests are being violated to different degrees by village elites, local governments, and some enterprises during the land transfers. This problem calls for further government action to protect the tenure security of farmers. International experience shows that securing land use rights of individuals *before* promoting rights tradability is a sound principle.

Therefore, it is recommended that the Guangdong provincial government take timely and concrete actions to strengthen farmers' land tenure security. One of the most effective ways to achieve this goal is to establish a plot-level rural land registration system and grant farmers land rights certificates. Such a registration system is strongly supported by the most recent policy changes, as reflected by the CPC's decision in mid-October 2008 and the No. 1 Document of 2009. Rich international experiences can be found in this field—Vietnam, for example, which has a land rights arrangement similar to China's, has endeavored to conduct a broader land administration reform and establish a nationwide digital cadastral record system (see box 5.1 in chapter 5). Guangdong could again be a national pioneer in establishing a provincewide rural land registration system to promote more equitable growth with a higher degree of social harmony.

Adopting a new system that maximizes the overall economic value of land. Farmland protection is a major challenge for Guangdong. Under the existing policy framework, all remaining farmland in Guangdong falls into the category of "basic farmland," and, hence, scope for further conversion from farmland to urban use is very limited. In addition, under the current policy, this conversion is subject to approval by the State Council, the Chinese cabinet. The 2007 census shows that Guangdong has 42.7 million *mu* of farmland, but the basic farmland quota assigned to Guangdong for protection is also 42.7 million *mu*.[8] Therefore, in theory, Guangdong must keep 100 percent of its remaining farmland to meet the "basic farmland" protection quota unless the State Council determines otherwise.

Given Guangdong's rapid urbanization, it is unavoidable that a certain amount of farmland will and should be converted for urban expansion. Two principles should be followed for farmland protection in Guangdong. First, the core of farmland protection should focus on improving land productivity. The potential to improve land productivity is huge: current data show that 62 percent of the remaining farmland is middle- or low-yield land. Second, a mechanism to maximize the overall value of land resources should be introduced. The decision on whether a plot of land should be converted to urban use should be based on the overall economic value of all plots of land involved, rather than on the agricultural value of the specific plot alone. Inflexible farmland protection in a rapid urbanization area could result in an inefficient urban development pattern with problems such as urban sprawl, overstretched infrastructure, and the coexistence of incompatible land uses. In short, Guangdong should be innovative in piloting more effective ways to achieve the farmland protection objective.

Piloting the transferable development rights mechanism. Environmental degradation has become a matter of urgency in two respects. First, the quality of the living environment has declined significantly in certain areas. Second, the quality of farmland is deteriorating, which has a significant

negative impact on the safety of agricultural products. Innovative land policy, such as land transferable development rights (TDRs), could be very
useful for addressing this issue (see box 5.2).

TDRs could be viewed as a tool for the government to purchase land
development rights from landowners. The core of TDR is to shift development rights from sending areas (where the development rights have
been bought by the government) to receiving areas (where the land could
be developed at a higher density). Similar to a marketable permit system,
TDRs are used to implement development restrictions on land designated
for environmental protection or as permanently agricultural (the sending
area). Owners of agricultural land in the sending area are granted TDRs
as compensation for the restrictions on their ability to develop the land
for higher-value urban uses. Owners of developable land in a designated
receiving area are typically allowed to exceed limits on density only by
purchasing a sufficient number of TDRs. In addition to facilitating environmental gains, compensation associated with TDRs will also help
reduce incentives for illegal land conversion and address increasing tensions among regions with different economic growth prospects. The
United States has a quite well-developed TDR system at both the federal
and state levels. Drawing on international experience, Guangdong could
pilot this mechanism, adapting it to the province's particular situation. If
the pilot is successful, the mechanism could be expanded province-wide.

Investing in People through More Equitable Service Delivery

While opportunities are important, they must be seized and fully utilized
by poor people to have a real impact on inequality. Therefore, the capacity of the poor to utilize opportunities is critical. Among the many factors
that determine such capacity, three are particularly essential and can be
influenced by government policies: educational attainment, skills, and
health. Better-educated people with better skills and health have greater
capacity to make use of the opportunities available to them. The government can therefore help poor people help themselves with a policy of
investing in people through equitable and effective service delivery in
basic education, vocational training, and health care.

Granting Rural Children Equal Access to High-Quality Education

Equal access to high-quality education is crucial for reducing inequality.
Given the increasing importance of educational attainment to young people's competitiveness in the labor market, it is very likely that today's

inequality in access to high-quality education will translate into inequality in income tomorrow. Based on an assessment of the current state of rural compulsory education, chapter 6 concludes with five recommendations.

First, Guangdong province needs to put more emphasis on measuring and monitoring multiple dimensions of educational performance, with a particular focus on gaps across groups to identify where the equity challenges really are. The current diagnostics are still very much focused on the school-age population, on average indicators or, at most, disaggregation across geographic areas, and on standard enrollment and transition rates, which provide only part of a more complex picture. It will be important to look at the educational performance of both the workforce and school-age populations, and across urban-rural areas, socioeconomic strata, and geographic areas. For a thorough diagnostic, a wider array of indicators should also be considered, such as dropout rate or standardized learning outcome indicators.

Second, the subsidy that was designed to replace miscellaneous fees, which were collected by schools from parents to finance school operation expenses, needs to increase over time to help close the gap. While making rural compulsory education free, the new scheme that was implemented recently has put greater pressure on rural and disadvantaged areas in the provision of compulsory education. The current minimum standards of subsidies, which are 288 yuan per student for primary school and 408 yuan per student for junior secondary school for rural areas, are very low and do not even reach the level of the miscellaneous fees they are supposed to replace in very poor counties. The province is well aware of this issue and of the increasing pressure on rural schools, and it has planned some increases with, for instance, standards set at 350 yuan per student for primary schools and 550 yuan per student for junior secondary schools in 2009. This measure is a step in the right direction, but, as shown in the simple simulations presented in figures 6.40 and 6.41 in chapter 6, it will not be enough to make a substantial difference.[9] The analysis in chapter 6 shows that about 390 yuan and 580 yuan per student, respectively, would be the minimum needed to fill the rural fee gap—that is, to make up for the average rural fees collected in 2004 at 2007 prices—and even that would only marginally help close the gap. What would really start to make a difference is a substantial increase in the minimum subsidies to rural schools that would allow their teacher salary allowances to reach the provincial average, and their operation and maintenance (O&M) budgets to reach the urban school standard.

Third, an improved funding formula for the subsidy in replacement of miscellaneous fees is needed. The high and increasing spending gaps between urban and rural areas in Guangdong clearly point to the need for differentiating urban and rural standards in replacement of miscellaneous fees to ensure that rural schools can satisfy basic needs. It is important to continue working, as the province currently is, with minimum and predictable subsidies per student that limit the scope for lengthy negotiations and provide strong incentives for efficient behavior. The issue is not about changing the subsidy per student approach, but, rather, getting a better grasp on what the subsidy "needs to buy" in rural areas and then adjusting the current minimum subsidy accordingly over the short to medium run. Rural school operation cost includes teacher cost, such as salary allowance/bonus for permanent teachers and substitute teachers, as well as O&M cost, such as basic school supplies, utilities, and simple classroom maintenance, which used to be covered, to the extent possible, by the miscellaneous fees that were collected by schools from parents. If the subsidy that is supposed to replace miscellaneous fees needs to allow rural schools to cover acceptable teachers' costs and O&M costs, then it would make sense to fix minimum acceptable standards for both—set at the provincial average or, more likely, other standard costs—and review the overall amount of the subsidy. As described in chapter 6, some useful examples of funding formulas from across the world could be used as a reference for Guangdong.

Fourth, there is strong justification for a systematic, predictable, and well-articulated maintenance scheme. The analysis in chapter 6 shows that regular funding for O&M budget per student is much lower in rural areas—which typically experience faster dilapidation of school buildings—and differs across counties without an apparent logic. The policies for financing are also fairly different. These findings provide strong justification for the more structured, systematic, and predictable longer-term maintenance plan proposed for rural areas and already implemented by the province in 2008. One question is how this new plan would be best articulated with the subsidy in replacement of miscellaneous fees, which also cover some O&M. These two subsidies could, in principle, be seen as complementary, with the subsidy in replacement of fees covering just the basic O&M (supplies, utilities, minor classroom maintenance) and the separate maintenance subsidy feeding into a longer-term fund for more in-depth refurbishment and renovation of the infrastructure when the time comes. The articulation between these two subsidies may need to be further reviewed to ensure their different purposes and mechanisms are well understood and implemented. Finally, the proposed 50-50 county-provincial cofinancing scheme (with a 100 percent county- and city-financed scheme in the PRD) seems to be a generally acceptable solution for ensuring rational infrastructure decisions and cost sustainability.

Fifth, the textbook and needy student subsidies need to be reviewed further and rationalized. As above, the subsidy in replacement of fees and the textbook subsidy, which was extended to almost all compulsory education students in 2008, should be well articulated to ensure that they are complementary and to determine if it is justifiable to keep them separate now that they have the same coverage. How to ensure that the current textbook gap between urban and rural areas is filled remains an open question, as the textbook scheme has been extended to urban areas. One option for closing the gap would be to factor in a one-time supplement to the subsidy in replacement of fees for rural areas.

The targeting of the subsidy for needy students may need to be reviewed. The planned 2008 increase in the subsidy for 20 percent of needy students in special difficulty—to include supplements of 500 yuan in primary and 750 yuan in junior secondary schools—is welcome, as it will help address the significant private education expenditure burdens faced by poor rural households. However, coverage of needy students still appears to be quite low and, more importantly, does not seem to adhere to very clear poverty logic when comparing beneficiary groups across counties and cities. The targeting of the subsidy may need to be reviewed to ensure it is at least allocated as equitably as possible.

Overall, all of these measures to improve the FCE scheme will need to be accompanied by improved management practices at all levels to ensure that funds always reach their intended beneficiaries and do so in the most efficient way. The move toward giving schools more budget management responsibilities is positive, as they generally have better knowledge of needs and are accountable to their communities, and this approach is also consistent with the use of block grants per student. This move will need to be accompanied by coaching and training in financial management and procurement.

Equipping Workers with Skills

Workers' skills and education are an important constraint on growth as viewed by employers in Guangdong. In the World Bank's 2006 investment climate assessment survey for China (World Bank 2006), which covered 120 cities and 12,400 firms,[10] 14 factors were ranked as potential constraints on growth. Workers' skills and education were ranked as either the first or second most important constraint on growth by one-third of the Guangdong firms surveyed. Only access to dependable electrical power exceeded this in importance (see figure 7.1 in chapter 7). At a national level, access to finance was ranked as the most important constraint on growth, followed by worker skills and education. Improvements in workers' skills are thus a high priority from the viewpoint of employers.

Chapter 7 finds that Guangdong faces a series of interrelated challenges in meeting the rapidly changing skill needs of its economy and ensuring that the poor have the skills necessary to take advantage of the opportunities available to them. As in the case of compulsory education, lower fiscal capacity in rural areas poses a major constraint, and the subsidies provided to reduce the urban-rural spending gap are limited. Given this context, it will be critical for Guangdong to use its public expenditures for skills development more effectively and efficiently, which will also involve stronger coordination of public and private skills initiatives, greater emphasis on demand-side financing, and other measures to address the skills development challenges, as described below.

Strengthening coordination with a new governance framework. To achieve the national and local objective of a skilled workforce, a strong governance framework is required to coordinate Guangdong's diverse provider community for skills development. Faced with a similar diversity of state and nonstate providers, governments in countries such as Australia, Chile, Singapore, and South Africa have created coordination bodies. Their governance frameworks include national and regional training authorities run by governing boards, which have public and private members with roles and responsibilities defined in legislation and decrees. The duties and powers of these authorities vary, but all have the overarching objective of creating a more coherent policy and operations framework for providers and consumers of education and training, whose purpose is helping a workforce prepare for employment. Guangdong could establish its own provincial training authority with oversight and advisory responsibilities and, possibly, implementation responsibilities for some activities. Such training authorities serve as umbrellas for other market institutions that improve the operation of training markets. Their creation would address the growing fragmentation in the provision of skills and lead to a more strategic use of public expenditures.

Making financing bring about results. Changing how skills are financed is a powerful tool to get better results from public expenditures. While governments are concerned with mobilizing more financing for skills development, improving how money is spent can be even more important to meeting an economy's objectives for skills development. Incentives need to be put in place to encourage public and private providers to deliver education and training of good quality that is responsive to market demand. The incentives are already in place for private providers, since consumers who pay for services are not expected to continue enrolling in programs that do not produce results in employment and earnings. The same types of incentives can be put in place for public providers by financing them in ways that hold them accountable for good performance. Performance-based budgeting (PBB), vouchers, and training funds are three instruments that Guangdong province may consider adopting.

PBB replicates for public providers of education and training the incentives available to private providers. Rather than combining quantities and costs of inputs in a budget, PBB calls for agreement first on the results to be achieved—for example, the share of students who can pass national certification exams for the program, or the share who can find work using their skills in a given period of time—or even on targets such as raising the percentage of program completers. The budgeting process focuses on strategies to achieve these objectives and the activities to produce the results. Success is judged by whether key performance outcomes are achieved, and, if they are not, sanctions hold those responsible accountable. At the same time, managers and teachers must be given the tools with which to succeed, including adequate training and operating resources to accomplish the agreed-upon task and achieve the key performance indicators.

Vouchers can be used to shift financing from the supply side of service delivery (that is, schools or training institutes) to the demand side (the end users). Those who receive government training vouchers can shop for training services and pay their service providers with the vouchers. Service providers can then get final payment from the government in exchange for the vouchers they have received. The vouchers thus help the government achieve two goals: first, they subsidize a targeted group of end users, such as young farmers with income below a certain threshold; and, second, they generate competition among providers. Some countries using such vouchers are Australia, Canada, Chile, Denmark, France, Germany, the United Kingdom, and the United States.[11] China has its own version, as found in the "Sunshine Program," which provides rural migrants with support for training and personal expenses but without promoting competition for delivery of the training services.

Some preconditions must be met for vouchers to meet their objectives. First, the user must have adequate information about the service to be bought. Second, there must be an adequate number of providers to promote competition. These conditions are often difficult to meet, in which case training funds provide an intermediate step to vouchers, using financing and competition to promote better outcomes for skills development. Training funds are used worldwide—Malaysia and Singapore offer good examples—to encourage more enterprises to offer training and to buy training services competitively on the open market from public and private providers (Dar, Canagarajah, and Murphy 2003). The financial sources of training funds often include a tax on employer payrolls of 1 to 2 percent, government budget provided by general taxation, and, in some countries, donors and financing agencies like the World Bank. The funds, in turn, buy training services for target groups, using competitive procedures or levy-grant arrangements in which they disburse funds to enterprises to carry out approved training programs.

Opening the market to nonstate provision. While skills development often requires government financing for reasons ranging from positive externalities to the need to support the poor, services in education and training can be supplied by both state and nonstate providers. Opening the market to nonstate providers reduces pressure on the government as a provider of services and mobilizes nonstate capital in building educational and training capacity. In Guangdong, nonstate providers of both education and training are relatively underdeveloped, with an estimated 7 percent of training capacity in secondary education being privately owned. The available evidence of this capacity highlights its responsiveness to market demand but also raises questions about the quality of services it provides.

The government can take steps to promote the expansion of nonstate capacity and strengthen regulations to safeguard quality. As a starting point, a clear set of regulations that do not discriminate against private providers—including, for example, opening access to public financing for private education and training—is needed. The intent of state regulation of private providers is to protect consumers from exploitation and abuse. Licensing, for example, is an instrument of the state that applies minimum standards for private training activities in return for the legal right to offer these services. Public information on performance and abuses can serve as a low-cost means of regulating private education and training. Information on accreditation, for example, can help consumers sort good from bad training, both public and private.

Developing market institutions. Guangdong would benefit from giving more attention to strengthening its market institutions. Functions of market institutions—such as producing and disseminating market information, setting competency standards and testing, certifying those who meet them, and licensing and accrediting education and training providers— help guide the decisions made by all participants in labor markets. A provincial qualifications authority, operating independently or under the direction of a provincial training authority, holds promise for improving the quality and relevance of education and training. Countries like Ireland and New Zealand have introduced national qualifications authorities for this purpose. These authorities play a role in defining qualifications, setting competency standards, and testing individuals and certifying skills— functions that are now performed by the Department of Labor and Social Security.

Carrying forward school-based reforms. Along with the measures outlined above, school-based reforms will influence how successful Guangdong is in adjusting the skills of its workforce to the changes taking place in the economy. With support from the World Bank, the province is currently piloting school-based reforms in several public training institutions. The reforms include strengthening links between schools and local industry, improving school management and instructional capacity, introducing a modular competency-based curriculum focused on competencies sought by employers, and upgrading instructional equipment and facilities. Successful implementation can help enhance the quality and relevance of skills training offered by public training institutions across the country and across line ministries, thereby improving the use of public resources.

Providing Adequate Health Care to the Poor and Disadvantaged

Inequality of income and wealth oftentimes stems from inequality of health outcomes. Not only have many of the poor been driven into poverty by illness, but less than satisfactory health conditions also hinder people from exploring economic opportunities for greater income and wealth. Equal access to good health care services is, therefore, crucial to reducing inequality. In this regard, chapter 8 finds a great deal of potential for improvement in Guangdong province, particularly in the financing of health care services.

How can an economy achieve a distribution of health care services that is more nearly equal than its distribution of income? Obviously, income redistribution or subsidies are inevitable. Such redistribution is often carried out in one of two ways. The first is through the government budget, which involves collecting revenue through taxation and spending disproportionately on health care to subsidize lower-income households and regions. The second is through health insurance schemes, which involves collecting revenue in the form of contributions and spending disproportionately on health care to subsidize higher-risk individuals. Substantial room for improvement exists in Guangdong's health financing system in both respects—for example, through the three policy actions described below.

First, the provincial government could review the current situation of intergovernmental finance for health care services to identify gaps and develop an action plan aimed at a much higher degree of equalization. For example, in the current regime, the general transfers from the provincial budget to counties are determined by a formula that has been designed such that counties with faster growth in fiscal revenues receive higher transfers. Although this formula may provide a good incentive for revenue creation, the fact that indicators of social sector development are missing deserves attention. Reducing inequality and building a harmonious society require the allocation of transfers to the needy.

Second, actions can be taken to strengthen the role of the Medical Assistance (MA) system. The MA system is a special program in China's health safety net, designed to provide financial assistance for medical expenses and contributions from the New Rural Cooperative Medical Scheme (NRCMS) to specific groups of the vulnerable population, mostly the neediest. It is therefore a very important instrument for reducing poverty and inequality. In Guangdong, the targeted population includes *Tekun, Wubao,* and *Dibao* households and those who suffer from large and potentially impoverishing medical expenses.[12]

However, this instrument appears to be seriously underutilized in Guangdong province. In terms of per capita MA, Guangdong province is the fifth lowest among all of China's provinces. With spending of only 200 yuan per capita, Guangdong falls far behind comparable provinces such as Shandong (984 yuan), Zhejiang (1,073 yuan), and Shanghai (2,184 yuan). Although it would be good news if the need for MA in Guangdong were really almost 5 times lower than in Zhejiang and 10 times lower than in Shanghai, this appears unlikely, given the annual spending on health of 96 yuan among the poorest 20 percent of Guangdong's population. The large number of migrants may have contributed to the low level of per capita spending, but this factor does not seem significant enough to explain the gap with other provinces, such as Shanghai and Zhejiang, which also have large migrant populations.

In addition, it appears that Guangdong's MA scheme is underdisbursed in some places. In one poverty-stricken county for which data were made available, the county's MA scheme spent 0.05 million yuan in 2005 and ended up with a surplus of 1.4 million yuan. In the following year, spending increased to 0.5 million yuan, while the surplus accumulated to 1.5 million yuan. In 2007, spending fell to 0.2 million yuan, while the surplus was 10 times larger at 2.2 million yuan. It is therefore important for the government to review the functioning of the existing MA system and take necessary action to strengthen its role.

Third, the provincial government could consider piloting greater pooling for the NRCMS. The NRCMS is an insurance scheme, and one of the most important functions of a health insurance scheme is to pool the health risks of its enrollees. Through pooling, it transforms the unpredictable risks of large amounts of expenses into predictable small and regular contributions for insurance premiums, which provides protection for its enrollees. In other words, it equalizes health risks among high-risk and low-risk individuals. A larger pool can bring lower costs and greater efficiency.

In this regard, neither Guangdong nor the rest of China has yet fully explored the potential of NRCMS, since the level of pooling remains very low—almost universally at the county level. If the political and economic obstacles—which are admittedly formidable—could be removed, and a greater pooling could at least be piloted, Guangdong could substantially increase the protection of its rural households against health risks without a proportional increase in government spending.

Like labor training services, health services can be financed by the government from the demand side or the supply side. In subsidizing patients, both the MA system and NRCMS are instruments of demand-side financing. With well-functioning demand-side financing, health service providers could find themselves in an environment in which the costs of services—including the costs of fixed assets such as buildings and equipment, as well as the true market costs of health workers—are fully recovered by the payments of users, who are covered by various financing programs. Health service providers would be able to finance their own investments and pay market-level compensation to their staff.

When demand-side financing is not functioning well and health services are underpriced in relation to real costs, health service providers have difficulty raising funds to finance investments. This seems to be the case in rural Guangdong and the non-PRD regions. For example, an average rural township health center in the PRD region has 2.44 beds per 1,000 population, while in non-PRD regions, this ratio is only 0.79. A clear regional disparity also exists in the density of health professionals among different municipalities and regions in Guangdong province. Out of the 21 municipalities, 12 have a physician density lower than the provincial average, and 8 have a physician density even lower than the mountainous neighboring province of Guizhou, one of the least developed provinces in China.

The Guangdong provincial government has the option to increase its health spending on the supply side in the short run, in which case the government would cover the costs of fixed-asset investments for public health providers in exchange for discounted prices of their services for users. In the long run, along with the scaling up of health insurance schemes as well as the development of purchasing services, the health services in the lagging areas could be fully financed through demand-side financing.

Conclusion

After three decades of continuous, fast economic growth, China has entered a new phase of development in which inequality has become one of the top challenges on its development agenda. Not only does the trend of rising inequality weaken social cohesion and fuel conflicts and instability, but it also undermines the credibility of market-oriented reform and hinders longer-term development.

While the economic downturn caused by the global crisis in late 2008 might have forced policy makers to focus on short-term actions needed to stimulate the economy and maintain growth, it is important to recognize that longer-term issues, such as unbalanced growth whose benefits have not been shared broadly, will determine the ultimate vitality of the economy and the cohesion of the society. Experience suggests that inequality, which tends to constrain domestic consumption, may ultimately hurt economic growth. As a result, GDP growth is forced to follow an unbalanced path, with an increasingly high reliance on investment and exports, until it becomes unsustainable.

As China's powerhouse for economic growth and a pioneer of reform and opening up over the past three decades, Guangdong province has the opportunity—and also bears the responsibility—to lead the nation again by exploring a new pattern of pro-poor and more equitable growth.

To this end, a comprehensive strategy is needed for Guangdong to reduce inequality.

While it is a common perception that reduction in inequality can only be achieved at the expense of efficiency and growth, the truth is more complicated. As described earlier, inequality needs to be viewed as having three aspects: absolute poverty, inequality in opportunities, and inequality in outcomes. Absolute poverty is in fundamental conflict with the social values of most societies, and certainly those of China. Elimination of absolute poverty has, therefore, its own value that is independent from efficiency and growth. Reducing inequality in opportunities enhances, rather than conflicts with, efficiency and growth. Containing inequality in outcomes can also promote efficiency and growth to the extent that it can help ensure an even playing field or prevent theft of public property and abuse of public power through corruption. It is only when the focus is on reducing the "good" element of inequality in outcomes—that is, the inequality in income and wealth that reflects performance variations—that efficiency and growth will be compromised.

Based on this conceptual framework, this study recommends that Guangdong province adopt a three-pillar strategy of reducing inequality: eliminating absolute poverty, reducing inequality in opportunities, and containing inequality in outcomes. Central to this strategy, and indeed central to the economic reform over the past three decades, is the role of the state. Defining the appropriate role of the government in relation to private individuals and the market is critical to the success of every aspect of this strategy.

The appropriate role and level of government intervention differs among the pillars of the strategy. Eliminating absolute poverty is a responsibility that falls squarely on the shoulders of the government. While the involvement of private individuals and civil society is to be promoted, and while social protection programs should be designed in a way to encourage individual efforts, the state should assume the ultimate responsibility. Reducing inequality in opportunities, however, requires the proper combination of government intervention with market forces. The high degree of complexity notwithstanding, the most frequently observed pattern is a coexistence of inadequacy and excessiveness of government action—inadequate in areas where the government has the responsibility to fulfill, such as financing social services and ensuring quality, and excessive in areas where the government has some power to exercise. A greater emphasis on accountability in government actions is the key to improvement.

With its strong will to reform and its solid economic foundation, Guangdong is well positioned to take on these new challenges and implement such a comprehensive approach to reducing inequality. A range of policies recommended in this study can be considered to eliminate absolute poverty, boost rural income by giving people opportunities, and invest in people through more equitable service delivery. Guangdong's success in fostering shared growth will not only position it again as the leader of China's new phase of development; it can also provide a valuable example to other countries that are grappling with similar challenges.

Notes

1. The PRD region comprises nine municipalities: Dongguan (DG), Foshan (FS), Guangzhou (GZ), Huizhou (HZ), Jiangmen (JM), Shenzhen (SZ), Zhaoqing (ZQ), Zhongshan (ZS), and Zhuhai (ZH). The five municipalities in the northern region are Heyuan (HY), Meizhou (MZ), Qingyuan (QY), Shaoguang (SG), and Yunfu (YF). The three municipalities in the western wing are Maoming (MM), Yangjiang (YJ), and Zhangjiang (ZJ). The four municipalities in the eastern wing are Chaozhou (CZ), Jieyang (JY), Shantou (ST), and Shanwei (SW).

2. For more detailed discussion of poverty lines, refer to World Bank (2009).

3. This poverty line is the median of all 75 national poverty lines for developing countries used in the World Bank (2009) study.

4. See chapter 1, box 1.1, for a description of the data. A two-stage probability proportionate to size (PPS) sampling approach, in which the probability of selecting a sampling unit is proportional to the size of its population, was used to draw samples of counties (cities) and rural (urban) households. The national sample is representative at the national level. The difficulty in capturing the migrant population has been a challenge for analysis of related subjects.

5. The only PRD city with a hospital delivery rate below the provincial average was Zhuhai, which has a relatively developed economy and good performance on health services. Its lower hospital delivery rate was mostly due to a different recording and monitoring approach. A hospital delivery rate is the number of hospital deliveries in a year as a percentage of the number of pregnant women recorded by health institutions in a city, including those who are recorded in one city and deliver their children in another. Zhuhai has pioneered a more effective approach to recording the number of pregnant women, which makes the number of pregnant women appear larger than otherwise.

6. This section draws on Zhang 2009.

7. It should be noted that in most OECD countries, the GMIs are of very modest level and coverage, as they usually represent one basic component of a broader social assistance system.

8. A Chinese unit of land area, one *mu* equals 0.16 acre.

9. These are admittedly very simplified simulations based on 2007 revenue data, since full data for 2008 are not yet available.

10. Cities in the Guangdong sample included Dongguan, Foshan, Guangzhou, Huizhou, Jiangmen, Maoming, Shantou, Shenzhen, and Zhuhai.

11. See, for example, Bruttel (2005); Gasskov (2000); West et al. (2000); Finkelstein and Grubb (2000); and Carnoy and McEwan (2001).

12. The term *Tekun* refers to households in extreme poverty identified by local authorities and therefore eligible for basic social assistance provided by the government. *Tekun* programs operated as the basic social assistance scheme in localities where basic living allowance programs did not exist. *Wubao* refers to households without income, family support, or working capacity, and therefore eligible for guaranteed protection by the local government in the form of support for food, clothing, medical care, housing, and burial expenses.

References

Bruttel, Oliver. 2005. "Delivering Active Labour Market Policy through Vouchers: Experiences with Training Vouchers in Germany." *International Review of Administrative Sciences* 71 (3): 391–404.

Carnoy, Martin, and Patrick J. McEwan. 2001. "Privatization through Vouchers in Developing Countries: The Cases of Chile and Colombia." In *Privatizing Education: Can the Marketplace Deliver Choice, Efficiency, Equity, and Social Cohesion?* ed. Henry M. Levin, 151–77. Cambridge, MA: Westview Press.

Dar, Amit, Sudharshan Canagarajah, and Paud Murphy. 2003. "Training Levies: Rationale and Evidence from Evaluations." Unpublished paper. World Bank, Washington, DC.

Finkelstein, Neal D., and W. Norton Grubb. 2000. "Making Sense of Education and Training Markets: Lessons from England." *American Educational Research Journal* 37 (3): 601–31.

Gasskov, Vladamir. 2000. *Managing Vocational Training Systems.* Geneva: International Labour Organization.

Gottret, Pablo, and George Schieber. 2006. *Health Financing Revisited: A Practitioner's Guide.* Washington, DC: World Bank.

Green, Stephen. 2008. "China—If Guangdong Were a Country . . ." Global Research, Standard Chartered Group. August 26.

Guangdong Provincial Bureau of Statistics. 2009. *Guangdong Statistics Yearbook (2008)*. Guangzhou: Guangdong Statistical Publishing House.

Ravallion, Martin, Shaohua Chen, and Prem Sangraula. 2008. "Dollar a Day Revisited." Policy Research Working Paper 4620, Development Research Group, World Bank, Washington, DC.

West, Anne, Jo Sparkers, Todor Balabanov, and Sarah Elson-Rogers. 2000. *Demand-Side Financing: A Focus on Vouchers in Post-Compulsory Education and Training: Discussion and Case Studies*. CEDEFOP dossier. Thessaloniki: European Centre for the Development of Vocational Training.

World Bank. 2005. *World Development Report 2006: Equity and Development*. Washington, DC: World Bank; and New York: Oxford University Press.

———. 2006. *Governance, Investment Climate, and Harmonious Society: Competitiveness Enhancements for 120 Cities in China*. Beijing: China Fiscal and Economic Publishing House.

———. 2008. *World Development Report 2009: Reshaping Economic Geography*. Washington, DC: World Bank.

———. 2009. *From Poor Areas to Poor People: China's Evolving Poverty Reduction Agenda: An Assessment of Poverty and Inequality in China*. Washington, DC: World Bank.

Xing, Shaowen, and Hua Mi. 2008. "Behind the 3.5 Million Migrant Workers Stuck in Guangdong: Pearl River Delta Remains the Largest Destination of Migrant Workers." *China Business News*, February 28. http://finance1.jrj.com.cn/news/2008-02-28/000003338349.html.

Zhang, Chunlin. 2009. "'Ride with the Tide': Facilitating the Spatial Transformation of Guangdong Industry." Unpublished policy note. June.

CHAPTER 1

Understanding Poverty and Inequality in Guangdong

Benefiting from years of economic reform, Guangdong has achieved remarkable growth relative to the rest of China and even other countries. Guangdong now has the largest economy among China's provinces and, in 2007, accounted for 11.3 percent of the country's aggregate GDP—a much greater proportion than other leading provinces and municipalities (figure 1.1). With an aggregate GDP of $328 billion (current international purchasing power parity [PPP]) in 2007, Guangdong outperformed the East Asian newly industrialized economies of Hong Kong, China; Singapore; and Taiwan, China (figure 1.2). The size of Guangdong's economy is even comparable to that of other developed countries around the world, such as Austria, Sweden, and Switzerland.

Although Guangdong's large population lowers its ranking in terms of per capita income, its per capita income level is still relatively high. In 2007, Guangdong ranked sixth among the leading provinces (cities) in terms of per capita income and, as shown in figure 1.3, below all the newly industrialized economies. However, it still had a per capita income of around 1.8 times the national average at $4,538 (33,151 yuan).[1]

This chapter was written by Dewen Wang of the Chinese Academy of Social Sciences. Substantial contributions were made by Gaurav Datt and Minna Hahn Tong. Information and advice of Shaohua Chen is gratefully acknowledged.

45

Figure 1.1   Comparison of GDP and Per Capita GDP across China's Provinces, 2007

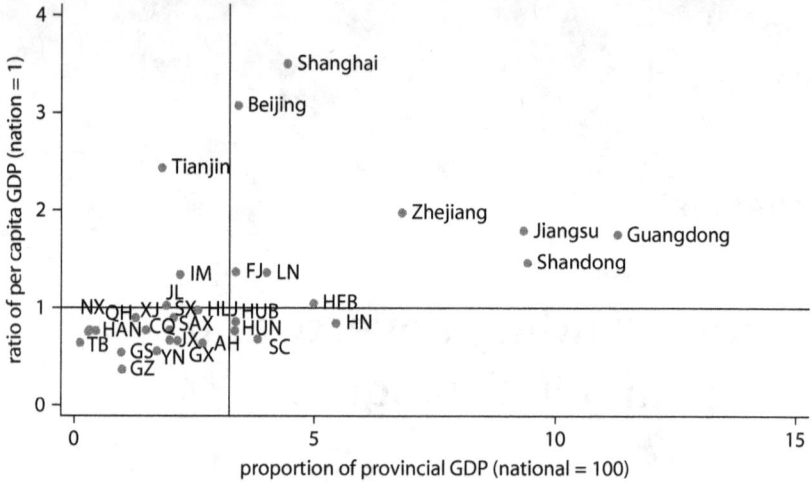

Source: National Bureau of Statistics 2008.

Note: Province names are abbreviated as follows: Anhui (AH), Chongqing (CQ), Fujian (FJ), Gansu (GS), Guangxi (GX), Guizhou (GZ), Hainan (HAN), Hebei (HEB), Heilongjiang (HLJ), Henan (HN), Hubei (HUB), Hunan (HUN), Inner Mongolia (IM), Jiangxi (JX), Jilin (JL), Liaoning (LN), Ningxia (NX), Qinghai (QH), Shaanxi (SAX), Shanxi (SX), Sichuan (SC), Tibet (TB), Xinjiang (XJ), Yunnan (YN).

Figure 1.2   GDP of Guangdong and East Asian Newly Industrialized Economies, 2007

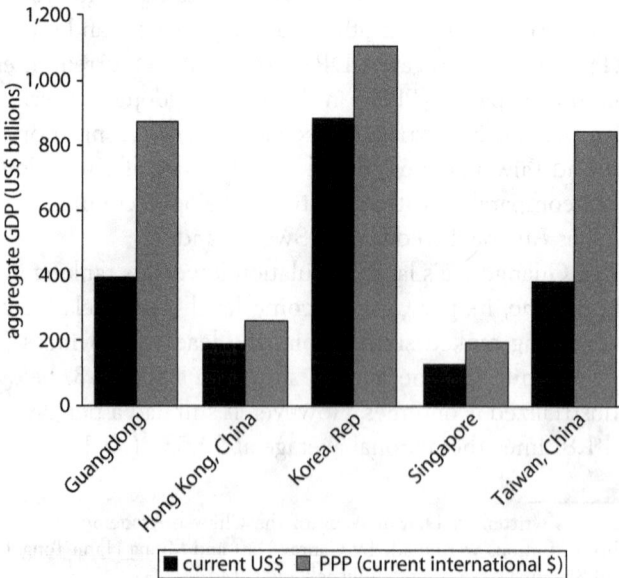

Sources: World Bank 2008; Guangdong Bureau of Statistics 2008; Council for Economic Planning and Development (Taiwan, China) 2008.

Figure 1.3   Per Capita GDP of Guangdong and East Asian Newly Industrialized Economies, 2007

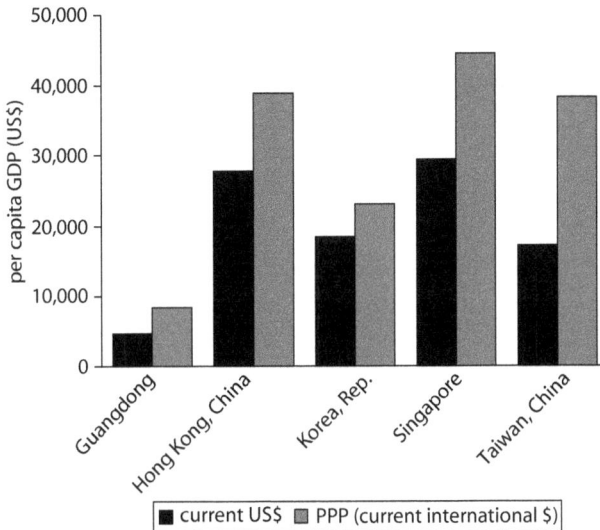

Sources: World Bank 2008; Guangdong Survey Department of the National Bureau of Statistics 2008; Council for Economic Planning and Development (Taiwan, China) 2008.

Despite these achievements, Guangdong still faces significant challenges with respect to poverty and inequality. As one of China's richest provinces, Guangdong is excluded from the national poverty alleviation program that targets the poor localities of China. However, Guangdong has designated 16 of its own counties—all located in the lagging northern mountainous region and eastern and western regions—as poor. Poverty is concentrated in rural areas, with 89.9 percent of Guangdong's poor living in rural areas. Development across the province has been uneven, and Guangdong's annual per capita GDP growth rate of 11.4 percent between 1978 and 2007 has not translated into commensurate growth in incomes—rural income grew at an annual rate of 6.8 percent, while urban income grew at 7.2 percent annually over the same period. As shown in figure 1.4, the ratios of both rural and urban incomes to per capita GDP have declined over time due to the uneven growth of per capita GDP with respect to rural and urban incomes, mirroring a similar trend at the national level and in other leading provinces.

To develop effective policies for addressing these challenges, a better understanding of the extent and nature of poverty and inequality is needed. This chapter assesses the current poverty situation in Guangdong, drawing on rural and urban household survey data (as described in box 1.1)

Figure 1.4   Ratio of Rural and Urban Incomes to Per Capita GDP

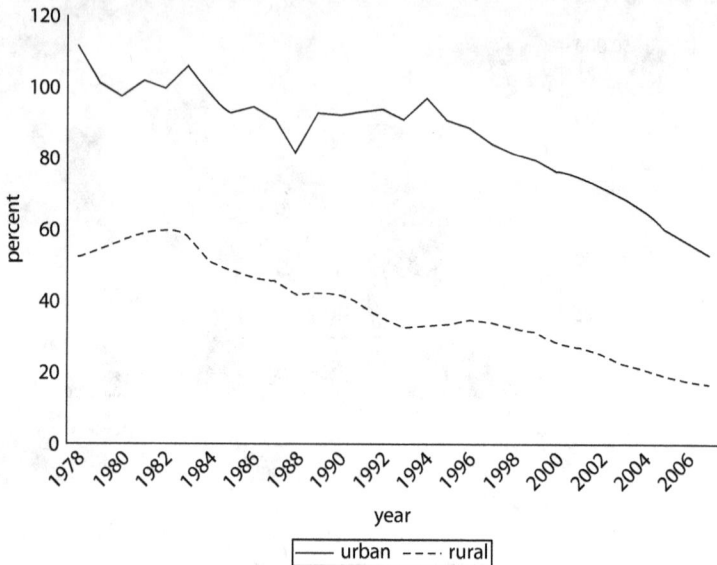

Source: Guangdong Bureau of Statistics 2008.

Box 1.1

Guangdong Rural and Urban Household Survey Data

Household data are crucial to poverty and inequality analysis. They contain disaggregated information on a series of important variables, including household size, demographic characteristics, income and consumption, education and health, transfers, and social welfare. This information can be used to develop a profile of poverty and to understand the extent and sources of inequality.

The Guangdong Survey Department of the National Bureau of Statistics is in charge of rural and urban household surveys at the provincial level and is part of the national rural and urban household survey network in China. This department follows the methodologies designed by the National Bureau of Statistics to draw counties (cities) and rural (urban) households. The sampling technique is a two-stage probability proportionate to size (PPS) approach—that is, the probability of selecting a sampling unit is proportional to the size of its population.

The rural household survey in Guangdong covers 30 counties and 2,560 rural households, of which 10 counties (830 rural households) are in the Pearl River

(continued)

Box 1.1 *(continued)*

Delta (PRD) area, 10 counties (890 rural households) are in the eastern and western areas, and 10 counties (840 rural households) are in the northern areas. The rural household survey is rotated completely every five years.

Before 2007, the urban household survey in Guangdong covered 18 cities and 1,600 urban households, of which 9 cities (950 urban households) were in the PRD area and 9 cities (650 urban households) were in non-PRD areas. Since 2007 (including 2007), Guangdong has expanded its sampling size of urban households in those cities to 3,150 households. Although the urban surveys, in theory, capture all residents, including those without urban local *hukou*, it should be noted that the data may not be fully representative, because it is difficult to capture those living in dormitories or places without street addresses.

It should be recognized that the 2,560 rural households and 1,600 urban households covered by the surveys represent a relatively small sample, accounting for only 0.019 percent of all rural and urban households in Guangdong. Although this sample size may be too small to draw detailed conclusions regarding a small subset of those surveyed at the provincial level, such as rural *Dibao* beneficiaries in Guangdong, it is still useful for examining poverty and inequality issues in general. The daily record accounting system helps ensure high-quality data: the sampled rural and urban households are asked to record their cash income (expenditures) daily and their noncash income (expenditures) monthly, and the information is reported to the statistical agencies quarterly and aggregated for every household annually.

Source: Guangdong Survey Department of the National Bureau of Statistics.

to determine the incidence and distribution of poverty and to develop a profile of the poor. It also looks at the current situation of income inequality and the various sources of this inequality. This analysis can inform the development of pro-poor growth policies in Guangdong, as well as policies related to the rural *Dibao* program, education and training, health, labor market development, land reform, finance, and industrial transfers.

Measuring Poverty in Guangdong

Before discussing specific poverty rates in Guangdong, it is necessary to explain the methodology used in this analysis, since poverty can be measured in several different ways, yielding very different results. One basic choice is whether to use income or consumption as an indicator of well-being. This analysis presents both income- and consumption-based poverty measures, when available. In general, income is considered to be a measure of welfare opportunity, while consumption is considered to be a measure of welfare achievement. If detailed information on consumption is available, consumption may be a better indicator, since actual consumption is more closely related to well-being in terms of having enough to meet current basic needs. Furthermore, getting an accurate measure of consumption may be easier than trying to estimate income, particularly in poor agrarian economies and urban economies with large informal sectors.

Both the income- and consumption-based approaches are justifiable, but, as described in World Bank (2009), a key economic issue is whether the poor save and why. Consumption-based measures give no weight to household savings, while income-based measures treat them on par with consumption. Under the same poverty line, consumption poverty incidence is often higher than income poverty incidence because individuals or households do not spend all their earnings, and they save some money for future consumption or to prepare for uncertainties.

Another central issue in poverty measurement is the selection of a poverty line. A range of poverty lines have been used in China. They are compared in table 1.1, and can be listed as follows:

- **Official poverty line**—traditionally used by the government to monitor rural poverty in China (value of 785 yuan per capita per year in 2007).

Table 1.1   Poverty Lines in China

	Year	Value (yuan per capita per year)	As percentage of mean rural per capita income in Guangdong (5,335 yuan in 2007)
Official rural poverty line	2007	785	14.7
Basic needs line	2003	864	16.2
Low-income line	2007	1,067	20.0
Dollar-a-day line	2007	1,132	21.2
Rural *Dibao* threshold (population-weighted average for Guangdong)	2007	1,520	28.5

Sources: Basic needs and dollar-a-day lines from World Bank 2009. Official poverty line and low-income line from the National Bureau of Statistics 2008. *Dibao* threshold from the Department of Civil Affairs of Guangdong, http://www.gdmz.gov.cn/.

- **Basic needs line**—developed by Chen and Ravallion (see Chen and Ravallion 2004), anchored to 2,100 calories per person per day, with 75 percent of the calories from food grains, and an allowance for basic nonfood consumption (value of 864 yuan per capita per year in 2003).
- **Low-income line**—introduced by the government in 2000 to monitor the situation of households above the official poverty line but below a low-income threshold (value of 1,067 yuan per capita per year in 2007).
- **Dollar-a-day line**—typically used for international poverty monitoring, and strictly corresponding to $1.08 per person per day at 1993 (PPP) (value of 1,132 yuan per capita per year in 2007).
- *Dibao* **threshold**—not a poverty line, per se, but significant because it represents the locally selected minimum living standard for the *Dibao* assistance program, which provides support for households living below the threshold level (population-weighted average threshold level of 1,520 yuan in 2007 for rural Guangdong).

As shown in table 1.1, all of these lines represent a small fraction of mean rural per capita income in Guangdong and are arguably too low for Guangdong, particularly given its level of development relative to other provinces in China and to other country economies. As argued in World Bank (2009), even at the national level, the official poverty line is low by international standards and relative to mean incomes and growing aspirations within China. In a comparison of the 76 countries for which national poverty line data are available, China was one of 11 countries with national poverty lines below a dollar a day (Ravallion, Chen, and Sangraula 2008). Figure 1.5 shows where China's poverty line stood relative to upper-middle-income countries[2]—a relevant comparison for Guangdong, given its movement into upper-middle-income status—and other East Asian countries. It also highlights the countries with poverty lines similar to China's poverty line of $25.89 per capita per month at 2005 PPP, such as Burkina Faso ($26.27), Chad ($26.60), and Malawi ($26.11). China's national poverty line was much lower than the poverty lines of other developing East Asian countries, as shown in table 1.2. To reflect Guangdong's movement into upper-middle-income status, this analysis uses a higher poverty line of $2 per day, equivalent to 2,263 yuan in 2007, for rural Guangdong. The selection of this poverty line is aligned with the World Bank's approach of using the $2-per-day line for monitoring poverty in economies where cost-of-living and income levels are

Figure 1.5 Comparison of National Poverty Lines

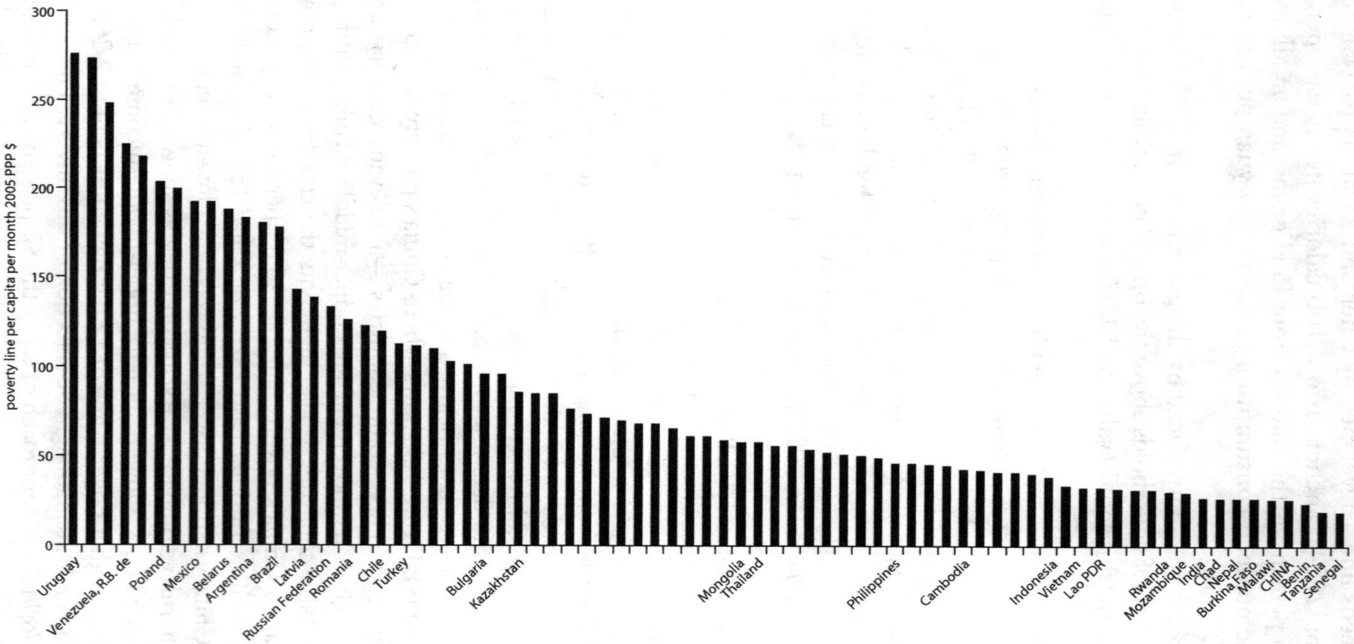

Source: Ravallion, Chen, and Sangraula 2008.

Note: The survey years for this poverty-line information ranged from 1991 to 2005. Urban poverty lines were used for some countries, because the 2005 PPP rates were from urban centers for these countries. Based on the International Comparison Program (ICP) sampling information, the 2005 consumption PPPs were treated as urban PPPs for Argentina, Brazil, Cambodia, Chile, China, Thailand, and Uruguay. For additional information, see Ravallion, Chen, and Sangraula (2008).

Table 1.2   Comparison of National Poverty Lines in East Asia, Selected Countries

Country	Survey year	Poverty line per capita per month (2005 PPP $)
Mongolia	2002–03	57.88
Thailand[a,b]	1992	57.58
Philippines	1988	46.02
Cambodia[a,b]	2004	42.80
Indonesia	1999	32.63
Vietnam	2002	32.52
Lao PDR	1997–98	32.10
China[b]	2002	25.89

Source: Ravallion, Chen, and Sangraula 2008.
a. Urban poverty lines were used, since the 2005 PPP rates were from urban centers for these countries. For Cambodia, the urban poverty line is a simple average of that for Phnom Penh and other urban poverty lines.
b. Based on International Comparison Program sampling information, the 2005 consumption PPPs were treated as urban PPPs. For these countries, both poverty lines and food poverty lines are urban poverty lines.

higher. To reflect the cost-of-living differences between rural and urban areas, this analysis applies a higher poverty line of 3,195 yuan in 2007 for urban Guangdong. These lines represent 42.4 percent and 20.2 percent of mean rural and urban per capita incomes, respectively, in Guangdong in 2007.

Once the poverty line was selected, different poverty indexes could be used to analyze poverty in terms of incidence, depth, and severity. As described in box 1.2, poverty incidence refers to the number of people who are below the poverty line. Poverty depth and severity take into account how poor the poor are, with poverty severity giving more weight to those who are very poor. This analysis uses all three indexes to assess the extent of poverty in Guangdong.

The Current Poverty Situation in Guangdong

This section aims to measure the level, distribution, and dynamics of poverty in Guangdong to gain a better understanding of the current overall situation and to develop a profile of the poor to identify what types of households and individuals may be more vulnerable to poverty.

Box 1.2

Measuring the Incidence, Depth, and Severity of Poverty

Three poverty indexes are often used in poverty measurement and analysis: poverty incidence, poverty depth, and poverty severity. Although the indexes measure different things, they are complementary and together can provide a multidimensional picture of the poverty situation.

Poverty incidence. Referred to as the poverty ratio, headcount index, or headcount ratio, poverty incidence measures the proportion of households or individuals whose incomes are below a given poverty line. This indicator shows how many people are living in poverty at a given poverty line, but it does not differentiate between two regions that have the same level of poverty incidence but different degrees of poverty severity.

Poverty depth. Referred to as the poverty gap, poverty depth measures the normalized income gap between the poverty line and the income of the poor. This indicator assumes the poverty gap for the nonpoor is zero. It only captures the income difference between the poverty line and the income of the poor, which reflects the resources required to eradicate poverty completely in a given location.

Poverty severity. Poverty severity measures the average value of the square of the depth of poverty for each individual or household. The poverty severity index gives more weight to very poor than to less poor, so it incorporates the income distribution of the poor into the poverty analysis. Along with other indicators, this index can be used to assess the effectiveness of poverty alleviation measures in reaching the very poor.

Source: Haughton and Khandker 2009.

Headcount

The incidence of poverty remains high in rural areas of Guangdong, at 10.28 percent in 2007 compared to only 1.65 percent in urban areas (table 1.3). Rural consumption poverty, which arguably provides a better sense of the well-being of rural households, was over 8.0 percentage points higher than income poverty in 2007. In contrast, the difference between the headcount indexes of urban income and consumption poverty was only 0.1 percentage points in 2007, suggesting that urban households in general enjoy fewer financial constraints, better social security support, and more stable employment and income than rural households.

**Table 1.3   Poverty Headcount, Depth, and Severity
in Guangdong, 2007 ($2-Per-Day Poverty Line)**
percent

Poverty indicators	Income poverty	Consumption poverty
Headcount index		
Rural areas	10.28	18.64
Urban areas	1.65	1.55
Poverty depth		
Rural areas	2.43	3.97
Urban areas	0.57	0.26
Poverty severity		
Rural areas	0.89	1.26
Urban areas	0.31	0.07

Source: Guangdong Survey Department of the National Bureau of Statistics 2007.

The large disparities between Guangdong's rural and urban areas are unsurprising, given the sizable differences in income levels. Figure 1.6 shows that, although the distribution of income follows the same pattern in rural and urban areas, urban median income is much higher than rural median income.

Depth

The poverty depth indexes also point to significant differences in rural and urban poverty in Guangdong. A particularly large gap between urban and rural areas can be seen in terms of consumption poverty—as shown in table 1.3, the consumption poverty depth index for urban areas was 0.26 in 2007, compared to 3.97 for rural areas. As in the case of headcount poverty, consumption poverty depth was higher than income poverty depth in rural areas, while income poverty depth was higher than consumption poverty depth in urban areas.

Severity

The poverty severity indexes also underscore the problem of rural poverty in Guangdong. Again, the consumption poverty severity index for rural areas, at 1.26 in 2007, was much higher than for urban areas, at 0.07. Again, as in the case of headcount poverty and poverty depth, consumption poverty severity was higher than income poverty severity in rural areas, while the opposite was true for urban areas. An analysis of household savings rates in 2007 suggests that one possible reason for these urban-rural differences across all three poverty measures is that the urban

Figure 1.6   Urban and Rural Income Distribution in Guangdong, 2007

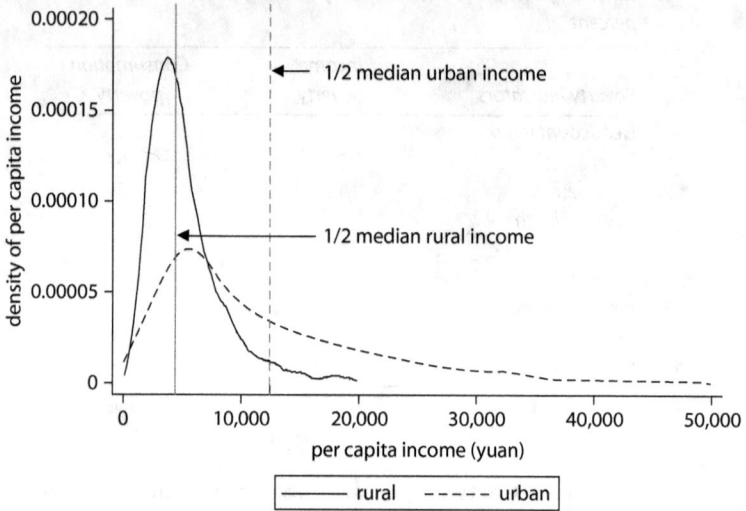

Source: Guangdong Survey Department of the National Bureau of Statistics 2007.
Note: The 2007 rural prices and the cost-of-living difference between rural and urban areas estimated by Brandt and Holz (2005).

poor try to smooth their consumption by drawing down from their savings, or dissaving. The same behavior is evident among rural households, but the dissavings rates are relatively lower.

Distribution

Another way to assess the poverty situation in Guangdong is to test the sensitivity of poverty incidence to shifts in the poverty line. As shown in figure 1.7, the incidence of rural income poverty rises rapidly as the poverty line level increases. In contrast, the incidence of urban income poverty is less sensitive to changes in the level of the poverty line. The difference in poverty incidence between urban and rural areas widens with the rise of the poverty line, again reflecting that rural poverty is more sensitive to the level of the poverty line.

In terms of geographic distribution, poverty in Guangdong is predominantly a rural phenomenon, with 89.9 percent of the poor living in rural areas. As one would expect, both rural and urban poverty are concentrated in the less developed parts of Guangdong, namely in the areas outside the Pearl River Delta (PRD) area. As shown in table 1.4, the western and eastern areas had the highest total rural poverty headcount indexes

Figure 1.7   Sensitivity to the Poverty Line in Urban and Rural Guangdong, 2007

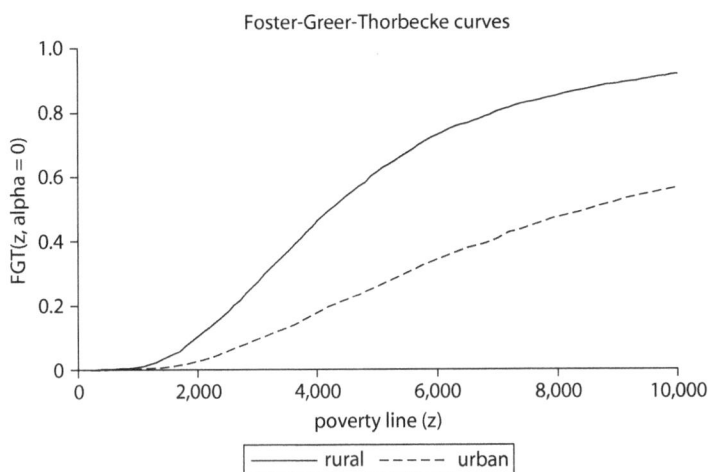

Foster-Greer-Thorbecke curves

Source: Guangdong Survey Department of the National Bureau of Statistics 2007.
Note: Foster-Greer-Thorbecke (FGT) curves are often used to illustrate the headcount index, depth, and severity of poverty with changes in the poverty line.

Table 1.4   Concentration of Rural Poverty in Guangdong ($2-Per-Day Poverty Line)

	Headcount index		Distribution of the poor	
Poverty indicators	*2005*	*2007*	*2005*	*2007*
Income poverty				
Pearl River Delta	5.8	4.7	12.1	13.2
West and east areas	23.1	18.1	62.5	67.0
North areas	11.0	6.2	25.4	19.8
Consumption poverty				
Pearl River Delta	9.4	10.4	13.6	16.2
West and east areas	33.1	32.4	62.6	66.3
North areas	14.8	9.9	23.8	17.5

Sources: Guangdong Survey Department of the National Bureau of Statistics 2005, 2007.

and the largest proportion of the rural poor in 2007, followed by the northern areas. The western and eastern areas also had the highest rates of rural consumption poverty, although, surprisingly, the incidence of rural consumption poverty in the PRD areas was higher than in the northern areas. This relatively higher rural consumption poverty rate in the PRD areas may be explained by savings differences among different regions of Guangdong. For example, the savings rate of rural households in 2007 was 30.7 percent in the PRD areas, compared to 19.8 percent in the northern areas.

The distribution of urban poverty between PRD and non-PRD areas differed according to income and consumption poverty, with PRD areas having a somewhat higher proportion of the urban population who were income poor in 2007, but a much lower proportion of the urban population who were consumption poor, due to larger discrepancies in the income and consumption poverty rates (table 1.5).

Interestingly, the less developed areas of Guangdong appear to have made greater strides in reducing headcount poverty in recent years. As shown in table 1.4, from 2005 to 2007, the rural income poverty headcount indexes fell by 5.0 percentage points in the western and eastern areas and 4.8 percentage points in the northern areas but only 1.1 percentage points in PRD areas, owing to faster growth in the non-PRD areas. Moreover, the incidence of rural consumption poverty in the PRD areas increased from 9.4 percent in 2005 to 10.4 percent in 2007 owing to the rapid increase in savings rates in this area, from 24.9 percent to 30.7 percent, over the same period. In urban non-PRD areas, with rapid wage growth, urban income poverty fell significantly between 2005 and 2007, reversing the distribution of urban poor between PRD and non-PRD areas (table 1.5).

The analysis also shows differences in rural poverty according to geographic topography. The rural poor were concentrated in the hilly and mountainous areas of Guangdong, where they were mainly engaged in farming and had fewer opportunities for labor migration, although the income poverty headcount indexes were similar across the different areas (table 1.6). Rural consumption poverty had a similar distribution, although the headcount index was higher in the plains areas than in the hilly and mountainous areas. This unexpected finding may again be explained by differences in savings rates among the different regions of

Table 1.5   Concentration of Urban Poverty in Guangdong ($2-Per-Day Poverty Line)

Poverty indicators	Headcount index		Distribution of the poor	
	2005	2007	2005	2007
Income poverty				
Pearl River Delta (PRD)	1.65	1.54	34.51	53.01
Non-PRD areas	4.21	1.79	65.49	46.99
Consumption poverty				
Pearl River Delta (PRD)	0.98	0.70	15.18	23.47
Non-PRD areas	7.33	2.67	84.82	76.53

Sources: Guangdong Survey Department of the National Bureau of Statistics 2005, 2007.

Table 1.6   **Rural Poverty by Geographic Topography, 2007 ($2-Per-Day Poverty Line)**

Poverty indicators	Headcount index	Distribution of the poor
Income poverty		
Plains areas	9.85	21.08
Hilly areas	10.98	44.14
Mountainous areas	9.76	34.78
Consumption poverty		
Plains areas	20.44	24.14
Hilly areas	19.93	44.21
Mountainous areas	16.10	31.65

Source: Guangdong Survey Department of the National Bureau of Statistics 2007.

Guangdong. For example, the savings rate of rural households in the plains areas was 31.8 percent in 2007, compared to 24.9 percent in hilly areas and 21.2 percent in mountainous areas.

Poverty Dynamics

An analysis of poverty dynamics in Guangdong shows that Guangdong has been making progress in poverty reduction. Because the 2005 and 2007 rural household surveys covered the same households, the data can be used to analyze the movement of rural households between poor and nonpoor status. As shown in table 1.7, only 7.5 percent of nonpoor rural households in 2005 had become poor by 2007, while 43.2 percent of poor rural households in 2005 escaped from poverty by 2007. However, of those rural households that were poor in 2007, 37.7 percent had been nonpoor in 2005.

Despite this progress in poverty reduction, it should be noted that the income mobility in Guangdong appeared to be constrained. Although rural income and consumption growth were relatively high for the lowest and second-lowest quintiles (figure 1.8), 52.5 percent of rural households in the poorest quintile in 2005 were still in the poorest quintile in 2007 (table 1.8). Because the poverty line falls between the lowest and second-lowest quintiles, it means that over half of rural households in 2005 were still poor in 2007. The overall immobility ratio—the proportion of rural households not changing income quintiles—was 0.426, which means that 42.6 percent of rural households in Guangdong remained in the same income quintile between the two years. In comparison, the immobility ratios in the United States were 0.377 in the 1980s and 0.406 in the 1990s (see Hungerford 2008).

Table 1.7   Rural Poverty Dynamics in Guangdong ($2-Per-Day Poverty Line)

Status in 2005	Nonpoor in 2007	Poor in 2007	Total
		Number of households	
Nonpoor	1,944	157	2,101
Poor	197	259	456
Total	2,141	416	2,557
		Percentage of households	
Nonpoor	92.5	7.5	100.0
Poor	43.2	56.8	100.0
Total	83.7	16.3	100.0
Status in 2007	Nonpoor in 2005	Poor in 2005	Total
		Number of households	
Nonpoor	1,944	197	2,141
Poor	157	259	416
Total	2,101	456	2,557
		Percentage of households	
Nonpoor	90.8	9.2	100.0
Poor	37.7	62.3	100.0
Total	82.2	17.8	100.0

Sources: Guangdong Survey Department of the National Bureau of Statistics 2005, 2007.
Note: Results in this table are based on consumption, as it is a more stable indicator than income.

Figure 1.8   Rural Income and Consumption Growth in Guangdong by Quintile, 2005–07

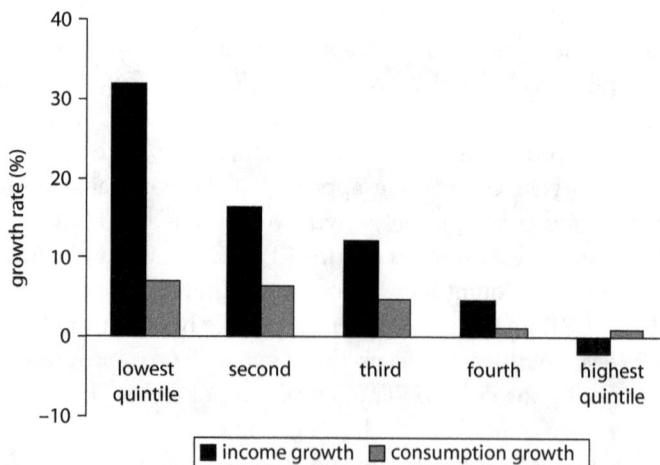

Sources: Guangdong Survey Department of the National Bureau of Statistics 2005, 2007.

Table 1.8   Rural Income Mobility by Quintile, 2005–07

Quintile in 2005	Lowest in 2007	Second in 2007	Third in 2007	Fourth in 2007	Highest in 2007	Total
	Number of rural households					
Lowest	269	126	65	36	16	512
Second	152	164	115	57	24	512
Third	45	139	157	115	56	512
Fourth	29	64	123	191	105	512
Highest	17	19	52	113	311	512
	Percentage of rural households					
Lowest	52.5	24.6	12.7	7.0	3.1	100.0
Second	29.7	32.0	22.5	11.1	4.7	100.0
Third	8.8	27.1	30.7	22.5	10.9	100.0
Fourth	5.7	12.5	24.0	37.3	20.5	100.0
Highest	3.3	3.7	10.2	22.1	60.7	100.0

Sources: Guangdong Survey Department of the National Bureau of Statistics 2005, 2007.

In light of these findings, a key question is whether poverty in Guangdong is more transient or chronic in nature. The national-level findings of the World Bank (2009) indicate that a large fraction of observed rural poverty in China is transient, which has important implications for policies aimed at reducing poverty and suggests that measures to help mitigate and manage the risks of falling into poverty are very important. However, it is difficult to draw such conclusions for Guangdong based on changes in the short time between 2005 and 2007. Data covering a longer time period would be needed to develop a more definitive understanding of the nature of poverty and poverty dynamics in Guangdong.

International Comparison

Although making cross-provincial comparisons is difficult due to lack of data using the $2-per-day poverty line in other provinces, it is possible to compare poverty levels in Guangdong with those in countries with similar mean levels of income. Per capita expenditures per month in rural and urban Guangdong in 2005 were about $130–$150 and $230–$250 (2005 consumption PPP), respectively. As shown in table 1.9, poverty rates varied considerably across countries with similar levels of income. The poverty rate in rural Guangdong was higher than in Algeria, Azerbaijan, and Morocco; the poverty gap was higher than in Morocco; and poverty severity was close to that in Algeria. The poverty rate in urban Guangdong was also higher than Bulgaria and Ukraine.

Table 1.9   International Comparison of Poverty, 2005 ($2-Per-Day Poverty Line)

Economies	Mean income (2005 PPP $)	Headcount index (%)	Poverty gap (%)	Poverty severity (%)
Rural Guangdong	130–150	20.20	3.99	1.66
Urban Guangdong	230–250	3.69	0.83	0.29
Azerbaijan	135	0.27	0.04	0.02
Algeria	136	18.07	4.54	1.67
Nicaragua	151	31.86	12.26	6.44
Morocco	156	16.16	3.69	1.27
Turkey	235	9.05	2.64	1.25
Bulgaria	236	1.63	0.69	0.65
Dominican Republic	245	15.09	4.32	1.68
Ukraine	250	0.48	0.12	0.06

Sources: Numbers for Guangdong from author's calculations. Numbers for other countries from World Bank staff calculations; see Ravallion, Chen, and Sangraula (2008).

Profile of the Poor

Beyond measuring poverty levels, one can develop a profile of the poor to understand what types of households and individuals may be more vulnerable to poverty. This understanding can help policy makers target poverty reduction efforts more effectively, as well as identify the types of interventions that could help alleviate poverty in the long run. This section provides a profile of the poor in Guangdong, with a focus on the rural households that comprise the vast majority of the poor.

Household Size and Structure

One common characteristic among the rural poor is larger household size. Larger rural households tend to have high poverty incidence, with poverty being particularly concentrated among households with four to eight members (table 1.10). This result is unsurprising, given that large rural households may have to support more dependents, resulting in lower per capita income.

In terms of household structure, households with a relatively higher number of dependents in 2007 were poorer on average. Single-headed households had the highest poverty incidence but comprised a relatively smaller proportion of poor rural households. Households consisting of a couple with three or more children had the second-highest poverty incidence and accounted for the largest proportion of poor rural households. Three-generation households accounted for the second-largest proportion of poor rural households and also had high poverty incidence.

Table 1.10   Profile of Household Poverty in Rural Guangdong, 2007 ($2-Per-Day Poverty Line)

percent

Household indicators	Poverty incidence of rural households	Distribution of poor rural households
Household size (number of members)		
1–2	5.26	0.76
3	5.99	3.65
4	6.20	13.09
5	8.06	20.93
6	12.09	23.29
7	15.32	18.11
8	22.50	10.96
9+	13.80	9.21
Household structure		
Single or couple	8.72	0.99
Couple with one child	4.30	2.13
Couple with two children	5.73	11.11
Couple with three or more children	13.72	45.13
Single family	15.14	2.89
Three generations	10.29	33.64
Other	9.51	4.11
Medicare scheme		
Participates	9.63	87.75
Does not participate	20.10	12.25
Rural **Dibao**		
Yes	28.16	4.41
No	9.99	95.59
Migration		
Yes	3.57	13.17
No	14.38	86.83

Source: Guangdong Survey Department of the National Bureau of Statistics 2007.
Note: Data on rural *Dibao* reflect income net of *Dibao* transfers.

Looking at characteristics of individual household members, poverty incidence was highest among households with children under 15 years of age (table 1.11). This result is unsurprising because it is an indication of larger households, which also tend to have more children and dependents and, thus, are likely to be poorer.

Human Capital Endowment

Poor individuals tend to have lower levels of education and health care. As shown in table 1.11, in over 85 percent of poor households in 2007, the highest level of education attained by household members aged

Table 1.11   Profile of Individual Poverty in Rural Guangdong, 2007 ($2-per-day Poverty Line)

percent

Individual indicators	Headcount index	Distribution of the poor
Gender of household members		
Female	10.37	48.36
Male	10.25	51.64
Age of household members		
0–14	15.90	29.48
15–24	8.95	21.75
25–34	6.70	9.11
35–44	12.62	16.62
45–54	6.53	9.80
55–64	8.53	6.51
65+	13.69	6.74
Education of household members ages 16+		
Illiteracy	16.88	11.90
Primary school	12.17	32.31
Middle school	7.37	41.04
High school	6.21	12.81
College +	6.07	1.93
Loss of ability to work		
Yes	14.96	12.08
No	7.83	87.92
Medicare scheme of household members		
Participate	2.76	0.80
Do not participate	10.21	99.20
Rural **Dibao** *of household members*		
Participate	31.43	3.29
Do not participate	10.19	96.71

Source: Guangdong Survey Department of the National Bureau of Statistics 2007.
Note: Data on rural *Dibao* reflect income net of *Dibao* transfers.

16 years or above was below the high school level. Poverty incidence was highest among the illiterate and progressively decreased at higher levels of educational attainment. These findings clearly suggest that better education is important for breaking the cycle of poverty.

Similarly, better health care also appears to play a role in rural poverty reduction. Poverty incidence among households participating in the New Collective Medicare Scheme was 9.6 percent in 2007, compared to 20.1 percent among households who did not participate (table 1.10). These numbers imply that participation in the New Collective Medicare Scheme may be helpful for the reduction of rural poverty.

Labor Situation

Households that lack able-bodied workers—and, in particular, migrant workers—tend to be poorer. As shown in table 1.11, poverty incidence was significantly higher among households whose adult members had lost the ability to work. Having one or more migrant workers was also significant, as poverty incidence among households with migrant workers was much lower at 3.6 percent, compared to 14.4 percent among households with no migrant workers, in 2007. The difference was even starker in terms of poverty distribution, with households that did not have migrant workers comprising over 86 percent of poor rural households (table 1.10).

Access to Assistance

Given the importance that is being placed on the rural *Dibao* program as a vehicle for delivering assistance to the poor, it should be noted that the program reached less than 5 percent of poor rural households. Furthermore, even with the *Dibao* benefits taken into account, as in table 1.11, poverty incidence was higher among rural households and individuals receiving *Dibao* support. Although this finding indicates that the *Dibao* program is targeted well, it also suggests that rural *Dibao* support is not sufficient for lifting the poor out of poverty.

Inequality in Guangdong

This section will offer a measurement of the current income inequality from different dimensions in Guangdong will decompose the overall income inequality by different sources and levels to understand the factors behind the rising inequality levels in Guangdong.

Current Situation

Authorities in Guangdong are concerned about the level and trend of income inequality there and, in particular, the gaps between urban and rural areas. A closer look at the inequality situation in Guangdong reveals a more complex picture.

As described in box 1.3, several different indexes can be used to gauge inequality. This analysis applies each of these indexes to Guangdong, providing comparisons to the national level and to the levels of other provinces, where data are available, to illustrate the current extent of inequality in Guangdong and recent trends. It should be noted that this analysis focuses on the income dimension of inequality, but inequality can also be examined from other dimensions, such as access to services. These other dimensions are discussed in depth in later chapters.

Box 1.3

Measuring Inequality

Inequality indexes are often applied to measure the inequality of income or wealth. These indexes include the following:

- *Lorenz curve*—a graphical representation of the cumulative income share (vertical axis) versus the cumulative population distribution (horizontal axis). If each individual had the same income—or total equality—the income distribution curve would be a straight 45-degree diagonal line. The deviation from the 45-degree diagonal line reflects the extent of income inequality.
- *Gini coefficient*—the area between the line of perfect equality and the observed Lorenz curve, as a percentage of the area between the line of perfect equality and the line of perfect inequality. The higher the coefficient, the more unequal the distribution is. It is sometimes argued that one disadvantage of the Gini coefficient is that it is not additive across groups, meaning that the total Gini of a society is not equal to the sum of the Ginis for its subgroups.
- *Theil index*—a less commonly used measure of income inequality, with a different formula for calculating the magnitude of income inequality. Unlike the Gini coefficient, the Theil index is additive across different subgroups or regions.

Source: Haughton and Khandker 2009.

Although inequality in Guangdong has increased in recent years, it does not appear to be exceedingly high compared to other countries. As in the rest of China, the level of inequality in Guangdong rose rapidly, from 0.246 in 1982 to 0.467 in 2004. Pooling rural and urban households together and adjusting for differences in cost of living, the overall Gini coefficient for Guangdong was 0.394 in 2007.[3] The measured levels of inequality in Guangdong and in China more generally were comparable to those in many other middle-income economies—including countries in East Asia, such as Malaysia and Thailand—and lower than those in many Latin American countries (figure 1.9).

One of the most significant inequality trends in Guangdong, as well as other parts of China, has been the increasing income gap between urban and rural areas. Figure 1.10, which shows changes in the nominal and real urban-rural income ratios since 1985, illustrates the widening urban-rural gap. Although the trend in Guangdong mirrored that at the national level, the ratio values in Guangdong were slightly lower than the national values. From 1985 to 2007, the nominal urban-rural income ratios rose from

Figure 1.9   Comparison of Gini Indexes of Income Inequality, 2007

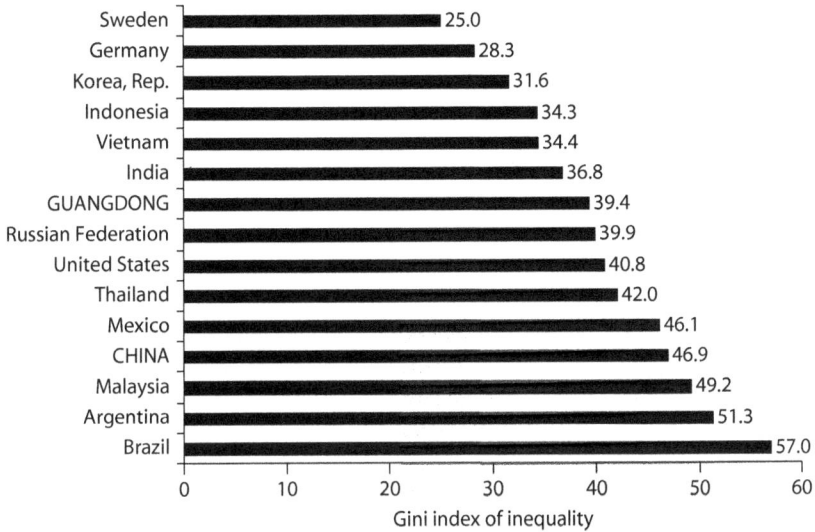

Sweden	25.0
Germany	28.3
Korea, Rep.	31.6
Indonesia	34.3
Vietnam	34.4
India	36.8
GUANGDONG	39.4
Russian Federation	39.9
United States	40.8
Thailand	42.0
Mexico	46.1
CHINA	46.9
Malaysia	49.2
Argentina	51.3
Brazil	57.0

Gini index of inequality

Sources: Country Gini data from World Bank 2007; Guangdong Gini data from Guangdong Bureau of Statistics 2007.

1.9:1 to 3.1:1 in Guangdong, while the real urban-rural income ratios rose from 1.5:1 to 2.2:1 in Guangdong.

Significant levels of inequality can also be seen within urban and rural areas in Guangdong. As shown by the Lorenz curves for rural and urban income inequality in figure 1.11, urban income inequality was greater than rural income inequality in 2007. The Gini coefficients of rural and urban household income inequality were 0.328 and 0.371, respectively. Similarly, the overall Theil index of rural household income inequality for Guangdong was 0.200 in 2007, compared to the overall Theil index of urban household inequality of 0.237. In contrast, at the national level, rural income inequality has been higher than urban income inequality (Li 2008). The Gini coefficients of rural and urban household income inequality at the national level were 0.38 and 0.34, respectively, in 2005. Higher urban income inequality in Guangdong may be explained by such factors as increasing returns to education, openness to global markets, and cost-of-living differences among cities. Further work is needed to identify the underlying reasons.

For rural areas, the ratio of the highest income quintile to the lowest income quintile decreased from 5.56 in 2005 to 3.07 in 2007 due to rapid

Figure 1.10   Trends in Rural-Urban Disparity: Guangdong and China

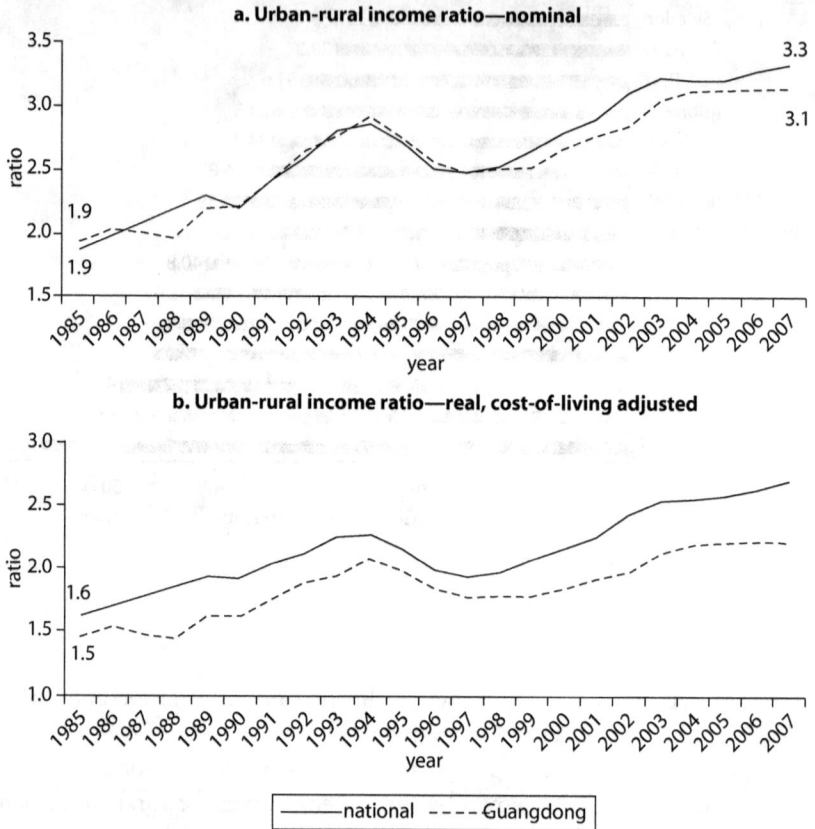

a. Urban-rural income ratio—nominal

b. Urban-rural income ratio—real, cost-of-living adjusted

——— national   - - - - Guangdong

Sources: National Bureau of Statistics 2008; Guangdong Bureau of Statistics 2008.
Note: Per capita incomes are adjusted for inflation using the rural and urban consumer price indexes (CPI) as well as the cost-of-living difference between rural and urban areas estimated by Brandt and Holz (2006).

income growth for the lowest and second-lowest quintiles. The ratios were higher for urban areas but decreased only slightly from 6.95 in 2005 to 6.82 in 2007, because there was no significant difference in income growth between the lowest and highest quintiles of urban households.

In terms of regional disparities, inequality among Guangdong's counties has been decreasing in recent years. As shown in figure 1.12, regional disparity reached a peak in 2003 with a Gini coefficient of per capita GDP among Guangdong's counties of 0.476—higher than the "cautious line" of 0.4 that is often selected internationally for monitoring inequality—then fell to 0.462 in 2007. A decomposition of inequality points to possible

Figure 1.11   Lorenz Curves for Per Capita Rural and Urban Income, 2007

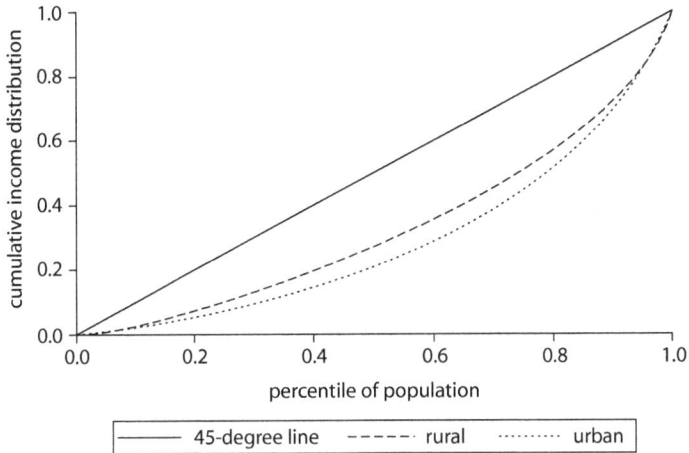

Source: Guangdong Survey Department of the National Bureau of Statistics 2007.

Figure 1.12   Regional Income Disparity in Guangdong and China, 1998–2007

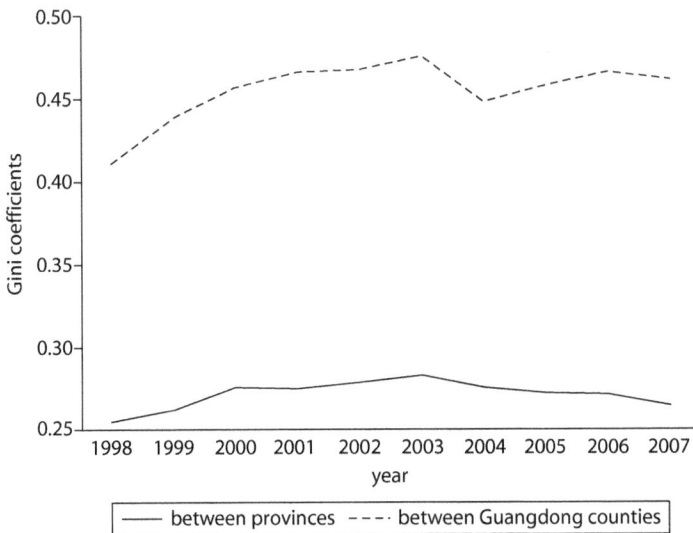

Sources: National Bureau of Statistics 2008; Guangdong Bureau of Statistics 2008.
Note: Per capita GDP at the provincial level and at the Guangdong county level was used to calculate the population-weighted Gini coefficients.

reasons for this decline, as discussed below. Notably, the trends in Guangdong have mirrored the trends at the national level, although the magnitude of regional disparities among counties in Guangdong has been much larger than that among provinces at the national level.

The main reason for the relatively high degree of regional inequality in Guangdong may be the imbalanced regional distribution of the province's population and economic activities. As shown in figure 1.13, nearly 80 percent of Guangdong's GDP in 2007 was generated in the PRD area, but the residents of this region accounted for only 35.1 percent of Guangdong's total population, pointing to a large difference in productivity. Similarly, over 80 percent of the province's GDP was created in urban areas, but urban residents accounted for only 38.3 percent of the total population in Guangdong (figure 1.14).

In sum, while significant between rural and urban areas and across different regions, income inequality in Guangdong is not exceedingly high in comparison with the rest of China. Inequality among Guangdong's counties has also seen some decrease in recent years. These observations imply that, rather than focusing narrowly on income equality, the government needs to assess degree and types of inequality of opportunities, and focus its intervention accordingly.

Figure 1.13   Distribution of Regional Population and Economic Activities in Guangdong, 2007

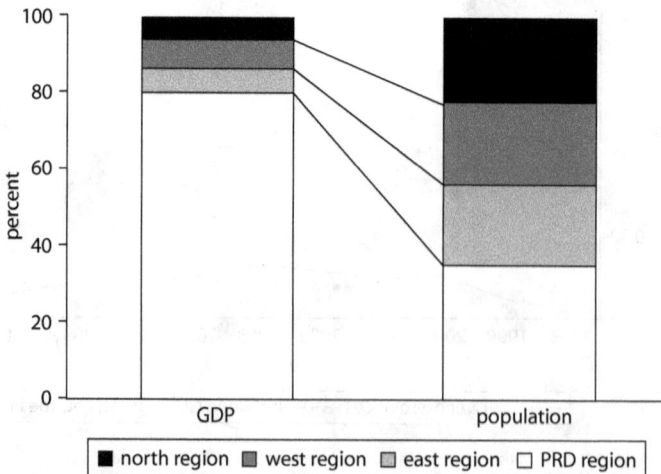

Source: Guangdong Bureau of Statistics 2008.

Figure 1.14   Urban-Rural Distribution of Population and Economic Activities in Guangdong, 2007

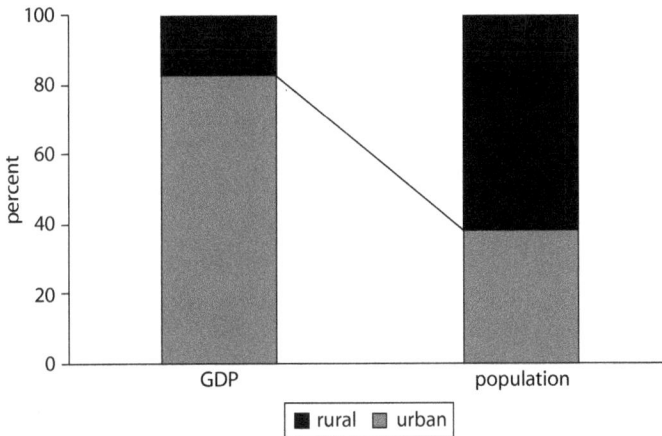

Source: Guangdong Bureau of Statistics 2008.

The Decomposition of Inequality

To determine what measures might be needed to address overall inequality, it is critical to understand the factors behind the rising inequality levels in Guangdong. Inequality decomposition techniques can be used to help identify the sources of inequality and the relative contributions of different factors to overall inequality. Inequality is often decomposed by population groups to assess its contribution within and among groups—for example, within and among households in urban and rural areas—to total inequality.

A decomposition analysis shows that the urban-rural income gap is the biggest component of overall household income inequalities in Guangdong. As shown in figure 1.15, overall inequality in Guangdong can be broken down into seven components: within rural (urban) households in the PRD areas; within rural (urban) households in non-PRD areas; among rural (urban) households; and between rural and urban households. The urban-rural gap comprised the highest share of overall inequality at 23.2 percent in 2007. Income inequalities within both rural and urban households also accounted for a large component of overall inequality in Guangdong.

The urban-rural disparity appears to be driven by the widening wage income gap between rural and urban households. Figure 1.16 presents the

Figure 1.15   Income Decomposition of Pooled Rural and Urban Households in Guangdong, 2007

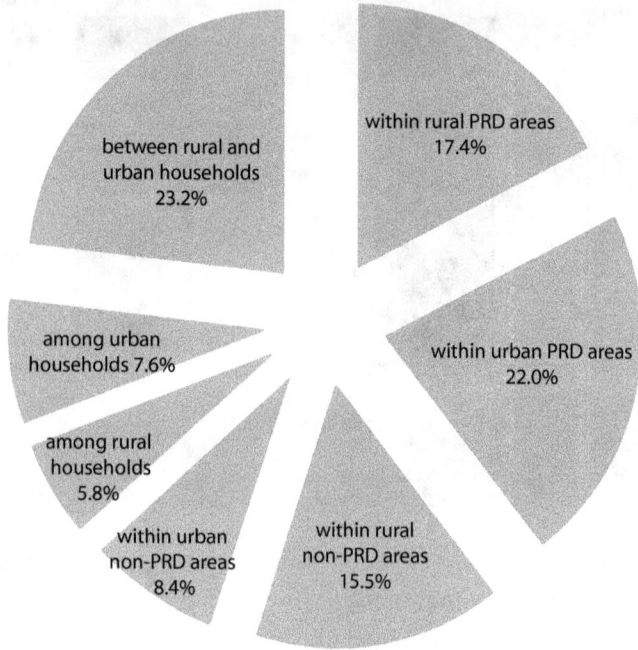

between rural and
urban households
23.2%

within rural PRD areas
17.4%

among urban
households 7.6%

within urban PRD areas
22.0%

among rural
households
5.8%

within urban
non-PRD areas
8.4%

within rural
non-PRD areas
15.5%

Source: Guangdong Survey Department of the National Bureau of Statistics 2007.

results of a decomposition of rural and urban household income from 1995 to 2007 into wage income; income generated by assets; and transfer income, which includes private and public transfers as well as some remittances from nonfamily members. Throughout this period, the wage income difference between rural and urban households accounted for nearly 70 percent of the urban-rural income gap.

A somewhat surprising finding from the household data is that inequalities within the PRD account for a very significant share of overall inequality in Guangdong, while the contribution of cross-regional inequality is not as high. Looking first at rural inequality, 45 percent of overall rural inequality came from within the PRD rural area, while income inequalities among the three geographic regions of Guangdong contributed only 15 percent to overall rural inequality in 2007. Similarly, income inequality within the PRD urban area contributed around 60 percent to overall urban inequality in Guangdong, while income inequalities

Figure 1.16   Sources of Urban-Rural Income Disparity

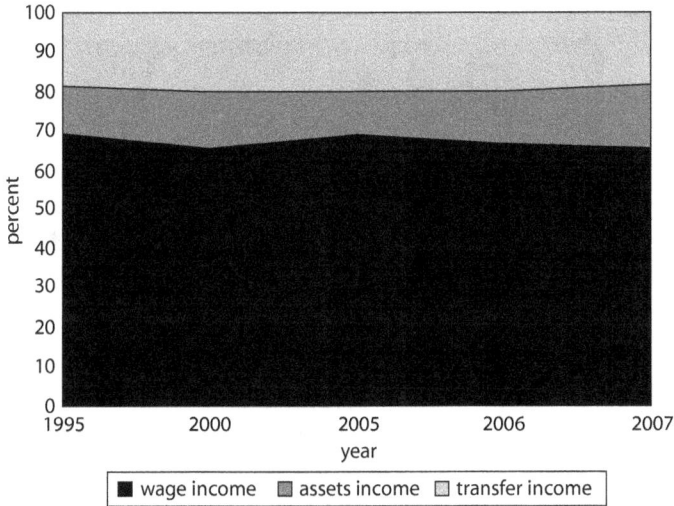

Legend: ■ wage income   ▨ assets income   □ transfer income

Source: Guangdong Bureau of Statistics 2008.

between the PRD and non-PRD regions contributed 19.9 percent to overall urban inequality in 2007.

It should be noted that the magnitudes of the contributions of intra-PRD urban inequality and intra-PRD rural inequality were influenced by relative income shares. The Theil index for intra-PRD urban households was 0.192—only 4.1 percentage points higher than that for non-PRD urban areas—but the larger income share of 71.6 percent raised the contribution to overall inequality. In contrast, the Theil index for intra-PRD rural households was 0.222—1.65 times higher than that for non-PRD rural areas—but the income share of 40.4 percent was relatively smaller, reducing the contribution to overall inequality.

The determinants and specific features of the high intra-PRD inequality need to be explored further. In particular, one needs to take a closer look at the poverty situation of peri-urban residents and that of migrants in the PRD area.

Decomposition analysis can also be used to understand the decline in regional income inequality that Guangdong has experienced since 2003, as mentioned in the previous section. In figure 1.17, the regional Theil indexes from 1998 to 2007 are decomposed into contributions from among regions and within regions. From 1998 to 2002, the inequalities among regions remained stable at around 60 percent of overall regional

Figure 1.17   County-Level Income Inequality Decomposition in Guangdong, 1998–2007

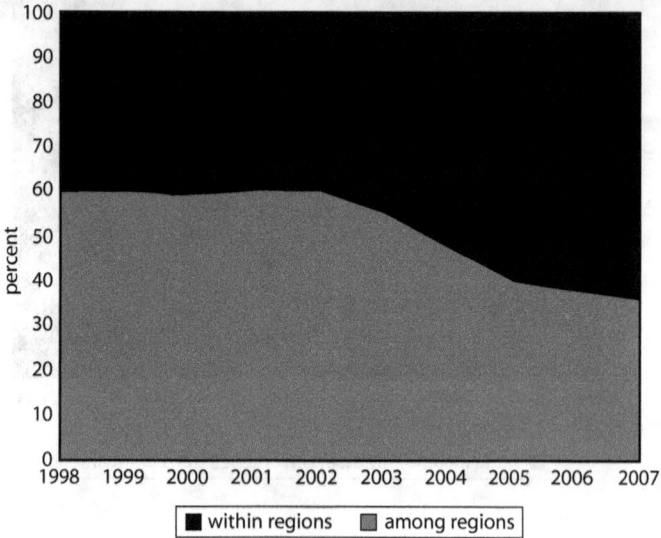

Source: Guangdong Bureau of Statistics 2008.
Note: Per capita GDP at the Guangdong county level was used to calculate the population-weighted Theil index and conduct the decomposition.

inequality. Since 2003, the contribution of inequality among regions has followed a downward trend, dropping to 36.2 percent in 2007. The decreasing overall inequality appears to reflect the "catching up" of lagging regions in the province, while the increasing contribution of inequality within regions indicates that the catching up has been quite different among the lagging counties or regions.

Summary and Policy Implications

The evidence presented above shows that while Guangdong has achieved phenomenal economic growth, this growth has not eradicated the problems of poverty and inequality in the province. Despite some progress in reducing the poverty headcount, poverty levels are still relatively high in Guangdong's rural areas and the regions outside the Pearl River Delta. Although some degree of inequality is natural during high growth periods, the levels of inequality both between and within rural and urban areas remain significant. Inequalities within the PRD region, in particular, now account for a large proportion of overall inequality in Guangdong.

Going forward, it will be important to develop a deeper understanding of poverty and inequality in Guangdong as a basis for designing policies to address these issues. As a starting point, selecting an appropriate poverty line for Guangdong and collecting the necessary household data to monitor poverty and inequality trends will be critical. Further investigation is needed to understand the nature of poverty—for example, whether it is transient or chronic in nature—and the underlying reasons for the differences between rural and urban areas. It will also be critical to develop a more detailed profile of households that are vulnerable to poverty, the factors that may push them into poverty, and the factors that help poor households to escape from poverty. Closer examination of the causes behind the increasingly significant within-region inequalities—including a closer look at the poverty situation of peri-urban residents and the situation of migrants in the PRD area, both from within and outside Guangdong—is also needed to help inform policies.

In terms of policy implications, this analysis underscores the central importance of fostering inclusive growth in Guangdong. As one of China's most developed provinces, Guangdong is in a very strong position to tackle the problems of poverty and inequality through balanced, pro-poor growth. A range of policies can be used to ensure that Guangdong's rapid growth is inclusive: economic reforms that make markets more competitive; measures to level the playing field in terms of labor, land, and capital markets; the expansion of employment opportunities and measures to foster mobility; and human capital investments in education and health. The following chapters describe such policies in detail, laying out an agenda for development in Guangdong going forward. In taking bold measures to promote pro-poor growth, Guangdong can provide an important example for other, less developed regions of China that are struggling with even more severe poverty and inequality.

The findings regarding higher intra-PRD inequality may also have important policy implications for reducing poverty and inequality. Clearly, the conventional focus on urban-rural inequality does not capture the complexity of the situation in Guangdong. In terms of social assistance to the poor, consistent with the message in World Bank (2009), this finding implies that to deal effectively with poverty and inequality, emphasis should shift from area-based approaches to household-oriented approaches for human capital investments and assistance. Understanding the situation of migrants may also shed light on the policy priorities in human capital investment.

Particularly given the high degree of transient poverty, it will also be critical for Guangdong to review and strengthen its social insurance and social assistance programs. Effective social safety nets can help vulnerable households manage the risks that threaten to push them into poverty. The rural *Dibao* program, one of Guangdong's most important assistance programs for the poor, is assessed in chapter 2. Clearly, greater efforts are needed to ensure that such programs have sufficient coverage of the poor population and provide a meaningful level of support.

Notes

1. The population figure of 94.5 million in 2007 that was used to calculate per capita income is from the National Bureau of Statistics (2008), and it includes migrants who lived for more than six months in Guangdong. According to the *Guangdong Statistical Yearbook 2008* (Guangdong Bureau of Statistics 2008), the total population with Guangdong rural and urban *hukou* (household registration) was 81.6 million. The difference amounts to 12.9 million.

2. Based on 2007 GNI per capita, the World Bank divides the global economies into four income groups: low income ($935 or less); lower middle income ($936–$3,705); upper middle income ($3,706–$11,455); and high income ($11,456 or more) using the Atlas method, a three-year average of exchange rates, to smooth the effects of transitory exchange rate fluctuations.

3. It should be noted that the Gini numbers for pre-2005 and the Gini numbers for 2005–07 come from different sources and are therefore not comparable. The pre-2005 numbers are from Guangdong Bureau of Statistics reports, while the numbers for 2005–07 have been calculated from household data.

References

Brandt, Loren, and Carsten Holz. 2005. "Spatial Price Differences in China: Estimates and Implications." *Economic Development and Cultural Change* 55 (1): 43–86.

Chen, Shaohua, and Martin Ravallion. 2004. "China's (Uneven) Progress against Poverty." Policy Research Working Paper 3408, World Bank, Washington, DC.

Council for Economic Planning and Development (Taiwan, China). 2008. Taiwan Statistical Data Book. http://www.cepd.gov.tw/encontent/m1.aspx?s No=0001453.

Guangdong Survey Department of the National Bureau of Statistics. 2005. Rural and Urban Household Survey Data unpublished.

———. 2007. Rural and Urban Household Survey Data, unpublished.

Guangdong Bureau of Statistics. 2008. *Guangdong Statistical Yearbook 2008*. Beijing: China Statistics Press.

Haughton, Jonathan, and Shahidur R. Khandker. 2009. *Handbook on Poverty and Inequality*. Washington, DC: World Bank.

Hungerford, L. Thomas. 2008. "Income Inequality, Income Mobility and Economic Policy: U.S. Trends in the 1980s and 1990s." Congressional Research Service, Washington, DC.

Li, Shi. 2008. "The Current Income Distribution in China." In *Green Book of Population and Labor: Linking up Lewis and Kuznets Turning Points*, ed. Cai Fang, 1–29. Beijing: China Social Sciences Academic Press.

National Bureau of Statistics. 2008. *China Statistical Yearbook 1998–2008*. Beijing: China Statistics Press.

Ravallion, Martin, Shaohua Chen, and Prem Sangraula. 2008. "Dollar a Day Revisited." Policy Research Working Paper 4620, The World Bank Development Research Group, Washington, DC.

World Bank. 2008. *2008 World Development Indicators*. Washington, DC: World Bank.

———. 2009. *China's Evolving Poverty Reduction Agenda: An Assessment of Poverty and Inequality in China*. Washington, DC: World Bank.

CHAPTER 2

Supporting the Poor through Rural *Dibao*

Despite impressive economic growth in recent years, poverty reduction remains a challenge for Guangdong, particularly in rural areas. In 2007, Guangdong had the highest provincial gross domestic product level at nearly 3.07 trillion yuan, accounting for 12 percent of national GDP, and it ranked sixth among provinces in terms of average per capita GDP. Nonetheless, absolute poverty remains significant, especially in rural areas of Guangdong. Measured against a poverty threshold of purchasing power parity (PPP) $2 per day[1]—equivalent to 2,263 and 3,195 yuan per person per year for rural and urban Guangdong, respectively—the income poverty rate stood at 10.3 percent and the consumption-based poverty rate at 18.6 percent in rural Guangdong in 2007 (see table 2.1). In terms of regional distribution, the eastern and western parts of Guangdong account for over 60 percent of the province's poor. Most are concentrated in the hilly and remote mountainous areas, which are home to around 80 percent of the rural poor.

In an effort to address the problem of extreme poverty, the *Dibao* program has been implemented in both rural and urban Guangdong over the

---

This chapter was written by Xiaoqing Yu and Meiyan Wang, with assistance from Minna Hahn Tong. Comments of the Guangdong counterparts on preliminary findings are gratefully acknowledged.

79

**Table 2.1   Poverty Rate and Distribution in Rural Guangdong, 2007
($2-Per-Day Poverty Line)**
percent

By region	Poverty rate	Poverty distribution
Income-based poverty		
Pearl River Delta	4.7	13.2
Eastern and western regions	18.1	67.0
Northern mountainous regions	6.2	19.8
Total	10.3	100
Consumption-based poverty		
Pearl River Delta	10.4	16.2
Eastern and western regions	32.4	66.3
Northern mountainous regions	9.9	17.5
Total	18.6	100

Source: Wang 2010.

past decade. As the main social assistance intervention to support the poor, the program provides direct cash transfers to households whose average net per capita incomes are below a minimum living standard threshold that is locally defined. *Dibao* complements other social safety-net interventions, such as the Five Guarantees (*Wubao*) program, which aims at guaranteeing a basic standard of living for the elderly, disabled, and orphans who lack family support, and the Medical Assistance (MA) program, which provides basic medical protection to the poor. Although the pace of implementation at the national level has been uneven, the *Dibao* system in Guangdong has grown steadily in both urban and rural areas since the inception of the first rural *Dibao* pilot in 1995.

As the "last resort" of the social protection system, has *Dibao* been able to achieve its stated objective of ensuring the minimum subsistence of the poor and eradicating extreme poverty in Guangdong? At this point, the answer is, unfortunately, no. A number of design and implementation challenges have arisen over the past decade, hindering the achievement of objectives. These challenges include inadequate program coverage, very low levels of support from the *Dibao* system, insufficient fiscal inputs, some arguably impractical policy design features, weak program governance, and limited administrative capacity.

With the ability to build on its extensive experience with *Dibao*, and, given its fiscal strength, Guangdong is in a position to lift the poor out of extreme poverty by expanding and improving the *Dibao* program. It will require determination in setting priorities, improvements in policy design to enhance efficiency, and strengthening of safety-net institutions to ensure that the program is well governed. Guangdong's success will offer valuable lessons and experience to other provinces of China.

Since extreme poverty is largely a rural phenomenon in Guangdong, this chapter will focus on the rural *Dibao* system. It will first describe the framework and criteria against which program design and performance will be assessed. It will then review the key design features of the *Dibao* system in Guangdong and identify the main policy and implementation issues. Finally, the chapter will provide recommendations to the Guangdong authorities on how to develop *Dibao* further into an effective policy instrument to achieve the goal of eradicating extreme poverty in the province.

How to Evaluate a Social Assistance Program

Before an assessment of the rural *Dibao* program in Guangdong, it would be useful to describe the framework and methodology used for such an assessment. This section highlights the key attributes of an effective social assistance program and lays out some basic questions to be considered in reviewing social assistance programs. It then describes the specific methodology and data used for the assessment of the *Dibao* program in Guangdong.

Important Attributes of a Social Assistance Program

What is a good social assistance program? In assessing the design and performance of any social assistance program, one needs to consider whether the program exhibits the following important attributes[2]:

- *Adequacy*—The overall social safety-net system is designed to assist various groups of society in need of assistance, such as the chronic poor; the transient poor; those affected by economic, natural, and social shocks; and other vulnerable groups. Individual social assistance programs should provide full coverage and meaningful benefits to the population they are designed to assist.

- *Equitability*—A safety-net intervention should treat beneficiaries in a fair and equitable manner. In particular, it should aim to provide the same benefits to individuals or households that are equal in all important respects (horizontal equity), and it may provide more generous benefits to the poorest beneficiaries (vertical equity). Support should be provided in a transparent manner.

- *Efficiency*—Efficiency of social assistance programs is required in several dimensions. A social assistance program is designed efficiently if it is incentive compatible for the beneficiaries. That is, instead of creating welfare dependency and significant disincentives to work, it should encourage beneficiaries to build assets actively, invest in their futures, and seek work and income opportunities. Keeping the benefit levels of the program modest and conditioning eligibility on desirable behaviors can help ensure such compatible incentives. By design, targeted social assistance programs also need to achieve a satisfactory level of targeting efficiency. Targeting efficiency is measured by the percentage of beneficiaries who should not have been eligible but get the benefits (error of inclusion) and the percentage of those who should have been eligible but do not get the benefits (error of exclusion). Finally, social assistance programs are implemented efficiently when most of the program resources are channeled to the intended beneficiaries at low administrative cost. Designing an effective administrative system and reducing program leakage are key to achieving a satisfactory level of cost-effectiveness.

- *Sustainability*—A social assistance program needs to be financially and politically sustainable. While it should be adapted to the evolving needs of the society, policy goals should be consistent and well communicated, and adequate monitoring and accountability mechanisms should be in place. Stop-and-go implementation should be avoided since it compromises the credibility of the program and lowers the confidence of the population, as well as results in lost opportunities for developing efficient and cost-effective administration.

Policy Questions to Answer

Against the principles laid out above, an assessment of a social assistance program should examine the following aspects of policy design and implementation:

- Did the program have clearly stated and achievable policy goals?
- Was the program designed and implemented in a way that ensured adequate coverage and the necessary level of protection?
- Were the key policy parameters (such as eligibility criteria and benefit levels) set in a way to ensure that the program was incentive compatible and well targeted?
- Was program administration cost-effective? Were the proper monitoring and evaluation mechanisms in place to assess results?
- Was the program financed and governed in a sustainable manner?

A full assessment clearly needs to look at the impact of the program on intended beneficiaries and its outcome for them—whether family welfare was protected effectively and what behavior changes resulted from the policy.

Methodology and Data Used

The analysis and findings presented in this chapter relied on a review of policy documents, visits and discussions with policy makers and program participants, analysis of the Guangdong rural household survey data, and review of some administrative data. While such a combination of approaches was appropriate for the questions at hand, the depth of the analysis was seriously affected by the limitations of the basic survey and administrative data. Therefore, the analysis can only partially answer the questions outlined above.

The analysis relied on the provincial rural household survey data, which covered 30 counties (cities, or districts) and 2,560 rural households. The survey adopted the standard questionnaire developed at the national level; the sampling approach was consistent with the procedures required by the National Bureau of Statistics. The data were collected by the rural survey team of the provincial statistical authority. While the survey was representative and the size sufficient for analyzing general poverty trends and policy implications at the national level, the small number of *Dibao* beneficiaries included in the sample made it impossible to draw robust conclusions regarding the characteristics of the beneficiaries or the targeting efficiency and welfare impacts of the program on beneficiaries in Guangdong. It was also not possible to carry out sensitivity analysis of changes in policy parameters.

To answer questions about the cost-effectiveness of program administration and to pinpoint the issues concerning financing, the research team required critical information on actual resource use and administrative costs, but it was not made available. To the extent possible, the study used data from various statistical yearbooks. Much more in-depth analysis is needed to present stronger evidence for some of the observations and to develop more specific recommendations.

Evolution and Main Policy Features of Rural *Dibao* in Guangdong

The rural *Dibao* system in Guangdong has a relatively long history compared to *Dibao* programs in other parts of China and thus has had more time to develop. This section provides a brief history of the *Dibao* system in Guangdong then summarizes the current policy objectives and key design features of the program.

Evolution

Guangdong was among the first provinces in China to establish a rural *Dibao* system and one of the few to maintain a stable program throughout the past decade. At the national level, rural *Dibao* was initiated at different times, and some provinces experienced stop-and-go operation during the piloting phase. Until very recently, the national government gave local governments discretion on whether to develop *Dibao* programs and on the specific policy parameters. The national government finally mandated the nationwide scaling up of the rural *Dibao* program in 2007.

Compared with those in other provinces, the rural *Dibao* program in Guangdong has a long history, partly because Guangdong's rapid economic growth has enabled it to afford such a program. Pilot *Dibao* projects were launched in Guangdong in 1995. In 1999, the issuance of regulations known as the "Implementation Approach Concerning the *Dibao* System for Urban and Rural Residents in Guangdong Province" marked the formal establishment of rural *Dibao* in Guangdong. Since then, the coverage of the program has expanded steadily, as shown in table 2.2.

Policy Objectives and Key Design Features

The 1999 provincial regulations outlined the objectives, principles, basic policy features, and implementation responsibilities for the urban and rural *Dibao* programs. These regulations are the ones still being implemented today.

The *Dibao* system is designed as a typical guaranteed minimum income program, similar to those found in many countries in the Organisation for Economic Co-operation and Development (OECD) and

Table 2.2   Basic Indicators for Rural *Dibao* in Guangdong

Year	Number of beneficiaries (10,000 households)	Number of beneficiaries (10,000 persons)	Dibao payment (10,000 yuan)
2004	32.46	78.22	31249.4
2005	50.04	130.00	38268.8
2006	53.48	133.90	55002.5
2007	56.29	138.86	75466.1

Source: Unpublished data provided by the Department of Civil Affairs of Guangdong Province.

some developing countries. The policy objective is to assist poor households whose per capita monthly income is below a locally determined minimum standard (the "*Dibao* standard"). The benefit is given in the form of a cash transfer equal to the difference between the minimum standard and the household income. The regulations lay out three main principles for the program: (1) it should be compatible with the level of economic and social development in that locality; (2) it should be combined with the intrafamily support required by the law; and (3) it should follow the principles of fairness, equity, and democracy.

The targeted beneficiaries of the program are local residents whose per capita household incomes are below the local *Dibao* standard. The beneficiaries must have local residency (*hukou*). Residents who have better living conditions, who have luxury consumption goods, who refuse to work without proper reasons, or who do not follow the family planning policies are excluded even if they meet the income-testing requirements.

The income-testing threshold (the *Dibao* standard) is expected to reflect the local living standard and what is required for minimum subsistence; price levels; local economic and fiscal conditions; and the standards used in other social protection programs. The threshold should be adjusted over time. However, the regulations do not specify a methodology for establishing and adjusting the threshold.

The household income that is used as a basis for means testing includes wage and nonwage income such as income from assets, inheritance, and transfers. It does not include certain sources of income, such as the veteran's subsidy, awards given by the government for outstanding contributions to the country, and transfers for funeral and family planning purposes.

The mandated eligibility review procedure involves four steps. First, the household files a household application in written form with the village committee in the household's place of *hukou* registration, along with any relevant documents proving eligibility, such as a certificate of employment income and household income. Second, the village committee investigates and verifies the information in the application, which is then submitted with the written opinions of the committee to the people's government at the township level. Third, the township government reviews the application and provides its opinions, then submits the application to the civil affairs bureau at the county level. Fourth, the bureau reviews and approves the application. To ensure transparency, the village committee must post the names of applicants and the approval decisions for public information on a timely basis.

The regulations stipulate that financing responsibility for the *Dibao* program shall be borne jointly by the fiscal authority and the village-level collectives. Subsequent documents have specified the proportion that each level of government is required to pay.

Challenges Faced by the *Dibao* Program in Guangdong

Despite the impressive progress made by Guangdong in sustaining and expanding its rural *Dibao* program, a review of implementation experience indicates that the program has yet to achieve its objectives. The key issues hindering the achievement of objectives include the level of program coverage, the amount of fiscal input, the design of some key policy features, and the governance and administration of the program.

Coverage

The *Dibao* program in Guangdong cannot lift the rural poor out of absolute poverty because its coverage is very limited. This is true when measured in terms of the absolute level and also relative to the level of poverty in Guangdong.

Administrative data show that rural *Dibao* beneficiaries accounted for about 3.54 percent of total residents with rural *hukou* in 2007. However, this figure masks substantial regional variation in coverage. As shown in figure 2.1, Guangzhou ranked first with a coverage rate of 9.5 percent, while Zhaoqing city was at the bottom of the list with a coverage rate of 1.9 percent.[3] Among the geographic regions, the five mountainous cities had the highest coverage rate of 4.1 percent, followed by the Pearl River Delta with a coverage rate of 3.2 percent. The eastern and western parts of the province, which, as noted above, account for over 60 percent of the province's poor, had the lowest coverage rate at 2.7 percent. Although these statistics do not reflect the magnitude of need among the poor in each region and therefore cannot be used to draw conclusions about the absolute adequacy of coverage, the fact that the coverage rate in the PRD region is higher than or similar to that in the eastern and western regions of the province, where poverty rates are much higher, does indicate geographic gaps in coverage.

Using rural household data rather than administrative data yields a significantly lower overall coverage rate of 1.6 percent for Guangdong in 2007. The large difference between the administrative data and household survey data calls into question the quality of the administrative data and also points to the need for larger surveys to ensure robustness of the survey data.

Figure 2.1   Regional Differences in Rural *Dibao* Coverage[3]

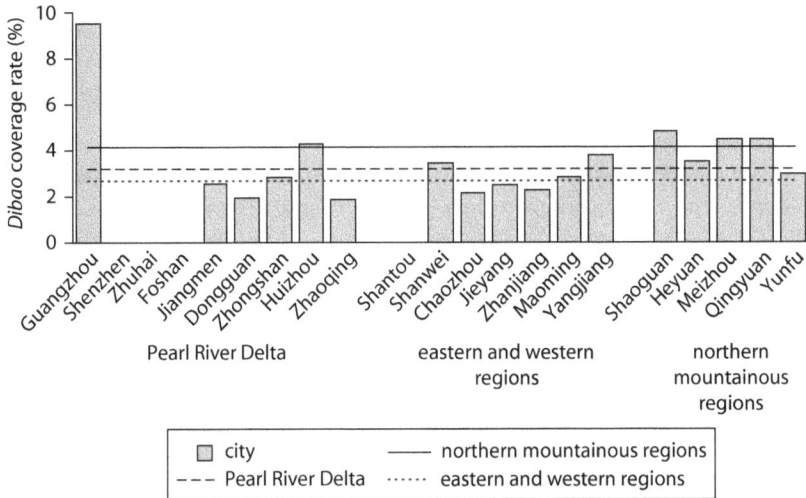

Source: Statistics on rural *Dibao* beneficiaries are as of December 2007 and were provided by the Department of Civil Affairs of Guangdong Province. Statistics on local farming population with *hukou* are as of 2007 and are from Guangdong Bureau of Statistics (2008).

Table 2.3   Rural *Dibao* Coverage Rates vs. Rural Poverty Rates 2007
percent

By region	Coverage rate	Income-based poverty rate	Consumption-based poverty rate
Pearl River Delta	3.19	4.7	10.4
Eastern and western regions	2.69	18.1	32.4
Northern mountainous areas	4.13	6.2	9.9
Total	3.25	10.3	18.6

Source: Rural *Dibao* coverage rates are from the Department of Civil Affairs of Guangdong Province and Guangdong Bureau of Statistics (2008); see figure 2.1, above. Poverty rates are from Wang 2010.

The proportion of the target population—in this case, the rural poor—receiving the *Dibao* benefit is perhaps one of the best indicators of program coverage. Based on rural household data, 4.5 percent of the poor population (measured against a $2-per-day poverty line) are covered by *Dibao*. Although the limited sample size makes it difficult to estimate this proportion by region, a simple comparison of the coverage of the local rural population and local poverty rates provides an indication of how well the program is covering the target population. Table 2.3 shows that at the provincial and local levels, large gaps exist between rural *Dibao* coverage rates and the income- and consumption-based poverty rates.

The Dibao *Standard*

Looking at the second dimension of adequacy, one can reach the same conclusion that the rural *Dibao* program in Guangdong is inadequate for meeting its policy objective. The *Dibao* standard is very low, and the way it is established does not always reflect the principles outlined in the regulations.

The *Dibao* standard adopted in rural Guangdong is low, especially considering the significant gap between rural and urban income levels. As shown in table 2.4, the average rural *Dibao* standard among the 114 counties was 137 yuan per month in 2007, equivalent to about 30 percent of average per capita net income in rural Guangdong. Responsibility for establishing the benefit level has been left to the county governments, and, as a result, levels have differed substantially across the province. In 2007, over 80 percent of the counties set the *Dibao* standard below 150 yuan per month, and 28 percent set it below 100 yuan per month.

Although national and provincial policies require that the *Dibao* standard reflect the cost of maintaining the minimum subsistence level and be adjusted over time according to changes in the cost of living, this principle is rarely followed. As elsewhere in China, no consistent method for determining the standard—such as using the cost of a certain minimum consumption basket and indexing to price changes—has been applied. In general, the *Dibao* standards in Guangdong are higher than the national poverty line and lower than the $2-per-day poverty line (measured using the PPP data, as discussed in chapter 1 of this volume). Table 2.5 illustrates that the *Dibao* standard does not appear to be linked to the poverty lines.

One factor that has really driven the level of the *Dibao* standard is the fiscal capacity of the local government. Figure 2.2 shows a strong positive correlation between the selected *Dibao* standards and per capita GDP levels. Similarly, the counties with the highest levels of per capita local government budgetary expenditures also have established higher *Dibao* standards.

Table 2.4   *Dibao* Standard and Rural Net Income, 2007

Parameter	Dibao *standard (yuan/month)*	*As percentage of average per capita net income of the rural population*
Minimum	100	21.32
Median	120	25.59
Mean	137	29.21
Maximum	320	68.23

Source: The minimum, median, and maximum values were calculated using unpublished data provided by the Department of Civil Affairs of Guangdong Province. Per capita net income is from the Guangdong Bureau of Statistics (2008).

Table 2.5   Comparison of *Dibao* Standard and Poverty Lines, 2007

Parameter	Dibao *standard* (yuan/month)	National poverty line	$2-per-day poverty line (2005 PPP $)
Median	120	65	189
Mean	137	65	189

Source: Dibao standard data are from the Department of Civil Affairs of Guangdong Province.
Note: PPP = purchasing power parity.

Figure 2.2   Correlation between *Dibao* Standards and Economic Strength, Selected Counties

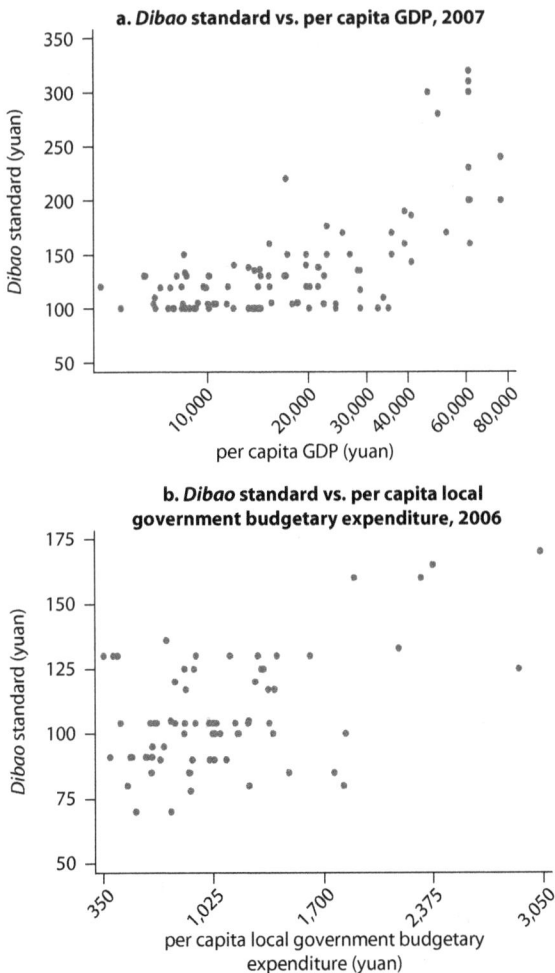

a. *Dibao* standard vs. per capita GDP, 2007

b. *Dibao* standard vs. per capita local government budgetary expenditure, 2006

Source: Dibao standard data are from the Department of Civil Affairs of Guangdong Province; per capita GDP is from Guangdong Bureau of Statistics (2008); per capita local government budgetary expenditure was calculated using data from National Bureau of Statistics (2007).

Dibao *Eligibility and Targeting*

Guangdong has also faced challenges in applying the eligibility criteria for the *Dibao* program and in improving targeting. The application of eligibility criteria has been hindered in part by information constraints as well as limited program resources. Although further analysis is needed to understand the program's targeting performance, it appears that several factors in the design and implementation of the program could contribute to targeting errors.

Eligibility. While the provincial regulations concerning the *Dibao* program in Guangdong explicitly lay out the key eligibility criteria—(1) holding an official residency (*hukou*) within the jurisdiction, (2) meeting the per capita household income-testing criteria, and (3) having actual living standards and a lack of assets that indicate great need—the implementation of such eligibility criteria and means-testing requirements has been a major challenge. The key issues are the following:

- Information on income and living conditions is very difficult to obtain, posing a major challenge to establishing eligibility according to the policy. Self-reported income information for each household member (including income from labor, asset inheritance, transfers, and so on) is often unreliable and difficult to verify. Rural income is particularly hard to track, since some outputs can be consumed directly. This challenge is certainly not unique to Guangdong, but the particular benefit policy design (top-up scheme) requires a certain level of precision for such information—an issue that could be tackled differently, as discussed below.

- The fiscal allocation to the *Dibao* program does not allow for faithful implementation of such eligibility criteria. As observed during visits and interviews conducted during preparation of this chapter, it seems that in many places, despite the fiscal matching or transfers from the provincial government, the program is often significantly underfunded. As a result, an entitlement program by design is, in practice, a program that must ration eligibility for benefits.

Targeting. Basic incidence analysis suggests that the current system is mostly benefiting the poorest segment of the population. Figure 2.3, using pretransfer income as the welfare variable, presents the distribution of beneficiaries across income quintiles by individuals and households. It shows that in 2007, 48 percent of the individual beneficiaries fell into the

Figure 2.3   Distribution of Rural *Dibao* Recipients across Income Quintiles, 2007

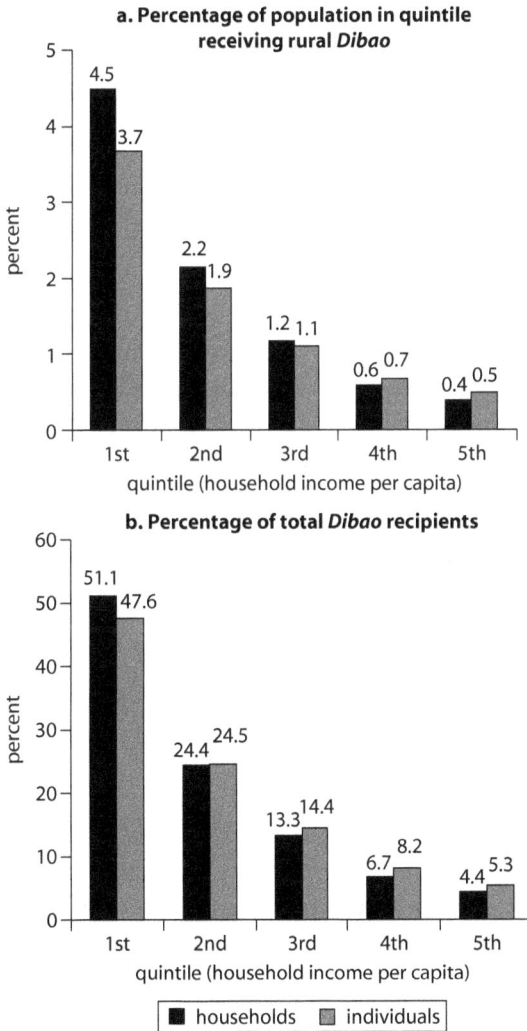

a. Percentage of population in quintile receiving rural *Dibao*

quintile (household income per capita)

b. Percentage of total *Dibao* recipients

quintile (household income per capita)

■ households   ■ individuals

Source: World Bank team analysis of Guangdong rural household survey microdata provided by the Guangdong Bureau of Statistics.

lowest quintile of the distribution, and over 72 percent belonged to the lowest two quintiles. The leakage to the nonpoor as measured by income was therefore relatively small.

An analysis of *Dibao* recipients using household survey data also reveals that a significant number of beneficiaries had per capita household incomes higher than the *Dibao* threshold. At the same time, many households that met the income criteria did not receive *Dibao*. Closer analysis of the data and a larger survey sample are needed to help identify patterns and the reasons behind what appear to be significant inclusion and exclusion issues.

Aside from the targeting errors that may arise from difficulties in verifying eligibility, several hypotheses regarding targeting deserve further study. First, while the data analysis used income as the eligibility criterion, in reality, significant weight may be given to criteria other than income, such as the ability to work and household consumption needs. Second, it is important to understand whether assumed income is applied when conducting means testing. If there are family members who are working as migrants elsewhere or who could provide support, is the receipt of that support assumed without further verification? It is also very important to determine, although perhaps from different sources of data, whether there is a high percentage of applicants who did not get approved for eligibility, which indicates the degree of awareness of the program and individuals' rights and responsibilities.

The discretion that the current system allows in establishing the eligibility of particular households and its implications are important to understand. At this point, substantial discretion is left to the village committee, which is below the lowest level of government. Communities are, in principle, involved in monitoring and providing feedback. Village committees can, in principle, take into account other factors and judge whether a particular household is eligible. Although such discretion allows for effective use of local knowledge, it also opens the system to potential abuse and credibility issues. As the system is scaled up and becomes the main social assistance program in China, the targeting policy and approaches need to become much less discretionary and much more rule-based.

Dibao *Financing*

The rural *Dibao* program is expected to be funded primarily by the municipal and county government budgets, supplemented by subsidies from the provincial fiscal authority. According to the "Interim Measures of Guangdong Province for the Management of the *Dibao* Program Fund," issued in 2005, for the 14 provincially designated poverty-stricken areas and Enping city, the provincial financial department subsidized 30 percent and 50 percent of the urban and rural *Dibao* benefit expenditures, respectively. These provincial inputs were increased to 40 percent and 60 percent, respectively, starting from January 2008. The prefecture-level cities are required to shoulder a certain proportion of financing responsibility for the program according to local capacity in order to reduce the fiscal pressure at the county level.

Overall Expenditure on Dibao. Guangdong as a province has dedicated a very small proportion of its government budget expenditures to the rural *Dibao* program, particularly compared to other provinces. Figure 2.4, panel a, shows rural *Dibao* payments as a percentage of government budget expenditures by province. At 0.24 percent, Guangdong's expenditure was lower than the national average of 0.27 percent in 2007. Figure 2.4, panel b, also shows that Guangdong had one of the lowest proportions of urban and rural *Dibao* payments as a percentage of GDP compared to other provinces. It is perhaps expected that as a province gets richer, the need for poverty reduction relative to the size of the economy is reduced. However, as illustrated earlier, Guangdong needs to and can provide more inputs to eradicate extreme poverty and improve the basic living conditions of the rural poor.

Financing by the Provincial Government. Provincial inputs in less developed regions are critical to the successful implementation of the *Dibao* program. Among the key questions regarding whether the financing needs of the programs are being addressed are the following: How well are the overall program financing needs established, and what incentive problems have been encountered when budgeting the program? Is the transfer of provincial inputs adequate and timely, and are the regional variations appropriate? Is the required matching amount by prefecture and county government secured, and if not, how much is lacking and why? To ensure that the program is adequately budgeted to meet the financing needs, does the provincial-local balance need to be adjusted further, and what steps are needed to ensure that local funds are devoted as required?

Financing data were too limited for the study to answer these critical questions fully and to obtain a systematic picture of the actual financing arrangements. Data from the statistical yearbook could only confirm the observation that the provincial government plays a major role in financing rural *Dibao* in poor areas. Meanwhile, the actual level of financing varied significantly across the province and differed from the required percentage in some cases. Figure 2.5, panel a, shows how financing responsibilities were shared among different levels of government. Among the seven cities in the Pearl River Delta, only Enping city (in Jiangmen) received a provincial subsidy, though at 44 percent of the total *Dibao* payments rather than the prescribed 50 percent. In underdeveloped areas, all cities except

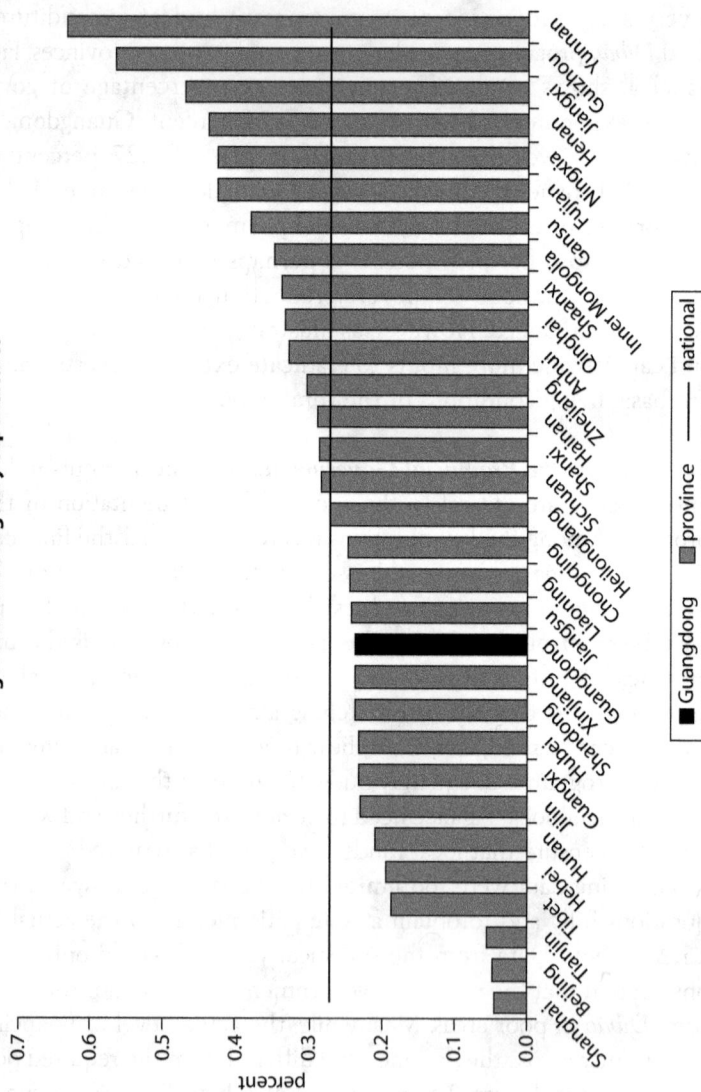

Figure 2.4 Rural *Dibao* Expenditure in Guangdong in Comparison with Other Provinces, 2007

a. Rural *Dibao* expenditure as a percentage of
government budgetary expenditures

■ Guangdong   ■ province   — national

b. Urban and rural *Dibao* expenditure as a percentage of GDP

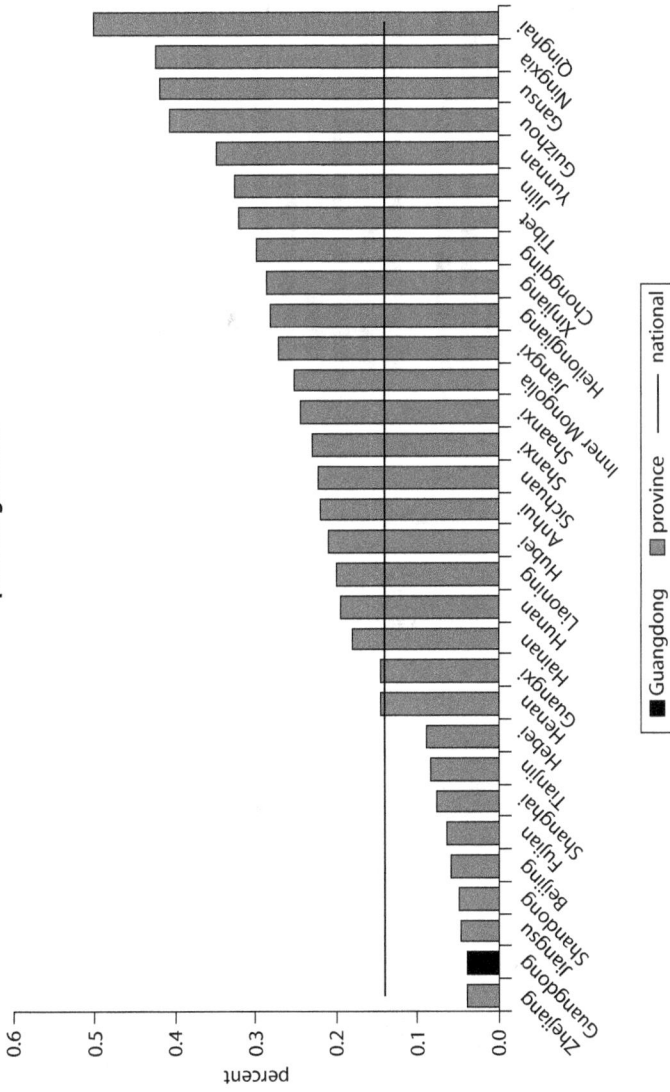

Legend: Guangdong ■ province ▨ national —

Source: Data on rural *Dibao* payments from the Ministry of Civil Affairs Web site. Data on GDP and government budgetary expenditures from the National Bureau of Statistics (2008).

Figure 2.5   Financing of Rural *Dibao* by the Provincial and Local Governments

a. Percentage of local and provincial budget inputs in rural *Dibao* payments, 2005

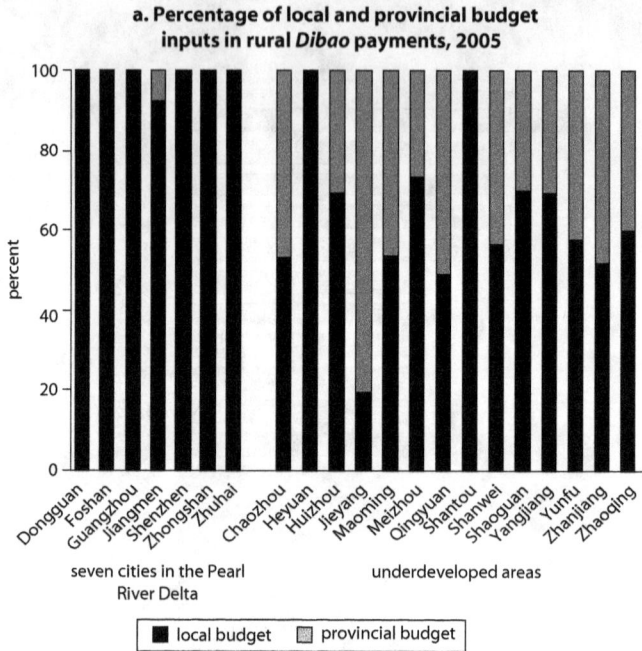

seven cities in the Pearl River Delta

underdeveloped areas

■ local budget   ▨ provincial budget

b. Percentage of rural *Dibao* payments in local budget expenditures, 2006

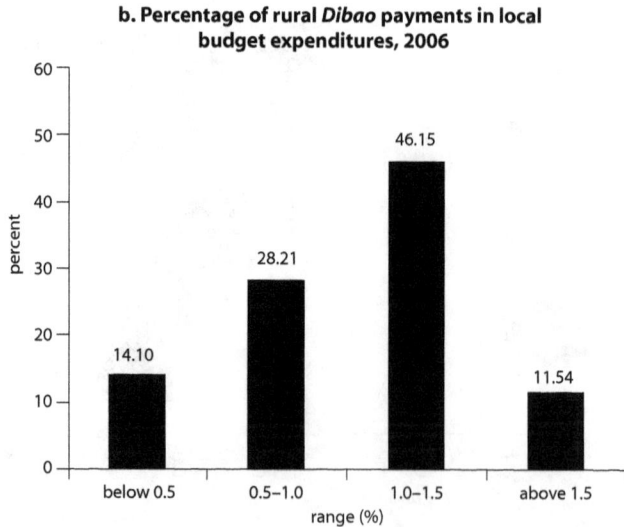

Source: Data on rural *Dibao* payments were provided by the Department of Civil Affairs of Guangdong Province. Data on local budget expenditures are from National Bureau of Statistics (2007).

Heyuan and Shantou received some provincial subsidy. The percentages in other cities, except Jieyang and Qingyuan, were below 50 percent, with the lowest in Meizhou at 27 percent.

Local Financing. Rural *Dibao* payments comprise a small fraction of general budget expenditures for most local governments in Guangdong. Figure 2.5, panel b, shows the percentage of rural *Dibao* payments in the general budget expenditures of local governments (county, city, or district level). By December 2006, this percentage was below 0.5 percent in 14.1 percent of counties (cities or districts) and above 1.5 percent in only 11.5 percent of counties (cities or districts). Although it is difficult to pinpoint what the "right" percentage should be, the proportion of budget expenditures that is allocated for the rural *Dibao* program is clearly very low.

Intergovernmental Fiscal Issues. Central to the success of all social assistance programs is the intergovernmental fiscal policy and framework. With the substantial variation in fiscal capacity and poverty situations within and across provinces, substantial redistribution of fiscal resources will be necessary. In the short to medium term, the government may need to develop a simple and transparent formula that helps set the level of redistribution and introduce the link between performance and allocation. In the early development stage of the urban *Dibao* system, such a formula was used when the national government allocated across provinces; however, some aspects of the formula were not clearly spelled out. Ring-fencing—that is, specifically allocating—such expenditure to protect the critical social programs became necessary. In the long term, as intergovernmental fiscal reform progresses, earmarking may need to give way to a well-defined, general transfer mechanism. In either scenario, a good measure of the needs and the performance of the *Dibao* program will be essential.

Dibao *Program Governance and Administration*
In studying the *Dibao* program in Guangdong, it appears that two sets of issues concerning program governance and administration require attention from the provincial authorities. If these issues are left unaddressed, what appears to be a well-designed and popular social program may not only fail to achieve its stated objectives, but also become a source of social tension.

Governance and Accountability. Perhaps characteristic of China's economic and social policies, *Dibao* is governed by national and provincial policies that leave substantial room for local interpretation. Less characteristic is the fact that many of the *Dibao* program decisions are made at the village level. With an average of one civil affairs officer at the township or county levels of government having to serve more than one thousand households, there is not sufficient capacity to check and ensure that policies are implemented consistently at the local level, leaving the program wide open to potential abuse and mismanagement, with limited channels for redress. No system has been put into place to track expenditures and assess efficiency.

Administrative Resources and Capacity. Little attention seems to have been given to estimating and monitoring the resources required to operate such a social assistance program as *Dibao*. Administrative costs at the very local level are not monitored and covered, as they are not part of the government system. Information management is not integrated vertically with the provincial authorities nor horizontally across core social protection and labor market programs. Human resources seem to be a major cause for concern. The civil affairs bureaus at the township and county levels have few full-time staff dedicated to the *Dibao* program. As a result, they have limited capacity to verify household situations, ensure that information is kept up to date, handle grievances, coordinate with other social assistance programs, monitor the expenditure situation, and ensure the proper participation of various stakeholders.

Building a *Dibao* Program for the Future: Policy Recommendations

Based on the incomplete data that are available, this analysis of the rural *Dibao* program in Guangdong yields the following main conclusions.

As the poverty and inequality situation evolves, and as Guangdong tackles its challenges of eradicating extreme poverty, it is highly appropriate to develop *Dibao* as the main social assistance program for the future. Programs targeted at particular geographic areas (for instance, the poverty-stricken counties) and programs focused on particular categories of individuals (for instance, the *Wubao* program for the elderly, disabled, and orphans without family support) can complement the overall effort but cannot alone be expected to tackle the entire poverty situation. Social assistance programs such as *Dibao* that are targeted at poor households are the appropriate instrument at this new phase of development.

However, the *Dibao* program in Guangdong today, particularly its rural component, falls significantly short of expectations. While this gap to some extent is only to be expected for a program that is relatively young and that for a long time had an unclear mandate at the national level, there is an urgent need for the Guangdong government to strengthen the program.

For development of *Dibao* into the basis and backbone of China's social assistance program for the future, attention is needed in four key areas: (1) ensuring adequacy of the system by expanding program coverage and raising the level of protection, (2) developing a policy and governance framework to ensure equity and accountability, (3) modifying some policy design features to ensure that the program is targeted efficiently and is compatible with individual work incentives, and (4) substantially strengthening the basic institutional infrastructure and human resources and ensuring that the program is administered efficiently and in a sustainable manner. These areas are described in greater detail below.

Aligning Policy and Financing Priorities to Ensure Adequate Support

Eradicating extreme poverty in rural Guangdong by further developing the *Dibao* program needs to be one of the top priorities of the Guangdong government. Guangdong has the need as well as the capacity to ensure the adequacy of the program, but the task requires determination and an approach based on solid policy design. Addressing the adequacy issue requires efforts in the following areas.

Setting the Appropriate Dibao *Standard.* This study recommends that the Guangdong government adopt a different approach to setting the *Dibao* standard. Rather than basing the standard primarily on local fiscal capacity, history, and position relative to neighboring counties, a systematic approach should be established and followed to ensure that the standard reflects the true cost of living and is adjusted accordingly over time. The *Dibao* standard should also be consistent with the poverty line. The provincial authorities could consider adopting a common benefit floor for all localities in Guangdong, while allowing local government to establish a higher level as capacities allow.[4]

Protecting Dibao *Financing.* Central to success in addressing the adequacy issue of the *Dibao* system is ensuring that the necessary financing arrangements are in place. First, although there is no golden rule for determining the appropriate level of spending, the unmet needs and the importance to Guangdong of the rural *Dibao* system suggest that the current level of total spending is too low. Second, in a decentralized setting, it is appropriate to require local governments to match the provincial-level transfer. However, the degree of redistribution by the provincial government may need to be higher. Finally, funds may need to be ring-fenced at the local level to ensure that they are used for the intended purposes. This would be particularly important as the program takes off, when basic rules and expectations are being formulated.

Developing a Policy and Governance Framework for Equity and Accountability

The success of the *Dibao* program requires a governance structure that involves all levels of government, grassroots administration, and communities. Coordination among different government agencies in areas such as civil affairs, finance, and statistics will be critical. The program should also encourage participation and have channels for ensuring that stakeholder voices are heard.

Going forward, a key challenge is to address the balance between flexibility and accountability. At every level of program implementation, the system needs to be less discretionary. More detailed criteria and procedures are necessary to ensure consistency in policy and implementation. Furthermore, there is an urgent need to establish a basic monitoring framework, track program execution, assess results and impact, and share information with the broad range of stakeholders.

Modifying Policy Design to Improve Efficiency

Drawing from the experience of urban and rural *Dibao*, Guangdong can help ensure that the program meets its stated objectives by addressing a range of policy and program design issues. Three major issues and the recommended solutions are highlighted here.

Eligibility Requirements. A combination of income testing and evaluation of other factors affecting the livelihoods of the poor (that is, assets and living conditions) seems to be an appropriate policy for the short to medium term. As the program is developed further, in addition to adopting a more systematic approach to establishing the *Dibao* standard and aligning it with the poverty line, it may be appropriate to introduce an equivalence scale that takes household size into account in determining thresholds.

Targeting Mechanism. Combining income and asset testing with community participation for targeting is a logical choice for Guangdong at this stage of development. Taking into consideration the major consumption needs of the poor and vulnerable (such as needs imposed by chronic disease) also seems appropriate in this context.

In light of the difficulties in verifying household income, as the program is scaled up, the Guangdong authorities could consider piloting a proxy means-testing mechanism. Proxy means tests basically require statistical analysis of data from detailed household surveys to identify the key determining and easily observable factors of poverty. They use a formula and relative weights to generate a score for applicant households based on easily observable characteristics, such as location and quality of dwelling, ownership of durable goods, demographic structure of the household, and the education and possible occupations of adult members. Eligibility is determined by comparing the household's score against a predetermined cutoff. Proxy means tests are useful for reducing discretion and ensuring greater transparency and fairness. They are also appropriate for addressing chronic poverty, which accounts for a significant share of the poor.

Benefit Structure. While the classic guaranteed minimum income (GMI) design adopted in the *Dibao* program is conceptually clean and well justified, the difficulty in determining the actual income of families—especially for rural households—makes it virtually impossible not to overshoot or undershoot in the provision of benefits and makes performance evaluation impossible. Addressing such inconsistencies between policy design and implementation is important for the credibility of the program.

Given the nature of income and the difficulty in fully recording household income, the authorities may wish to consider adopting a simpler benefit structure. The benefit structure could have two to three benefit levels, or it could start with a base amount that would then be adjusted for each household member or child. It would be a more honest and realistic approach and administratively feasible to implement.

Strengthening Institutional and Administrative Capacity

As the rural *Dibao* program expands, it will be critically important to ensure sufficient administrative capacity to handle the workload. Additional resources will be needed to strengthen the civil affairs departments, which will involve developing the information management system, increasing staffing levels according to the population or families served, and developing business processes and performance standards.

Notes

1. Two dollars per day measured in PPP terms is used to analyze the poverty situation in Guangdong, given its level of development relative to other provinces in China and other economies.

2. For a much more in-depth introduction to the concepts, principles, and main instruments of social assistance and safety nets, refer to Grosh and others (2008).

3. The coverage rate in Shenzhen cannot be calculated because the city has introduced an integrated *hukou* system for its rural and urban residents, and the city does not divide beneficiaries into urban and rural groups. Coverage rates in Foshan city and Zhuhai city cannot be calculated because the Guangdong Provincial Bureau of Statistics (2008) has no information on the total number of the local farming population with a *hukou* in these two cities. Figure 2.1 excludes Shantou city due to data problems—according to the Department of Civil Affairs of Guangdong Province, the number of rural beneficiaries in Shantou city was 66,587 in 2007, but the Guangdong Provincial Bureau of Statistics (2008) indicates that Shantou city had only 45,200 people with a rural *hukou* in 2007, yielding a coverage rate of 147.32 percent.

4. If localities are allowed to set a higher standard, the financing responsibility for this enhanced protection should be assigned to the local authority to ensure that the appropriate incentives for the local authority are in place.

References

Department of Civil Affairs of Guangdong Province. 2005. "Interim Measures of Guangdong Province for the Management of the *Dibao* Program Fund," downloaded from the website of the Department of Civil Affairs of Guangdong Province.

Grosh, Margaret, Carlo del Ninno, Emil Teslivc, and Azedine Overghi, ed. 2008. *For Protection and Promotion.* Washington, DC: World Bank.

Guangdong Bureau of Statistics. 2008. *Guangdong Statistical Yearbook 2008.* Beijing: China Statistics Press.

National Bureau of Statistics. 2007. *China County (City) Socio-Economic Statistical Yearbook.* Beijing: China Statistics Press.

———. 2008. *China Statistical Yearbook 2008.* Beijing: China Statistics Press.

Wang, Dewen. 2010. "Understanding Poverty and Inequality in Guangdong." In *Reducing Inequality for Shared Growth in China: Strategy and Policy Options for Guangdong Province,* chapter 1. Washington, DC: World Bank.

CHAPTER 3

Developing an Efficient and Integrated Labor Market in Guangdong Province

For Guangdong to achieve its proposed plan of doubling the average income of its residents in five years, accelerating income growth for rural residents will be a key priority. Despite remarkable economic achievements over the past three decades, the income gaps between rural and urban areas are still significant in Guangdong. As Guangdong's economy has grown, income inequality between rural and urban households has also grown, mirroring the trend at the national level. The empirical study, "Understanding Poverty and Inequality in Guangdong," finds that this urban-rural disparity comprises the largest share of overall income inequality in the province (Wang 2010). Clearly, rapid growth in rural incomes is needed to narrow the income gap and raise the average income of Guangdong's residents.

In determining how to promote this income growth among rural households, one finds it is clear that labor market income is of central importance. This holds true especially in Guangdong, where wage income accounted for 56.9 percent of net income for rural households in 2007, compared to 38.6 percent for China overall, 52.5 percent for Jiangsu province, and 48.5 percent for Zhejiang province. As shown in figure 3.1, labor market

The chapter was written by Du Yang of the Chinese Academy of Social Sciences, with substantial support from Minna Hahn Tong.

Figure 3.1   Rural Household Income in Guangdong by Source, 2007

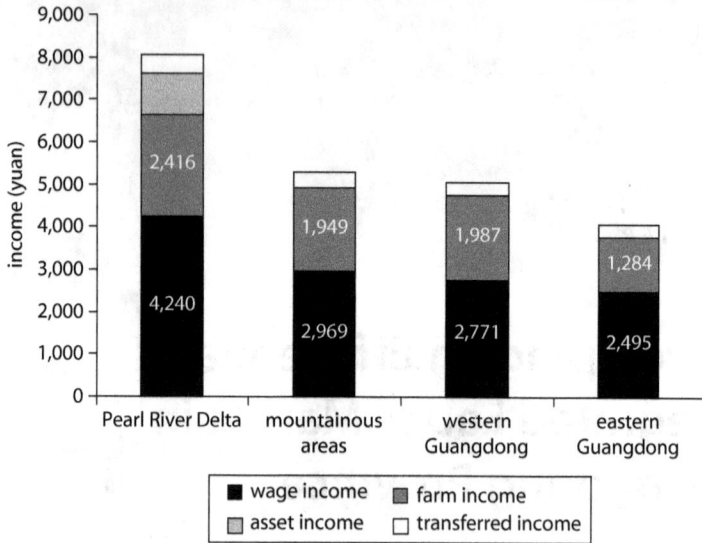

Source: Author's calculations from Quangdong Bureau of Statistics 2007.

activities dominated the income composition for rural households across all regions of Guangdong in 2007. Regression analysis results using rural household survey data for Guangdong also indicate that spending more time on off-farm activities—particularly for migration work—raised average rural household income.[1] Going forward, it is expected that rural income growth will rely mainly on labor income, since the average size of cultivated land is very limited in Guangdong.

Analysis of household survey data underscores the importance of rural household income for reducing inequality. Using various indexes for inequality, figure 3.2 shows that income inequality indexes fall as the ratio of labor income increases, implying that income gaps will be reduced as the share of income from the labor market grows.

Because wage income is a major component of income for most rural residents in Guangdong, the labor market situation has a significant influence on rural incomes. The availability of off-farm employment and the degree of labor mobility have become critical determinants of income for Guangdong's rural residents. Policies to stimulate labor demand, and labor market regulations and policies that affect mobility, therefore play a key role in expanding—or limiting—opportunities to earn wage income, which in turn can affect poverty and inequality, as well as economic growth prospects.

Figure 3.2   Income Inequalities and Share of Labor Income, 2007

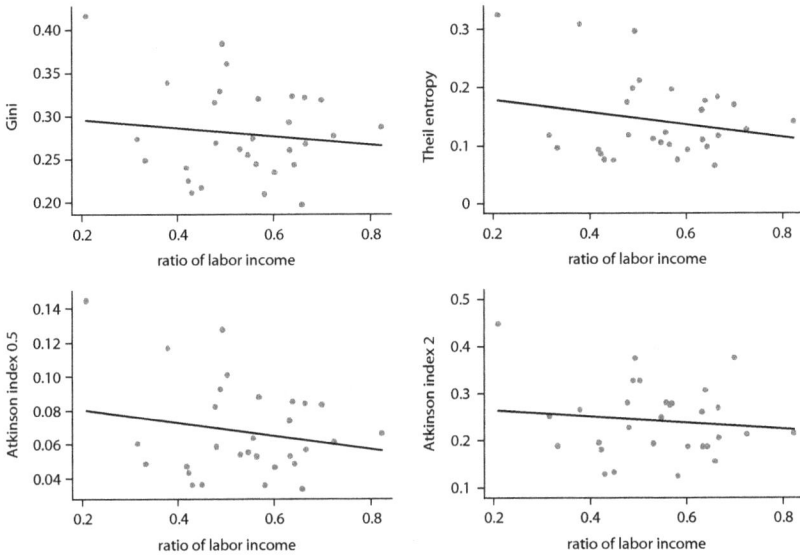

Source: Author's calculations from Quangdong Bureau of Statistics 2007.
Note: For a description of inequality indexes, see box 3.1.

Box 3.1

Measuring Inequality

Inequality indexes are often applied to measure the inequality of income or wealth. These indexes include the following:

- *Lorenz curve*—a graphical representation of the cumulative income share (vertical axis) versus the cumulative population distribution (horizontal axis). If each individual had the same income—or total equality—the income distribution curve would be a straight 45-degree diagonal line. The deviation from the 45-degree diagonal line reflects the extent of income inequality.
- *Gini coefficient*—the area between the line of perfect equality and the observed Lorenz curve, as a percentage of the area between the line of perfect equality and the line of perfect inequality. The higher the coefficient, the more unequal the distribution is. It is sometimes argued that one disadvantage of the Gini coefficient is that it is not additive across groups, meaning that the total Gini of a society is not equal to the sum of the Ginis for its subgroups.
- *Theil index*—a less commonly used measure of income inequality, with a different formula for calculating the magnitude of income inequality. Unlike the Gini coefficient, the Theil index is additive across different subgroups or regions.

Although Guangdong has made significant progress in expanding employment opportunities and developing its labor market, the recent global economic crisis has shown that Guangdong's economy is very vulnerable to external shocks, which could undermine such progress. Although the effects of the crisis have been felt in other parts of China, the impacts on economic growth and employment in Guangdong were particularly severe given the province's export orientation. The crisis has underscored the importance of further efforts to strengthen the labor market and to improve flexibility and openness for Guangdong to maintain its long-term competitiveness. Greater attention to social protection institutions will also be critical to preparing Guangdong for any future crises that may occur.

To help fill knowledge gaps and inform policy making, this chapter assesses the current labor market situation in Guangdong and draws out implications for future policy. Given the importance of raising rural incomes to address the problem of urban-rural inequality, the chapter focuses primarily on issues related to the rural labor force. It first provides a brief overview of Guangdong's labor market and discusses recent trends, including the impacts of the global economic crisis. It then identifies the main factors that have hindered the functioning of the labor market, with a particular emphasis on factors affecting labor mobility. The chapter concludes by laying out a range of policy options to address these challenges and ensure the development of an efficient and integrated labor market.

Labor Market Overview

Key Trends

As China's largest provincial economy, Guangdong has a massive labor market and has created the most employment opportunities of all the provinces. In terms of overall labor market trends, employment has shifted increasingly to the manufacturing and services sectors of the economy. As shown in figure 3.3, a steady decrease in the proportion of employment in the primary sector has been accompanied by a steady increase in employment in the secondary and tertiary sectors. Similarly, rural farm employment has decreased while rural off-farm employment has increased.

Labor Supply

Recent Trends in Labor Allocation. With the development of the nonagricultural sectors in Guangdong, a pronounced shift in labor supply has

Figure 3.3   Employment by Sector in Guangdong

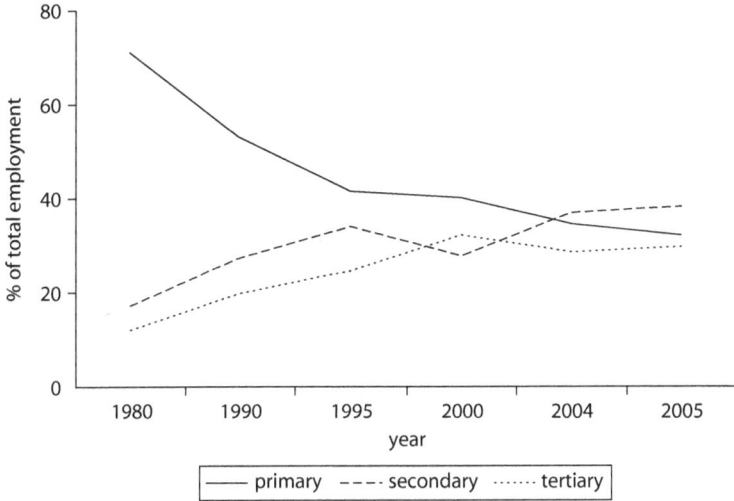

Source: National Bureau of Statistics 2006.

Table 3.1   Labor Allocation by Region, 2007
percent

Labor allocation	Pearl River Delta	Mountainous areas	Western Guangdong	Eastern Guangdong	Guangdong overall
Labor transfer	65.6	54.9	48.9	65.6	59.4
Local off-farm work	46.7	19.8	16.4	55.5	34.7
Migration work	18.9	35.1	32.5	10.1	24.7

Source: Author's calculations from rural household survey data (Quangdong Bureau of Statistics 2007).

taken place out of agriculture and even out of rural areas. As shown in table 3.1, about 60 percent of Guangdong's rural labor force in 2007 was "transferred labor," defined in this chapter as the rural labor force that spends time on off-farm activities, including local off-farm activities and migration work. The pattern differs by region: regions with developed local nonagricultural industries generate demand for rural labor,[2] while the rural labor force in mountainous regions tends to work in other regions.

The time spent on each category of work activity, which is another dimension of labor allocation, shows a similar movement away from farm work toward local off-farm or migration work. As shown in figure 3.4,

Figure 3.4   Labor Allocation, 2005 and 2007

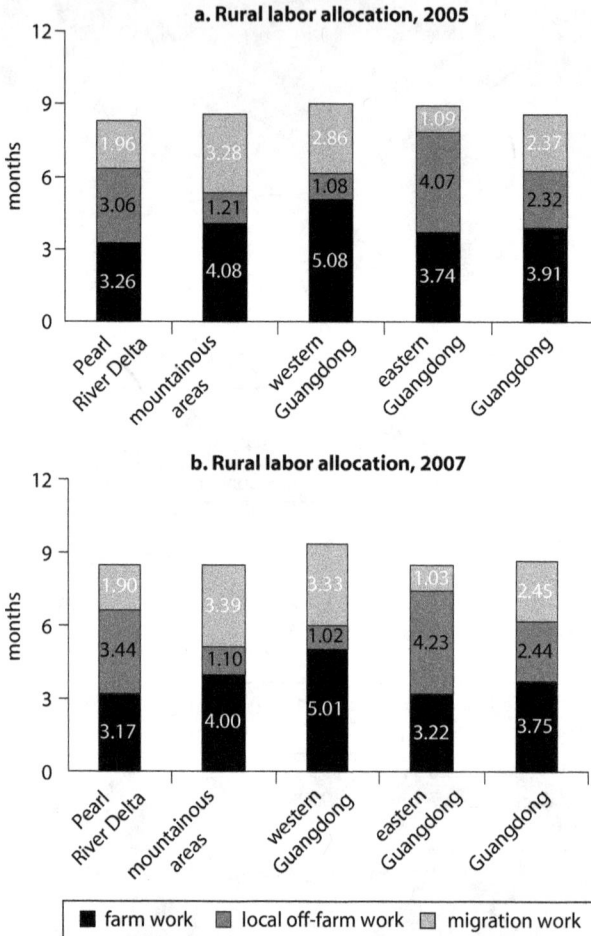

a. Rural labor allocation, 2005

Pearl River Delta: farm work 3.26, local off-farm work 3.06, migration work 1.96
mountainous areas: farm work 4.08, local off-farm work 1.21, migration work 3.28
western Guangdong: farm work 5.08, local off-farm work 1.08, migration work 2.86
eastern Guangdong: farm work 3.74, local off-farm work 4.07, migration work 1.09
Guangdong: farm work 3.91, local off-farm work 2.32, migration work 2.37

b. Rural labor allocation, 2007

Pearl River Delta: farm work 3.17, local off-farm work 3.44, migration work 1.90
mountainous areas: farm work 4.00, local off-farm work 1.10, migration work 3.39
western Guangdong: farm work 5.01, local off-farm work 1.02, migration work 3.33
eastern Guangdong: farm work 3.22, local off-farm work 4.23, migration work 1.03
Guangdong: farm work 3.75, local off-farm work 2.44, migration work 2.45

■ farm work   ■ local off-farm work   ☐ migration work

Source: Author's calculations from Quangdong Bureau of Statistics 2007.

changes in the pattern of rural labor allocation took place even in the two-year interval between 2005 and 2007. The average time allocated to farm work per laborer in Guangdong was 3.91 months in 2005, dropping to 3.75 in 2007. Meanwhile, the total months spent on off-farm activities increased from 4.69 months to 4.89 months.

Determinants of Labor Allocation. What factors influence this labor allocation in Guangdong? A regression analysis of the rural household survey data points to a number of individual and household characteristics that affect the decision to engage in labor transfer. In terms of individual characteristics, young workers are, in general, more likely to participate in off-farm activities. The analysis shows that in 2007, one additional year of age reduced the probability of participation in off-farm activities by about 1.7 percent (table 3.2). Young workers were more likely to prefer migration work, while older workers preferred local work. A breakdown of working time allocation by age is consistent with these findings: for people below age 60, time allocated to farm work increased with aging while showing an inverted U-shape for local off-farm activities (table 3.3).

The analysis also shows that males are more likely to engage in off-farm activities. Holding other things constant, the probability of a male

Table 3.2   Change in Determinants of Labor Allocation
% difference in probability

Determinant	2005	2007
Labor transfer from agriculture		
1 additional year of age	−1.6	−1.7
Gender: male	20.0	18.3
1 additional year of schooling	2.3	2.4
1 additional percent of ratio of children below age 6	−4.9	−13.3
1 additional percent of ratio of the elderly above age 65	5.0	−1.4
1 additional percent of ratio of labor force	−26.0	−17.6
1 additional household member	−0.86	0.7
1 additional *mu* of cultivated land	−1.07	−1.7
Local off-farm work		
1 additional year of age	0.3	0.2
Gender: male	8.7	6.8
1 additional year of schooling	2.6	2.8
1 additional percent of ratio of children below 6	12.5	2.1
1 additional percent of ratio of the elderly above 65	−20.6	−29.1
1 additional percent of ratio of labor force	−52.8	−39.6
1 additional household member	−3.2	−2.2
1 additional *mu* of cultivated land	−1.9	−2.0
Migration work		
1 additional year of age	−1.3	−1.6
Gender: male	5.7	7.1
1 additional year of schooling	1.0	0.7
1 additional percent of ratio of children below age 6	−14.0	−12.9
1 additional percent of ratio of the elderly above age 65	2.0	8.9
1 additional percent of ratio of labor force	7.5	6.3
1 additional household member	0.9	1.5
1 additional *mu* of cultivated land	0.5	0.0

Source: Author's calculations from Quangdong Bureau of Statistics 2007.
Note: 1.00 *mu* = 0.16 acre.

Table 3.3   Working Time Allocation by Group, 2007
months per year

Group	Farm work	Local off-farm work	Migration work	All working time
Age				
20 and below	1.31	2.01	4.92	8.24
21–30	1.52	2.18	5.81	9.50
31–40	3.62	3.56	2.43	9.61
41–50	5.93	3.19	0.51	9.63
51–60	6.28	2.35	0.12	8.76
60 and above	2.85	0.52	0.05	3.42
Education				
Primary and below	5.14	1.65	0.70	7.50
Jr. high school	3.40	2.47	3.44	9.31
Sr. high school	3.21	3.84	2.08	9.13
College and above	0.33	4.86	3.36	8.54
Gender				
Male	3.38	2.80	2.82	9.00
Female	4.14	2.07	2.07	8.28

Source: Author's calculations from rural household survey data, Quangdong Bureau of Statistics 2007.

worker participating in labor transfer is 18.3 percent higher than that of his female counterpart. The same trend is evident for migration work, and these findings are again consistent with the working-time allocation presented in table 3.3.

Unsurprisingly, workers with higher levels of education are more likely to transfer. In 2007, one additional year of schooling increased the probability of labor transfer by about 2.4 percent (table 3.2). The marginal impact of years of schooling is larger for local off-farm work than for migration work. The allocation of working time also shows that educated people prefer off-farm work—in particular, local off-farm work.

In terms of household characteristics, the analysis shows that between 2005 and 2007, households with a higher ratio of children to household size became less likely to engage in labor transfer. Workers with preschool children preferred local work, and the data reveal a significant influence on the migration decision, with rural farmers being less likely to migrate if they had preschool children. These findings suggest that access to social services such as child care may be an important determinant of rural labor transfer.

The effect of having elderly household members is mixed. The analysis shows that a household with a higher ratio of elderly is less likely to engage in local off-farm work. However, it also shows that a household with a higher ratio of elderly is more likely to migrate for work. The reason for this discrepancy may depend on the role of the elderly members in the household. The elderly could be dependents who need care, making off-farm labor transfer less likely, or the elderly could help facilitate off-farm labor transfer if they provide child care for the children in the household.

Does Guangdong Have Surplus Labor? At the national level, the question of whether China is reaching the end of its labor surplus phase is controversial. Anecdotal evidence indicates that many growing markets in China, particularly in the coastal areas, are facing shortages of cheap labor. In those areas, wages for informal sector and migrant workers are starting to rise (Du, Cai, and Wang 2006). Cai (2007) also finds that in certain areas, the annual growth rate of average monthly wages for migrants has increased significantly, from 2.8 percent in 2004 to 11.5 percent in 2006, and points to this trend as a sign that China is exhausting its population dividend and reaching a "Lewis" turning point, which means the era of unlimited labor supply is going to end soon. Others, however, argue that the tightening of the labor supply is artificial and caused by fragmented labor markets and regulatory constraints on labor mobility.[3]

The size of rural surplus labor is a critical issue for Guangdong, particularly in light of the measures that have been proposed to restructure the economy. One of the most prominent measures is the "dual transfer" program, which aims to transfer agricultural labor to urban areas and relocate industries to less developed regions of the province. The success of this program, which is being supported by government funding of 50 billion yuan, depends on the size of rural surplus labor.

In a determination it whether Guangdong has surplus labor that can be transferred from rural to urban areas and from agriculture to industry, the method of measurement is critical. Most studies estimate the size of surplus labor based on the difference between the total rural labor force and the total labor demand for agriculture. However, this methodology is flawed because the labor allocation to agriculture is determined not only by agricultural productivity, but also by prices of agricultural outputs, job opportunities in the nonagricultural sector, and other factors. Furthermore, the estimation is based on aggregated data that do not capture the variations caused by individual characteristics. As described above, labor allocation decisions depend to a large extent on individual characteristics, such as age and education. In addition, estimating actual labor use in agriculture based on aggregated data is very difficult.

Using an alternative measure that predicts surplus labor in rural areas by looking at working-time allocation, it appears that Guangdong still has a large pool of transferable rural labor. Using the probability of migration for each individual based on his or her personal characteristics, one can calculate the predicted average probability of migration for each age group. In table 3.4, the first row shows the current labor resources in rural Guangdong. The fourth row ("probability of transfer") presents average group probability according to the predicted individual probability. The seventh row ("potential migrants") displays the predicted amount of migration from current labor resources. The summation in the fifth row ("transferable") gives a total of about 4.3 million workers who are available for transfer to nonagricultural industries.

Notably, the actual amount of transferable labor for off-farm activities is lower than the estimate used by policy makers, indicating that the scope for using the dual transfer program to transfer labor may be more limited. The analysis estimates that Guangdong has about 1.5 million rural workers who could potentially migrate. It should also be recognized that while Guangdong still has a very large number of rural workers in

Table 3.4   A New Estimation of Surplus Labor in Rural Guangdong, 2007

	Age 20 and below	Age 21–30	Age 31–40	Age 41–50	Age 51–60	Total
Rural labor (thousands)	2,221	7,294	6,975	6,047	3,988	28,456
Percentage of nontransferred	23	17	29	45	59	41
Number of nontransferred	511	1,240	2,023	2,721	2,353	11,667
Probability of transfer	0.82	0.67	0.54	0.4	0.29	0.38
Transferable (thousands)	427	825	1,086	1,105	679	4,346
Probability of migration	0.71	0.5	0.18	0.075	0.027	0.13
Potential migrants (thousands)	362	614	365	203	64	1,544
Remaining in agriculture (thousands)	84	415	937	1,616	1,674	7,321

Sources: The data in the first row are from the National Bureau of Statistics 2008b. The other numbers are the author's estimations based on data in Quangdong Bureau of Statistics 2007.

agriculture, the willingness of all of these workers to transfer is question-able. Many young and well-educated workers have already transferred to nonfarm sectors, while the workers between ages 41 and 60 have a low propensity to transfer. These issues are discussed further in the policy implications section below.

Labor Demand

The Nature of Labor Demand in Guangdong. Labor demand in Guangdong has been determined to a large extent by the province's posi-tion as an important "world workshop," which has given rise to a very labor-intensive economy. Guangdong was the first place to receive the industries that were transferring out of the newly industrialized economies, so labor-intensive industries took root in Guangdong earlier than in other coastal areas of China. Thanks to this economic structure, a unit of GDP creates more employment in Guangdong than in other parts of China. As table 3.5 shows, 10,000 yuan of value added in secondary industry created 0.17 job vacancies in Guangdong in 2004, compared to 0.13 in the Yangtze River Delta, which has been another engine of China's economy, and in China overall.

Notably, with its high demand for low-skilled workers, Guangdong has attracted more migrants from other parts of rural China than from within Guangdong itself. As shown in table 3.6, migrant workers accounted for 58.3 percent of off-farm employment in 2005, and most of these migrants were from rural areas of other provinces. This phenomenon was even more pronounced in the manufacturing sector, where migrant work-ers accounted for 71.8 percent of employment, and rural migrant work-ers from other provinces alone accounted for 53.8 percent of employment. The percentages of migrant workers—and migrants from outside the province, in particular—were much higher in Guangdong than in the Yangtze River Delta and China overall. Since the low-skilled jobs offer low pay, rural workers in the Pearl River Delta (PRD) who have

Table 3.5   Economic Structure and Employment

	Guangdong	Yangtze River Delta	China
Value added/GDP (2007)	0.48	0.48	0.43
Exports/sales (2004)	0.43	0.25	0.19
Employment/value added (2004, person/10,000 yuan)	0.17	0.13	0.13

Sources: The first row is calculated from National Bureau of Statistics 2008a. The data in the second and the third rows are from National Bureau of Statistics 2008b.

Table 3.6   Distribution of Employment by Locality, 2005
percent

Origin of workers	Guangdong	Yangtze River Delta	China
	Nonagricultural employment		
Local	41.8	69.0	70.9
Migrants			
Urban migrants of other provinces	5.5	1.3	2.0
Urban migrants from within province	6.4	5.5	8.0
Rural migrants of other provinces	**36.0**	**16.2**	**10.9**
Rural migrants from within province	10.4	8.0	8.2
Total	58.3	31.0	29.1
	Employment in manufacturing		
Local	28.2	64.9	63.9
Migrants			
Urban migrants from other provinces	6.0	1.2	2.2
Urban migrants from within province	3.1	3.6	5.2
Rural migrants of other provinces	**53.8**	**23.1**	**20.8**
Rural migrants from within province	8.9	7.3	7.9
Total	71.8	35.2	36.1

Source: Author's calculations based on 1% Population Sampling Survey 2005.
Note: Local workers are defined as those who work within the township of their *hukou* locality.

income from assets, as represented in figure 3.1, and high reservation wage rates are reluctant to accept those jobs. As a result, rural "surplus" labor can be found in the developed areas of Guangdong, which have the most employment opportunities.

In Guangdong, demand for labor is driven by the export-oriented sectors, which is unsurprising, given the export-oriented nature of its economy. Even compared to the Yangtze River Delta, Guangdong's economy is highly export-oriented. Guangdong and the Yangtze River Delta have similar proportions of secondary industry; the share of secondary industry in GDP was 48 percent in 2007. However, data from the 2004 economic census show that the ratio of export value to total sales in secondary industry was 43 percent for Guangdong, compared to only 25 percent for the Yangtze River Delta and 13 percent for China as a whole.

It should be noted that while the export-oriented sectors have played an important role in generating employment in Guangdong, the heavy export orientation has left industries and their workers vulnerable to shocks that affect demand for exports. A clear example is the recent global economic crisis, which has already affected growth and employment in China, and in Guangdong in particular. Unlike the 1997 East

Asian financial crisis, which affected most of Guangdong's competitors, this crisis has affected the economies that are buyers of Guangdong's export products. Faced with declining orders, many manufacturing firms have closed down. Given the labor-intensive nature of Guangdong's economy, the impact of the shock has been even greater on employment than on GDP. Over 15,000 small and medium-size enterprises were shut down in the first eight months of 2008, and the trend continued. The impact on migrant workers who, as noted above, are the majority of workers in manufacturing, has been particularly severe. As in many other countries, the shock has resulted not in pay decreases, but in the reduction of positions, and migrants have been the first to be laid off. It has been reported that the large return migration flow that usually takes place prior to the Spring Festival happened sooner in 2009 (Chen 2009). Estimates based on surveys conducted by the Ministry of Agriculture indicate that about 38.5 percent of migrants nationwide returned home early; of those, 39.6 percent had lost jobs. The PRD region is where massive return migrations were observed first and where the magnitude was the highest among all coastal regions (Sheng 2009). In general, migrant workers were more vulnerable to the decline in the economy, since they work mainly in the informal sector and have less access to social protection.[4]

Regional Changes in Labor Demand. Given the challenge of reducing inequality in Guangdong, it is important to assess the recent shifts in labor demand across different regions of the province. A number of factors have contributed to a change in employment structure across the regions, such as rising wages and higher land costs in certain areas of Guangdong. According to interviews with firms in the PRD, substantial increases in land costs and higher land use fees have aggravated the situation for firms. At the same time, the appreciation of the yuan against the U.S. dollar in 2007 and 2008, as well as soaring energy and raw material prices, have negatively affected export-oriented firms.

Driven by these factors, labor demand has shifted from the PRD to other areas of Guangdong in recent years. As shown in figure 3.5, employment in the PRD comprised half of total employment in Guangdong in 2000, then dropped to 42 percent in 2005. Meanwhile, the mountainous region had a significant increase of employment opportunities. Because this shift took place before the implementation of government labor transfer programs, it appears the changes were driven by market forces.

Figure 3.5   Regional Employment Structure, 2000 and 2005

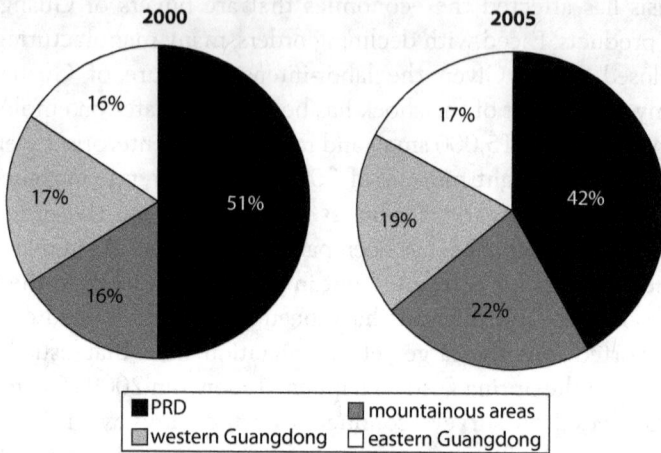

Sources: Author's calculations from Population Census in 2000 and 1% Population Sampling Survey in 2005.

Barriers to a Mobile and Flexible Labor Market

In the course of its economic reforms, Guangdong has reaped tremendous benefits from having an open and competitive labor market. Thanks to the development of non-state-owned enterprises (SOEs) in the early stages of reform, the enterprises there broke out of the rigid employment system much earlier than those in the rest of China. By simplifying tedious personnel procedures, firms in Guangdong easily attracted many skilled and talented workers from other provinces. In terms of hiring and firing decisions, firms introduced the market mechanism in Guangdong much earlier than in the other regions. Clearly, having an open and flexible labor market has been critical to economic growth in Guangdong, particularly with its labor-intensive industries.

However, Guangdong still faces a number of challenges in developing a true labor "market." Significant barriers to labor mobility—for example, in the household registration (*hukou*) system and the social protection system—continue to exist within Guangdong and across provinces. These barriers compromise the efficient allocation of labor and limit wage-earning opportunities for rural workers, thereby posing a threat to Guangdong's goal of reducing inequality. It also appears that recent national-level regulations, such as the Labor Contract Law and minimum wage regulations, have imposed significant burdens on firms in Guangdong and may be reducing labor market flexibility.

Hukou *Restrictions*

Despite measures to reform it, the *hukou* system in Guangdong still poses a barrier to labor mobility. As early as 2001, Guangdong first proposed to abolish agricultural, nonagricultural, and other types of *hukou* and integrate them as residential *hukou*. Since then, many provinces have followed Guangdong's example in reforming their *hukou* systems. However, reforming the *hukou* system is not simply a matter of changing the registration system. Barriers to obtaining a *hukou* and unequal access to public services and welfare programs associated with *hukou* can discourage workers who would otherwise migrate.

One problem with the current *hukou* system in Guangdong is the restrictions placed on obtaining *hukou*, particularly in the developed areas of Guangdong. Given Guangdong's heavy reliance on migrant labor as described above, this issue is particularly serious for Guangdong as compared to other provinces. A recent case study found that even a well-educated manager has difficulties obtaining a *hukou* in developed parts of Guangdong such as the PRD (Cai and Du 2008). The barriers for unskilled migrants are presumably even higher.

For rural workers migrating within Guangdong, another problem is that access to services and programs is not equal for rural and urban residents. Furthermore, the provision of services varies across different parts of Guangdong. Migrants are concerned not only about wage rates, but also about whether they can meet family needs in cities in a stable and affordable way. Lack of access to affordable health care, to good-quality schools that are free for the compulsory education period or accessible at a reasonable cost, and to decent affordable housing are major deterrents to migration. These restrictions contribute to labor market segmentation between rural and urban areas, lowering the overall efficiency of Guangdong's labor market.

Labor Market Regulations

Labor Contract Law. Although the new Labor Contract Law was enacted with the aim of protecting workers, these regulations appear to be having adverse effects on Guangdong's firms. Those effects may in turn hurt workers and contribute to labor market rigidity. Under the law, which took effect January 1, 2008, all firms are required to have written contracts with employees. Interviews with firms in the PRD indicate that the associated increases in hiring and firing costs have hurt Guangdong's labor-intensive industries (Cai and Du 2008). The increased labor costs come as a blow at a time when export-oriented firms are also struggling with the appreciation of the yuan and rising raw material prices.

The requirement that employers assume social security contributions for their employees has also added to labor costs. Firms in Guangdong hire a large number of migrant workers who are unable to transfer their social security accounts when they move, as discussed below. In these cases, strict implementation of the law simply increases labor costs for enterprises without significantly improving the well-being of employees.

Struggling with these increased costs, firms in Guangdong have reduced labor demand through a number of channels. To save on labor costs, enterprises in the formal sector tend to outsource some parts of production to the informal sector, which contributes to rising informality in the economy. Firms might even collude with migrant workers to have an informal employment relationship without a contract, again contributing to informality and weakening worker protection from other perspectives. The increasing price of labor relative to capital also pushes employers to find ways of using more capital rather than labor. In the most extreme cases, a significant increase in labor costs can lead to the shutdown of enterprises and reduce labor demand.

Minimum Wage Increases. Although the minimum wage system was introduced into the urban labor market 15 years ago, enterprises have started feeling the impacts only recently. One reason is that at the local level, the minimum wage standard has risen more rapidly in recent years. Another reason is that both the central and local governments have been giving greater attention to enforcement of the regulations than previously.

Since 2004, when the Ministry of Labor and Social Security issued new minimum wage regulations, the minimum wage standard in Guangdong has been raised significantly. As shown in figure 3.6, the average minimum wage standard in Guangdong was slightly higher than the national average in 2004. Since then, Guangdong has raised the standard more rapidly compared to the national average, with the average minimum wage standard in Guangdong reaching 655 yuan per month by 2007.

While a higher average minimum wage for Guangdong may be appropriate, given its level of development and costs of living, the frequency and size of the adjustments impose a significant burden on the province's labor-intensive industries. Firms that cannot afford the frequent adjustments may need to shut down, pushing down labor demand. The method of calculating the minimum wage standard also may be problematic. The

Figure 3.6   Average Minimum Wage Standards in Guangdong and China

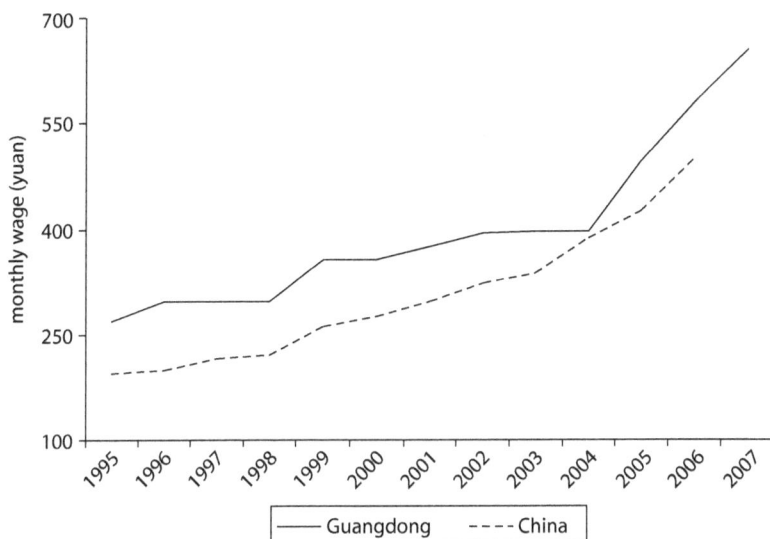

Source: Du and Pan 2009.

minimum wage level should be established relative to the average wage, but because a larger number of migrant workers are concentrated in Guangdong, the average wages based on the current reporting system are overestimated. Therefore, the calculated minimum wage level may be higher than what is actually appropriate. Although higher minimum wages may help Guangdong attract more migrant workers, it may be detrimental to low-skilled workers if their labor becomes unaffordable for firms.

Limited Social Protection
Labor mobility to and within Guangdong is also hindered by the limited social protection for migrant workers. As discussed in World Bank (2008), migrants in China tend to be concentrated in occupations that expose them to greater risk of work-related injury and illness, particularly in the manufacturing and construction industries. In China overall, migrant workers accounted for 80 percent of deaths in construction, mining, and chemical factories and for approximately 90 percent of patients suffering from workplace-related diseases (*China Daily* 2006; ILO 2006). However, few migrants are covered by any social insurance programs, so any serious injury or illness can impose an immense burden on migrant workers and their families. In the China Urban Labor Surveys conducted in 12 cities in 2004 and 2005, only a very small proportion of migrant

workers reported participating in the main social insurance programs—6.8 percent for medical insurance and 4.4 percent for unemployment insurance, compared to 52.3 percent and 18.8 percent, respectively, among local residents (World Bank 2009).

Another issue for migrants in Guangdong, as in other provinces of China, is the portability of social insurance benefits, such as pensions. Rather than paying a large portion of their payroll into a pension scheme that may provide little or no benefit to them in the future, migrant workers may prefer not being covered. However, if they could take their accounts with them when they moved, workers might feel less compelled to stay in the same job when a better opportunity arose elsewhere, and they might be more willing to contribute to the system out of their payroll.

Policy Implications

The above analysis indicates that while Guangdong has made tremendous strides in developing an open and competitive labor market, further efforts are needed to help raise rural incomes and reduce poverty and inequality in the province. Given the importance of wages from off-farm and migrant work for rural households, fostering urban-rural labor market integration and greater mobility for Guangdong's rural surplus labor will be critical. Taking into account the determinants of labor allocation and the barriers to mobility discussed above, this section highlights a range of labor market policies that Guangdong can use to remove barriers to mobility, facilitate migration, and protect against future shocks, thereby strengthening its overall labor market and improving its longer-term competitiveness. Intensified investments in human capital will also be critical in this regard, namely for improvements in general education and skills development, which are discussed in chapters 6 and 7.

Notably, Guangdong's government has already recognized the importance of labor mobility in its "dual transfer" strategy, which focuses partly on transferring labor or moving people to jobs. Continuing to build on its success in developing a flexible labor market, the government can play a crucial role in facilitating the movement of workers while allowing market forces to work. Given the complex issues involved in the migration decision at the individual and household levels, it is not possible or appropriate to set a simple target for how many individuals will be moved. Nor can it be expected that government interventions will persuade all rural surplus labor to move, since the decision to migrate involves a host of individual and household considerations and should be market-driven. However, by removing barriers to migration and creating a friendly environment for migrant workers, the government can help improve the functioning of the labor market itself.

It should be emphasized that, to be effective, measures to facilitate labor transfer must be tailored carefully to different groups of rural surplus labor. As described earlier, rural surplus labor is not a homogeneous group, and the decisions to engage in off-farm or migrant work depend to a large extent on individual and household characteristics. The incentives and disincentives for labor transfer vary depending on age, number of dependents, and other factors. Therefore, a one-size-fits-all approach is unlikely to have a meaningful impact.

The other part of the "dual transfer" strategy, which is to transfer labor-intensive industries from the PRD to the "lagging" regions of Guangdong, is riskier and may be more difficult to implement successfully. The transfer of industries involves a high degree of government intervention, which may work against market forces. Another risk is that the enterprises will relocate to lagging regions without adequate efforts to upgrade their technology, making it likely that the lagging regions will someday face the same difficulties that the PRD is now facing. In addition, despite the strong commitment of each level of government to protecting the land and environment, local governments still have strong incentives to suppress land prices and trade environmental protection for GDP growth.

Whatever policies the government chooses to pursue, it will be important to sequence the measures properly and undertake them in a gradual process to minimize any adverse effects for rural and urban areas. The exact timing will depend on the policy priorities of the different levels of government. Some reforms—for example, to the *hukou* system—might be politically sensitive and will require very careful phasing and management.

Reducing Institutional Barriers to Migration
Understanding the Impacts of Labor Market Regulations. Given the potentially adverse impacts the Labor Contract Law and minimum wage regulations may have for employers and, hence, workers, a better understanding of how these regulations affect Guangdong's labor market should be developed. Although such regulations are very important for safeguarding worker interests, they need to be implemented carefully so the flexibility of the labor market is maintained. Further research is needed on the direct and indirect costs imposed on firms by the Labor

Contract Law, the way hiring and firing decisions have been affected, and the impact on labor demand. For the minimum wage standard, more scientific ways of calculating the level should be explored to ensure that it is appropriate to the local situation in Guangdong.

Reforming the Hukou *System.* Given the importance of migrant labor to Guangdong's economy, Guangdong should explore ways to push ahead with *hukou* system reform and lower the remaining institutional obstacles to a fully integrated labor market. Although China is unlikely to eliminate the *hukou* system entirely in the near future since it provides an instrument for controlling labor flow and coordinating rural and urban development, the existence of the system in and of itself is not the main issue. Rather, it is the unequal access to benefits and social services tied to *hukou* that needs to be addressed.

Drawing on the experiences of other provinces, Guangdong could lower the restrictions on *hukou* eligibility to encourage the continued flow of migrants from other provinces. In some towns and cities, migrants are able to obtain *hukou* if they have stable incomes and legal housing. Given the large number of external migrants already in Guangdong, local governments may be concerned about the fiscal sustainability of opening the door to even more migrants from other provinces. The lowering of restrictions would have to be undertaken gradually to avoid a flood of migration that could overwhelm urban infrastructure and services and cause social tension.

It will also be important to equalize the provision of public services to encourage migration among Guangdong's rural surplus labor, as well as reduce inequality between rural and urban areas. Eventually, *hukou* status needs to be delinked from public services and programs so that it simply serves as a record of residence. Improving the level and quality of social and human services across all areas of the province will also be critical so potential migrants can be assured access to affordable health care, good-quality education at no or reasonable cost, and decent housing. As one of China's richest provinces, Guangdong has the capacity to provide basic and equal public services for all of its rural and urban residents.

Facilitating Migration through Active Labor Market Policies

To ensure the smooth integration of rural surplus laborers into receiving areas and to help improve their employability, Guangdong must prepare them for off-farm employment and migration. Improvements in human capital will also help Guangdong upgrade the overall quality and skill level of its workforce, which is vital for Guangdong to maintain its competitiveness. One important measure in this regard will be to improve rural education. As noted earlier, rural workers with higher levels of educational attainment are more likely to pursue off-farm employment and to migrate. Although rural education reform is a longer-term effort, it should be given a high level of priority.

Short-term training is another important instrument for improving the employability of potential migrants for higher-skilled and better-paying jobs in urban areas. This training should be relevant to the demands of the labor market and tailored to the particular needs of younger and older migrants. In addition to teaching entry-level vocational skills, training could include basic life skills courses, such as those provided under the Sunshine Project, to help migrants manage the transition to a new locality.

Efforts are also needed to improve the flow of information on job opportunities from urban areas to rural areas. First-time migrants often must rely on family and personal networks to find employment, which limits their job prospects. For provision of access to a wider range of employment opportunities, job search assistance and placement services could be extended both to potential migrants in sending areas and to migrants in receiving areas of Guangdong.

Improving Social Protection for Migrant Workers

Improving social protection for migrant workers would help boost the incentives for migration. Since young workers are already more likely than older workers to migrate, ensuring social protection for migrant workers may be particularly important in encouraging older rural surplus labor to migrate. However, Guangdong, like other provinces, faces a dilemma: while providing social protection to migrant workers is desirable, social security contributions impose high costs on firms and may drive them to cut back on hiring or to hire labor on an informal basis, weakening worker protection and contributing to informality.

As a starting point, making social insurance benefits portable among different areas and municipalities, as stated in the Labor Contract Law, would be an important step. For portability to work effectively, the administration of social insurance programs would need to be strengthened and better integrated across sending and receiving areas to ensure that contribution and account records are transferred as workers move.

The critical role of social protection in providing support during times of crisis should also be underscored. Although strengthening labor regulations is critical for Guangdong and the rest of China, relying on tools such as minimum wage increases and tighter restrictions on hiring and firing decisions may not be the most effective response to crisis. Instead, already having in place strong social protection institutions and other measures to protect workers can be much more effective in helping to mitigate the impacts of shocks, such as the recent global economic crisis, when they occur. For example, the issue of wage arrears resurfaced when some firms were closed down suddenly. Thanks to the Wage Arrears Warning system established in some cities, the problems were resolved. Such initiatives should be expanded to ensure that workers will be protected in case of future shocks, which will, in turn, improve the well-being of workers and make the prospect of migration more attractive.

Notes

1. For a description of the rural household survey for Guangdong, see box 1.1.
2. The National Bureau of Statistics defines those who are out of their township more than six months as migrants. The share of local off-farm workers increases more significantly for the Pearl River Delta than for other regions if the geographic scope of migration definitions is extended.
3. For more discussion of the debate and issues regarding China's labor surplus, see World Bank (2008).
4. For further discussion, see Du, Cai, and Wang (2006).

References

Cai, Fang. 2007. *The Coming Lewisian Turning Point and Its Policy Implications.* Beijing: Social Science Documentation Press.

Cai, Fang, and Du Yang. 2008. "The Impacts of Financial Crisis on Firms: A Case Study in Guangdong." Working paper, Institute of Population and Labor Economics, Beijing.

Chen, Xiwen. 2009. "Maintaining Stable Agricultural Development and Promoting Increases of Incomes for Farmers." Speech for a news conference held by the State Council Information Office of the People's Republic of China.

China Daily. 2006. "Occupational Diseases Haunt Migrant Workers," February 17.

Du, Yang, Fang Cai, and Meiyan Wang. 2006. "Marketization and/or Informalization? New Trends of China's Employment in Transition." Background paper, World Bank AAA Program on China's Labor Market Development, World Bank, Washington, DC.

Du, Yang, and Weiguang Pan. 2009. "Minimum Wage Regulation in China and Its Applications to Migrant Workers in the Urban Labor Market." *China and World Economy* 17 (2): 79–93.

Guangdong Bureau of Statistics. 2007. Rural Household Survey Data. Unpublished.

ILO (International Labour Organization). 2006. "Internal Labour Migration in China: Features and Responses." Beijing: International Labour Organization.

National Bureau of Statistics. 2006. *Guangdong Statistical Yearbook 2006*. Beijing: China Statistics Press.

———. 2007. 1% Population Sampling Survey.

———. 2008a. *China Statistical Yearbook 2008*. Beijing: China Statistics Press.

———. 2008b. *The Summary of the Second Agricultural Census*. Beijing: China Statistics Press.

Sheng, Laiyun. 2009. "Migrants Are Faced with New Challenges on Their Employment during the Financial Crisis." Unpublished memo.

Wang, Dewen. 2010. "Understanding Poverty and Inequality in Guangdong." In *Reducing Inequality for Shared Growth in China: Strategy and Policy Options for Guangdong Province*, chapter 1. Washington, DC: World Bank.

World Bank. 2008. *China's Modernizing Labor Market: Trends and Emerging Challenges*. Washington, DC: World Bank.

———. 2009. *China's Evolving Poverty Reduction Agenda: An Assessment of Poverty and Inequality in China*. Washington, DC: World Bank.

CHAPTER 4

Making Finance Work in Reducing Inequality and Poverty in Guangdong

Despite spectacular economic growth in the past decades, inequality and urban-rural divergence in Guangdong have worsened. In 2007, the average disposable income of urban dwellers was 3.2 times that of rural, and per capita gross domestic product (GDP) in the rich Pearl River Delta region[1] was 7.2 times that of the rest of Guangdong province. The rates at which the population fell into poverty were 10.3 percent for rural and 1.7 percent for urban. Poverty was especially acute in the east and west wings and in the mountainous and remote areas of Guangdong.

Financial sector development plays a crucial role in reducing inequality and boosting regional development in many ways. One way in which it can have direct and significant impacts is through promoting access to finance by rural households and micro- and small enterprises (MSEs) in both rural and urban areas (box 4.1). It is agreed that enormous potential exists in economic growth and development in counties in Guangdong and China, where rural households and MSEs

This chapter was prepared by Wang Jun and Zhao Luan. The authors wish to thank the following reviewers without implication: Michael J. Goldberg, Senior Private Sector Development Specialist, the World Bank; Feng Xingyuan, China Academy of Social Sciences; and Aurora Ferrari, Senior Private Sector Development Specialist, the World Bank.

Box 4.1

Understanding Finance

Finance is widely misunderstood in China. It means different things to different people, and its role is underestimated and overestimated at the same time. Reflecting the misunderstandings, financial policies and government practices are sometimes misdirected and produce unintended results. The purpose of this box is to provide an analytical framework for discussion in the remainder of the chapter.

How Finance Helps in Reducing Inequality and Poverty

The impact of finance on growth and poverty reduction has been well documented.[a] Broadened financial services help reduce poverty and inequality through several channels. First, financial deepening has been shown to cause growth, thus raising overall income levels. Second, finance can help the poor more specifically by distributing opportunities more fairly, especially to those rural and urban households and small businesses that have opportunities to engage in productive economic activities but lack the necessary funding to do so (Beck, Demirgüç-Kunt, and Levine 2007; Clarke, Xu, and Zou 2006).

Improved access to finance is believed to help the poor reduce their vulnerability to shocks and enable them to invest in health and education, thereby increasing their opportunities to grow out of poverty. Such belief has been borne out by ample, though sometimes anecdotal, evidence in many countries (Littlefield, Morduch, and Hashemi 2003). In this connection, improving access to finance is considered a responsibility of the government, like its obligation to provide basic health care and education.

Microfinance has, over time, proved a useful instrument in poverty reduction, but it is not the only means. Other forms of finance, including microinsurance, leasing, deposit and savings services, and money transfer and remittance services, are indispensable to the rural poor. That is because, like the financial needs of urban dwellers, those of the rural poor are diverse, as many demands may pop up in people's lifetimes, ranging from emergencies to consumption to business investments. Remittances from family members and relatives from elsewhere or even outside of China can go a long way in improving their livelihood.

The Limitations of Finance

However, while finance can help raise economic growth and income levels and reduce poverty and inequality, there is also a limit to what it can do (Dichter and Harper 2007). In microfinance, there is a consensus that while microfinance may

(continued)

Box 4.1 *(continued)*

help reduce poverty, it is not an effective instrument in helping the "poorest of the poor."[b] All it does is to push the poorest borrowers into deep indebtedness without raising their welfare. On the supply side, forcing financial institutions to provide financial services to the unbankable will only undermine the institutions' financial positions, and in cases where public resources are used to bail out failed financial institutions, the financial risks spill over to the fiscal accounts. In case of a financial crisis, the poor and vulnerable are hurt more than the average population, just as microfinance could help them disproportionately.

The difficulty in broadening access should not be underestimated. It has been proved time and again that providing financial services to households and small businesses in poor and remote rural areas is an arduous endeavor, and, indeed, the road is littered with more failures than successes worldwide and over time. The reasons behind the failures are well documented in the economic and finance literature. In short, high transaction costs, information asymmetries, and associated moral hazard and adverse selection problems are prevalent, making it difficult if not impossible for financial institutions to serve the market profitably. Those that try to do so often end up failing because of many factors, one of which is the lack of appropriate lending technology that can effectively deal with the soft information of micro- and small borrowers. Indeed, in the past many financial institutions did try to lend to micro- and small borrowers, only to find the numbers of their nonperforming loans rising to unacceptable levels, in part because the lending techniques appropriate for large corporate borrowers did not work with micro- and small borrowers.

In an emerging economy like China, the gap between supply and demand has been widened by the withdrawal of state-owned banks from counties and towns, as well as by the increasingly commercial orientation of the rural credit cooperatives, which drives them toward urban rather than rural clients.

Notes: a. For succinct reviews of the literature on the relationship between finance and growth, see Claessens (2006); Rajan and Zingales (1998); Beck, Levine, and Loayza (2000); and Levine (2005).
b. Helms and Matin (2000) indicate that none of the microfinance institutions in Bangladesh, Bolivia, the Philippines, or Uganda reach out to the destitute, and only some reach out to the extreme poor. In contrast, many serve the moderate poor and the vulnerable nonpoor.

concentrate. Improvement in the welfare of rural households and further growth of the MSEs are essential for achieving the goal of reducing poverty and urban-rural divergence. Without improvement in access to finance, neither rural households nor MSEs will be able to break out of the poverty trap.

Despite differences in geographic locations and scales, rural households and MSEs share certain similarities as far as difficulties in access to finance are concerned. Both categories are small in size, usually have a short history, do not maintain or issue formal financial statements, and lack credit records. They do not possess the kinds of collateral and guarantees required by banks, but have multiple sources and uses of funds. Because of those features, formal financial institutions are usually deterred by the high transaction costs and risks in repayment caused by asymmetric information. It has been proved time and again that formal financial institutions would suffer from huge credit losses if they attempted to use the same credit techniques in lending to rural households and MSEs as they do with corporate clients.

Despite impressive progress in financial reform and development, rural and MSE finance as measured in outreach has remained limited in China in general and in Guangdong in particular. So far, the financial institutions in China have been unable to meet the demands for financial services and products by the rural households and MSEs in a convenient, expedient, and reliable fashion. The Chinese governments at all levels have attached great importance to financial services to the poor and vulnerable groups in the society and have implemented various policy actions. Unfortunately, these efforts have not produced the desired results; in certain situations, the policies have hampered rather than helped the outreach of financial services.

The overarching goal of this chapter is to promote effective and sustainable access to finance by the rural households and MSEs in Guangdong province so as to reduce poverty and curb the gaps between the poor and the wealthy and between the rural and urban areas, and among regions. The focus is not on any particular financial products or operations of financial institutions, important as they are. Instead, it is on policy actions of the government—on the paradigm supporting them and on their impacts— with the objective of building a consensus on what should be done and what should not be done, and how to implement the right policies going forward. The reason behind this intended focus is an observed tendency for the government to impose incorrect and often distorting financial policies that tend to get in the way of improving access to finance.

The chapter is arranged as follows. The first section, "The Current Situation," describes the current conditions of access to finance in Guangdong, with a focus on access to bank loans, as they are still the main form of financing demanded by households and businesses. Based on evidence, the section argues that what is lacking in Guangdong in general and the rural areas in particular is not financial resources, but the ability of the financial institutions to turn savings into productive loans. It also highlights the lack of public infrastructure essential to efficient financial intermediation. This section also examines access to other financial services, such as savings deposits and remittances.

"Issues and Problems" discusses issues that are central to the promotion of access to finance in Guangdong province. Increasing access to finance by the rural households and MSEs is not an easy task. The task is made more complicated by prevalent misconceptions about finance and by government measures that actually hurt rather than help the rural households and MSEs. This section identifies a number of issues and problems that get in the way of access to finance.

The chapter concludes with a number of recommendations for the Guangdong government to pursue in its drive to promote access to finance, making note of a number of pitfalls Guangdong may wish to guard against and describing some actionable policies, both short and long term. The chapter acknowledges that certain policies are the prerogatives of the central government, and it would be unreasonable to expect the Guangdong government to undertake such initiatives. Nonetheless, Guangdong can provide positive feedback and influence on solutions.

The Current Situation

Leakage of Funds

Chinese banks are good at taking savings deposits, but not at lending the deposits out effectively. The financial institutions in Guangdong—including branches of state-owned commercial banks (SCBs)—are no different. At the end of 2007, their combined loan-to-deposit (L/D) ratio stood at 58 percent, indicating that they were able to lend out slightly more than half of what they had collected in deposits. This compared poorly with similar provinces and with the national average. The L/D ratio for the rural area was even lower, at 0.32, which was less than half of that in comparator provinces (see figure 4.1).

Obviously, there was no lack of financial resources in Guangdong, including in the rural area. What was lacking was the means to allocate the savings to households and micro- and small businesses that were both willing and able to repay the loans. The rural credit cooperatives (RCCs) in Guangdong were reluctant to tap into the People's Bank of China (PBC) window for agriculture support loans, even though the interest rates were only a fraction of the market rates. This is additional supporting evidence

Figure 4.1   L/D Ratio of Financial Institutions in Urban and Rural Areas, 2007

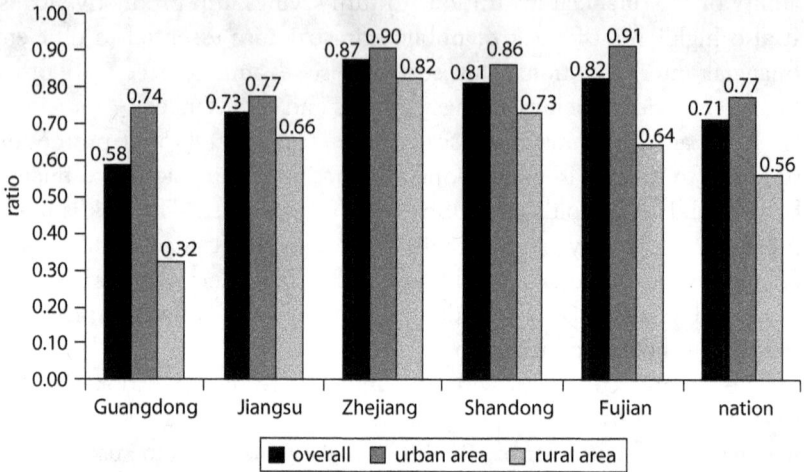

Source: Author's calculations using data in China Banking Regulatory Commission (2007).

that funding is not a problem for the RCCs, and that they are flush with savings deposits. Another conclusion that may be drawn is that the RCCs lack the motivation to disburse the agriculture support loans, as they are more interested in lending to corporate borrowers in cities and towns.

The L/D ratio is a meaningful indicator of the effectiveness of intermediation because if the actual ratio is lower than the prudential threshold by a wide margin,[2] there is reason to believe that an undue amount of the savings has either gone to investment in fixed-income financial instruments, such as government securities and bonds issued by policy banks, or has flown to other parts of the country through the intrabank funds transfer systems. In either case, the end results are the same: an undersupply of loans for the local market, especially the rural households and micro- and small businesses. At the end of 2007, the difference between savings deposits and loans in Guangdong was 1.5 trillion yuan, of which over 1 trillion yuan could be traced to the five largest national banks.[3] That the L/D ratio of the five largest banks in other provinces was way above that in Guangdong suggests a massive outflow of funds from Guangdong, including to those provinces (see figure 4.2). If it is not a surprise that the national banks were the channels of outflow, the roles played by the RCCs should be, as they were touted as the mainstay of rural finance. Of the 924 billion yuan difference between deposits and loans, the RCCs contributed 209 billion

Figure 4.2   L/D Ratio of Selected Financial Institutions, 2007

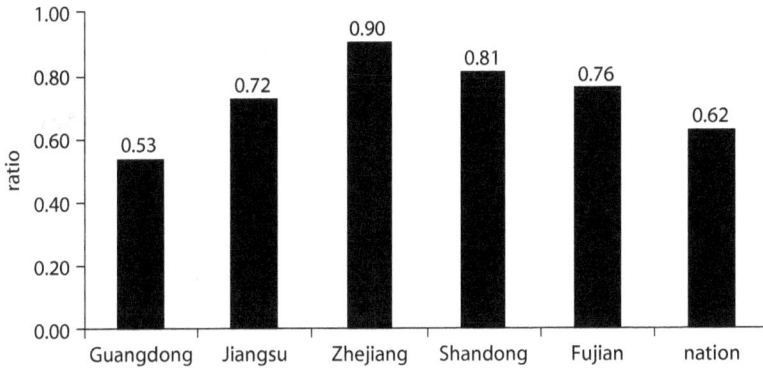

Source: Author's calculations using data in China Banking Regulatory Commission (2007).

yuan, with the remaining amount coming from the Agriculture Bank of China (ABC) and the Postal Savings Bank (PSB). Suffice it to point out that there is little the Guangdong government can do to influence the decisions of the national banks directly. What it can do, though, is to make conditions more conducive to lending by the banks.

Steep NPL Ratios

The leakage of funds is not the only problem. The savings that did find their way to lending in Guangdong registered a lower rate of repayment than elsewhere in China. Despite faster than average economic growth and spectacular urban prosperity in Guangdong, the quality of the loan portfolio has been notoriously bad for many years. The poor loan portfolio quality may be the root cause of poor access indicators (see below) and the low L/D ratio of banks in Guangdong, because the poorer the loan quality, the less lending authority the local bank branches receive from their headquarters. At the end of 2007, the combined nonperforming loan (NPL) ratio of all financial institutions in Guangdong stood at 9.3 percent, higher than those of the comparator provinces and the national average (see figure 4.3). Among them, the ABC and RCCs exhibited even poorer loan quality. Measured by the risk-based loan classification criteria, ABC's NPL ratios were as high as 26.5 percent, while RCC's were 19.3 percent (see figure 4.4).

During most of the 1990s, fast economic growth and accumulation of wealth coexisted with steep NPLs of branches of national banks in

Figure 4.3   NPL Ratio of Financial Institutions, 2007

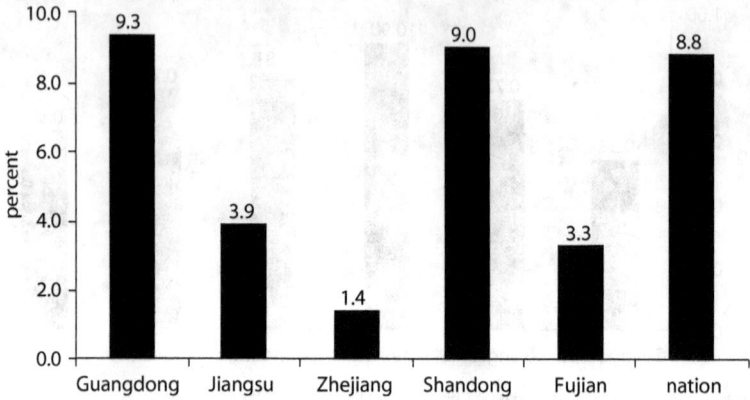

Source: Author's calculations using data in China Banking Regulatory Commission (2007).

Figure 4.4   NPL Ratio of Five Largest Banks, ABC, and RCC, 2007

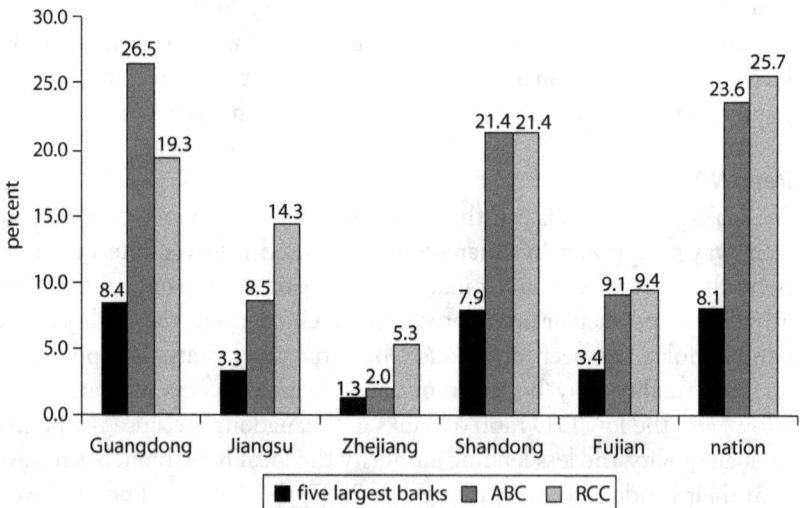

Source: Author's calculations using data in China Banking Regulatory Commission (2007).

Guangdong. Guangdong has been among the fastest growing provinces in China and was once among the pioneers in financial liberalization and innovation. Unfortunately, the province suffered setbacks, as frauds and irregular financial behaviors caused several notable failures and pushed Guangdong into a hazardous financial zone (see box 4.2).

Box 4.2

The Financial Crisis Legacy in Guangdong

Guangdong continues to suffer from a poor track record in handling finance. Up to this day, it is still haunted by what had happened during the 1990s, a period marked by financial chaos, abuse, and frauds. Guangdong has had its share of "ponzi games," "pyramid schemes," and numerous willful defaults on bank loans by its citizens and businesses. For example, a former mayor of Enping municipality whimsically ordered a branch of an SCB to lend to pet projects, resulting in severe losses. The residents of Enping have ever since been deprived of financial services, as no FI is willing to set up a presence in that municipality. In an example of a highly visible fraud, the managers of a branch of the Bank of China succeeded in embezzling US$4.83 billion to squander in casinos in Macao, China, and the United States. The list is long.

It cost Guangdong and the central government heavily to clean up the mess. In 1999, Guangdong borrowed 38 billion yuan under a PBC facility, with guarantee from the Ministry of Finance, to resolve failed urban credit cooperatives, trust and investment companies, and other local financial institutions. The money mainly went to the settlement of foreign debts and individual deposits. Even the Guangdong branch of the PBC suffered heavy losses from failed investments in FIs and nonfinancial businesses, on the order of 7 billion yuan. All told, Guangdong has thrown more than 50 billion yuan into cleaning up financial failures.

No wonder Guangdong has been labeled a "hazardous financial region" by the financial regulatory authorities and national financial institutions. There are several consequences of the financial crisis legacy. One is that a general paranoia has seized the Guangdong government at all levels, and officials have become extremely "risk averse" in general where financial matters are concerned. For example, Guangdong may have led other provinces in economic reform and opening, but it has certainly lagged in financial sector reform and developments. The shift from frivolous treatment of finance to extreme caution has prevented the government from financial innovation and from taking bold but necessary actions. Over time, it has also become hostage to poorly performing RCCs, ready to submit to their unreasonable demands.

Another consequence is that, deterred by the (both real and perceived) unfavorable conditions, especially the default culture, none of the SCBs, including the PSB, has chosen Guangdong as the testing ground for financial innovation, such as the "one bank, two system" experiment by the ABC and the new lending products from PSB.

Source: Compiled by the author from various sources.

Many businesses and individuals became prosperous but defaulted on bank loans willfully. Viewed from that angle, Guangdong's fast growth was sustained at least partly by financial savings of other provinces channeled through the national banks. As a matter of fact, some businesses enriched themselves at the expense of financial institutions and, as a result, poisoned the economic ecology of Guangdong province.

To some extent, the current problems in financial access can be traced in large measure to a chaotic episode of financial history in Guangdong. Since about a decade ago, the direction of funds flow has been reversed, as all the SCBs tightened risk management in lending and investment. Together with the downsizing of networks and staff, credit authorization has been standardized, based on a set of qualitative and quantitative criteria. Until their portfolio quality is noticeably improved, the head offices of national banks, especially the SCBs, will not relax credit controls in their branches in Guangdong. Viewed from the standpoint of prudential risk management, the restricted credit authorization to branches with poor credit management represents progress in China's banking reform and development.

Limited Access to Credit by Rural Households and MSEs

As indicated by China Banking Regulatory Commission (CBRC) statistics, only 13.6 percent of rural households borrowed from formal financial institutions in 2007, compared with 13.5 percent in Zhejiang, 17.3 percent in Jiangsu, 23.4 percent in Shandong, 36.7 percent in Fujian, and a national average of 34.6 percent (see figure 4.5). Most important, it seems not to be the case that Guangdong rural households are less bankable than the national average or their counterparts in other provinces. In the Pearl River Delta (PRD) region, only about 8.1 percent of the rural households had borrowed from banks by the end of 2007. The provincial household survey data indicate that the percentage of rural households with outstanding debt to informal moneylenders in 2007 was 4.6 times that of those who had unpaid loans to formal financial institutions (see figure 4.6).

MSEs did not fare any better than rural households. Although the micro- and small businesses contributed importantly to economic growth and employment,[4] their access to bank lending remained extremely limited, as only about 5.0 percent of small businesses had ever borrowed from banks (see figure 4.7), while 7.5 percent had done so nationally, 8.2 percent in Fujian, 5.5 percent in Jiangsu, 11.2 percent in Shandong, and 10.2 percent in Zhejiang. In the PRD region, the ratio was even

Figure 4.5   Rural Households with Access to Bank Loans, 2007

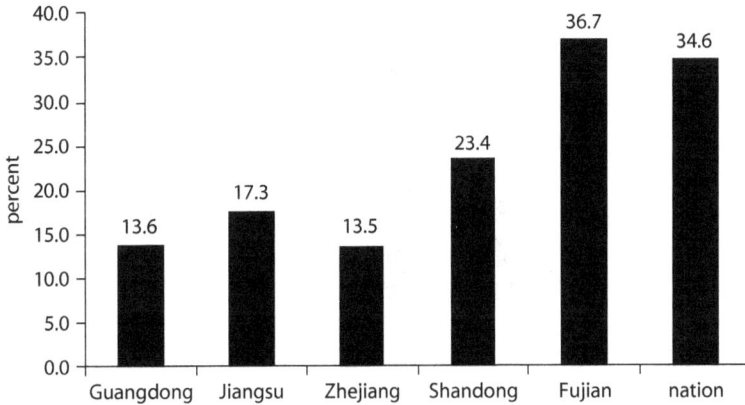

Source: Author's calculations using data in China Banking Regulatory Commission (2007).

Figure 4.6   Rural Households with Access to Informal and Formal Channels, 2007

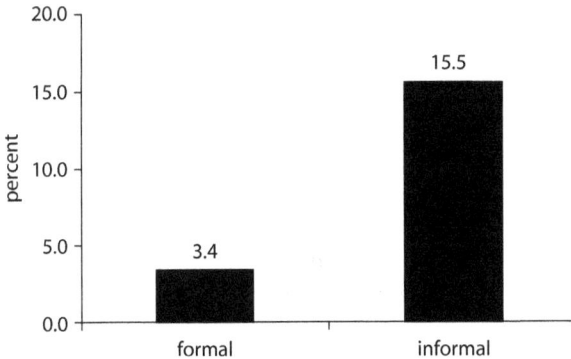

Source: Author's calculations using data in China Banking Regulatory Commission (2007).

smaller: only about 4.4 percent of the businesses had ever borrowed from banks by the end of 2007.

There are several factors contributing to poor financial outreach to rural households and MSEs in Guangdong. First, the relatively poor loan-to-deposit ratio of financial institutions in Guangdong has mainly been due to the lack of capacity in intermediation by the RCCs, which, over time, became a leakage of funds as their savings deposits found their way

Figure 4.7   Small Businesses with Access to Banks Loans, 2007

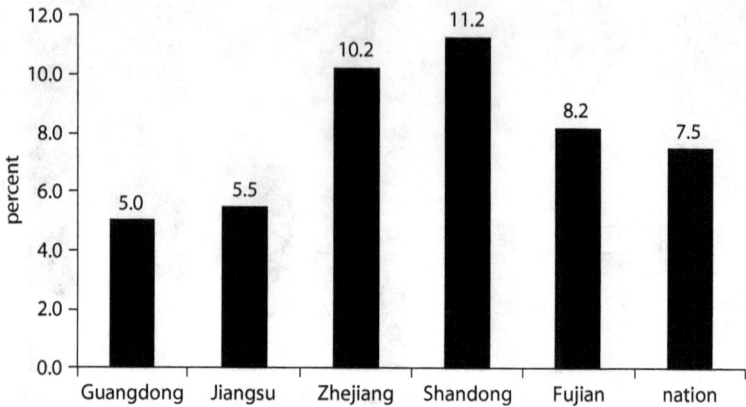

Source: Author's calculations using data in China Banking Regulatory Commission (2007).

into government securities and policy bank bonds. Second, none of the national banks, including the ABC and the Postal Savings Bank (PSB), chose to include Guangdong in their experiments in lending to rural households and MSEs, on account of perceived high risks posed by Guangdong as a whole. Exclusion from the pilots also resulted in lags in financial reform and innovation, which in turn negatively affected the level of financial access in the province. Finally, the indiscriminate shutting down of all the rural credit foundations that emerged in the late 1990s, together with newly created financial intermediaries, caused great damage to the supply side of financial services. As an example of the stifling effect of the earlier financial chaos and resultant depression, it was not until early 2009 that only two village and township banks were established in Guangdong, one in Enping, the other in Zhongshan.

Overview of Other Financial Services

The need for credit is not the only demand placed on financial services by rural households and MSEs. Like those of urban dwellers, the demands of rural households are also diverse, ranging from savings deposits, payments, remittances, insurance, and supplier financing services. It's particularly true as Guangdong is undergoing rapid industrialization and urbanization.

Access to deposit services for the poor farming households is limited. According to a 2002 household survey by the Guangdong Bureau of Statistics, only 34.8 percent of the farming households in the lowest income quartile had savings deposit accounts, with 46.5 percent in the second-lowest income quartile and 63.2 percent in the third-lowest income quartile (see figure 4.8). Among those farming households in the lowest income quartile that did not have savings deposits in banks, average cash holdings were as high as 5,425 yuan at the end of the year (7,759 yuan for the second-lowest income quartile).

Deposit services are important not only because they help smooth out intertemporal consumption patterns, but also because they serve to reduce the need for debt. But, as shown below, the reduced banking presence in remote rural and mountainous areas could have been an important hindrance to savings deposit services in Guangdong. Only 36.7 percent of rural households had access to deposit finance in the non-PRD area in 2007, compared with 82.6 percent in the PRD area (see figure 4.9).

Remittance services are particularly important for Guangdong, as it is the leading host for migrant workers. According to a 2005 survey, about 61.5 percent of the residents had their household registration, or *hukou*, from other provinces. Intraprovince migration seems a dominant choice for the rural households simply because there are more opportunities within towns, counties, and municipalities in Guangdong province than in other provinces. About one-fourth of the population—almost one per household—are intraprovince migrant workers, and about one-half of the workers ages 16 to 30 seek employment in the cities of Guangdong. Their remittance constitutes about one-third of rural household annual incomes. In remittance services, the financial institutions, notably the

Figure 4.8   Farming Households with Access to Savings Deposit Accounts, 2002

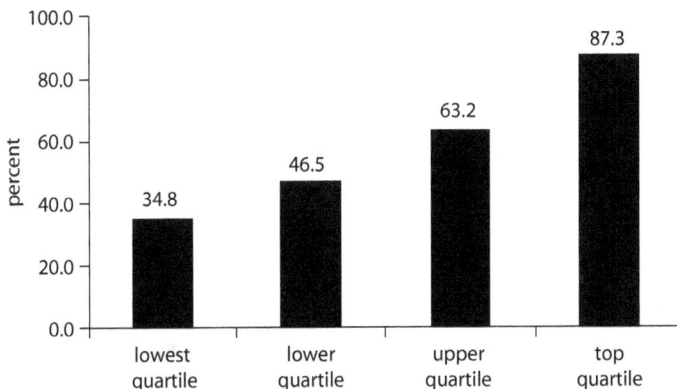

Source: Author's calculations using data in Guangdong Bureau of Statistics 2007.

Figure 4.9   Farming Households with Access to Savings Deposit Accounts, PRD Area vs. Non-PRD Area, 2007

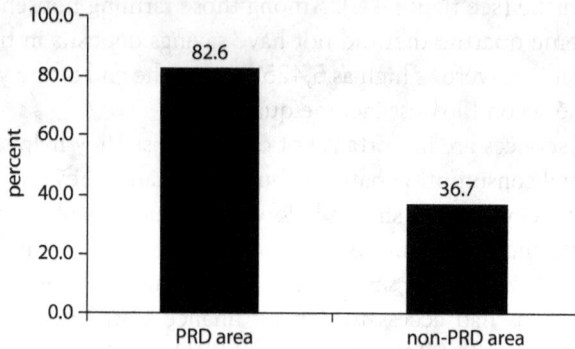

Source: Author's calculations using data in Guangdong Bureau of Statistics 2007.

Figure 4.10   Average Holdings of PSB Banking Cards, 2006

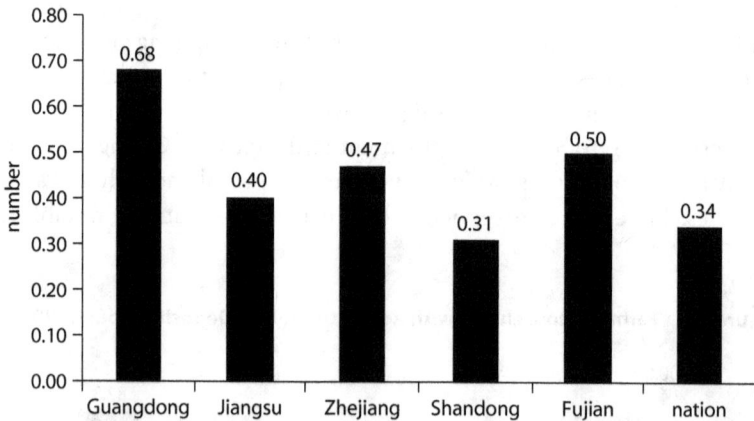

Source: Author's calculations using data in People's Bank of China 2007.

PSB, have performed better than their peers in comparable provinces, as measured by the average holdings of postal savings deposits, average amount of a single remittance, average holdings of the PSB banking cards and deposit accounts (figures 4.10 and 4.11).

There is an inherent need for commercially sustainable rural and microinsurance, especially in the rural areas, but rural and microinsurance remain underdeveloped in Guangdong. Disaster insurance is unavailable

Figure 4.11   Average Holdings of Deposit Accounts, 2006

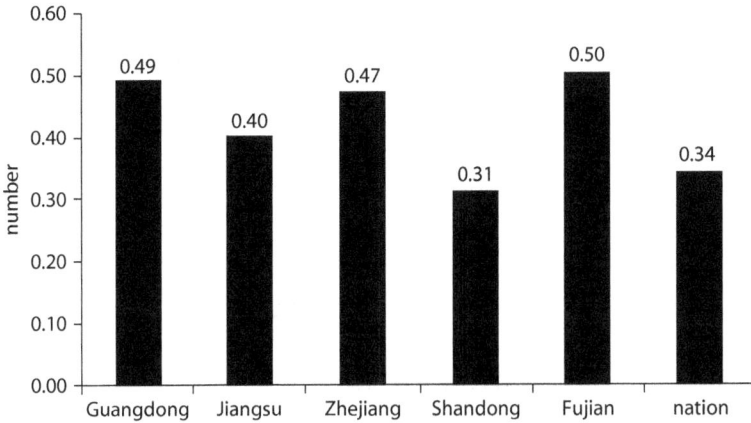

Source: Author's calculations using data in People's Bank of China 2007.

because a catastrophic insurance scheme has yet to be established in China as a whole, and other types of insurance have not enjoyed a level of penetration in keeping with potential demands. Providers of rural insurance products in Guangdong tend to provide comprehensive hazard coverage, which exposes them to potential losses, and a widely implemented practice of subsidizing insurance premiums exposes the government to open-ended risks. Subsidization of premiums tends to create artificial demands and exacerbates moral hazards. China must draw upon both lessons and experiences from other countries if it is to promote commercially sustainable rural and microinsurance.

What is not well known about rural and microfinance is the role of trade finance, as it is often not on the horizon of financial regulatory authorities and fails to be captured in official statistics. In reality, trade finance, including that provided by wholesale suppliers and purchasers of agricultural products, has played an important role in facilitating agricultural production and rural economic activities in general. The existence of trade credit may explain the perceived funding gap between economic growth and rural credit supply in China, including in Guangdong.

Shrinking Number of Banking Outlets

The history of central planning explains why Chinese banks have a more extensive network than those in other developing countries of similar standing (see figures 4.12 and 4.13). In Guangdong, the coverage of the

Figure 4.12   Number of Bank Branches in Selected Countries

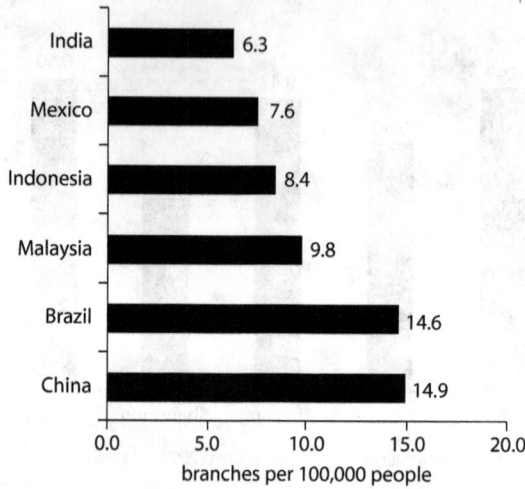

Source: Beck, Demirgüç-Kunt, and Honohan 2007.

Figure 4.13   Number of Bank Branches in Selected Countries

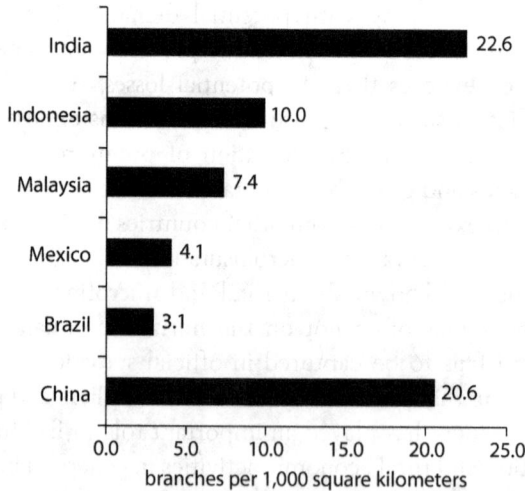

Source: Beck, Demirgüç-Kunt, and Honohan 2007.

financial institutions network is similarly impressive and compares no less favorably with its peers and the national average (see figures 4.14 and 4.15). In 2007, there were about 6,633 banking outlets at county level and below, of which 3,440 belonged to the RCCs, 1,136 to the PSB, and

Figure 4.14   Number of Bank Branches, 2007

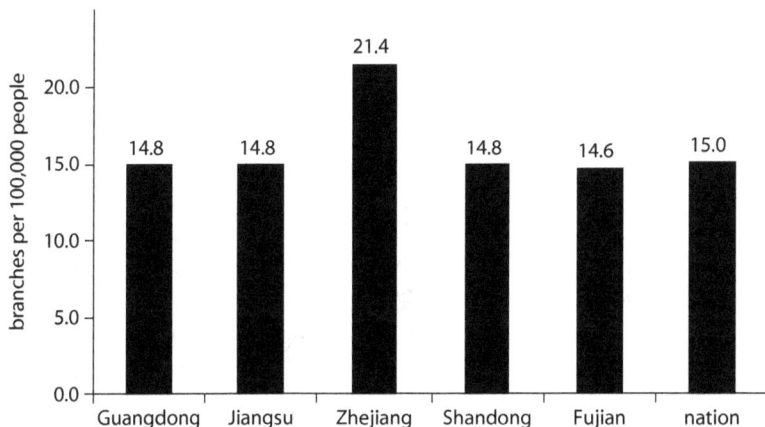

Source: Author's calculations using data in China Banking Regulatory Commission (2007).

Figure 4.15   Number of Bank Branches, 2007

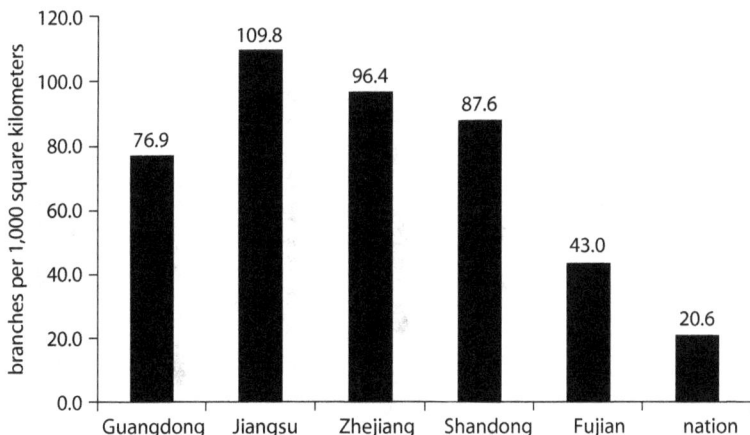

Source: Author's calculations using data in China Banking Regulatory Commission (2007).

the remaining 694 to the ABC. This implies that for every township in Guangdong, there were about 0.3 banking outlets, and for every administrative village, there were about 4.2 banking outlets. In terms of coverage of banking outlets, Guangdong fared better than most of its peers and the national average (see figures 4.16 and 4.17).

However, it should be noted that the banking outlets were concentrated in the urban area and the PRD area, where every 100,000 of the

Figure 4.16   Average Number of Banking Outlets Per Township, 2007

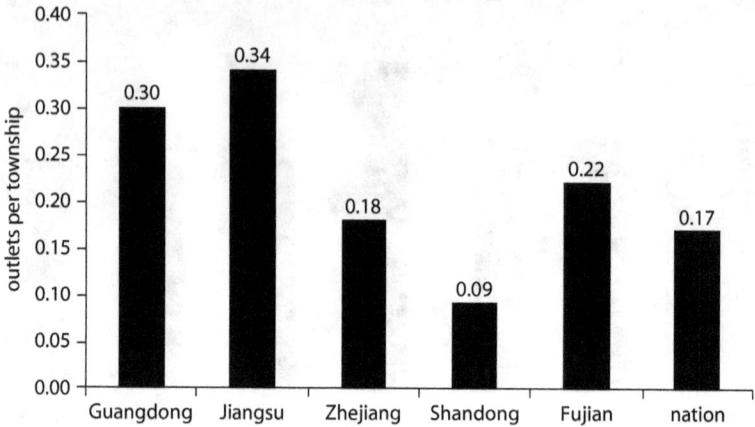

Source: Author's calculations using data in China Banking Regulatory Commission (2007).

Figure 4.17   Average Number of Banking Outlets Per Administrative Village, 2007

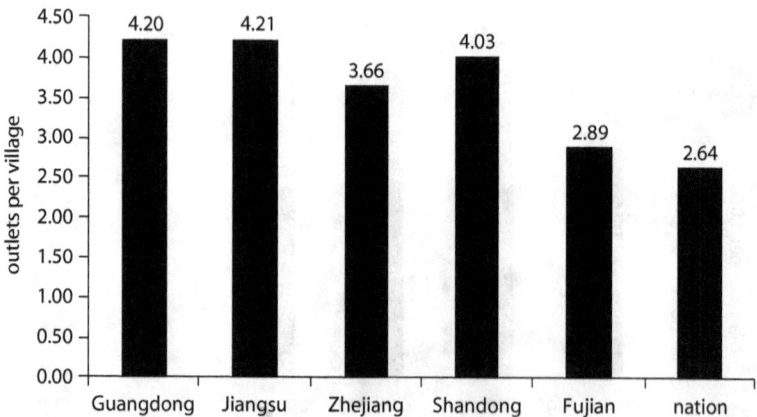

Source: Author's calculations using data in China Banking Regulatory Commission (2007).

population shared 27.1 banking outlets, as compared with 9.8 outlets in the non-PRD area (see figure 4.18). The geographic picture of banking coverage was similar. In the PRD area, there were 155.0 banking outlets per 1,000 square kilometers, compared with 46.9 in the non-PRD area (see figure 4.19). What is more striking is the total absence of banking in 73 townships and the single banking outlet for all of 162 townships.

Figure 4.18   Number of Bank Branches, PRD Area vs. Non-PRD Area, 2007

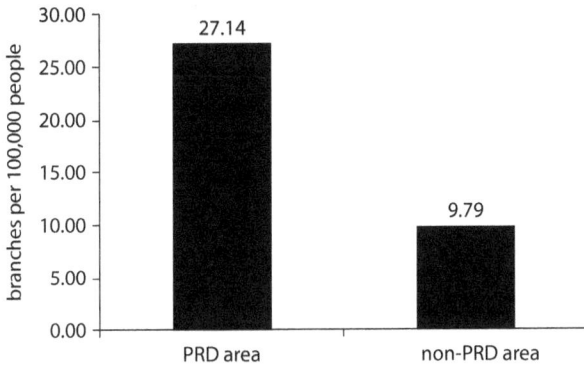

Source: Author's calculations using data in China Banking Regulatory Commission (2007).

Figure 4.19   Number of Bank Branches, PRD Area vs. Non-PRD Area, 2007

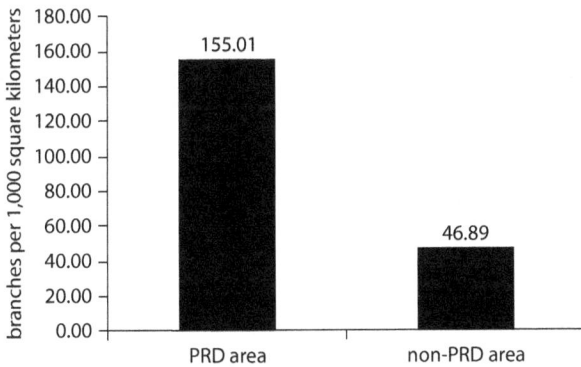

Source: Author's calculations using data in China Banking Regulatory Commission (2007).

Together, these townships were about 15 percent of the total townships in Guangdong. Rural households and small businesses in them have to travel long distances to access financial services, including basic services such as deposits and loans.

It should be pointed out that, just as it is wrong to force financial institutions to withdraw from certain locations for whatever reason, it is inappropriate, and may even be illegal, to order financial institutions to establish their presence in desired locations for whatever reason. One lesson learned from China and other countries is that it will never work for the government to dictate who is to be served by commercially oriented financial institutions and where the institutions are to operate. The void in financial services created by the withdrawal of banking outlets does not need to be filled by reestablishing brick and mortar banking offices. Nowadays more innovative channels are available to provide access to finance to rural households and businesses without physical presence. Branchless banking, as it is called, has proved a less costly and more efficient means for providing financial services and products in the rural and remote areas. Developing bottom-up village-level, member-based financial cooperatives in selected rural and mountainous areas is also a potential solution.

Changing the Landscape in Access to Finance

Since 2004, there have been several noticeable changes that hold important implications for access to finance in China. One is the liberalization of lending interest rates by the central bank in October 2004 (with the exception of RCCs and UCCs, which continue to be subject to a lending interest rate ceiling of 230 percent of the PBC base rates). Another is the campaign to promote commercially oriented lending to small businesses by the CBRC, which has led to a mushrooming of various experiments. A third is the relaxation of entry control in the rural financial market, as CBRC has created a variety of licenses for microcredit companies, village and town banks, and village-level, member-based financial cooperatives (see annexes 4.1 and 4.4). A fourth is the creation of the PSB on the basis of the previous postal savings and remittance arm of the State Post Bureau. The PSB, with its huge savings deposits, a nationwide network linked up by a state-of-the-art computer system, a clean balance sheet, and, most important, a dedication to microfinance, holds enormous potential to scale up microfinance in China. Already the PSB has shown impressive initial success in its experiments in microlending (see box 4.3 for a summary description). A fifth is the reorientation of ABC to focus on microfinance in markets at and below county level, in parallel with its urban finance—a model that has been proved successful by the well-known Bank Rakyat Indonesia in Indonesia. Transition economies in Eastern Europe and Central Asia have shown that former SCBs, once reformed, can become successful MSE lenders through downscaling.

These positive developments should lessen the pressure on the Guangdong provincial government to take hasty measures to promote access to finance. Instead, it should focus on improving investment conditions in Guangdong to make the province market-friendly for the financial institutions that would scale up their operations there of their own volition. This way, scarce financial and fiscal resources could be better

Box 4.3

The Microlending Experiments by China Postal Savings

In 2006, China Postal Savings began to experiment with granting certificate of deposit (CD)–backed microloans up to 200,000 yuan to meet the financing needs of small borrowers or to bridge the maturing CDs. A year later, it made this product available across the whole nation. In 2007, the Postal Savings began to provide uncollateralized microloans in seven provinces on a pilot basis, targeting borrowers such as small rural households, self-employed business owners, and private business owners. Those uncollateralized products were basically general guarantee loans or joint guarantee loans of less than 200,000 yuan. As of the end of 2008, 359,000 loans totaling 2.4 million yuan were disbursed, and the past-due ratio was 0.3 percent. From 2008, the Postal Savings began to finance the business operations of self-employed business owners and small business owners, accepting operation rights of real estate and business property as collateral. Individual credit volume could be as much as 500,000 yuan. Since the end of November 2008, all types of products provided by China Postal Savings have been available in Guangdong. With its 120 outlets, Guangdong Postal Savings has disbursed 10,551 loans totaling 744 million yuan, among which 6,553 loans with a volume of 391 million yuan were disbursed by outlets in counties or rural areas.

The success of the pilot program benefited from the competitive edge of Postal Savings in rural finance with respect to its large deposits, nationwide electronic network, clean balance sheet, and already established reputation. With such potential, the Postal Savings is expected to expand substantially the outreach of microcredit in China. However, caution should be taken in the sound operation of the institution, as massive credit risk may lead to problems should effective risk management not be in place.

Source: Compiled by the author from various sources.

targeted for better results. To meet that objective, the Guangdong government should be careful to adopt the right policies. This is the main theme of the next section.

Issues and Problems

How Risky Are Rural and Microfinance?

Finance may be one of the most—if not the most—misunderstood disciplines in China. One striking misunderstanding is over the nature of financial risks. Fear of financial instability has prevented government agencies from taking the needed steps in financial reform and liberalization. Following the financial chaos of the late 1990s that led to heavy losses, there was a general reluctance on the part of the government agencies and regulators to open up the rural financial market, especially the microfinance market. The financial repression at the same time reflected by closing down the rural credit foundations and the ban on newly emerged informal or semi-informal financial organizations and activities, eventually left the rural and microfinance financial market in a state of monopoly for more than a decade. While vigilance against systemic risks in finance is needed, excessive concern over nameless financial risks at the microlevel goes against the interests of the rural population and MSEs.

For example, the guidelines issued by both central and local governments in the campaign to promote microcredit companies contained provisions that would hinder rather than help the microfinance industry. The guidelines issued by the PBC and CBRC were already stringent. Yet the provincial authorities, including Guangdong, made those even more restrictive (see annex 4.2). It should be noted that with respect to microcredit companies that do not take public deposits, the risk to the public is minimal, if not nil. There is no need to apply the same level of scrutiny to this class of microlenders as to deposit-taking institutions.

Just like anything else in life, there exists a certain degree of risk in finance. But compared with the high leverage embedded in transactions involving derivatives, rural and microfinance is much less risky, especially viewed from a systemic point of view. Lending to MSEs in trade and services is even less risky because of their diversity and lack of covariance with the general economy. It is true that some rural, micro-, and small borrowers may be vulnerable to external shocks for various reasons, such as in rural finance, where one can face a much higher degree of covariance; but in that sense they are no riskier than large, urban-based corporate borrowers. In this regard, four factors should be clarified:

- First, the goal of rural and microfinance should not be to satisfy the needs of *all* rural and microclients, but only those that are creditworthy (both willing and able to repay the loans). It is up to the financial institutions to identify creditworthy borrowers, provide them with suitable products, and ensure timely repayment of principal and interest.
- Second, it has been proved that sound incentives to both borrowers and bank staff will help mitigate credit risks, as shown in the case studies contained in annex 4.3.

- Third, what the government can do to promote access to finance is to refrain from direct interference in the operations of rural and microfinance institutions. Instead, the government can and should reduce credit risk by providing public infrastructure that facilitates contract enforcement and reducing transactions costs.
- Finally, the government may wish to draw a line between what is commercially feasible and what is not. In remote and sparsely populated rural areas with inhospitable natural conditions, commercial rural and microfinance may be an infeasible proposition, which explains the perennial reluctance of rural financial institutions (RFIs) to set up and maintain banking outlets in such places. In such cases, the government is well advised to invest in public infrastructure, allow the RFIs to price their services and products without interference, promote free entry and impose discipline on failures. A combination of conducive financial policies, enabling public infrastructure, a reasonable degree of competition, and the threat of bankruptcy goes a long way toward bringing down transaction costs and providing the right incentives for RFIs to step up efforts to serve segments of rural markets that would otherwise be deemed as commercially infeasible.

Why Do Certain Policies Hurt Rather Than Help?

Despite all the good intentions, some policies actually hurt rather than help the poor, the rural households, and the MSEs, and serve to widen the poverty gap and inequality.

The interest rate ceilings often hurt rather than protect the most vulnerable by shrinking poor people's access to financial services. Interest rate ceilings make it difficult or impossible for formal and semiformal microlenders to cover their costs, driving them out of the market (or keeping them from entering in the first place). Poor clients either are left with no access to financial services or must revert to informal credit markets, such as local moneylenders, which are even more expensive. Ceilings can also lead to less transparency about the costs of credit, as lenders cope with interest rate caps by adding confusing fees to their services.

Another common mistake is the misuse of fiscal subsidies. Like elsewhere in China, Guangdong has set up reward programs aimed at attracting financial institutions, both foreign and Chinese, to move to Guangdong. The amount of monetary compensation offered to senior executives of financial institutions that move to Guangdong can run as high as several million yuan. The truth is that few if any financial institutions would decide to move to Guangdong because of the monetary compensation paid to senior executives. On the other hand, they would move to Guangdong if the move were consistent with their strategy, regardless of monetary compensation. One may ask, why give scarce fiscal resources away to those commercial banks that would locate in Guangdong anyway? Why not use the fiscal resources for better purposes, such as leveraging outreach by financial institutions to rural households and MSE borrowers?

There are also monetary awards granted to financial institutions that have increased their lending in a given year. Obviously, the design of such awards favors large, corporate borrowers instead of MSEs, because it is based on the volume rather than the number of clients. Should the Guangdong government wish to stimulate credit supply to rural households and MSEs, the authorities are better advised to base such awards on the number of loans or customers rather than the amount of the loans.

For example, in March 2009, MOF launched a pilot program to reward incremental supply of rural credit (Guangdong was not among the pilot provinces). In contrast to subsidizing lending interest rates, this pilot represents progress. But the drawback is that the definition of rural credit is too broad, leaving room for nonrural and large loans to pass as rural credit. The danger is that scarce fiscal resources may leak to unintended borrowers who might be engaged in real estate development and manufacturing and can afford commercial terms of borrowing. In such a scenario, the gap between the rural and urban, and that between the rich and poor, will not be narrowed by such loans.

Further, the government should refrain from extending interest rate subsidies to the targeted clients. As it has been proved time and again, subsidized credit usually does not reach the intended clients, as it is prone to being grabbed by the rich and influential, which defeats the purpose of poverty reduction because it widens rather than narrows the poverty gap.

Altogether, 0.34 billion yuan were given to the RCCs as a grant, from 2005 to 2007, to enable them to pay dividends to shareholders. This subsidy was on top of in-kind payments by government at various levels to the RCCs as part of the reform program sanctioned by the State Council in 2003. It is difficult to understand the rationale behind giving a subsidy to 100 percent privately owned financial institutions that are expected to become commercially oriented. Aside from wasting taxpayers' money, the generous subsidy also defeats the purpose of RCC restructuring, as it takes away the RCCs' incentives to stand on their own. One hidden motive behind the subsidy could be to qualify the RCCs for PBC promissory notes. If that is the case, it serves to reveal the loopholes in and the perverse incentives caused by the design of the restructuring program.

The Nature of RCC Problems

No policy discussion is complete without dealing with the RCCs. RCCs remain the largest formal lender in China's rural market. In Guangdong, as a result of the restructuring that consolidated the RCCs at the county level, there are now 99 county-level RCCs that together have invested in the shares of the provincial RCC union. At the end of 2007, the combined assets of the RCCs were about 695.3 billion yuan and the total deposits were about 542.4 billion yuan, or about 15.6 percent of the market share in the province. The NPL ratio was 19.8 percent, with a loan loss reserve rate of 12.8 percent. The leverage ratio of the Guangdong RCC system was only 3.1 percent.

The analysis here shows that the Guangdong RCC system fails to satisfy the financial needs of the farmers and MSEs. Access to finance is constrained by a lack of demand-driven and attractive products, a lack of monitoring, adequate staff training, and a well-designed management information system. But seen from another angle, all the problems can be traced to the corporate governance of the RCCs. Although the RCCs have installed the structure of corporate governance, including annual general meetings, boards of directors, and boards of supervisors, corporate governance has been established only in form, not in substance.

The RCCs remain heavily politicized and perceived as state owned, despite the fact that they are fully privatized. The restructuring since 2003 did transform their government ownership right, but because of the dispersed ownership structure,[5] in reality the shareholders have little or no incentive or power to exercise their rights in governance matters, especially when the RCCs continue to receive heavy intervention in their day-to-day operations. As a result, the RCCs continue to operate under ambiguous and conflicting objectives as they are asked to serve the so-called *sannong* (the farmers, agriculture, and rural developments). On the one hand, the local government is supposed to be responsible for their profits and losses. Over time it became a vicious circle. The continued ambiguity and conflicting objectives would not put the RCCs on the path to safety and soundness.

In the meantime, policy requirements and interference from both the government and the bank regulator entitled the RCCs to protracted protection against bankruptcy and competition from new entrants, domestic or foreign. The protection and fiscal subsidy, as well as the perception that local governments would be held responsible for the failure of RCCs, provided government officials with justification for interference. The protracted interference further weakened the RCCs' governance and distorted their incentives. And the lack of good governance and capacity for risk management also gave the bank regulatory authority—the CBRC—a reason to be intrusive in regulation and supervision, which further weakened the RCCs. Today, despite numerous and repeated reform measures and massive bailout funds, a breakthrough in this vicious circle is nowhere to be seen.

What is not ambiguous is the fact that, despite good intentions and expectations and the heavy subsidies they received,[6] the RCC systems actually failed to serve *sannong*. The number and amount of loans made by the RCCs were insignificant in terms of agricultural production, rural households, and MSEs (see figures 4.20 and 4.21). They actually became a channel of capital flows away from rural Guangdong.

Not long after the massive capital injection in 2003, there emerged pleas for another round of bailout on the grounds that old losses had not been fully absorbed. Even bank regulators joined RCC managers in the complaint that the government had not done enough for the RCCs—even though nearly 2,000 billion yuan had been paid out of government coffers—because they were looking at a bigger number: the amount of NPL carve-out and the recapitalization handed to the SCBs. Such sentiment is like a disease that holds the potential to sap the

Figure 4.20   Proportion of Rural Household Loans, 2007

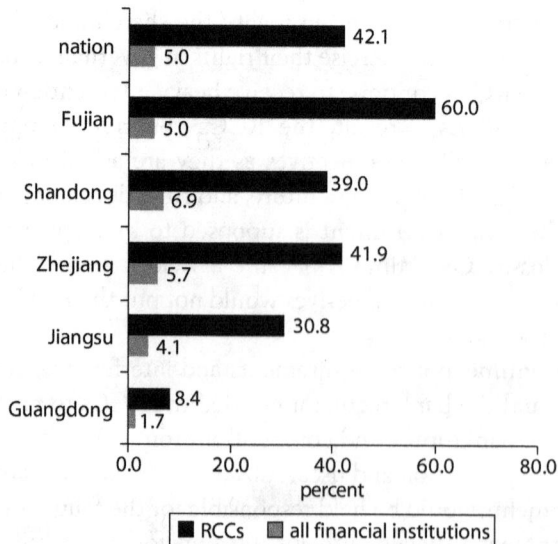

Source: Author's calculations using data in China Banking Regulatory Commission (2007).

Figure 4.21   Proportion of Loans on Agricultural Production, 2007

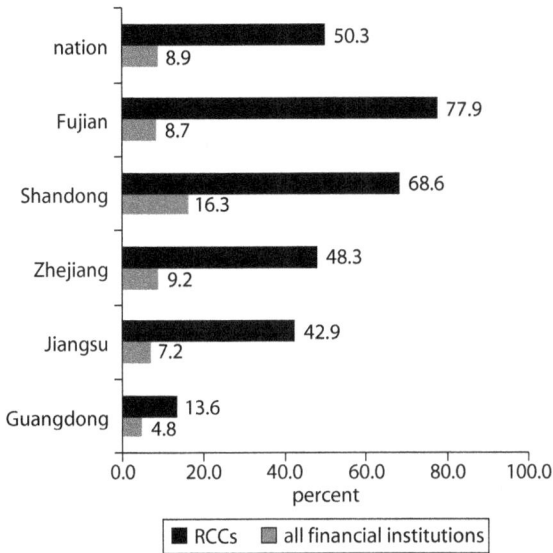

nation	50.3
	8.9
Fujian	77.9
	8.7
Shandong	68.6
	16.3
Zhejiang	48.3
	9.2
Jiangsu	42.9
	7.2
Guangdong	13.6
	4.8

percent

■ RCCs   ▨ all financial institutions

Source: Author's calculations using data in China Banking Regulatory Commission (2007).

morale of the RCC staff and managers and, more important, serves to discredit reform policies.

In 2007, following the Third National Finance Conference, a new round of restructuring was launched in Chongqing and Ningxia, among other provinces, this time focusing on the reform of the provincial rural credit cooperative unions (RCCUs). The provincial RCCUs were formulated by provincial governments to manage the member RCCs on their behalf, and over time they became a problem themselves. With a few exceptions, the provincial RCCUs became a burden to their members, interfering with the daily operations of members and viewed by them as a hindrance.

Will Credit Guarantee Schemes Work?

In their pursuit of solutions to promote rural and MSE finance, governments at all levels in China turn to credit guarantee schemes as a matter of course. In general, there is a blind belief in the role of credit guarantee schemes, and the danger of overinvestment in this industry is on the rise. In response to the ongoing financial crisis and a need to boost confidence, the pace of creating additional credit guarantee schemes has been accelerated.

There is a need to take a closer look at the credit guarantee industry and put it in perspective.

There were about 3,729 credit guarantees in China at the end of 2007, of which 703 were exclusively government owned and 682 were partially government owned. Together they leveraged bank lending on the order of 1.35 trillion yuan to about 700,000 MSE borrowers.

Among the main problems confronting the credit guarantee companies is that their leverage ratio has remained extremely low—at about two to three times, much lower than the industry average in countries like Japan (19 times) and Korea (10 times).

Very few credit guarantee companies are dedicated to the business they were set up to do—that is, the provision of guarantee to those borrowers that need credit enhancement in order to access bank credit. Many credit guarantee companies engage in nonguarantee businesses, such as real estate investment, primitive investment banking, and even stock market speculation. The 441 or so credit guarantee companies in Guangdong have performed no better than the national average, with a leverage ratio of 2.6.

According to news reports, Guangdong created a provincial reguarantee company in February 2009, with a paid-up capital of 2 billion yuan, half of which was contributed by the provincial fiscal bureau and the other half from a provincially owned finance company (the Yuehai Stock Holding Company). This followed in the footsteps of several other provinces, including Anhui, Beijing, Chongqing, and Jilin.

The call for a national reguarantee company as a "guarantor of last resort" went out several years ago, following the adoption in 2003 of the MSE Promotion Act, but to no avail. The central government is fully aware of the risks that could be transferred to it from the local governments through such a reguarantee regime. Already the industry is suffering moral hazard as the credit guarantee companies are forced to bear more than a lion's share of the credit risks—oftentimes over 80 percent or even 90 percent of the losses, should the loans go sour. Credit risks could soon accrue to the policy-oriented reguarantee companies, at either the provincial or national level.

The government control over lending interest rates before 2004 provided a business reason for credit guarantee schemes, as the policy provided convenient circumvention of interest rate regulation by banks and borrowers. Following the liberalization of lending interest rates, that justification became no more.

A key question is what a credit guarantee company can do in analyzing the credit risks of borrowers that cannot be done by the lending banks. The technical skills required of credit guarantee companies and banks are essentially the same. In reality, a credit guarantee company may well add to the costs of borrowing (usually on the order of 2 to 3 percentage points) without introducing the desired "additionality" to credit supplies.

Those credit guarantee companies set up or dominated by the government are beset with problems in governance, incentives, and risk management, similar to those that confronted state-owned banks prior to their restructuring. These problems further complicate the matters surrounding the credit guarantee industry. The industry also suffers from fragmented and ambiguous regulation and supervision, as several central government authorities are involved in both the promotion and regulation of the industry—an institutional arrangement recognized as a sure recipe for failure, based on lessons learned in China and elsewhere. The high-profile turbulence observed not long ago at a Shenzhen-based credit guarantee company, Orienwise, provides an example.

In view of the pros and cons of credit guarantee schemes, Guangdong is advised to take care to avoid the pitfalls of such schemes as the provincial reguarantee company, including increases in transaction costs to MSE borrowers, moral hazards, and waste of public resources.

Reshaping the Role of Provincial Government in Finance

China practices a centralized financial regulation and supervision system, with separate regulatory authorities overseeing the banking, insurance, and securities industries. Key financial policies and reform programs are formulated at the central government level. One would think, under this governance structure, there is little that a provincial government can do to influence the direction and impact of financial reform and developments. To the contrary, a closer look finds ample room for provincial governments to exert influence. Consistent with the overall trend of decentralization in economic policies and management, the central government has granted increasingly more authority to local governments, especially since the late 1990s. One driver of change came about when the central government started to involve the local governments in failure resolution and in sharing of the costs of rescuing insolvent financial institutions. Another wave of financial decentralization took place in 2003, when the State Council handed over the liabilities of the RCCs to provincial governments while retaining regulation and supervision authority. The most recent wave of decentralization came about in 2008, when the joint guidelines by the PBC and CBRC authorized local governments to license microcredit companies on the condition that the local governments bear the ultimate responsibility for any financial failures.

Thus, in reality, there exists a huge area where local governments can play a role in promoting access to finance. Such a role is just inescapable, because already the importance of locally registered financial institutions is rising, creating room as well as pressure for the local governments to intervene. The question is what role they will play, and how they will play it. Without a proper understanding of the basic principles of finance, many local governments have revealed a tendency to turn to quick fixes without achieving needed outreach and sustainability—two of the central criteria of successful rural and microfinance. Some are repeating the mistakes made by the central government about a decade ago. This chapter will show that the provincial governments are ill prepared for the role because they lack proper understanding of finance, institutions, and skills.

As mentioned above, several categories of financial institutions have been put under the jurisdiction of provincial governments. Some of them are locally registered, with licensing issued by the CBRC system through the local offices. In all cases, the provincial governments are supposed to bear the responsibility if things go wrong.

Unfortunately, that responsibility is ill defined, as nobody knows for sure what qualifies as "wrong." One of several possible criteria is insolvency resolution, as indicated by the slogan that "parents should take care of their own kids." In part because of a nameless fear and in part because of ignorance, many provincial governments have become extremely risk averse where financial reform, development, and innovation are concerned.

Lacking the means and capacity to ensure the safety and soundness of local financial institutions, provincial governments resort to heavy intervention in their governance and operations, either through the provincial RCCU in the case of RCCs, or through the Financial Affairs Office, or *Jinrongban*, with regard to other local financial institutions. In nature, the provincial governments assume an intensive ownership function, at the expense of a regulatory function.

Now is the time for the provincial governments to consider seriously rebalancing their roles in finance. Especially in the case of fully privatized financial institutions, such as the RCCs, there is no ownership role for the government to play. Ownership functions, by law and logic, belong to the shareholders. Putting governments in the shoes of owners not only deprives the owners of any incentives to monitor and exert pressure in governance matters, but it also creates friction and sows the seeds for failure. It also unnecessarily implicates the government should the RCCs fail in operations and end up with heavy losses. The provincial government should concentrate on (a) the regulatory function, in coordination with the central authorities, and (b) the gradual building up of a regulatory capacity, including a regulatory framework, a continuous supervisory capacity supported by on-site examination and off-site surveillance, and a cadre of professional supervisors. To date, no provincial government has done so, and Guangdong would set the pace should it decide to embark on the path of building up a local financial regulatory system to complement and free the already strained central government regulatory regime.

Another role appropriate for the provincial government (and government at all levels, for that matter) is to create an environment conducive to finance. In addition to meeting the well-exposited need to improve the investment climate, in finance the government could productively engage in activities that help improve the credit culture and contract enforcement and reduce transaction costs. Admittedly, some of those are the responsibility of the central government, such as the consumer credit information system and a modern secured transactions framework. But areas exist where a provincial government can help without undue interference in the internal affairs of financial institutions, such as by promoting consumer protection and financial literacy. There are also areas where experimentation can be made in testing new models of financial institutions and new products and instruments through sensible fiscal and taxation policies. These will be dealt with below.

Conclusions and Summary of Recommendations

Pitfalls to Avoid in Promoting Access to Finance

Before engaging in a discussion on what should be done, we believe it is essential to discuss what should *not* be done in the drive to promote access to finance in Guangdong. What prompted us to start with the "don'ts" is that over time we have observed a tendency to seek quick fixes by engaging in superficial and short-term policy measures that are wasteful and harmful.

A good starting point would be to reconsider policies and practices that perpetuate distorted incentives and behaviors in the financial industry. Such policies and practices not only waste public resources but also hamper healthy development of the financial sector, at the expense of the numerous rural households and MSEs.

- Giving monetary rewards to foreign and Chinese financial institutions to attract them to Guangdong is one such policy, as explained earlier. At present, several municipalities and provinces have engaged in competition to attract financial institutions to move to their jurisdictions, but the merit of such competition is dubious. Instead of giving out monetary rewards, it would be advisable to work toward improving the investment climate, which would provide a preferred incentive for all potential financial institutions.

- The government should not waste fiscal resources on the bankable groups in society and should focus on the nonbankable groups instead. Should the Guangdong government wish to stimulate credit supply to rural households and MSEs, it should consider replacing the volume of loans with the number of loans as the basis for monetary awards granted to financial institutions that have increased their lending in a given year. Awards based on volume of loans actually encourage banks to lend to large borrowers at the expense of MSEs. And such subsidies or tax treatments should not be institution-specific. That is, they should be awarded without discrimination among existing and potential financial institutions.

- It is recommended that the Guangdong government reconsider the policies geared toward encouraging the proliferation of government-owned credit guarantee companies and policy-oriented reguarantee companies. The role of such credit guarantee companies is dubious at best, as they may well add to transaction costs without raising overall credit supply. The wide spread of credit guarantee schemes tends to perpetuate moral hazard in the credit market and erode the fragile credit culture, without bringing about the intended additionality of credit.

- It would also be wise to take a sober-minded approach to the creation of government-dominated financial holding companies by amalgamating the existing RFIs and local government or SOE FIs. Such top-down conglomeration rarely works unless fundamental changes are introduced in governance and incentives.

The fiscal resources released by the above programs, estimated to be on the order of 10 billion yuan, will go a long way in funding the right programs, including pilots to test new ways of promoting access. This is the focus of the following paragraphs.

Recommendations for Policy Measures

There are several areas where Guangdong government can take immediate action, keeping in mind its impacts and implications for the medium and long term:

- Launch a pilot program for village-level, member-based financial cooperatives in selected rural and mountainous areas. The pilot should provide a solution to the void of basic financial services, deposits, and loans for the rural households that have been denied access as a result of the withdrawal of presence by the SCBs, starting in 1998, and the diminishing role of RCCs as they are being restructured into joint-stock rural commercial banks and becoming increasingly urban. There are several such experimental financial cooperatives in China, notably those promoted by the Leading Office for Poverty Alleviation and Development of the State Council and the Agriculture Department of the Ministry of Finance, with support from the World Bank, in Henan and Sichuan. In order for them to be successful, care should be taken to preserve the autonomy and initiatives of members and avoid willful interference by government officials at all levels. It is also advisable for the provincial government to set up an auditing unit to protect the interests of members through periodic audits as a public service to the newly established financial co-ops.

- Revise the policies and guidelines to promote microcredit companies under the overall sponsorship of the PBC and CBRC. It is critical that the provincial policies avoid the mistakes made by other provinces that chose to set even higher thresholds than those stipulated by the PBC and CBRC. Based on the discussion above on the nature of risks, it should be clear that the systemic risks posed by such microcredit companies are minimal, as they do not take public deposits. Artificially constraining their ability to formulate and to borrow will cause a systemic risk because few if any such companies can even hope to be sustainable. The Guangdong government should broaden its thinking and take a pragmatic approach to the promotion of microcredit companies. To promote competition and provide a level playing field, Guangdong should consider allowing multiple microcredit companies to be set up in all the counties, with lower thresholds of paid-up capital and the restriction over their funding limit and geographic expansion relaxed. The microcredit companies should be established at township as well as county level. It should be understood that microcredit companies require economies of scale in order to achieve meaningful outreach and commercial sustainability.

- Redesign fiscal incentive programs to promote access to finance by rural households and MSEs, away from the previous bias in favor of urban-based, large corporate clients. The fiscal incentive programs should focus on the reduction of transaction costs, on the introduction of innovative products and instruments such as microleasing and factoring (or reverse factoring), and on branchless banking models. The intended beneficiaries of fiscal subsidies should be well defined, and their welfare enhancement should be subject to monitoring and evaluation. Any existing or potential financial service providers wishing to serve rural and MSE borrowers should have equal access to the fiscal stimulus. As argued earlier, public resources spent on education, health care, and public infrastructure generate better economic and social returns than credit subsidy. Therefore, the government should not resort to interest rate subsidy but rather to nondistortive policy actions that help bring down transaction costs. In addition, in certain geographical locations with inhospitable natural conditions, it makes better economic sense to move the people to more habitable locations than to force the RFIs to set up or maintain outlets without commercial prospects or social benefits.

- Restructure the *Jinrongban* to balance its roles and functions as an owner and regulator of local financial institutions and markets. As discussed earlier, the increasing responsibilities of the provincial government in maintaining local financial stability and providing access to finance justify the addition of regulatory and supervisory functions. The CBRC does not have enough capacity to oversee the numerous local financial institutions, which continue to proliferate as the experiments with new types of financial institutions progress. In the meantime, the provincial government does not have an explicit regulatory and supervisory function. The resultant vacuum not only creates uncertainty and opportunities for regulatory arbitrage, but also potential risks. Guangdong will be a pioneer in charting new waters in the next generation of financial reform if it takes initiative in this important aspect.

- Plan a thorough study of the issues and problems surrounding the RCCs to explore a real pilot of restructuring, one aimed at making the RCCs truly resilient financial institutions with good governance and sound control systems. The RCCs should be freed from ambiguous roles and become real commercial financial institutions without the label of serving *sannong*. Local governments and the CBRC should make a commitment not to interfere with the internal operations of the postrestructuring RCCUs and RCCs. The shareholders, directors, and management should be allowed to execute their responsibilities fully under the new governance framework. In exchange for granting RCCUs this much-needed autonomy, the regulatory authorities should be correspondingly decisive and prompt in closing down failing RCCUs, and should announce their policy in this regard in advance to make it a credible deterrent to mismanagement. The recommended pilot on village-level financial cooperatives could be combined with the pilot on dealing with insolvent RCCs, as the two are complementary.

It should be pointed out that some financial and public policies that may affect access to finance are functions of the central government, and it would be inappropriate to expect the Guangdong government to take direct and specific policy actions. Nonetheless, there exists considerable room for Guangdong to provide positive feedback and constructive tension, including the following:

- Further improve the consumer credit reporting system to help expand outreach and sustainability of financial services as it facilitates credit discipline and brings down transaction costs. Enormous progress has been achieved in the consumer credit reporting system by the central bank since 1999, but further improvement is needed to enable better access and usage at the provincial level.

- Remove the remaining barriers to promoting a modern, secured-transactions framework to allow movable assets to be used as collateral for bank lending. Great breakthroughs have been made since 2007, when the Real Rights Law was adopted, but further reforms are essential to facilitate out-of-court settlement.

- Turn Guangdong into a special pilot zone for experiments with liberalizing the lending rate ceiling for rural financial institutions and in informal finance. Regulations should not focus on interest rates, but rather on disclosure standards and prevention of abusive techniques in loan recovery. Liberalizing interest rates can encourage outreach to previously unbanked customers. Allowing financial institutions to charge interest rates that allow provision of commercially sustainable financial service can foster competition by giving incentives to new institutions to enter financial markets.

The World Bank will stand ready to provide technical assistance to Guangdong in the design and implementation of the recommended reforms and experiments, should the need arise.

Annex 4.1 Comparison of the Regulation Framework for Commercial Banks and Rural Financial Institutions, 2008

	Commercial bank		Rural cooperative financial institution				New rural financial institutions			Nonfinancial institutions
	National commercial banks	City commercial banks	Rural commercial banks	Rural cooperative banks	Rural credit cooperatives	Rural credit cooperative unions	Village banks	Loan companies	Rural mutual cooperatives	Microcredit companies
Licensing regulation — Initial registered capital requirements	≥ 1 billion yuan	≥ 100 million yuan	≥ 50 million yuan	≥ 20 million yuan	≥ 1 million yuan	≥ 10 million yuan	At county (city) level ≥ 3 million yuan; at township level ≥ 1 million yuan	≥ 500 thousand yuan	At county level ≥ 300 thousand yuan; at village level ≥ 100 thousand yuan	For limited liability company ≥ 5 million yuan; for joint-stock company ≥ 10 million yuan
Number of shareholders	Subject to the company law		≥ 1,000 persons	≥ 1,000 persons	≥ 500 persons	≥ 1,000 persons	Subject to the company law	The capital should be contributed by commercial banks or rural cooperative banks.	≥ 10 persons Farmers or rural-small enterprise	Subject to the company law
Qualification of shareholders	/	/	Transform from Rural Credit Cooperatives, Rural Credit Cooperative Unions, or Rural Cooperative Banks.	Transform from Rural Credit Cooperatives, Rural Credit Cooperative Unions.	/	/	The sponsor should be a banking financial institution.			
Shareholding structure	/	/	Provincial government not allow to invest in				The largest single bank shareholder ≥ 20%; other single nonbank shareholders ≤ 10%		Single shareholder ≤ 10%	Single shareholder ≤ 10%

		Col 1	Col 2	Col 3	Col 4	Col 5	Col 6	Col 7
Prudential ratios	*Capital adequacy ratio (CAR)*	≥ 8%	/	/	≥ 8%	≥ 8%	≥ 8%	/
	Core capital adequacy ratio	≥ 4%	/	≥ 2%	/	/	/	/
	Deposit reserve ratio	17.5%	16.5%	12% or 15%	According to Rural Credit Cooperatives	/	/	/
Regulatory restrictions	*Deposit rates*	From zero to central bank benchmark interest rate						
	Lending rates	0.9–4.0 times central bank benchmark interest rate	0.9–2.3 times central bank benchmark interest rate		0.9–4.0 times central bank benchmark interest rate			
	Others	Operate nationally	Mainly operate locally	Restricted to local geographic area	Cannot lend to borrowers outside of the local geographic area	Restricted to local area; deposit taking not allowed	Deposit taking allowed only from members	Restricted to local area; deposit taking not allowed

Source: PBC Rural Finance Research Team 2007.

Annex 4.2 Different Requirements for Microloan Companies by Central versus Local Authorities

		Central authorities	Guangdong	Shandong	Shanghai	Zhejiang
Licensing requirements	Registered capital	Limited liability company ≥ 5 million yuan; company limited by shares ≥ 10 million yuan	Limited liability company ≥ 30 million yuan (≥ 15 million for mountain area); company limited by shares ≥ 50 million yuan (20 million for mountain area); ≤ 200 million yuan in either case	Limited liability company ≥ 50 million yuan (20 million for underdeveloped counties); company limited by shares ≥ 70 million (30 million yuan for underdeveloped counties)	Limited liability company ≥ 20 million yuan (10 million in Chongming); company limited by shares ≥ 50 million yuan (20 million in Chongming)	Limited liability company ≥ 150 million yuan (120 million for underdeveloped counties); company limited by shares ≥ 80 million yuan (30 million for underdeveloped counties)
	Qualifications of shareholders		Net assets of lead sponsor ≥ 50 million yuan (20 million for mountain area); leverage ratio ≤ 70%; positive income account for 3 consecutive years; 3-year total profits ≥ 10 million yuan (5 million for mountain area); last year's profits ≥ 3 million yuan (1.5 million for mountain area)	Net assets of lead sponsor ≥ 50 million yuan (20 million for underdeveloped counties); leverage ratio ≤ 70%; positive income account for 3 consecutive years; 3-year total profits ≥ 14 million yuan (5.5 million for underdeveloped counties)	Net assets of lead sponsor ≥ 50 million yuan (20 million for underdeveloped counties); leverage ratio ≤ 70%; positive income account for 3 consecutive years; 3-year total profits ≥ 15 million yuan (6 million for underdeveloped counties); lower requirements for Chongming county	Net assets of lead sponsor ≥ 50 million yuan (20 million for underdeveloped counties); leverage ratio ≤ 70%; positive income account for 3 consecutive years; 3-year total profits ≥ 15 million yuan (6 million for underdeveloped counties)

Shareholding structure	Single shareholder ≤ 10%	Shareholding of a lead sponsor ≤ 45%; other single shareholders and related shareholders ≤ 20%; single shareholder ≥ 1%	Shareholding of a lead sponsor ≤ 20%; other single shareholders and related shareholders ≤ 10%	Less than two lead sponsors, shareholding of a single lead sponsor ≤ 20%; total shareholding of two lead sponsors and other related parties ≤ 15%; total shareholding of other single sponsors and related parties ≤ 10%; single shareholder ≥ 1%	Shareholding of a lead sponsor ≤ 20%; other single shareholders ≤ 10%; single shareholder ≥ 5%
Regulatory requirements *Borrowers*	Small-size loan; diversify enough; lending to single borrower ≤ 5% of net capital	Small-size loan; diversify enough; lending to single borrower ≤ 5% of net capital and the amount ≤ 5 million	Small-size loan; diversify enough; lending to single borrower ≤ 5% of net capital; 70% of the funds lent to small borrowers with single maximum amount of 500,000 yuan, the single borrower of the other 30% ≤ 5% of net capital, lending to shareholders not allowed	Small-size loan; diversify enough; lending to single borrower ≤ 5% of net capital; money lent to 50% of the borrowers ≤ 500,000 yuan; lending to shareholders not allowed	Small-size loan; diversify enough; 70% of the funds lent to small borrowers with single maximum amount of 500,000 yuan, the single borrower of the other 30% ≤ 5% of net capital; lending to shareholders not allowed

(continued)

Annex 4.2 Different Requirements for Microloan Companies by Central versus Local Authorities *(continued)*

	Central authorities	Guangdong	Shandong	Shanghai	Zhejiang
Lending rates	0.9–4.0 times basis rate	0.9–4.0 times basis rate	0.9–4.0 times basis rate	0.9–4.0 times basis rate	0.9–4.0 times basis rate
Managements	No criminal history	Specific academic requirements and industry working experience requirements, as well as age requirements	Senior management should be familiar with financial sector businesses, should have industry experiences, and abide by the laws and regulations.	Senior management should have appropriate knowledge and industry experience.	Specific academic requirements and industry working experience requirements for board of directors and senior managers
Number of institutions	/	Only 1 allowed in each county	Experiment in 1 county	Only 1–2 allowed in each county	Generally only 1 allowed in each county, 2 exceptionally
Geographic restrictions	/	Operate within county territory	Operate within county territory	Operate within county territory	Operate within county territory

Regulatory authorities	*Regulatory structure*				
	The provincial governments should designate an agency to supervise the microloan companies; the government should commit to taking care of the financial risks brought about by the microcredit companies before licensing the microloan companies.	The provincial financial office is responsible for piloting the microloan companies; municipal government is responsible for the daily supervision of the microloan companies; county-level governments are responsible for the resolution of possible problems with microloan companies.	The provincial financial office is responsible for piloting the microloan companies; municipal government is responsible for the daily supervision of the microloan companies; county-level governments are responsible for the resolution of possible problems with microloan companies.	The Shanghai municipal financial office is responsible for the piloting of microloan companies; county-level governments are responsible for licensing and supervising microloan companies, as well as resolving possible problems with microloan companies.	The provincial financial office is responsible for the piloting of the microloan companies; municipal government is responsible for the daily supervision of the microloan companies; county-level governments are responsible for the resolution of possible problems with microloan companies.

Source: Compiled by the author from various sources.

Annex 4.3 Innovative MSE Lending Project in China

Jointly with the World Bank, the China Development Bank hired a microcredit consulting firm to help select financial institutions to participate in the lending project for micro- and small enterprises (MSEs) and build up institutional capacity to extend noncollateralized credit to on a sustainable basis. By the end of April 2007, 7,953 loans were disbursed (amounting to over 453 million yuan) and 6,753 loans were outstanding (with an average size of 57,000 yuan) from three participating banks, namely, Baoshang Bank, Jiujiang City Commercial Bank, and Taizhou City Commercial Bank. The outstanding volume of arrears over 30 days was less than 0.2 percent. The 7,953 loans disbursed benefited over 7,000 MSE customers. About 70 percent of the borrowers had no previous experience borrowing from banks, and 54 percent had never borrowed at all. The lending interest rates for the three banks were from 15 percent to 18 percent.

Supported by the consulting firm, the participating banks set up separate MSE lending departments at both the head offices and branches. A set of standardized MSE lending products was developed, and standardized loan administration, training, marketing, and risk management policies and procedures, and incentive mechanisms were put into place to promote the effective extension of MSE lending. The preliminary results of the project showed that MSE lending could be profitable and could be sustained by changes in credit philosophy and innovation in credit techniques. In summary, the differences between the lending methodologies promoted by this project and the common practices in the Chinese banking industry are shown in the accompanying table.

The innovative MSE lending model has existed for some time in Guangdong. Shenzhen Zhong An Credit Investment Co. Ltd. is one of the leading MSE lending companies, providing noncollateralized loans to individuals and small private business owners through its more than 30 outlets in Shenzhen city. By the end of 2008, 40,000 loans were disbursed, amounting to 1.2 billion yuan. A total of 12,400 loans were outstanding, amounting to 260 million yuan and averaging 40,000 yuan for each borrower. The maximum amount for each individual loan was no more than 150,000 yuan. The past-due rate over 90 days was 2.1 percent, and the average interest rate was around 15.6 percent.

Differences between the Technology Promoted by the SME Lending Project and Lending Practices among Chinese Banks

Lending practices among Chinese banks	Practices promoted by the MSE credit technology
Loan approval mainly based on collateral or guarantee	Loan approval based on cash-flow analysis and debt capacity of client
Credit analysis based on official documentation (financial statements)	Credit analysis based on financial information retrieved by loan officers by "auditing" and interviewing the borrowers and checking the information gathered for consistency and plausibility
Excessive documentation requirements that lead to high transaction costs and processing time	Only core documents required, with MSEs having no difficulty presenting them
Low interest rates without fees but with high hidden costs	Market-based lending rates, which tend to be higher than those to large borrowers but typically lower than those charged by informal moneylenders
Large loans, usually over 1 million yuan	Micro- and small loans with average loan size of 40,000 yuan
Business plans and feasibility studies required, which tend to turn MSE borrowers off, as they usually do not have them	Business plans and feasibility studies never requested, as they are not essential for the very small borrowers
Complex loan procedures involving many departments and hierarchy levels, leading to processing times of three months or more.	"Time to cash" crucial to compete successfully with informal finance providers and to reach sufficient lending efficiency; loans typically disbursed in one to three days after application
Short loan maturities with frequent rollover of loans	Loan maturity matched with cash flow and debt capacity and finance needs; no rollover of debt
Incentives for loan officers to go after large corporate borrowers to disburse large loans	Motivation for loan officers to lend to MSEs with small loans, with incentives built into their compensation schemes accordingly to disburse loans and ensure repayment
Immovable assets required as collateral, with their evaluation by third parties increasing transaction costs for clients	Flexibility in collateral requirements, allowing items of emotional value to qualify as both collateral, with their evaluation conducted by loan officers
Bullet repayment of loans, making it difficult for the lender to offer incentive to and monitor the borrowers	Equal monthly installment loans serving as both a monitoring and an incentive device

Source: International Project Consult (IPC) company training materials.

Annex 4.4 Mutual Societies in Poor Villages

In 2005, with the technical assistance of the World Bank, the Poverty Reduction Office of the State Council began a pilot project to organize mutual societies in poor villages in Henan and Sichuan provinces. These mutual societies are not-for-profit organizations that are owned and managed by rural households and aimed at financing their production activities and emergency needs. These societies are not allowed to take deposits.

The funding sources of the societies include fiscal funds, membership contributions, and donations. The members of the societies are farmers who voluntarily contribute to the fund, and every five members compose a group that is jointly liable for their borrowing. It is the group meeting that decides who is eligible for the credit. The loan sizes are usually no more than 10 times the borrower's contribution, or lower than 4,000 yuan. The maximum maturity is one year, and the monthly rate of the commitment fee is at least 0.8 percent. Both principal and commitment fee should be paid down each month. Members of the societies are eligible for emergency borrowing in the event of sickness, injury, or death of family members. The maximum that can be borrowed for an emergency is 1,000 yuan, with less than three months maturity and one balloon repayment. The commitment fee is the same as that for production credit. At the same time, guarantee is required. The societies give preferential treatment to the poorest farmers who have a financing need and the willingness and capability to repay, and the borrowing must be used for profit-generating businesses. The credit line and level of commitment fee vary across regions with differing levels of prosperity.

The pilot project has been expanded to Gansu, Hubei, and Yunnan provinces and basically is going well. However, there is concern that the governance of the societies is being distorted by improper government intervention. The pilot program and articles of association extensively discussed among members cannot be put into practice at all, and the elected governance board and management team cannot perform effectively. In effect, the societies have been too much controlled or influenced by the government. Moreover, training is obviously inadequate for the governance board members of the mushrooming mutual societies in terms of fund management, loan origination and repayment, monitoring, treasury, accounting, and so forth, and that inadequacy effectively destroys the efficiency and sustainability of the societies.

Notes

1. The Pearl River Delta region consists of Dongguan, Foshan, Guangzhou, Huizhou, Jiangmen, Shenzhen, Zhaoqing, Zhongshan, and Zhuhai municipalities.
2. The Commercial Banking Law stipulates that the loan-to-deposit ratio of banks should not exceed 75 percent.
3. These are the Agriculture Bank of China (ABC), Bank of China (BOC), Bank of Communications (BOCOM), China Construction Bank (CCB), and Industrial and Commercial Bank of China (ICBC).
4. According to an economic census of Guangdong, at end of 2004, there were 337,000 registered businesses in Guangdong, of which 133,000 had less than seven employees and 110,000 had total assets below half a million yuan. In addition, there were about 2.7 million individual businesses, employing about 8 million people and accounting for about 17 percent of total employment in Guangdong.
5. The RCCs' shares became extremely fragmented following the reform of 2003 because of restrictions imposed on shareholdings (below 0.5 percent for individual investors, including both membership and investment shares, and 5 percent for legal-person shareholders).
6. These included (1) a special note issued by the PBC in exchange for NPLs of RCCs in Guangdong amounting to 23 billion yuan, which was unmatched among all the provinces; (2) a subsidy from the Provincial Fiscal Bureau to the RCCs totaling 1.2 billion yuan from 2005 to 2007; (3) grants in kind by the local government at various levels (land and real estate) equivalent to 14.67 billion yuan; and (4) concessionary tax treatment received by Guangdong RCCs from January 2005 to December 2007 amounting to 2.34 billion yuan, of which 1.89 billion yuan was granted by the central government and 449 million yuan by the local government.

References

Beck, Thorsten, Asli Demirgüç-Kunt, and Patrick Honohan. 2007. *Finance for All? Policies and Pitfalls in Expanding Access*. World Bank Policy Research Report. Washington, DC: World Bank.

Beck, Thorsten, Asli Demirgüç-Kunt, and Ross Levine. 2007. "Finance, Inequality, and the Poor." *Journal of Economic Growth* 12 (1): 27–49.

Beck, Thorsten, Ross Levine, and Norman Loayza. 2000. "Finance and the Sources of Growth." *Journal of Financial Economics* 58 (1): 261–300.

China Banking Regulatory Commission. 2007. "CBRC Rural Finance Service Map." Unpublished. Beijing.

Claessens, Stjin. 2006. "Access to Financial Services: A Review of the Issues and Public Policy Objectives." *World Bank Research Observer* 21 (2): 207–40.

Clarke, George, L. Colin Xu, and Heng-fu Zou. 2006. "Finance and Income Inequality: What Do the Data Tell Us?" *Southern Economic Journal* 72 (3): 578–96.

Dichter, Thomas, and Malcolm Harper. 2007. *"What's Wrong with Microfinance?"* Britain: Practical Publishing.

Guangdong Bureau of Statistics. 2007. "Rural and Urban Household Survey Data." Unpublished. Guangdong, China.

Helms, Brigit, and Imran Matin. 2000. "Microfinance and Risk Management: A Client Perspective." Focus Note 17, Consultative Group to Assist the Poor, Washington, DC.

Levine, Ross E. 2005. "Finance and Growth: Theory and Evidence." In *Handbook of Economic Growth*, ed. Philippe Aghion and Steven Durlauf, 865–934. Amsterdam: North-Holland Elsevier.

Littlefield, Elizabeth, Syed Hashemi, and Jonathan Morduch. 2003. "Is Microfinance an Effective Strategy to Reach the Millennium Development Goals?" Focus Note 24, Consultative Group to Assist the Poor, Washington, DC.

PBC Rural Finance Research Team. 2007. *China Rural Financial Service Report.* Unpublished. China.

People's Bank of China. 2007. *China Financial Statistics Yearbook.* Beijing: China Statistics Press.

Rajan, Raghuram, and Luigi Zingales. 1998. "Financial Dependence and Growth." *American Economic Review* 88 (3): 559–87.

CHAPTER 5

Guangdong: Reforming Land Policy for Better Rights Protection and a Healthier Development Pattern

Guangdong has achieved remarkable success in economic and social development since the early 1980s. As of 2007, with a per capita gross domestic product (GDP) above $4,200, Guangdong accounted for 13 percent of China's national GDP, made up about 33 percent of international trade; contributed more than 14 percent of total fiscal revenue; and created more than 2 million new jobs in a single year. By maintaining an annual growth rate of 13.8 percent in the past three decades, Guangdong has firmly secured its leadership position as one of the biggest and most dynamic regional economies in China and defined a good example for less developed provinces to follow.

There are many factors to explain Guangdong's success, such as its geographic location and a level of social and economic development

This chapter was written by Guo Li of the World Bank. The author would like to thank Chengri Ding of the University of Maryland, Dzung The Nguyen of the World Bank, and Li Ping of the Rural Development Institute (Seattle) for their help and constructive comments on draft versions of the chapter. The author would also like to thank Li Shuyuan and Zeng Xiaohong of the Guangdong Provincial Finance Department and Wen Haifeng and Lin Ying of the Guangdong Provincial Department of Policy Research for their great assistance during the author's field visits in Guangdong.

higher than those of many other provinces, going back as far as the early 1970s. However, the proactive pursuit of innovative policy and institutional changes, with a forward-looking mindset to accommodate economic and social transformations, is the most important factor behind Guangdong's success. Whenever such changes have been deemed necessary, the provincial government has always demonstrated a strong political will to introduce them. The history of changes to Guangdong land policy could serve as a good example. Guangdong was the first province in China to introduce marketable urban land use rights in the mid-1980s; Guangdong was the first province to enable farmers to form shareholding cooperatives by using land rights in the early 1990s; Guangdong was the first province to recognize and normalize the market of collective construction land in 2005; and Guangdong was one of the first few provinces to pilot innovative schemes, such as reserving land for farmers' nonfarm uses to compensate farmers affected by land acquisitions. In short, these land policy and institutional changes have represented adaptation to rapidly changing economic and social circumstances brought about by the emergence of a market economy and accelerating urban expansion.

As Guangdong endeavors to establish a new development model for more equitable and healthier growth, land will continue to assume a crucial role. Land is implicated in Guangdong's ongoing economic and social transformations in numerous important ways such as a key factor in its quest for a new round of economic growth, rapid urbanization, better environmental protection, sustainable rural development, and a higher degree of social harmony. Therefore, how to strike a balance among competing land-related interests is a daunting challenge facing the provincial government. The answer to this challenge will play a central role in determining the shape and trajectory of Guangdong's economic and social future.

A New Platform for Pursuing Bolder Innovations

On October 12, 2008, the Communist Party of China (CPC) Central Committee approved a broad policy document aimed at more balanced and integrated urban-rural development. Most important, under the new policy farmers' leases on land would be extended from the then-current 30-year term to an open-ended one. The new land policy established the objective of narrowing the scope of land expropriation by distinguishing between use of land for public interests and use of land for commercial purposes. The policy expressed a clear, central willingness to limit land expropriations to needs for public interests. Plot-level land registration and certification would also be introduced to grant farmers a higher degree of tenure security as well as better protected land use rights, including the right of land transfer. The policy also reconfirmed the government's priority of national food security. To this end, it committed to adoption of a stringent farmland protection system and urged local authorities to safeguard the 1.8 billion *mu* deemed as a minimum for overall food self-sufficiency.[1] This document set up a new platform for Guangdong to pursue bolder land-related policy innovations.

Purpose of the Chapter

The purpose of this chapter is to present the main policy recommendations that have emerged from discussions with provincial and local governments and during field visits to several municipalities in Quangdong, conducted in November 2008. The chapter gives special attention to challenges such as land tenure security, farmland protection, land-related environmental concerns, urban land use efficiency, and enhancement of the role of land as a sustainable foundation for local government finances. Wherever appropriate, the chapter tries to introduce relevant international experiences. The intended audience is provincial-level government agencies responsible for land administration and management. The chapter is not, however, intended to be comprehensive, since some land policy issues can only be effectively addressed at the national level.

Rural Land Challenges

Land tenure security. Farmers in rural China generally do not enjoy a high degree of land tenure security. Guangdong is no exception. During the field visits, it was noted that some local governments continued to support, or at least allow, community-level land readjustments with different justifications. Frequent land readjustments, even on a small scale, weaken farmers' perceptions of land tenure security. Both domestic research and international experiences unambiguously demonstrate that a low degree of tenure security will negatively affect farmers' long-term investment in and production behavior on land and impede development of land markets. Land readjustments at the community level will also create rent-seeking opportunities for local elites. In consideration of all the negative impacts, the Rural Land Contracting Law of 2003 basically prohibited land readjustment, and this legislative intention was reinforced in the Property Rights Law of 2007. Extension of the farmer's land lease from a 30-year term to an open-ended one, which was announced by the

CPC Central Committee in mid-October 2008, sent a clear and strong signal of the central government's determination to grant farmers a higher degree of land tenure security.

Tenure security is also crucial for the healthy development of the land market in both rural and urban areas in terms of protecting interests of land rights holders, as well as reducing land conflicts. Guangdong has been enjoying an increasingly active rural land market since the 1990s. For example, as of 2007, the province had about 15–20 percent of rural land engaged in the rental market, with huge variation across different regions. In the Pearl River Delta area, more than 90 percent of rural land was in the market (mainly through shareholding cooperatives), while in less developed areas, the rate was about 5–10 percent. About 20 percent of farm households were involved in the land rental market province-wide. An emerging phenomenon, confirmed by the field visits, is the violation of farmers' interests to different degrees by village elites, local governments, and some enterprises during land transfers. For example, it was reported that some community leaders forced farmers to rent out their land for so-called large-scale farming. It was also reported that some enterprises grabbed farmers' land in the name of commercial farming. However, the land was actually being used by the enterprises for speculative activities and real estate development. Obviously, these worrisome phenomena will obstruct healthy development of the rural land market and result in serious land conflicts. International experience shows that securing land use rights of individuals *before* promoting the transferability of such rights is a sound principle.

It is recommended, therefore, that the Guangdong provincial government take timely and concrete actions to strengthen farmers' land tenure security further. One of the most effective ways to achieve this goal is to establish a plot-level rural land registration system and grant farmers land rights certificates. Establishing such a registration system is strongly supported by the most recent policy changes, as reflected by CPC's decision in mid-October 2008, and the No. 1 Document of 2009. There are rich international experiences in this field. Vietnam, which has a similar land rights arrangement to that of China, has endeavored to conduct a broader land administration reform and establish a nationwide digital cadastral record system (see box 5.1). Guangdong could again be a national pioneer in establishing a provincewide rural land registration system to promote more equitable growth with a higher degree of social harmony.

Box 5.1

Vietnam: Land Policy Reforms and National Land Registration Program

A well-functioning land administration system is a fundamental institutional arrangement for sustainable economic and social development. Rural land administration reform was among the most important initial steps of *doi moi*—a gradual, market-oriented economic reform process in Vietnam. Like what happened in China in the early 1980s, the reform process started with the introduction of the "household responsibility system," characterized by the granting of long-term land use rights to farm households in an egalitarian way. The government legalized this arrangement through the 1987 Land Law. The Land Law was revised in 1993 to recognize land use rights of households and individuals in both rural and urban areas and to introduce a national land administration system (LAS) based on unified land use right certificates (LURCs). In 2003, the Land Law was again amended to deepen LAS reform by expanding land use rights of households and individuals, recognizing land use rights of institutions (such as enterprises and organizations), and establishing the LAS regulatory and institutional framework at all levels. All these changes promoted the development of the land market.

Although Vietnam maintains state ownership over the land, the holders of land use rights are the de facto owners. They enjoy a rich bundle of rights: exchanging, transferring, leasing, subleasing, inheriting, donating, mortgaging, guaranteeing, using land rights as capital contribution to form shareholding companies, and receiving compensation upon land taking by the government. There are also some restrictions, however, on land use rights. For example, there are ceilings on the agricultural land area one household can have (3 to 4 hectares in delta areas), limited durations of land use rights (for example, 20 years for cropping and 30–50 years for forestland), predetermined land use purposes, and limitations on land conversion.

Registration of land use rights is the cornerstone of the LAS. The format and procedures of land use rights registration are unified nationwide. The 2003 Land Law requires that a LURC be issued for each plot and contain the names of both spouses. The registration is carried out by land registration offices established at the provincial and district levels. Initial registrations are generally carried out in a systematic manner (for example, commune by commune) for the scale of economy

(continued)

Box 5.1 *(continued)*

as well as to avoid the exclusion of disadvantaged groups. To ensure the information is updated, the land registration offices are also responsible for subsequent registration of land transactions and changes of land use. However, subsequent registration is carried out sporadically—that is, on a demand basis.

Some challenges remain, however. They include incomplete granting of LURCs to land users; insufficient infrastructure for effective and efficient operation of the land administration system from cadastral mapping, land titling, registration of land transactions, and record management; and the lack of public awareness of the LAS. There also exist a number of pending improvements in land policies, ranging from the expansion of agricultural land use rights and land valuation to the reconciliation of a gap between the Land Law, on the registration of land use rights, and the Housing Law, on the ownership of buildings.

According to data from the Ministry of Natural Resources and Environment, which is responsible for land administration, about 82 percent of agricultural land area, 62 percent of urban residential land area, 76 percent of rural residential land area, and 62 percent of forestland area had been issued LURCs as of December 2007. The number of LURCs still to be issued was almost double the 30 million LURCs already issued. Cadastral records, including cadastral maps, were largely incomplete, inaccurate, and not updated and, thus, could not support the need for land management and services. By the end of 2007, only 15 percent of LURCs had been issued with the names of both spouses as specified by the Land Law, of which 11 percent are agricultural LURCs and 18 percent are rural residential LURCs. The system itself is cumbersome and inefficient, lacks transparency, and does not provide a quality of services on which end users can rely. As a result, it is difficult and costly to conduct land transactions or to use LURCs for collateral. The weaknesses represent one of the most serious constraints to business development and transparent governance in Vietnam.

To address these issues, the government of Vietnam outlined a comprehensive Program for the Development and Modernization of the Land Administration (PDMLA) for the next 15 years. The program's objective is to modernize the existing land administration system to meet the demands of the economy and maintain social equity. The program includes the following:

• Completing the issuance of LURCs, the digital cadastral record system, and, based on these, the land information system
• Completing the legal system for a more mature market economy

(continued)

Box 5.1 *(continued)*

- Streamlining land use planning and completing land use plans at all levels
- Establishing a comprehensive land finance system
- Strengthening the capacity of the land administration system. In addition, a comprehensive land code will be developed to meet demands from a more mature and dynamic market economy around 2010.

Source: Dzung The Nguyen, senior agricultural economist East Asia and Pacific Region of the World Bank, personal communication.

Farmland protection. Farmland protection is another major challenge facing Guangdong. Under the existing policy framework, all remaining farmland in Guangdong has fallen into the category of "basic farmland," and, hence, the land available for further conversion for urban uses is very limited. In addition, according to current policy, this conversion is subject to approval by the State Council. The census of 2007 showed that Guangdong had 42.7 million *mu* of farmland; however, the basic farmland quota assigned to Guangdong for protection was also 42.7 million *mu*. Therefore, theoretically, the current situation means that Guangdong has to maintain 100 percent of its remaining farmland for agricultural uses to meet the quota of basic farmland protection, unless the State Council determines otherwise. In the Pearl River Delta area (comprising the cities Dongguan, Foshan, Guangzhou, Shenzhen, Zhongshan, and Zhuhai), the fact is that the remaining farmland area is much less than the amount of basic farmland the Delta area is supposed to maintain. In Guangdong, the potential for acquiring more farmland through reclaiming or consolidating land is also limited. In many areas, fish ponds and orchards have already been categorized as basic farmland.

Given Guangdong's rapid urbanization, it is unavoidable that a certain amount of farmland will be converted for urban expansion. In Guangdong, it appears that two principles should be followed in terms of farmland protection. First, the core of farmland protection should focus on improving land productivity. There is huge potential to improve land productivity since the current data show that 62 percent of the remaining farmland is middle- or low-yield land. More investment should be made to improve irrigation systems, land consolidation, fertility enhancement, and the extension of new technology. The focus should be on the eastern and western parts of Guangdong, where agriculture still enjoys a comparative advantage.

Second, a mechanism should be introduced to maximize the overall value of land resources. A decision on which plot of land is to be converted to urban use should be based on the overall economic value of all the plots of land involved, instead of the agricultural value of a specific plot. For example, assume there are two plots of land, A and B. One will be used for agriculture and the other for urban use. Assume that plot A's value is 50 for agricultural use and 300 for urban use, and B's is 40 and 200, respectively. If only the agricultural value of land is considered, plot A will be used for agriculture and plot B for urban use. If such a decision is made, the overall land value of the society will be 250. However, from the perspective of maximizing the overall value of land, plot A should be designated for urban use and B for agricultural, as long as the cost of improving B's agricultural productivity to that of A is less than 90. In that case, the total economic value of the land will be always bigger than 250. In addition, inflexible farmland protection in an area of rapid urbanization could result in an inefficient urban development pattern (featuring, for example, urban sprawl and overstretches of infrastructure, as well as the coexistence of incompatible land uses). Therefore, farmland protection policy, if it considers only the farmland's agricultural value, will not necessarily ensure the highest overall economic value of land use.

It is recommended, therefore, that Guangdong be innovative in piloting more effective ways to achieve the objective of protecting farmland. Policy should be directed toward introducing a system that maximizes the overall economic value of land while maintaining the overall stability of agricultural production. In short, more economic incentives should be built in when addressing the challenge of farmland protection. Great efforts should also be made to improve the quality of existing farmland. Successful breakthroughs in this area will not only create additional space for Guangdong's more integrated urban-rural development, but will also make a great contribution to national policy development for balancing demands for land between the competing priorities of food self-sufficiency and urbanization.

Environmental concerns. Environmental degradation has become a matter of urgency. There are two aspects to the issue. First, the quality of the environment in certain areas has significantly declined. For example, it is quite alarming that the number of hazy days in the Pearl River Delta area exceeds 100 per year, although the area enjoys a rich annual rainfall (1,800–2,200 millimeters). Water pollution is also a serious issue as a result of a relatively low percentage of wastewater processing and overuse of pesticides and chemical fertilizers. Other outstanding environmental issues are air pollution and drinking water quality, as well as the rapid increase of electronic waste. Therefore, it is quite encouraging to see that some local governments have introduced the idea of the "nondevelopment zone." For example, the nondevelopment zone accounts for 36 percent of the geographic area of Foshan municipality.

Second, the quality of farmland is also deteriorating, which has a significant negative impact on the safety of agricultural products. It was reported by the Provincial Agricultural Bureau in 2005 that out of 260 monitoring points, over half (53 percent) registered a clear decline in the quality (including the fertility) of land. Innovative land policy, such as land transferrable development rights (TDRs; see box 5.2), could be very

---

Box 5.2

Transferable Development Rights (TDRs)

TDRs have been developed to balance conflicting development goals and objectives of farmland and open-space preservation, on one hand, and land supply for urban economic growth, on the other, through incentive-based mechanisms. Regulatory approaches—land use zoning that specifies permitted types of land use (agricultural, commercial, industrial, and residential) and places limits on the density and extent of development—often turn out to be too rigid to be efficient and effective.

Similar to marketable permit systems, TDRs are used to implement restrictions on development of land designated as environmentally protected as well as permanently agricultural. Owners of agricultural land in the sending area are granted TDRs as compensation for the restriction on their ability to develop their land for higher-value urban uses. Owners of developable land in a designated receiving area are typically allowed to exceed limits on density only by purchasing a sufficient number of TDRs.

TDRs offer a number of advantages over land use regulations that are implemented in a purely administrative fashion. First, they provide a means of obtaining compensation for those whose property cannot be developed and, hence, is presumably lower in value. Second, they help defuse political opposition to development restrictions on the part of farmers who want to sell for development and on the part of developers. Third, they help reduce the time spent and costs incurred on appeals of regulatory land use decisions.

(continued)

Box 5.2 *(continued)*

TDRs offer a number of potential advantages in the case of China:

- A TDR system can accommodate different prospects for economic growth, allowing more conversion of farmland in areas with high growth potential, in return for farmland preservation in areas with low growth potential. In other words, a TDR system can reduce or eliminate inefficiencies in economic growth created by farmland preservation policies.
- A TDR system offers a means of redistributing some of the gains from economic growth by making land conversion in areas with high growth potential contingent on the purchase of land conversion rights from areas with low growth potential. Compensation of this kind might help reduce incentives for illegal land conversions as well.
- A TDR system can be used as an effective policy tool for managing and addressing multiple objectives associated with land use and development. This incentive-based approach helps to implement farmland preservation policies by allowing people on preserved land to benefit, at least partially, from rapid urbanization and industrialization. This will be valuable in addressing increasing tensions among regions with different economic growth prospects.

Source: Ding Chengri, professor, University of Maryland and National Center for Smart Growth, personal communication.

useful in addressing the issue of environmental degradation, although the issue itself is a cross-cutting one that requires a much stronger and broader intervention beyond land-related agencies per se.

A TDR could be viewed as a tool for the government to purchase land development rights from landowners. The core of TDR is to shift development rights from sending areas (where the development rights have been bought by the government) to receiving areas (where the land could be developed at a higher density). In sending areas, land can never be developed since it loses its development rights, although the original use will be kept. TDRs do not affect ownership or other land use rights (for example, the use of the land as collateral). Through this market mechanism, a good balance among many conflicting objectives, such as farmland protection and rational urban development, could be achieved. The United States has a quite well-developed TDR system at both the federal and state levels.

It is recommended that the Guangdong provincial government conduct a pilot of the TDR mechanism and expand it provincewide, subject to a successful pilot. By doing so, Guangdong not only will be in a better position to address its environmental issues, but also will make a significant contribution to national policy development regarding TDR.

Urban Land Challenges

Improvement of land use efficiency. Guangdong is experiencing very rapid urbanization, and this is leading to the expansion of the built-up area of cities.[2] Between 1990 and 2003, many cities tripled their built-up areas in China. Four of the 10 cities that have expanded their built-up areas the fastest are located in Guangdong (Foshan, Guangzhou, Santou, and Shenzhen). According to Guangdong's provincial urbanization plan for 2006–20, the level of urbanization will reach 75 percent by 2020 (85 percent in the PRD area).

Urbanization is inevitably linked to the process of suburbanization, which increases the spatial size of cities. However, the World Bank's study on metropolitan management clearly shows a huge potential for Chinese cities to improve their land use efficiency (World Bank 2008). The current model of land supply for urban expansion in China is not sustainable. Although intensity has increased in Chinese cities over time, as measured by the gross floor area ratio (FAR),[3] there is considerable room for further increase because the gross FAR in major Chinese cities is lower than in urban centers like Seoul, Tokyo, and New York. Overly strict limits on FAR values in central urban areas force cities to accommodate the demand for space by spatial expansion, increasing both land consumption and average commuting times. For example, provincial data showed that the land demand for urban expansion in 2009 was around 50,000 hectares, but the construction land quota, allocated from the Ministry of Land and Resources to Guangdong, was only 12,000 hectares. There is a huge gap between the demand for and the supply of land.

Urban spatial form is largely irreversible and has long-term consequences for economic, social, and environmental sustainability. Given the irreversibility of the built form of cities, it is important to incorporate efficient policies at the outset rather than rely on expensive retrofitting later (see box 5.3 on Atlanta, Georgia). Improving land use efficiency will directly affect motorization-related energy use and the volume of greenhouse gas emissions. Therefore, a higher degree of land use efficiency will both contribute to a better environment and mitigate the negative impact of global climate change.

Box 5.3

The Case of Atlanta

The built-up shape of cities is largely irreversible. A stark reminder of this fact is provided by an analysis of Atlanta, Georgia, where the population density in the suburbs is too low to support public transit. It has been calculated that for the density to reach the threshold required, "the current built-up area would have to shrink by 64 percent. [This would mean] about two-thirds of the existing real estate stock would have to be destroyed [and] two-thirds of the built-up area would have to revert to nature, and its population and jobs would have to be moved into the 36 percent of the urban area which would remain." Clearly, this is not a feasible choice for a city that was suburbanized in the era of cheap energy and relative innocence about the dangers of global warming. Chinese cities have to make choices at the outset that will prove to be sustainable in the new environment.

Source: Altaf and Shah 2009.

Lessons from international experiences about metropolitan land management can be summarized as follows:

- Governments should always aim to enable good outcomes rather than prevent bad outcomes. Experience from both Seoul and Tokyo confirms that placing physical barriers in the path of rapid economic growth is not effective. Market forces find a way of circumventing obstacles and physical barriers. Incentive- and market-based instruments work better in such environments.

- It is better to organize and channel the major forces of change than to fight them. Suburbanization accompanied by motorization will prove a powerful impetus for a move away from the city. It is immensely important to direct and channel this force to prevent employment imbalances and to keep the resulting spatial form as efficient as possible. New towns uncoordinated with transport infrastructure can impose heavy economic and environmental costs (as reflected by the Atlanta case).

- It is important to sequence transport infrastructure and housing. The building of new housing developments following public transit investments raises efficiency; new developments in advance of transit investments cause residents to make alternative automobile-dependent transport arrangements that are difficult to give up. Subsequent investments in public transport often suffer from low ridership.

- Finally, it is plain fact that there is no one optimal urban spatial form. The objective should not be to search for the optimal spatial form but to employ land use principles that would make alternative spatial forms as efficient as possible. Changes in technology, communications, and decentralization of work are too rapid to commit to any one particular spatial form in advance (see box 5.4 on smart growth). Residential patterns and choices are also specific to cultural practices and demographic specificities.

Box 5.4

Smart Growth

According to Wikipedia, urban sprawl refers to the spreading of a city and its suburbs over rural land at the fringe of an urban area, and the consequent creation of single-family homes and dependence on automobiles for commuting. There are increasing concerns over sprawling patterns characterized by low-density and leapfrogging urban land use development because of enormous impacts on the well-being of urban residents and the community in general. The substantial negative consequences of urban sprawl include (1) environmental and public health impacts (including increasing dependence on automobiles, lack of transportation choices in the sprawling community, rising energy consumption, increasing obesity, decreasing social capital, depletion of farmland and open space, and deterioration in land and water quality); (2) infrastructure cost impacts; (3) deterioration in tax bases for inner cities; and (4) neighborhood impacts (it is essential to have a successful balance of urban life by making workplace, retail, and restaurant space accessible to daytime customers).

In response to issues associated with urban sprawl, smart growth as a land use strategy was developed in the United States, primarily as part of an overall strategy on land use intervention and growth management to make urban development better. The "betterness" is measured in terms of the environment, land use, economic growth, fiscal development, and social concerns.

(continued)

Box 5.4 *(continued)*

Smart growth often focuses on the basic issues of location and design of development; transportation and land use integration; and development procedures. The following are 10 widely applied principles for smart growth promotion and implementation:

- Mix land uses.
- Take advantage of compact building design.
- Create a range of housing opportunities and choices.
- Create walkable neighborhoods.
- Foster distinctive, attractive communities with a strong sense of place.
- Preserve open space, farmland, natural beauty, and critical environmental areas.
- Strengthen and direct development toward existing communities.
- Provide a variety of transportation choices.
- Make development decisions predictable, fair, and cost-effective.
- Encourage community and stakeholder collaboration in development decisions.

The idea of smart growth is relevant to cities in many countries. However, concrete principles may not be universally viable. The overall effect of mixing land uses depends upon the cost-benefit ratio. Therefore, the applicability of mixed land uses, particularly in cities outside the United States, is an empirical question that should be carefully examined.

Source: Ding Chengri (professor), University of Maryland and National Center for Smart Growth, personal communication.

Therefore, it is recommended that the Guangdong provincial government be proactive in considering the alternative land uses possible and the policy choices that are open to it to ensure sustainable futures. This process needs to begin now because expansion of urban areas has been underway since the reforms of the early 1980s. These alternatives include adopting a regional perspective instead of a city-centric approach to lead to a more optimal use of land; introducing a more flexible system to trade the urban construction land quotas; prioritizing land conversion within growth boundaries and in strategic corridors to allow contiguous development to prevent urban fragmentation (for example, urban villages); correcting distortions in the pricing of land by introducing a more competitive market for land use rights; using the availability of infrastructure to guide development in order to prevent the fragmentation of urban space; encouraging local governments to use FAR regulations to channel growth to desired locations and enable the emergence of high-density nodes; and conducting a more detailed investigation of alternatives and options, since the uniqueness of the Guangdong context limits the applicability of global experience.

Property taxation. An overreliance by local governments on revenues from land granting and land-related financing is a widespread phenomenon in China. Different studies consistently show that land transfer fees account for at least 30–50 percent of total subnational government revenues, particularly in coastal areas. Revenues from the land transfer fees have increased significantly in recent years. Data show that the total amount of land transfer fees was 590 billion yuan in 2004. It reached 551 billion yuan in 2005, 700 billion yuan in 2006, and 1,200 billion yuan in 2007. A substantial amount of revenues is retained by local governments and is mainly used for financing infrastructure construction related to urban expansion. In addition, before 2007, revenues from land transfer fees were counted as off-budgetary revenue, whose use generally lacked transparency and accountability. A similar pattern has existed in Guangdong. In 2006, total revenue from land transfer fees was about 68.5 billion yuan, and it increased to 107 billion yuan in 2007. Data provided by local governments show that land transfer fees have generally accounted for a high percentage (around 40 percent) of local governments' total revenues. Data also show that at least 70–80 percent of the revenues have been used for urban infrastructure construction and related activities. At the same time, there has been an increasing reliance on mortgage loans by local governments using requisitioned land as collateral through the vehicle of "land banks."

Since land-related revenues account for a major part of local government revenue, it is not difficult to understand why local governments have a strong incentive to acquire more land. This strong incentive is reinforced by a huge price difference between urban land and rural land. Empirical research by the University of Maryland on the Yangtze River Delta area (Lichtenberg and Ding 2009) has shown that the marginal value of land for urban areas is about 4 million yuan per hectare (in Shanghai it is 6.6 million yuan). However, in rural areas, the marginal value is only around 7,000 yuan. There is reason to believe that similar price differences have existed in many areas of Guangdong, particularly in the Pearl River Delta area. The current land administration system, characterized by a monopoly over the primary land market by the governments at local levels, provides local governments with an easily used and effective tool to take more land. This practice underscores the incentives for local governments to pursue aggressively the requisitioning of rural land in a manner that is potentially risky, while contributing to potentially unsound forms of urban growth.

Although the nature of the property market in China in recent years—dominated by the state's monopoly on land supply, the local government's access to development land at agriculture-related values, and the sustained buoyancy of the economy of China—has made this an area of relatively risk-free involvement for local government, it is nonetheless an area of speculative activity. The substantial risks taken by local governments include that they are not in a position to determine final demand for land and that they are exposed to interest rate fluctuations, particularly given that the land banking sectors borrow substantially against the appraised "market value" of the land. The nature of the rules governing the property market massively distorts local government incentives, at both the institutional and the personal levels, encouraging the conversion of agricultural-collective land into urban-state land as swiftly as possible. The rate of growth of the urban areas in recent years and the rate of increase in investment in fixed assets both tend to confirm this.

There are three major concerns—the potential volatility of local government income from this area and its sustainability in the event of significant changes in the factors affecting market demand, the finite nature of the land resource for expansion, and interest rate fluctuations—that go significantly beyond local government in their potential implications. In addition, while it has been understood that, starting in 2007, land transfer revenues would be treated as normal budgetary income and, hence, be subject to auditing and monitoring, the result of enforcement of the new regulation has not been clear. In general, there has been less accountability and transparency in relation to the administration and expenditure of land transfer revenues.

The general level of dependence of local government finances on profits resulting from trading in land, in large part through land banking operations, is unsustainable and creates undesirable incentives that are resulting in extensive and inefficient use of land. In China, the taxes, charges, and fees on land and real estate are complex and are predominantly based either on transactions or on statutorily fixed, usually cost-based, assessments, and thus, they do not relate to current market values of assets. Therefore, they fail to provide the sound, asset-based tax source for local government revenue that is provided in many countries by market value–based property taxes. It is understood that, in China, a large proportion of households do not pay any tax on the residential property that they occupy.

Therefore, market value–based property taxes should be explored as a matter of urgency as an alternative source of local government finance. This would provide a long-term, sustainable substitute as receipts from land trading are reduced. Property taxation is well developed in developed countries, and its revenues account for a major part of local government budget income (see box 5.5).

Box 5.5

Property Tax as Good Local Tax

A good local tax has the following characteristics:

- The tax should cover the cost of services financed by local governments. In other words, taxes should be the price local residents pay for services and goods received from local governments.
- The tax should be levied on local residents and not be exportable to other jurisdictions.
- The tax bases should be immobile so that tax policy has little impact on land use and economic development decisions.
- The tax should represent a stable and sufficient revenue source for local government.
- The tax should be administered easily and inexpensively.

Property tax scores well in each of these respects. First, there is theoretical and empirical support for the view that the property tax is a benefit tax. Experts point out that both benefits from local public programs and their cost through property tax liabilities are capitalized into property values. Property values are composed of structural, location-related, and neighborhood variables, such as schools, roads, the crime rate, and so forth.

Second, tax bases for property tax cannot be hidden, and local ownership can be easily identified. The physical aspects of property make tax evasion difficult, if not impossible.

Third, the property tax can provide stable and sufficient revenue to local government. Even though property taxes represent a small percentage of all taxes throughout the world, they play an important role in local public finance in many

(continued)

Box 5.5 *(continued)*

developed countries. For instance, in 1999, the share of property taxes among all taxes was 9.2 percent in the United States, 8.4 percent in the United Kingdom, 8.3 percent in Canada, 5.7 percent in New Zealand, 4.4 percent in Australia, and 4.2 percent in France. But the property taxes account for a high percentage of local government revenues. In 1997, it was 73 percent in the United States, 99 percent in the United Kingdom, 84 percent in Canada, 91 percent in New Zealand, 100 percent in Australia, and 23 percent in France. Due to a relatively low elasticity and a positive correlation with GDP, property tax tends to be more stable than other taxes, such as sales and income taxes.

Finally, in many countries, property tax is administered and used by local governments. This promotes public influence over and participation in local public affairs. Perhaps for the majority of residents, their biggest asset is the value of their housing, which capitalizes property taxes and public expenditures. Residents, therefore, have a strong incentive to protect their properties through involvement and participation in elections, public hearings, and expression of preferences and opinions to affect decisions about local programs and budgetary choices.

Source: World Bank and Development Research Center of the State Council 2006.

It is recommended that the Guangdong provincial government design and implement a pilot to test the feasibility of introducing property tax. A computer-based, large-scale virtual pilot in many represented areas might be a good option. Using the results from the pilot, the government could make an informed decision on many aspects of this important topic, such as the timing for introducing the tax, the tax base, the tax rate, mass appraisal methods, and possible impacts on different social groups. Guangdong's successful virtual pilot on property taxation would certainly make a significant contribution to national policy development.

Conclusions

Guangdong's new endeavor for establishing a more equitable and healthy growth model calls for innovative land policy changes. This chapter, based on discussions with local government officials and findings from field visits in early November 2008, presents five key policy recommendations on land administration and management. These five policy recommendations correspond to five major land-related challenges facing Guangdong's next round of development. In consideration of international experiences and Guangdong's stage of development, it is believed that now is a good time for Guangdong to tackle these challenges. Given Guangdong's status in the whole of China's economy, it is also believed that pursuing these innovative policy changes will generate national influence, which is Guangdong's responsibility.

The major policy recommendations could be summarized as follows:

- For strengthening of farmers' land tenure security, it is recommended that the Guangdong provincial government establish a plot-level rural land registration system and issue land use right certificates to all farmers within its jurisdiction who hold 30-year land rights. Establishing such a registration system is strongly supported by most recent policy changes, as reflected by the CPC's decision in mid-October 2008 and the No. 1 Document of 2009.

- With respect to farmland protection, it is recommended that Guangdong be innovative in piloting more effective ways to achieve the farmland protection objective. Farmland protection policy should introduce more economic incentives to maximize the overall economic value of land while maintaining a stable and functioning agricultural production base. Great efforts should also be made to improve the quality of existing farmland.

- For addressing of land-related environmental concerns, it is recommended that the Guangdong provincial government conduct a pilot of the mechanism of transferrable development rights and expand it to the whole province once the pilot demonstrates success. TDRs will also be a useful tool for achieving farmland protection targets.

- To improvement of land use efficiency in urban areas, it is recommended that the Guangdong provincial government be proactive in considering alternatives for land use and the policy alternatives that are politically available to ensure sustainable futures. Many alternatives could be considered, such as adopting a regional perspective instead of the city-centric approach to lead to a more optimal use of land; introducing a more flexible system to trade the urban construction land quotas; correcting distortions in the pricing of land by introducing a more competitive market for land use rights; and using the availability of infrastructure to guide development to prevent the fragmentation of urban space.

- There is an urgent need to explore the feasibility of introducing market value–based property taxes as an alternative source of local government finance. It is recommended that the Guangdong provincial government design and implement pilots to test the feasibility of introducing property taxes. Computer-based, large-scale virtual pilots in selected areas could be a good option.

Notes

1. Fifteen *mu* equals one hectare.
2. This discussion of land use efficiency is heavily drawn from the *China Urban Land Use report* prepared by the World Bank (2008).
3. The floor area ratio (FAR) is the ratio (or the limit imposed on such a ratio) of the total floor area of buildings on a certain location to the size of the land of that location. A limit of a FAR of 2.0 would mean that the total floor area constructed is not allowed to exceed two times the gross area of the plot. A FAR of 2.0 could be achieved in different ways, for example, by constructing two floors on the entire plot; four floors on half the plot; or eight floors on a quarter of the plot.

References

Altaf, A., and F. Shah. 2009. "The Spatial Growth of Metropolitan Cities in China: Issues and Options in Urban Land Use." Unpublished manuscript, World Bank, Washington, DC.

Lichtenberg, E., and C. Ding. 2009. "Local Officials as Land Developers: Urban Land Expansion in China." *Journal of Urban Economics* 66 (1): 57–64.

World Bank. 2008. *China Urban Land Use.* Washington, DC: World Bank.

World Bank and Development Research Center of the State Council, People's Republic of China. 2006. China: Land Policy Reform for Sustainable Economic and Social Development. Beijing.

CHAPTER 6

Spending for Compulsory Education in Guangdong

Guangdong has made great strides in providing access to universal compulsory education. However, access to universal "quality" education is still by no means granted and is likely to be an important determinant of the broader disparities across areas and individuals in Guangdong. For example, while the access to and coverage of primary education has become increasingly homogeneous across urban and rural areas, coverage of junior and senior secondary schooling is still significantly higher in the Pearl River Delta than in other areas, as are indicators that can proxy for the quality of the education received, such as teachers' qualifications and spending per student. Additionally, initial data suggest that migrant children do not have access to the same level and quality of education as nonmigrant children.

Government policy aimed at narrowing the gap between urban and rural schools was implemented in 2001, namely the "two exemptions and one subsidy" policy. This effort was followed in 2005 by the gradual application of the free compulsory education (FCE) program, which followed

This chapter was prepared by Emanuela Di Gropello. Support, advice, and comments were also provided by Liping Xiao. Many thanks go to the Education Finance Bureau of Guangdong province for sharing updated education expenditure data on the province and counties.

the national scheme and pattern but was shared by provincial, city, and county governments. In 2005, the FCE program was piloted in 16 provincial poor counties; by fall 2006, all rural students were exempted from miscellaneous fees; by fall 2007, all rural students further benefited from free textbooks; and, finally, since spring 2008, all urban students have also been covered by the FCE program. The implementation of the FCE program aimed to promote the equalization of compulsory education in Guangdong. However, there has been no assessment or quantitative analysis to demonstrate to what extent the gaps among schools, urban-rural areas, counties, and regions—at least in education spending—have narrowed, or how to adjust the program to improve its impact and implementation.

In this context, this chapter focuses on providing a diagnostic of compulsory education (grades 1–9) in Guangdong and some initial evidence on how the new free compulsory education scheme has been implemented and is contributing to reducing gaps in the province.

Four main gaps generally characterize compulsory education in lagging and rural areas around the world: an outcome gap (reflecting quality and coverage of education), a human resource gap (teacher numbers and qualifications), a spending gap, and a management gap. These gaps are deeply interrelated (see figure 6.1). According to many international studies, teachers are the most important supply-side determinant of completion and learning outcomes of basic education students. While less

Figure 6.1   The Four Gaps of Rural and Lagging Compulsory Education

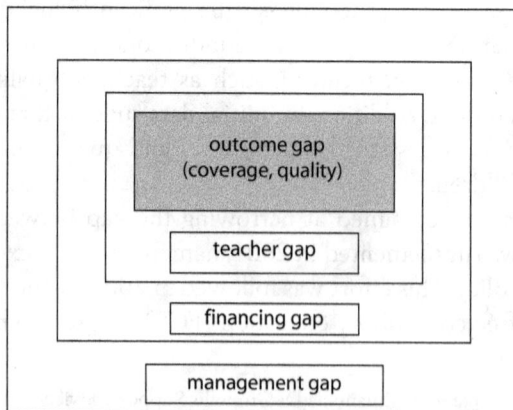

directly correlated with basic education outcomes, financing is central to ensuring access to high-quality infrastructure, facilities, and teaching and learning materials, and can certainly help attract good teachers. Finally, effective management is essential to ensure efficient and equitable use of funds and human and physical resources. Unfortunately, rural and lagging areas are generally characterized by shortages of qualified teachers, lower spending per capita and per student, and lack of management skills, all of which together are detrimental to education performance. This chapter will attempt to document the extent of the compulsory education outcome and spending gaps in the province, showing when possible how they are interrelated.

Key Outcome Gaps in Compulsory Education

This section will examine what and where the key outcome gaps are in the province of Guangdong, as well as suggest better strategies to measure them.

While it has been ascertained that gaps in education outcomes exist in Guangdong, the defi nition of outcomes is fairly limited (gross enrollment and completion rates), totally dependent on the official statistics, largely based on regional differentiations, and inward-looking. We will therefore explore or recommend other outcome dimensions (such as net enrollment rates, dropout and survival rates, and test scores), recalculate the main outcomes using other data sources (urban and rural household survey data), look at the distribution of outcomes over different equity dimensions (urban-rural, poverty levels), and undertake some minimal international benchmarking, to reach a better diagnosis of the outcome gap in Guangdong.

Enrollment and Internal Efficiency Indicators Based on Administrative Data

This section explores enrollment and internal efficiency indicators using administrative data. The next one will turn to more comprehensive indicators using survey data.

Administrative data show high enrollment and completion rates in primary, less so in junior secondary. Current administrative statistics of the Ministry of Education (see tables 6.1 and 6.2 and figure 6.2) point to high and generally constant gross enrollment rates and net enrollment rates in primary education in Guangdong, and, using similar statistics to

Table 6.1   Gross and Net Enrollment Rates in Primary and Junior Secondary Education, Administrative Data

10,000 persons

Indicators	1995	2000	2004	2005	2006
Primary					
Primary school–age population	832.4	905.4	1,010.1	1,026.9	1,014.6
Students enrolled in primary (of whatever age)	883.2	929.9	1,049.6	1,067.0	1,057.0
School-age children enrolled	830.0	902.7	1,006.6	1,023.6	1,011.8
Gross enrollment rate	106.1	102.7	103.9	103.9	104.2
Net enrollment rate	99.7	99.7	99.7	99.7	99.7
Junior secondary					
Secondary school–age population	—	—	—	579.2	—
Students enrolled in junior secondary (of whatever age)	—	—	—	462.7	—
Gross enrollment rate	—	—	—	79.9	—

Sources: Guangdong Bureau of Statistics 2008 and Census, various years.
Note: Numbers in italics are estimated. — = not available.

Table 6.2   Internal Efficiency Indicators, Administrative Data

10,000 persons

Indicators	1995	2000	2004	2005	2006
Number of primary graduates (of whatever age)	121.6	148.5	162.9	167.4	175.5
Number of new enrollees in primary (of whatever age)	151.6	155.7	168.5	164.2	155.6
Number of students entering junior secondary (of whatever age)	121.6	142.8	158.6	162.7	170.7
"Proxy" gross primary survival rate	—	98.0	—	107.5	—
Transition rate to junior secondary—same-year basis	100.0	96.2	97.4	97.2	97.3
Transition rate to junior secondary—two-year basis	—	—	—	99.9	101.9

Sources: Guangdong Bureau of Statistics 2008; author's elaborations.
Note: — = not available.

calculate some internal efficiency indicators—such as survival and transition rates—also point to high primary completion rates and transition to junior secondary. This is also confirmed by high and homogeneous enrollment and transition data at the city area level (table 6A.1.1 in annex 6.1). Data at the junior secondary level, however, show an estimated lower gross enrollment rate in junior secondary education—about 80 percent (unfortunately, available data do not allow us to capture time trends and

Figure 6.2   Gross and Net Enrollment Rates in Primary Education, 1995–2006

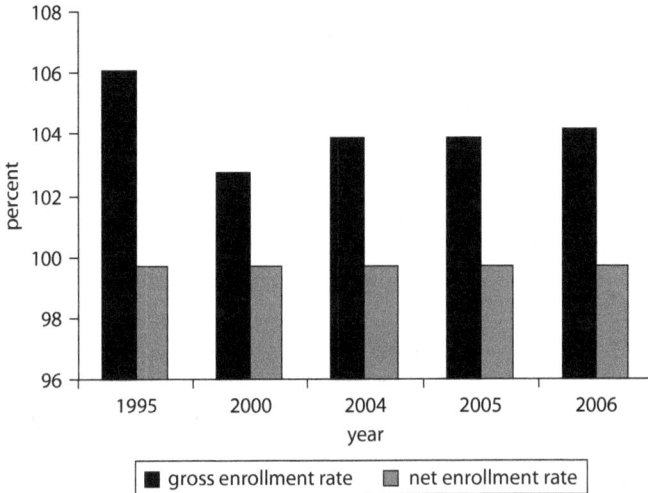

Source: Guangdong Bureau of Statistics, various years.

the net enrollment rate in lower secondary) and lower and more hetero-geneous rates of junior secondary to primary graduates across areas—from about 70 percent to 90 percent (table 6A.1.1), which point to lesser coverage and higher dropout rates in junior secondary.

Diagnostic of Educational Attainment Gaps in Guangdong Based on Survey Data

This diagnostic is constrained by the lack of comprehensive data on jun-ior secondary education, on quality dimensions at all levels, and on per-formance by key groups (urban and rural populations, wealthy and poor, nonmigrant and migrant, male and female). While there is scope to improve data collection and the elaboration and use of indicators using administrative school-based data along the lines indicated above, household survey data can also help provide a very useful complemen-tary source of information to (a) double-check some of the information (by comparing schools and household-generated data), (b) support more complete (along more varied dimensions, such as household income quintiles) and reliable (by being household based and therefore taking care of migration flows) equity diagnostics, and (c) calculate stock indi-cators on different age cohorts that provide useful longer-term measures of the evolution of education systems. Below are the key findings of the survey analysis.

Access to junior secondary education has improved across generations. Recent data from the urban and rural household surveys of Guangdong allow us to undertake an interesting diagnostic of the status of and evolution and gaps in educational attainment in the province. All data are shown in tables 6A.1.2, 6A.1.3, and 6A.1.4 in annex 6.1. Clearly, access to compulsory education has improved across generations, with about 91 percent of the 25–35 age cohort attaining at least junior secondary education, versus only about 80 percent for the 25–55 age cohort (figure 6.3). More people are also getting access to postsecondary and tertiary education. While about 9 percent of the 25–35 age cohort still has primary or less, this ratio has also been further reduced in the current school-age population (ages 15–20).

However, when looking more deeply at educational attainment in the 25–35 age range by urban and rural areas, income quintiles, and geographic areas, we see a more worrisome picture, where gaps in performance become very evident. While almost 100 percent of young adults of urban areas have attained at least junior secondary education, this ratio falls to about 87 percent in rural areas—with therefore about 13 percent of young adults with primary or less (figure 6.5). This ratio has, however, been decreasing in the 15–20 age range in rural areas to about 7 percent. The country is therefore on the right track to ensure universal primary in rural areas as well, although continued effort is needed. Compared to some other countries in Asia and Latin America, Guangdong's inequities between urban and rural areas in attaining lower secondary education are moderate (figure 6.4). It is, however, particularly noticeable that while

Figure 6.3   Educational Attainment of Different Age Cohorts, 2007

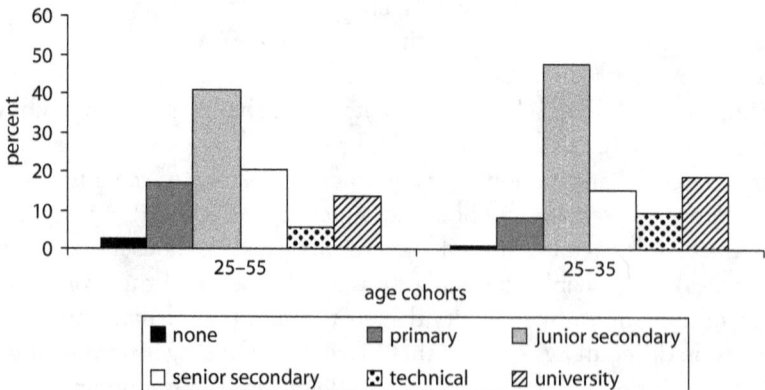

Source: Guangdong Bureau of Statistics 2007.

Figure 6.4   International Comparisons of Urban and Rural Educational Attainment among Young Populations

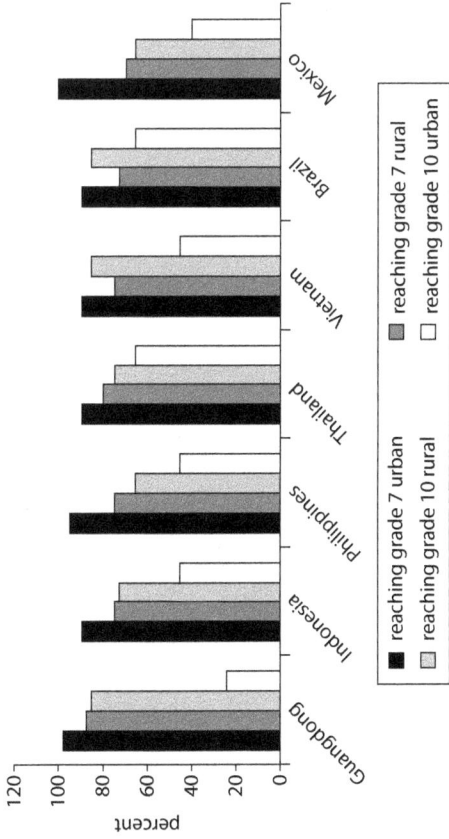

Legend:
- reaching grade 7 urban
- reaching grade 10 rural
- reaching grade 7 rural
- reaching grade 10 urban

Sources: Guangdong Bureau of Statistics 2007; Di Gropello, 2006b.

Figure 6.5   Educational Attainment for 25–35 Age Cohort in Urban and Rural Areas, 2007

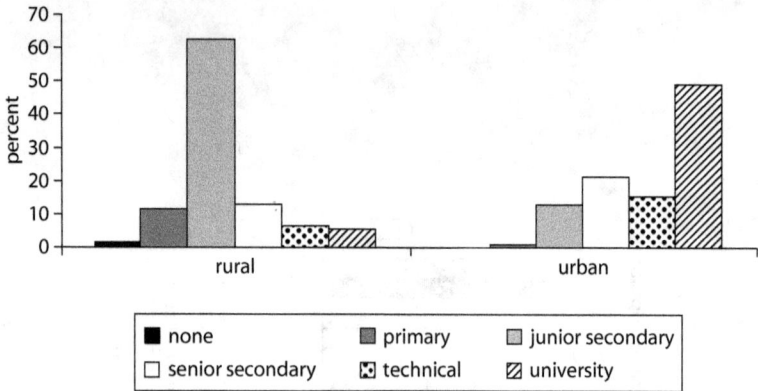

Source: Guangdong Bureau of Statistics 2007.

rural populations in Guangdong hardly go above junior secondary (either because they do not complete the cycle or because they drop out in the transition to senior secondary), about 85 percent of urban populations reach at least senior secondary. This implies very strong inequities in completion of junior secondary or transition to senior secondary and above (above what is seen in some other countries, although the data may not be strictly comparable given the different length of secondary cycles; see figure 6.4), which need to be urgently addressed.

Gaps are great among income quintiles and even more so across urban-rural areas. Similarly, there are also significant inequities across income quintiles in Guangdong, with about 77 percent of the 25–35 age cohort reaching at least senior secondary education in the upper quintiles versus only about half that reaching senior secondary in the lowest quintile (figure 6.6). Looking at performance by income quintile within urban and rural areas, we clearly see that the socioeconomic dimension is important and needs to be taken quite seriously into account, although urban-rural inequities appear to be even greater, as illustrated by the fact that the upper quintile in rural areas performs much less well than the lowest quintile in urban areas (figure 6.7). A similar pattern can also be seen for indicators of spending per student.

Gaps are also significant between the "top" areas of the Pearl River Delta (PRD) and the rest. Another dimension of inequity that comes out clearly from the survey data is the geographic one (table 6A.1.4 and figure 6.8). When we rank city areas by GDP per capita, we see clearly that educational

Figure 6.6   Educational Attainment for 25–35 Age Cohort by Income Quintile, 2007

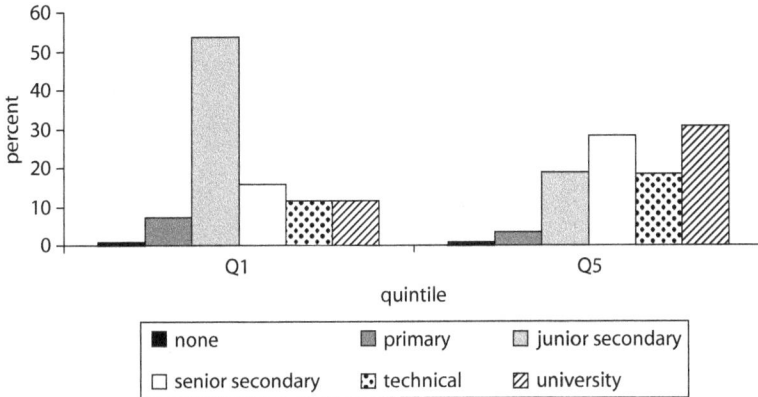

Source: Guangdong Bureau of Statistics 2007.

Figure 6.7   Educational Attainment for 25–35 Age Cohort by Urban and Rural Areas and Income Quintile, 2007

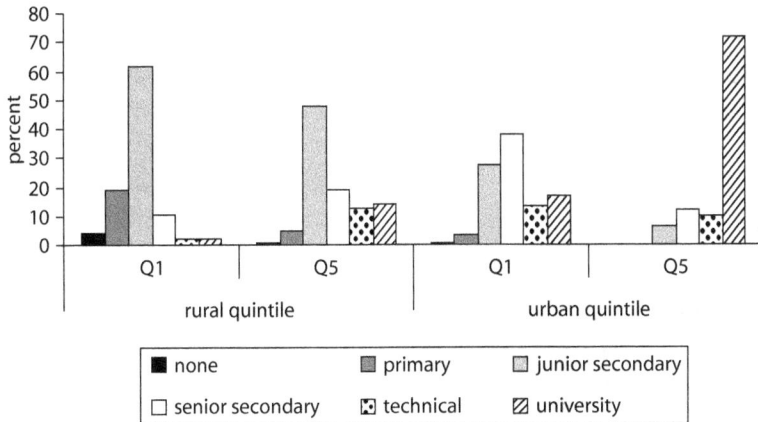

Source: Guangdong Bureau of Statistics 2007.

attainment is higher in the wealthier areas of Guangdong than in the other areas. Interestingly, the difference is really between the "top" five or six areas of the PRD and the rest, with income not necessarily being a determinant of performance below a certain threshold (in fact, the very poor Meizhou is doing better than the less poor Maoming). It is important to note that, by measuring educational attainment at the household level, the survey allows us to adjust for biases in the school data that may result from

Figure 6.8   Educational Attainment across Selected City Areas Ranked by GDP Per Capita, 2007

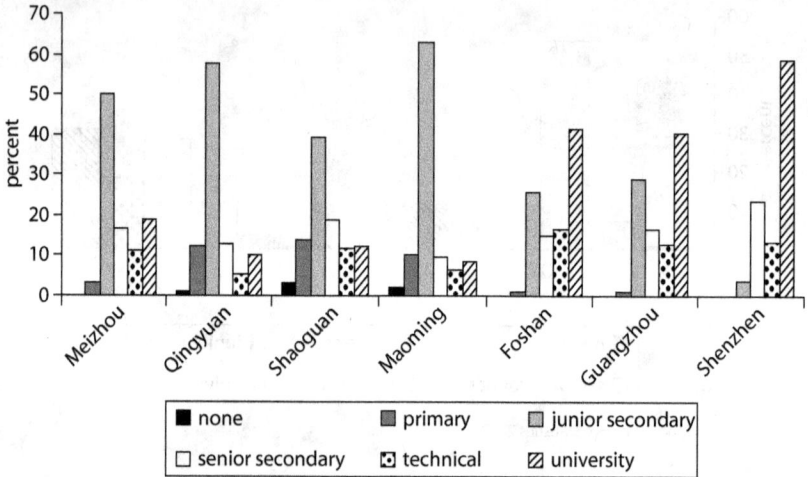

Source: Guangdong Bureau of Statistics 2007.

student movements in and out of a certain area—which explains why the survey data provide a different, more regressive, picture than the administrative data (compare tables 6A.1.1 and 6A.1.4). Finally, within city areas, the gap between urban and rural areas remains evident (figure 6.9).

Although not reported here, survey data also show gender inequities, with males performing better than females in the province.

A limitation of the Guangdong surveys is that they cannot properly account for household registration status in urban areas and therefore cannot be used to differentiate between the educational performance of migrants and nonmigrants, which is bound to be quite different, as shown by some administrative data on migrant workers indicating that only about 20 percent of them had reached at least senior secondary in 2006.

While helping provide more comprehensive diagnostics, Guangdong household surveys are missing some important variables on education. Other important limitations of Guangdong surveys for the education sector concern the lack of information on students currently enrolled in school—completely in the case of the urban survey, which does not even ask if children and youth are currently attending a school, and partially in the case of the rural survey, which asks about current attendance but does not allow for differentiation by attendance or enrollment by grade. This constrains the generation of enrollment, attendance, dropout, and survival

Figure 6.9   Educational Attainment for Two City Areas and across Urban-Rural Areas, 2007

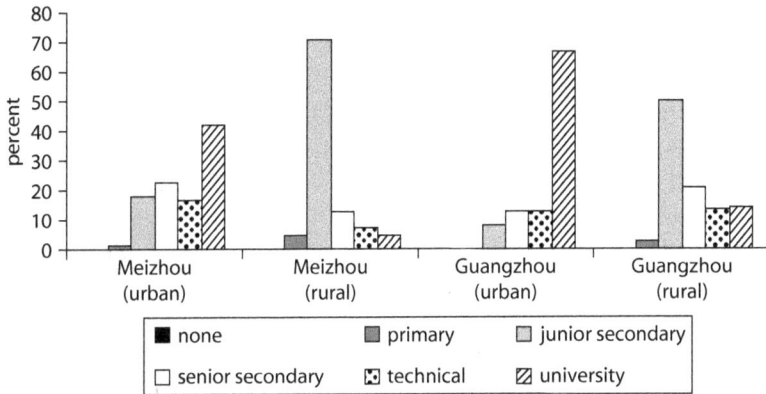

rates—so-called flow indicators—which would be useful to document the current school situation and to double-check some of the administrative or school-based data. The only information we were able to produce was estimated gross and net enrollment rates in primary and junior secondary education in rural areas, which are shown in figure 6.18 later in the chapter to illustrate the initial effects of the new rural compulsory education policy.

Educational Quality: The Missing Element

This last section reviews evidence on measures of educational quality in Guangdong, pointing to the lack of data on learning outcomes and the need for complementary quality measures.

Comparable measures of learning outcomes are not available. Beyond measures of educational attainment and coverage, it is very important also to have available measures of educational quality, since providing expanded opportunities for school enrollment and attendance is not necessarily synonymous with providing a high-quality educational experience. In other words, children may attend school but still learn little. Unfortunately, we have no data on learning outcomes for Guangdong, because of both the lack of standardized learning assessments at the national, provincial, and local levels in China and the lack of collection of existing—although not standardized—testing results. In this context, we can only recommend developing such measures as a next step to complete the education diagnostic of Guangdong. Beyond national testing, Guangdong should also consider participating in international assessments of learning outcomes, such as Trends in International Mathematics and Science Study (TIMSS) and Programme for International Student Assessment (PISA), which would provide useful international benchmarking.

Only "proxies" for educational quality are available. There are also a couple of other ways we can get around this constraint. One is by acknowledging that, to a significant extent, grade attained and cycle completed will also reflect educational quality, as it is more likely that children and youth will drop out from a poor than a good school (and there is very significant evidence of that all around the world). Another one is by reviewing proxy intermediate indicators of quality—such as measures of teacher quality, availability of teaching-learning materials, and quality of the school infrastructure and facilities—or somewhat broader indicators of quality (noted earlier), such as measures of spending per student and management capacity of the system. We will focus below on educational spending levels, as well as their sources of funding and uses in Guangdong—with a particular focus on spending gaps—to help complete a quality and quantity diagnostic of the province. Issues of teacher quality and management are beyond the scope of this chapter.

Spending Gaps in Compulsory Education and the New Free Compulsory Education Scheme

This section will look at trends, sources, and patterns of compulsory education expenditure in Guangdong province, with particular focus on spending gaps and the effects of the new FCE scheme.

Trends, Sources, and Patterns of Compulsory Expenditure on Education in Guangdong

This section reviews trends, sources, and patterns of compulsory expenditure on education in Guangdong to set the stage for the analysis of the FCE scheme. The following findings stand out.

Both total and public education expenditure grew in terms of GDP from 2004 to 2007 and, at the same time, public compulsory education grew as well, as indicated by an increasing share of compulsory education in total public education expenditure over the same period (table 6.3). This was likely the result of renewed emphasis on public compulsory education under the new FCE scheme.

Expenditure on education per student also increased from 2004 to 2007 (also adjusting for inflation). This renewed emphasis on compulsory

Table 6.3   Education Expenditure Indicators in Guangdong Province, 2004 and 2007

Education expenditure indicators	2004 (%)	2007 (%)
Total education expenditure/GDP	2.9	3.1
Public education expenditure/GDP[a]	1.8	2.0
Share of compulsory education/total education expenditure	52.9	47.0
Share of compulsory education/public education expenditure[a]	57.4	60.4

Sources: Guangdong Bureau of Statistics 2008; Guangdong Education Finance Bureau 2004–07; author's elaborations.
a. Only financed by public sources.

education can be seen even more clearly from the fact that total expenditure on primary education per student increased by about 25 percent from 2004 to 2007, and expenditure on junior secondary education per student increased by about 30 percent over the same period (see tables 6.4 and 6.5).

Expenditure composition has shifted toward a higher share going to salaries and a lower share to capital expenditure. While primary and junior secondary education expenditures per student have increased, their composition across expenditure categories has also changed somewhat, toward a higher share of funds spent on salaries and welfare and a correspondingly lower share spent on equipment and capital investment. Overall, therefore, it is mostly salary-related spending that has increased, representing close to 70 percent of overall spending on primary and 60 percent on junior secondary. Although it may be a bit of a concern that capital expenditure has decreased in both absolute and relative terms for both education levels, the balance between salary and nonsalary recurrent costs (about 65–70 percent of salaries and 25–30 percent of nonsalary) remained rather favorable compared to most other countries.

Expenditure sources have consisted of a higher share of public revenues and very significantly decreasing miscellaneous fees. Turning to the sources of this expenditure, the highest financing share has come from public revenues (about 82–85 percent, counting regular operational and budgetary revenues, the education appendix, and capital revenues), with the remaining 15–18 percent financed with private funds (fees, donations, and so forth) (tables 6.6 and 6.7). In line with the new FCE scheme (see below), the amount and share of miscellaneous fees have very significantly decreased since 2004 at both education levels, compensated by a significant increase in public budgetary revenues and, to some extent, other school-raised private funds. This changing composition is also illustrated in figures 6.10 and 6.11.

Table 6.4   Primary Education Expenditure Trends and Uses
yuan

Expenditure and uses of funds	2004		2004 (2007 yuan)		2007	
	Per student	%	Per student	%	Per student	%
Total primary education expenditure	2,115	100.0	2,284	100.0	2,854	100.0
Operational expenditure	1,971	93.2	2,129	93.2	2,799	98.1
Salaries and welfare expenses	1,252	59.2	1,352	59.2	1,936	67.8
Basic salaries	478	22.6	516	22.6	671	23.5
Other[a]	774	36.6	836	36.6	1,265	44.3
O&M	611	28.9	660	28.9	786	27.5
Equipment	108	5.1	117	5.1	77	2.7
Capital expenditure	144	6.8	156	6.8	55	1.9

Sources: Guangdong Education Finance Bureau 2004–07; author's elaborations.
a. Includes subsidy, social security, other salaries, and employee welfare.

Table 6.5   Junior Secondary Education Expenditure Trends and Uses
yuan

Expenditure and uses of funds	2004		2004 (2007 yuan)		2007	
	Per student	%	Per student	%	Per student	%
Total junior secondary education expenditure	2,836	100	3,063	100.0	3,985	100.0
Operational expenditure	2,614	92.2	2,823	92.2	3,856	96.8
Salaries and welfare expenses	1,514	53.4	1,635	53.4	2,388	59.9
Basic salaries	629	22.2	679	22.2	836	21.0
Other[a]	885	31.2	956	31.2	1,552	38.9
O&M	934	32.9	1,009	32.9	1,338	33.6
Equipment	166	5.9	179	5.9	130	3.3
Capital expenditure	222	7.8	240	7.8	129	3.2

Sources: Guangdong Education Finance Bureau 2004–07; author's elaborations.
a. Includes subsidy, social security, other salaries, and employee welfare.

In spite of these generally positive changes, Guangdong still spends little on education. These are positive changes, which indicate increasing priority given to the public financing of education in the province; but, as we will see below, these efforts may still be insufficient to address fully the

Table 6.6   Primary Education Expenditure Sources
yuan

Expenditure and sources of funds	2004 Per student	2004 %	2004 (2007 yuan) Per student	2004 (2007 yuan) %	2007 Per student	2007 %
Total primary education expenditure	2,115	100.0	2,284	100.0	2,854	100.0
Total primary education revenue	2,152	100.0	2,324	100.0	2,918	100.0
Type of revenue						
In budget[a]	1,334	62.0	1,441	62.0	2,303	78.9
Education appendix[b]	105	4.9	113	4.9	137	4.7
Tuition and miscellaneous fees	424	19.7	458	19.7	162	5.6
Capital revenues	119	5.5	129	5.5	44	1.5
Other[c]	170	7.9	184	7.9	272	9.3

Sources: Guangdong Education Finance Bureau 2004–07; author's elaborations.
a. Includes mostly fund allocation on operating expenses.
b. Includes urban, rural, and local appendix.
c. Includes mostly other school income and donations.

Table 6.7   Junior Secondary Education Expenditure Sources
yuan

Expenditure and sources of funds	2004 Per student	2004 %	2004 (2007 yuan) Per student	2004 (2007 yuan) %	2007 Per student	2007 %
Total junior secondary education expenditure	2,836	100.0	3,063	100.0	3,985	100.0
Total junior secondary education revenue	2,891	100.0	3,122	100.0	4,051	100.0
Type of revenue						
In budget[a]	1,705	59.0	1,841	59.0	3,012	74.4
Education appendix[b]	158	5.5	171	5.5	193	4.8
Tuition and miscellaneous fees	594	20.5	641	20.5	254	6.3
Capital revenues	163	5.6	176	5.6	110	2.7
Other[c]	271	9.4	293	9.4	482	11.9

Sources: Guangdong Education Finance Bureau 2004–07; author's elaborations.
a. Includes mostly fund allocation on operating expenses.
b. Includes urban, rural, and local appendix.
c. Includes mostly other school income and donations.

Figure 6.10   Primary Education Expenditure Sources, 2004 and 2007

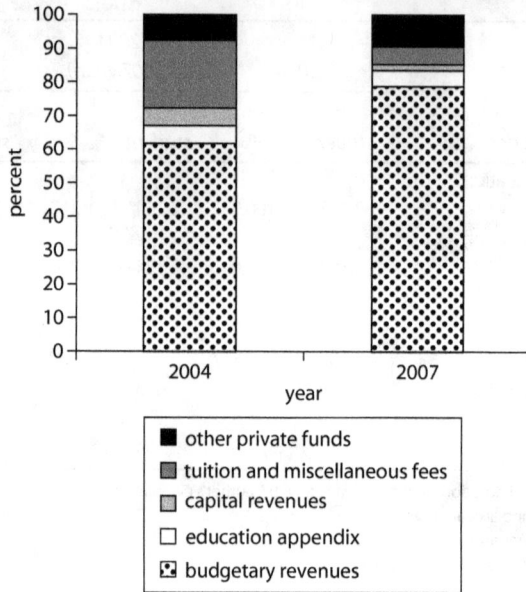

Sources: Guangdong Education Finance Bureau 2004–07; author's elaborations; see table 6.6 in this chapter.

Figure 6.11   Junior Secondary Education Expenditure Sources, 2004 and 2007

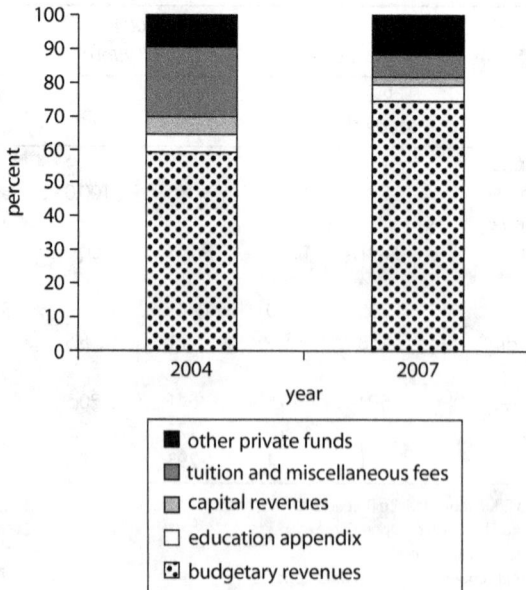

Sources: Guangdong Education Finance Bureau 2004–07; author's elaborations; see table 6.7 in this chapter.

rural–low income compulsory education gap in Guangdong. It is also very noticeable that, if Guangdong were a country and compared with other countries in Asia and Latin America—with just 1.8 percent of GDP spent on public education and 7.3 percent of GDP per capita spent on public primary education—it would rank very poorly (figure 6.12). The modest increases experienced between 2004 and 2007 would not significantly change this ranking.

The New Free Compulsory Education Scheme in Guangdong

Guangdong has been putting much emphasis on compulsory education spending through its new FCE reform, whose main aim, in line with broader Chinese policies, is to reduce the financial burden of compulsory education on rural families and improve access to and completion of compulsory education in these same areas. We review below the broader Chinese context and the policy in Guangdong.

The China context. This section briefly reviews the context of rural compulsory education reforms in China to set the stage for the analysis of the FCE scheme in Guangdong.

After a decade of growing inequities, the central government began in the mid- to late 1990s to address concerns over inequities, particularly those

Figure 6.12   Public Education Expenditure Indicators in Guangdong Province and a Sample of Countries, 2004

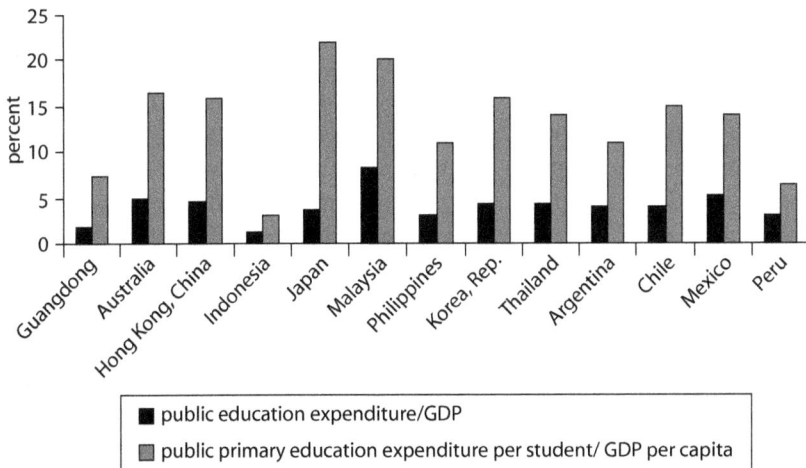

Sources: UNESCO Institute of Statistics 2006; Guangdong Education Finance Bureau 2004–07; see tables 6.3 and 6.5 in this chapter.

between rural and urban areas. Financial subsidies to local governments earmarked for the development of basic education in poor areas increased gradually. Though ad hoc in usage and small in scale, these categorical grants for basic education represented the first attempt by the government to use intergovernmental grants in the financing of education. Programs targeting poor regions and needy students focused largely on access. Between 1995 and 2005, the central government gave more than 38 billion yuan (in grants and matching funds) to poor counties for school reconstruction and other programs to improve enrollment. In 2004, the central government also started to offer targeted subsidies for needy students, covering mainly school fees for textbooks. Currently, 10 billion yuan have been earmarked for construction of boarding schools in areas with adverse geographic conditions, mainly targeting 372 western counties without universal nine-year compulsory education (as of 2003) and some minority districts in central China.

The Eleventh Plan Period of 2006–10 involved major increases in intergovernmental grants to support basic education (the FCE scheme). Totaling 218 billion yuan from central and local government levels, the new funding would provide for exemptions from school fees, textbooks for children from poor backgrounds, and living subsidies for boarding students; support essential nonpersonnel spending and school maintenance and reconstruction; and contribute to the payment of teachers' salaries in poor counties. Funding for miscellaneous fees would be shared proportionally by the central and local governments (proportion of 8 to 2 in the western region and 6 to 4 in the central region). Funds for free textbooks would be totally provided by the central government in the central and western regions. Subsidies for living costs of boarding students would be financed by local governments. Funds for school maintenance and reconstruction would be jointly financed by the central government and the local governments in the proportion of 5 to 5, and funds for teacher salaries would be largely financed by the central government. Finally, the new reform promoted by the plan would also aim at establishing a basic per-student expenditure standard in rural compulsory education (according to calculations, the base amount would be 300 yuan for primary students and 500 yuan for junior secondary students), as well as leading the provinces to set their own base standards. This new FCE reform is an extension of the 2004 "two exemptions and one subsidy" policy, with substantially increased amounts from the central government for miscellaneous fees (previously only covered by the local governments), adding a new, longer-term mechanism for school maintenance and reconstruction (with increased central government funds, although now at a proportion of 5 to 5 with local governments) and the consolidation of transfers for teacher salaries in poor counties.

The Two Exemptions, One Subsidy (TEOS) and the new FCE scheme in Guangdong. As a wealthy eastern province, Guangdong did not qualify for participation in this new scheme. However, the Guangdong government has been active in promoting different policies to support rural compulsory education in line with the central policy. In 2001, the government introduced the "two exemptions and one subsidy" policy aimed at reducing miscellaneous fees, granting textbook exemptions, and providing subsidies for needy students in financial difficulty.

This effort was followed in 2005 by the gradual application of the FCE program, following the national scheme and pattern but shared by provincial, city, and county governments. In 2005, the FCE program was piloted in 16 poor provincial counties. By fall 2006, all rural students were exempted from miscellaneous fees, and the subsidy in replacement of the miscellaneous fees was fixed at 288 yuan per student for primary and 408 yuan per student for junior secondary. By fall 2007, all rural students further benefited from free textbooks, extending drastically the coverage of the program at a standard yearly rate of 100 yuan per student for primary and 180 yuan per student for junior secondary. Subsidies for boarders and other needy students from rural families with net per capita income below 1,500 yuan would continue to be granted—at a rate of 200 yuan per student, slightly increased from the fall of 2007. Finally, some transfer payments to underdeveloped counties would also help ensure that rural school teachers would be paid at least as much as other local civil servants and receive their salaries in full and on time. With respect to maintenance, after very significant ad hoc efforts to refurbish the most dilapidated buildings in the west and east wings and mountainous region counties in 2007, it was decided that a long-term maintenance scheme would be introduced in 2008. Finally, all urban students would also be covered by the FCE program by spring 2008.[1]

Provincial financing of the subsidy in replacement of miscellaneous fees was set at four different levels (100 percent, 80 percent, 40 percent, and 10 percent), with gaps to be filled by the county or city—depending on the county or district or city fiscal capacity, location, and income, and the city or county nature. Specifically, the 16 poorest counties would be subsidized at 100 percent by the province; the 53 counties in the west and east rings and the northern mountainous areas would be subsidized by the province at 80 percent and all remaining areas of these regions at 40 percent; and the 7 cities of the PRD would only be subsidized at 10 percent. All subsidies for textbooks and needy students would be financed with provincial revenues (except for textbooks in the Pearl River Delta). As far as maintenance is concerned, the long-term maintenance mechanism would be seen as a shared scheme between the province and the county or district (applying a 50-50 share), with a standard of 30 yuan per student in primary education and 50 yuan per student in junior secondary education (scheduled to increase by 10 yuan per student each year), while all 2007 maintenance effort was financed out of provincial revenues.

Initial achievements. The new FCE scheme has already had some significant achievements, but a more comprehensive assessment is needed.

According to the recent government report on the implementation status of the new scheme, three main outstanding achievements have been made since the implementation of the new scheme. First, coverage of the rural areas has been expanded. According to statistics, by the end of 2007 the new scheme covered 22,733 rural schools, including 19,335 primary schools and 3,398 junior secondary schools, and benefited 10.25 million rural students and 1.03 million rural students from poor families with allowance subsidies. Second, the burden on farmers has been alleviated. In 2007, the scheme translated into a reduction of nearly 2.4 billion yuan in the farmer's burden. And third, a reduction has occurred in the dropout rate in rural primary and junior secondary education. Apparently, about 110,000 primary education students and 20,000 junior secondary education students returned to school.

The effects of the new scheme need to be broadly assessed, looking at several dimensions. While it is very relevant to look at these dimensions when assessing the effects of the new scheme, and there are strong grounds for concluding that at least the first two beneficial effects of the reform have taken place and some grounds to believe that the third one has happened at least partially, a more complete assessment is needed. This assessment should aim to measure the implications of the new scheme on the size, source, and composition of spending per student in compulsory education across urban and rural areas and counties of different socioeconomic level in the province to assess the potential for closing gaps in education completion and quality across areas, and the sustainability of that effort, beyond the effects of the scheme on access and fees paid by the families. This is all the more important as access to compulsory education is not the first challenge anymore. We would also like to start assessing the effects of the scheme on some other intermediate indicators of education quality.

Evaluating the Effects of the FCE Scheme in Guangdong on the Urban-Rural Gap

This section provides a more comprehensive assessment of the FCE scheme in Guangdong, with focus on urban-rural spending and enrollment gaps and the effects of the new scheme.

Urban-rural spending gap. As a first exercise, our data allowed us to differentiate information by urban and rural areas within the province for compulsory education, so we could compute expenditure trends, sources, and patterns across these two areas. Results are reported in tables 6A.2.5–6A.2.8 in annex 6.2. There are several key findings that stand out from the analysis.

First, primary and junior secondary education spending per student has increased in both areas over 2004–07, and miscellaneous fees have been effectively discontinued in rural areas (see tables 6A.2.7 and 6A.2.8 and figures 6.13 and 6.14). This is an important achievement, which also confirms the decreased burden on rural areas and farmers mentioned above. By 2007, all rural compulsory education students were exempted from paying any

Figure 6.13   Primary Education Spending and Revenue Per Student across Rural and Urban Areas in Guangdong Province, 2004 and 2007

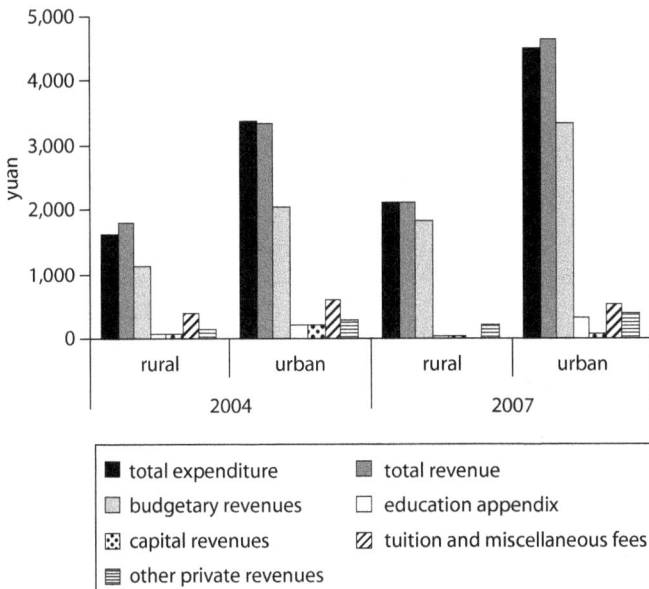

legend:
- total expenditure
- total revenue
- budgetary revenues
- education appendix
- capital revenues
- tuition and miscellaneous fees
- other private revenues

Sources: Guangdong Education Finance Bureau 2004–07; author's elaborations; see table 6A.2.7 in this chapter.

Figure 6.14   Junior Secondary Education Spending and Revenue Per Student across Rural and Urban Areas in Guangdong, 2004 and 2007

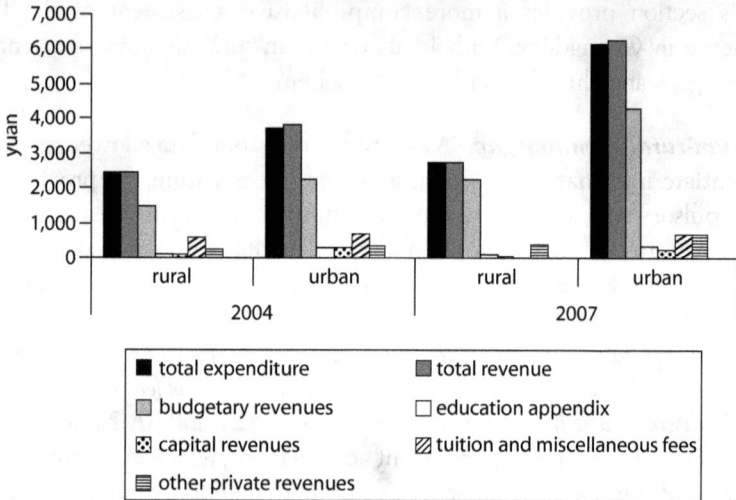

Sources: Guangdong Education Finance Bureau 2004–07; author's elaborations; see table 6A.2.8 in this chapter.

miscellaneous fees, and this was granted while maintaining a positive rate of increase in rural spending per student. The rural household survey data confirm that this exemption (together with the exemption on textbooks that we will review below) brought about a significant decrease in private expenditure on education for the average rural household, from about 1,900 yuan per household to about 1,280 yuan per household—although some care needs to be taken in interpreting these data, since they refer to spending on education as a whole.

Second, however, and on a less positive note, spending has increased proportionally more in urban areas over the same time period (see tables 6A.2.5 and 6A.2.6 and figures 6.13 and 6.14). As a result, the urban-rural gap in primary education spending, which was already fairly pronounced in 2004 (with spending per student in urban areas about double that in rural areas), has increased, with urban areas spending now more than double the rural ones; and the urban-rural gap in lower secondary education has increased significantly, with urban areas also spending more than double the rural areas per student, while they were spending only about one-third more in 2004.

While spending per student has therefore increased in rural areas from 2004 to 2007—which is a positive trend—it is nonetheless worrisome that the gap with urban areas has increased. Some tentative explanations for the increasing gap can be advanced. As a matter of comparison, why was rural primary education spending per student in Gansu province (a poor province) about 65 percent of rural primary education spending per student in Guangdong, while urban primary education spending per student was only about 38 percent of urban spending in Guangdong (compare figures 6.13 and 6.15)? What factors could be behind the increasing gap in Guangdong? When we look at expenditure sources (tables 6A.2.7 and 6A.2.8 and figures 6.13 and 6.14), we see that although regular budgetary revenues have increased significantly everywhere, they have increased more in urban areas. This trend, combined with the continuity of fees in urban areas and discontinuity in rural areas, can explain the increasing gap, suggesting two possible explanations.

A first explanation is that the new FCE scheme, with or without any additional regular budgetary revenues raised at whatever level, has managed to compensate rural areas for the loss of fees; however, independently of the new FCE scheme, regular budgetary revenues have increased faster for urban areas—although fees are still there—reducing the beneficial effects on overall equity. This could point to the small relative importance (or magnitude) of the FCE scheme, with limited redistributive

Figure 6.15   Primary Education Revenue Per Student across Rural and Urban Areas in Gansu Province, 2006

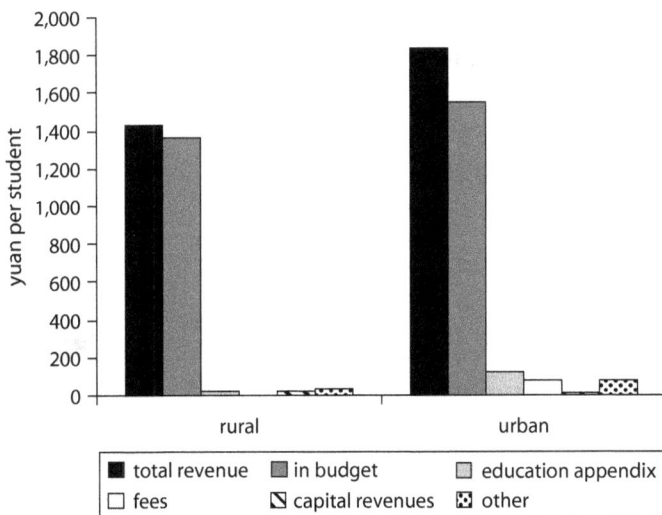

effect because of its mere relative size. A second possibility is that while a portion of the FCE transfers in substitution of fees manages to compensate, probably in combination with other additional regular budgetary revenues, for lost fees in rural areas, another portion of the FCE transfers has, in fact, benefited the urban areas of counties and districts, contributing to an increase in their budgetary revenues, and not only the rural areas that they should have more logically benefited. This would point, rather, to issues in the implementation of the new scheme, which ends up benefiting the urban areas too much.

There is a large and increasing gap in teachers' salaries per student between urban and rural areas. Finally, while spending per student has increased more in urban than in rural areas, expenditure composition has varied in a similar way across areas, with a similarly increasing share of salary-related expenditure in both areas—from about 60 percent to 68 percent in primary and 53 percent to 60 percent in junior secondary (see tables 6A.2.5 and 6A.2.6)—indicating similar spending priorities in both areas. However, when looking at average salaries per student in primary, we still see a very important and increasing gap across urban and rural areas—in particular for nonbasic salary components such as social security and other allowances—which points to the persistent and increasing gap in teachers' remuneration and benefits across urban and rural areas (figure 6.16; the trend is similar for junior secondary). While transfers and local efforts may have kept relative priority on teacher salary in rural areas, the reduction of

Figure 6.16   Teachers' Salaries Per Student in Primary Education in Urban and Rural Areas, 2004 and 2007

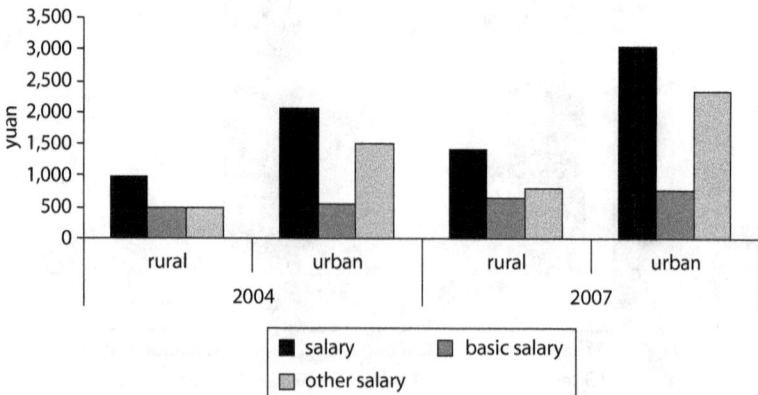

Sources: Guangdong Education Finance Bureau 2004–07; author's elaborations; see table 6A.2.5 in this chapter.

school fees, often used for additional teacher compensation, still may have had detrimental effects on teachers' benefits in rural areas. Overall average teacher salary in rural areas was falling below 50 percent of the average teacher salary in urban areas in 2007 (from a ratio of 53 percent in 2004).

Urban-rural enrollment gap. This section reviews evidence on urban-rural enrollment gaps. The following findings stand out.

Rural enrollment in junior secondary has been increasing. It is difficult to disentangle the different explanations that could be behind the increasing gap in Guangdong at this stage, but a more detailed analysis of the new scheme and of a few county cases will help cast some light on these issues. The ongoing movement of school consolidation in compulsory education may explain the relative concentration of resources in urban areas, but the data show that schools are becoming larger in both urban and rural areas, without any clearly apparent school reduction in rural areas. An important factor that more clearly contributed to some of the gap in spending per student in junior secondary education was the increase in rural enrollment at that level, by about 50 percent between 2004 and 2006 (see figure 6.17).

This is a positive result that, however, has still not been translated into an increase in the gross enrollment rate at that level—at least not according to the rural household survey. While, as expected, rural gross enrollment rates in primary have been high, they have decreased very significantly in junior secondary, where they have been well below the provincial average (although the sources of data are different) and have remained stable

Figure 6.17   Rural Enrollment Share in Compulsory Education, 2004 and 2007

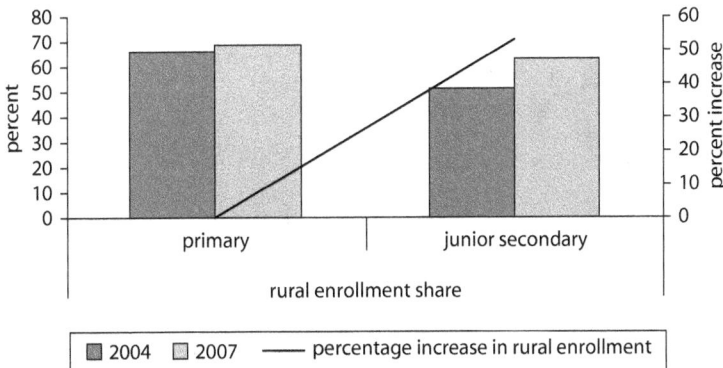

Legend: ■ 2004   □ 2007   —— percentage increase in rural enrollment

Sources: Guangdong Education Finance Bureau 2004–07; author's elaborations.

from 2005 to 2007. In combination with the fact that access to junior secondary has continued to increase in rural areas, this suggests that permanency is the real problem now, and that more will need to be done to keep children in the cycle once they are in. On the other hand, increased enrollment in rural areas also puts downward pressure on spending per student (for the non-student-based items), explaining at least part of the increasing spending gap.

Probably as a product of already high enrollment rates, rural enrollment remained stable in primary education, both in dynamic terms and total enrollment share (see figure 6.17). Nonetheless, primary gross enrollment rates increased very slightly over 2005–07 (although they decreased a bit in net terms; figure 6.18), probably because of decreased school-age population and some new students due to the new rural compulsory education scheme. It is important to point out that internal efficiency still seems to be a problem in rural primary education, judging from the difference between the gross and net enrollment rates—which may suggest late entrance, dropouts and returns, and so forth. This is a serious issue because it leads to higher dropout rates in junior secondary because of overage, and, in fact, similar gross and net enrollment rates in junior secondary illustrate this point.

Effects of the FCE scheme. We report in tables 6A.2.9 and 6A.2.10 the latest available information on the application of the TEOS and the new FCE schemes in 2006 and 2007 in the overall Guangdong province to derive insights into how the policy was applied and what its effects were.

Figure 6.18   Gross and Net Enrollment Rates in Rural Areas, 2005 and 2007

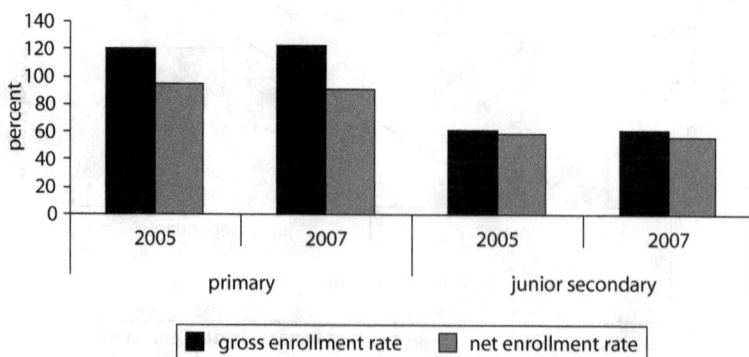

Source: Guangdong Bureau of Statistics 2007.

Note that in these tables all subsidies have been recalculated per student or rural student to be able to compare actual amounts on a same denominator, which would take into account both yearly and semester standards and student coverage. Several findings stand out from an analysis of the new policies since 2006.

Subsidies in replacement of miscellaneous fees and other subsidies have been increasing. The extension of the new scheme to all rural students in the fall of 2006 brought a massive increase in the total subsidy and the subsidy per student for miscellaneous fees, compared to the only application of the TEOS in 2006 (and of the TEOS and the targeted application of the new scheme in 2005), going from a de facto subsidy of about 10–13 yuan per rural student for the TEOS to about 162–230 yuan per rural student for the new scheme.[2] Along the same line, as better exemplified in figures 6.19 and 6.20, subsidies continued to increase in 2007. The subsidies for miscellaneous fees reached their yearly target levels of 288 yuan and 408 yuan per rural student, respectively, by being applied over the whole year. Subsidies for free textbooks increased substantially due to the combination of the new policy to provide free textbooks to most rural students in the fall of 2007 and an increase in the standard yearly rate. Subsidies for needy students remained allocated to the students and counties covered by the TEOS scheme but with an increased value per student in the fall of 2007, and an across-the-board subsidy for building renovation (which was practically null in 2006) was introduced in 2007 as part of the new scheme.

Figure 6.19   New FCE Scheme and TEOS for Primary Education per Student, 2006 and 2007

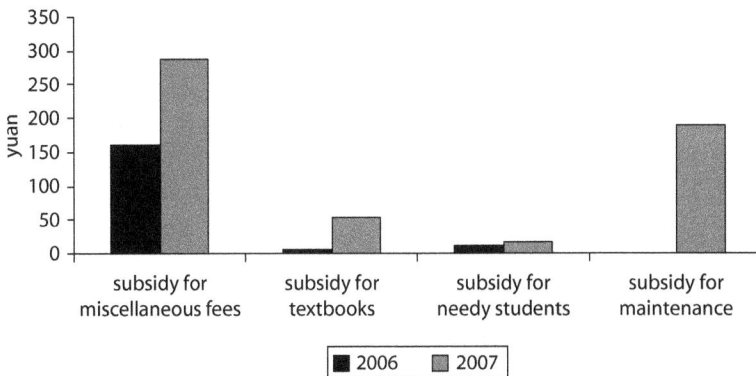

Sources: Guangdong Education Finance Bureau 2004–07; author's elaborations; see tables 6A.2.9 and 6A.2.10 in this chapter.

Figure 6.20   New FCE Scheme and TEOS for Junior Secondary Education per Student, 2006 and 2007

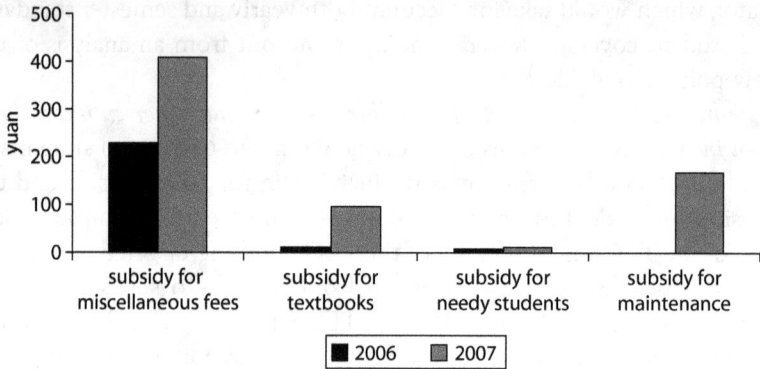

Sources: Guangdong Education Finance Bureau 2004–07; author's elaborations; see tables 6A.2.9 and 6A.2.10 of this chapter.

In spite of the increase, subsidies remained small compared to budgetary revenues, and subsidies in replacement of miscellaneous fees did not even make up for lost fees. It is important to highlight that although the subsidies for fees, textbooks, and maintenance have increased following the extension of the new FCE scheme—which is a positive trend—these subsidies remain small compared to budgetary revenues. Figure 6.21 indicates, for instance, that subsidies for miscellaneous fees represented only about 16–18 percent of rural provincial budgetary revenues in 2007, although they were responsible for about 40 percent of the increase in budgetary revenues over the 2004–07 time period. Along a similar line, these subsidies did not even make up for the miscellaneous fees in rural primary and junior secondary education that were collected from households in 2004, as shown in figure 6.22, raising an issue of which minimum standard was applied. We have seen that although budgetary revenues have increased for rural areas, they have increased faster for urban ones. Part of the explanation may indeed be the insufficiency of the subsidy in replacement of rural fees. Higher subsidies would bring budgetary revenues for rural areas up. This is all the more necessary, as enrollment in junior secondary is increasing in rural areas, bringing higher potential for collecting subsidies for fees but also a larger student population that needs to be attended to, producing downward pressure on revenues and spending per student.

Higher subsidies in replacement of miscellaneous fees would also help ease the burden on the counties for providing the additional budgetary

Figure 6.21   Subsidy for Miscellaneous Fees and Budgetary Revenues in Rural Areas, 2007

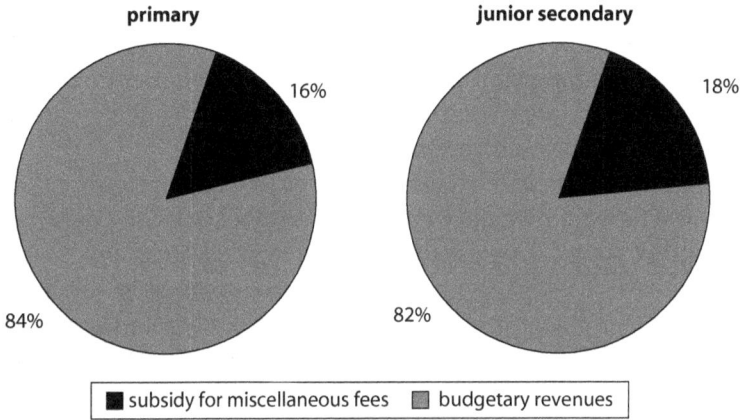

primary

16%

84%

junior secondary

18%

82%

■ subsidy for miscellaneous fees   ■ budgetary revenues

Sources: Guangdong Education Finance Bureau 2004–07; author's elaborations; see tables 6A.2.7, 6A.2.8, and 6A.2.10 in this chapter.

Figure 6.22   Miscellaneous Fees and Subsidies for Fees in Rural Areas

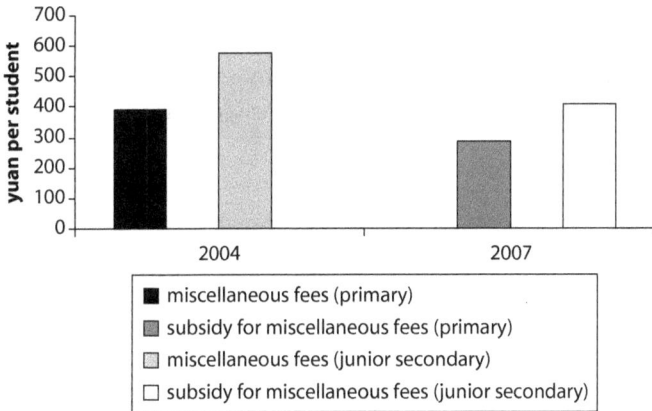

yuan per student

2004   2007

■ miscellaneous fees (primary)
■ subsidy for miscellaneous fees (primary)
▨ miscellaneous fees (junior secondary)
□ subsidy for miscellaneous fees (junior secondary)

Sources: Guangdong Education Finance Bureau 2004–07; author's elaborations; see tables 6A.2.7, 6A.2.8, and 6A.2.10 in this chapter.

revenues—at least for the group of counties with the least fiscal capacity. Indeed, it is likely that counties had to make up for the low minimum and homogeneous standards in replacement of miscellaneous fees with their own resources, increasing their financial burden. Mostly rural and poor counties would, in fact, end up being at an increasing disadvantage compared to more urban and wealthier counties, which have higher potential for mobilizing resources from all levels (including households). This leads us to the equity analysis of the next section, where we assess—in a purely illustrative way, given the small sample size—how spending has evolved in a sample of poor and highly rural counties from 2000 to 2007, how this spending compared to a much wealthier county, and what the effect of the new scheme was on this evolution.

There is still a gap in textbooks and operation and maintenance (O&M) per student across urban and rural areas. Textbook subsidies have helped increase the stock of books for students in rural areas, but the stock seems to have increased more in urban areas, pointing to the need for further support (figure 6.23). More clearly, according to the provincial statistics, the 2007 subsidy for building renovation helped reduce the ratio of seriously dilapidated buildings from about 3 percent to nil in the province, with larger decreases in rural areas. This is a positive finding, but the indication that in 2007 O&M per student in rural areas was only about 60 percent or even 50 percent of the amount spent in urban areas (while about 80 percent of the compulsory education schools are in rural areas; figure 6.24) makes it imperative to think about a longer-term mechanism—in particular for the benefit of rural areas—to ensure regular maintenance.

The standard rate of the subsidy for needy students is still low in relation to costs. While all other subsidies have increased, this has not been the case

Figure 6.23   Books Per Student and Ratio of Dilapidated Buildings Overall and in Urban and Rural Areas, 2004 and 2007

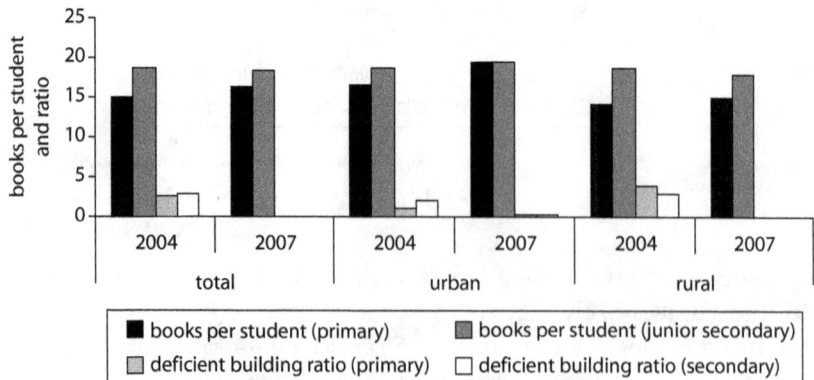

Sources: Guangdong Education Finance Bureau 2004–07; author's elaborations.

Figure 6.24   O&M Per Student Overall and in Urban and Rural Areas, 2004 and 2007

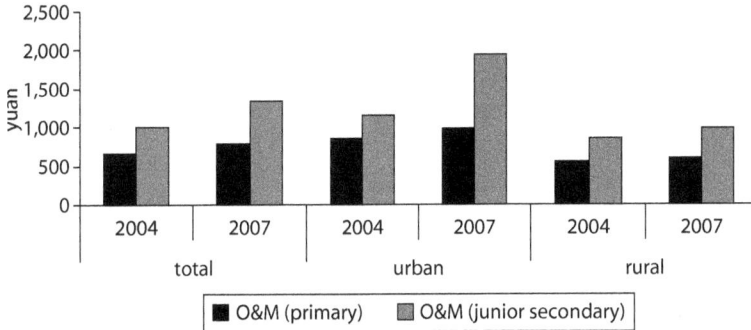

Sources: Guangdong Education Finance Bureau 2004–07; author's elaborations.

for the subsidy for needy students. While the standard rate has increased over time, the subsidy still covers a very small fraction of the student population—about 6 percent of the overall primary student population in a province with about 65 percent of rural primary student population, and we will see below that the rationale behind the student coverage by county is also not clear—and may still not be enough to cover students' basic needs. Unfortunately, the rural household survey does not allow us to calculate the exact amount and composition of private expenditure on compulsory education by rural households so we can assess how much per student they still need to pay for nonfee and textbook-related expenses, such as transportation, uniforms, and school supplies. However, if we make the assumption that an average rural household in 2007 had just one child and enrolled the child in compulsory education, we find that, after fee and textbook exemptions, about 1,300 yuan still need to be spent to keep him or her in school. This is substantial in proportion to the total expenditure of poor rural households and compared to a subsidy of just 200 yuan. In that respect, the province made the right decision in adding a supplement of 500 yuan for primary and 750 yuan for junior secondary for about 20 percent of the needy students in special difficulty. It is a pity that this concerns only 20 percent of an already reduced pool of students.

Finally, the distribution of the subsidies across institutional levels confirms the predominance of provincial funds, which in the case of miscellaneous fees reflects provincial contributions proportional to local fiscal capacity, income, and geography. All textbook and needy students' subsidies are financed only by the province,[3] and the Pearl River Delta finances textbooks out of its local revenues. Maintenance subsidies in 2007 were financed by the province, although some counties—see below—declared some to be cosharing.

Evaluating the Effects of the FCE Scheme in Guangdong on the Socioeconomic Gap

We present below an analysis performed on a sample of seven counties across the mountainous, west wing, and Pearl River Delta regions of the province. Together these seven counties represent about 5 percent of the total student population of the province (figure 6.25). This is, therefore, a small sample that can be used only for illustrative purposes. Zengcheng city in the Pearl River Delta is well above the provincial GDP per capita average, while all other counties are well below this average. This will allow us to draw some inferences on the spending gap across areas with different socioeconomic situations, with a focus on poor counties.

Spending gap across counties and cities of different socioeconomic levels. This section reviews the evidence on spending gaps across socioeconomic levels, with emphasis on both primary and junior secondary spending. The following findings stand out.

Increases in spending per student are driven by budgetary revenues. Tables 6A.2.11 and 6A.2.12 in annex 6.2 show spending per student, as well as main revenue sources per student, in primary and junior secondary education

Figure 6.25   GDP Per Capita and Share of Provincial Population of County Sample

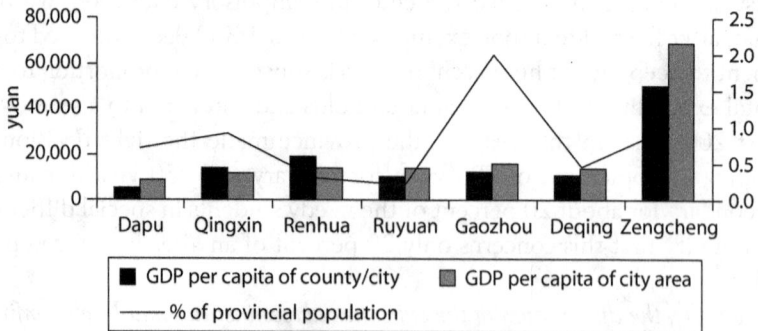

Sources: Guangdong Education Finance Bureau 2004–07; author's elaborations.
Note: Dapu city area = Meizhou; Qingxin city area = Qingyuan; Renhua city area = Shaoguan; Ruyuan city area = Shaoguan; Gaozhou city area = Maoming; Deqing city area = Zhaoqing; Zengcheng city area = Guangzhou.

for the county sample. The pattern of change in spending per student and sources of revenues by county confirms very much what is seen at the provincial level, with spending per student increases largely driven by an increase in regular budgetary revenues for education and an increase in other private funds, which more than make up for the overall decrease in miscellaneous fees. This positive pattern is illustrated for primary education in figure 6.26.

Gaps in spending per student across socioeconomic levels are less acute than urban-rural gaps. It is also noticeable that spending per student in primary education of some poor counties like Dapu and Ruyuan is at the provincial average in spite of much lower income per capita, or even at the Zengcheng average in the case of Dapu for junior secondary education. This makes urban-rural gaps in spending more serious than intercounty gaps—which may also indicate that beyond lack of fiscal capacity, lack of prioritization of rural areas within counties may also be an explanation for low spending.

However, a deeper look at the data for primary education reveals some more worrisome patterns. Similar trends, although a bit less clear-cut, can also be seen in junior secondary.[4]

Trends for primary education. This section reviews the evidence for primary education. These are the key findings that stand out.

First, the data on primary education show that spending per student was more inequitably distributed across the county sample in 2007 than in 2004, as shown by the relationship between GDP per capita and spending per student in 2004 compared with the same relationship in 2007 (figures 6.27 and 6.28). This result seems to be attributable to the fact that spending and budgetary revenues per student increased proportionally more in the counties with higher income per capita in 2004, and in particular Zengcheng (figures 6.29 and 6.30).

Clearly, this analysis needs to be conducted with care, given the very low number of observations; but it nonetheless indicates that the gap between the poorest counties and a wealthy city of the Pearl River Delta, like Zengcheng, has been growing since 2004, which is an alarm bell. Only the poor county of Renhua—which, however, also experienced a substantial increase in GDP per capita between 2004 and 2007—experienced an increase in spending per student comparable to that of Zengcheng. The different shapes in figure 6.26 also point to higher increases in spending per student in Zengcheng, Renhua, and the province in general in comparison with the other counties.

Figure 6.26   Change between 2004 and 2007 in Spending and Revenue Sources in Primary Education for the County Sample, Yuan Per Student

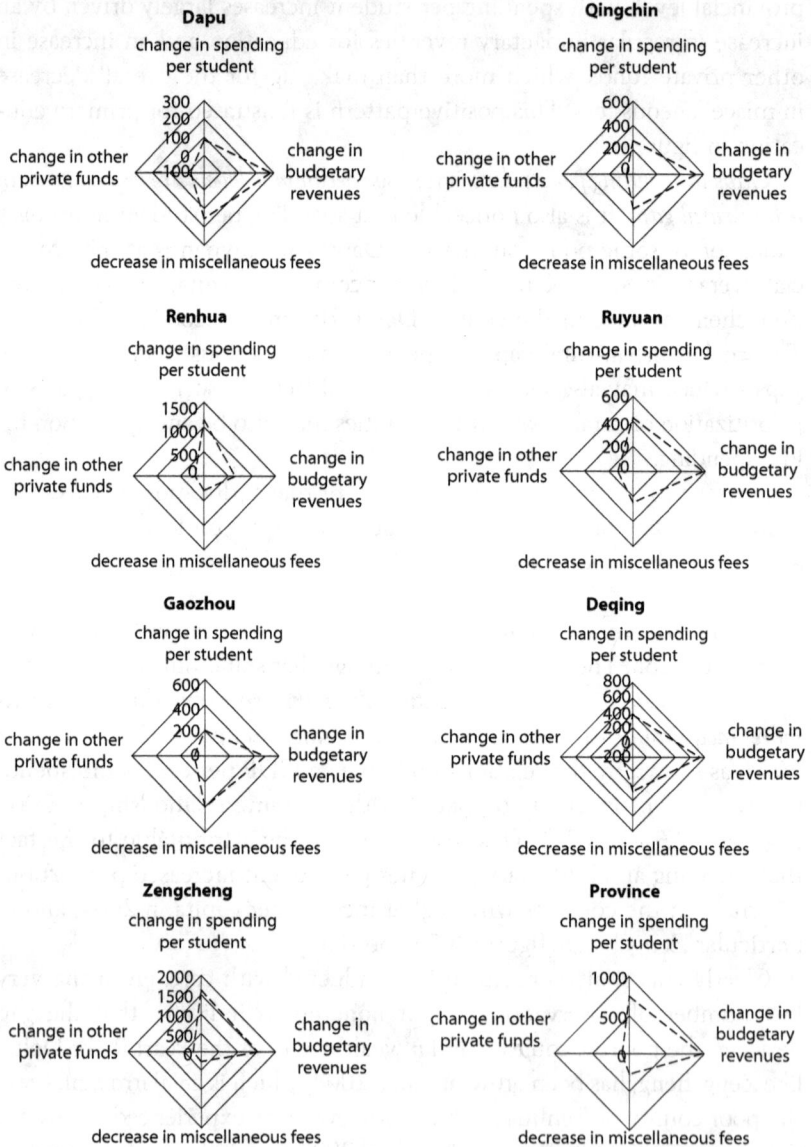

Sources: Guangdong Education Finance Bureau 2004–07; author's elaborations; see table 6A.2.11 in this chapter.

Figure 6.27   Relationship between GDP Per Capita and Primary Spending Per Student, 2004

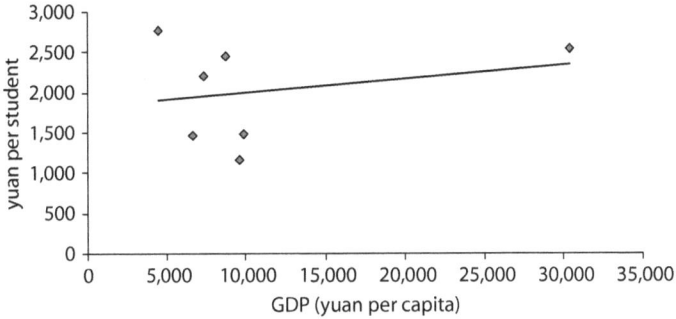

Sources: Guangdong Education Finance Bureau 2004–07; author's elaborations; see table 6A.2.11 in this chapter.

Figure 6.28   Relationship between GDP Per Capita and Primary Spending Per Student, 2007

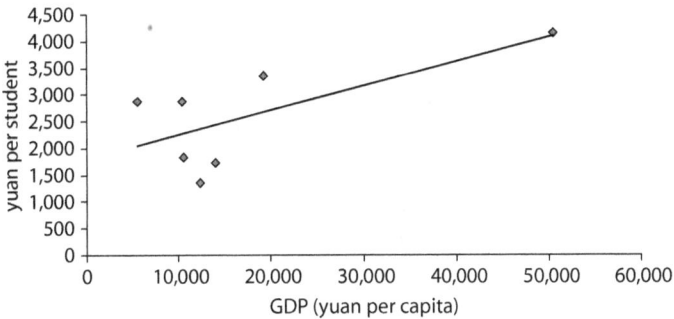

Sources: Guangdong Education Finance Bureau 2004–07; author's elaborations; see table 6A.2.11 in this chapter.

Figure 6.29   Relationship between GDP Per Capita in 2004 and Percentage Increase in Spending Per Student

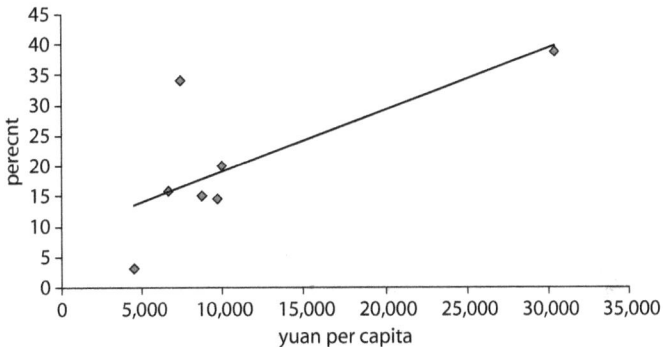

Sources: Guangdong Education Finance Bureau 2004–07; author's elaborations; see table 6A.2.11 in this chapter.

Figure 6.30   Relationship between GDP Per Capita in 2004 and Percentage Increase in Budgetary Revenues Per Student

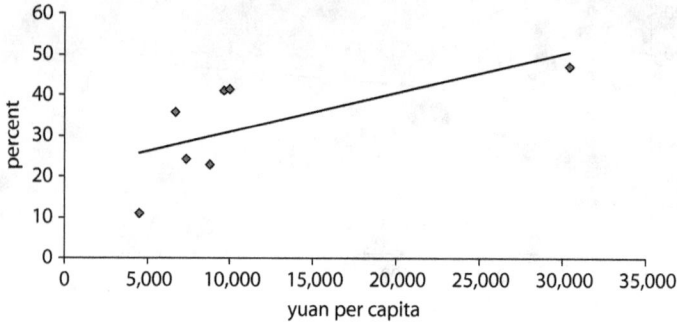

Sources: Guangdong Education Finance Bureau 2004–07; author's elaborations; see table 6A.2.11 in this chapter.

The subsidy in replacement of miscellaneous fees does not even make up for lost fees in poor counties. While there may be several explanations for this trend, what is nonetheless noticeable is that—with the exception of the two poorest counties in 2007, Dapu and Ruyuan—the subsidy in replacement of miscellaneous fees (288 yuan per rural student in 2007) did not make up for the lost fees in any of the other counties, with gaps fluctuating between 17 and 262 yuan per rural student (figure 6.31). This indicates that the subsidy had been fixed at a very low minimum which could not even cover lost fees in poor counties such as Qingxin, Gaozhou, and Deqing, which were lagging behind in terms of spending per student in 2007. While it is correct that Zengcheng has experienced a fee gap higher than the average for the county sample, wealthy counties have had more leeway to compensate for lost fees with some alternative sources of revenues, which is what Zengcheng has done (in terms of regular budgetary revenues and other private funds). There is even some evidence that the city invested about 336 yuan per student in primary education to replace the loss of fees, which would halve the current fee gap. Overall, therefore, fixing low subsidy levels penalizes, if not the poorest, certainly what are still by, all measures, poor counties. This is all the more true if we consider that two poor counties like Gaozhou and Deqing also have to finance about 20 percent of this already low subsidy themselves (see table 6A.2.13).

Related to the above is also the fact that the amount allocated for the new scheme is fairly low in proportion of in-budget revenues in all counties, going from about 2 percent in Zengcheng to 17 percent in a poor county like Dapu, which also constrains its impact. This also explains why, in spite of

Figure 6.31   Decrease in Miscellaneous Fees, Fee Gap, and Change in Rural Enrollment in Primary, Yuan Per Student

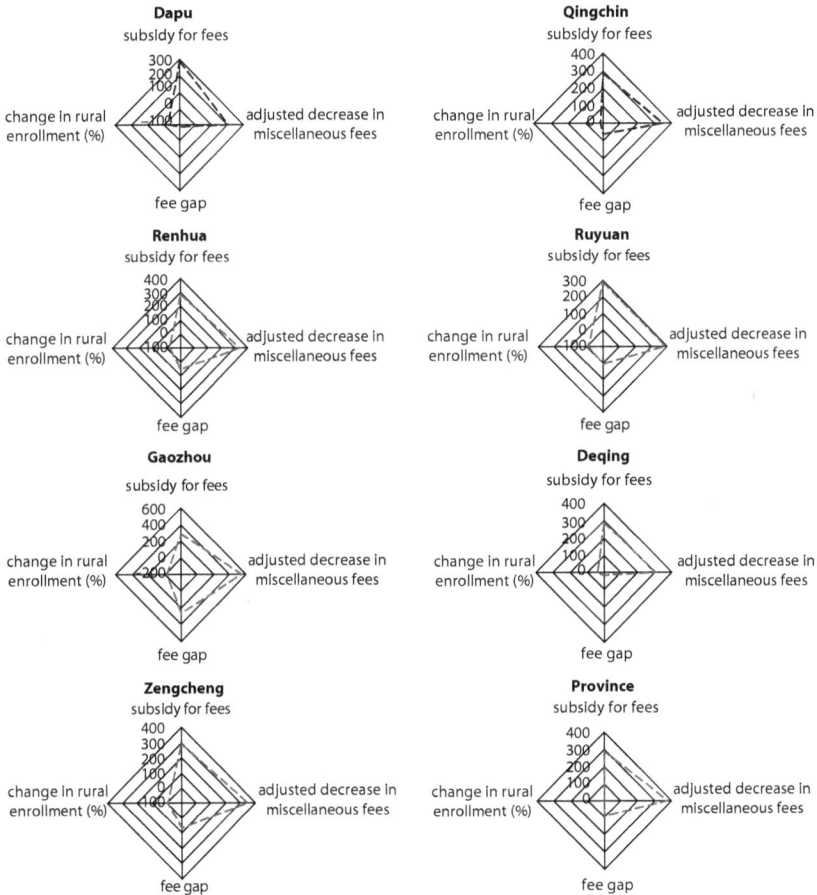

Sources: Guangdong Education Finance Bureau 2004–07; author's elaborations; see table 6A.2.11 in this chapter.
Note: The fee gap has been calculated as the difference between the subsidy for fees and the decrease in miscellaneous fees (of table 6A.2.11 in this chapter), adjusted for the share of rural student population to work on the same denominator.

the "positive fee transfer" in Dapu (see figure 6.31), the effects on overall spending per student remain limited.

Second, while spending inequities have increased—in part because of the insufficient impact of the new scheme—we also do not see clear evidence that in the short term the decrease in miscellaneous fees in rural areas has brought about increases in rural enrollment (see figure 6.31). In fact, while the province overall has seen no change in primary rural enrollment, five out of seven sample counties have experienced a slight negative percentage change in rural enrollment. Without reliable data on school-age population by county, it is difficult to say how enrollment rates have evolved (they may still have increased somewhat), and, moreover, a couple of years of operation of the new scheme may not be enough to show all results yet; but this trend, together with a generally decreasing trend of the overall primary education population in poor counties, makes the rising inequity in spending per student particularly worrisome.

Trends for junior secondary education. This section reviews the evidence for junior secondary education. These are the key findings that stand out.

Spending per student in junior secondary is also inequitably distributed, in part related to the fee gap and low relative magnitude of the new scheme. The data on junior secondary education also show a positive relationship between spending per student and GDP per capita, although this relationship did not necessarily worsen with time. This fact is due to the lack of relationship between increase in spending and GDP per capita in 2004 (although there was still a positive relationship between in-budget revenue increases and GDP per capita in 2004; figures 6.32–6.35). Although not worsening, spending per student remains inequitably distributed. As in primary, this is due, in part, to the generally low relative magnitude of the new scheme in proportion to budgetary revenues and, related to that, to the existence of fee gaps (subsidy for fee of 408 yuan per rural student minus adjusted decrease in fees per student) in all poor counties for which we can compare loss of fees between 2007 and 2004 and subsidy for fees. An exception is Dapu, which increased fees on urban students to compensate for loss of rural fees (figure 6.36). In fact, there was much less of a gap in a wealthy city like Zengcheng, raising equity concerns.

Finally, in a situation of lesser coverage, the reduction in miscellaneous fees seems to have had more of an effect on rural enrollment—which increased overall in the province—and in some counties, such as Zengcheng and Gaozhou (on the order of about 15–25 percent, difficult to discern in figure 6.36 because of the scale). The increase in junior secondary enrollment in Gaozhou can partly explain the lagging spending per student.

Effects of the FCE Scheme
By looking in more detail at the new scheme in table 6A.2.13, we can confirm some of the findings for the overall province, while making some additional considerations.[5]

Figure 6.32   Relationship between GDP Per Capita and Junior Secondary Spending Per Student, 2004

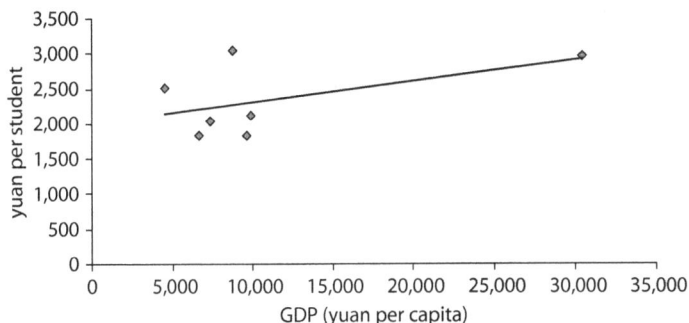

Sources: Guangdong Education Finance Bureau 2004–07; author's elaborations; see table 6A.2.12 in this chapter.

Figure 6.33   Relationship between GDP Per Capita and Junior Secondary Spending Per Student, 2007

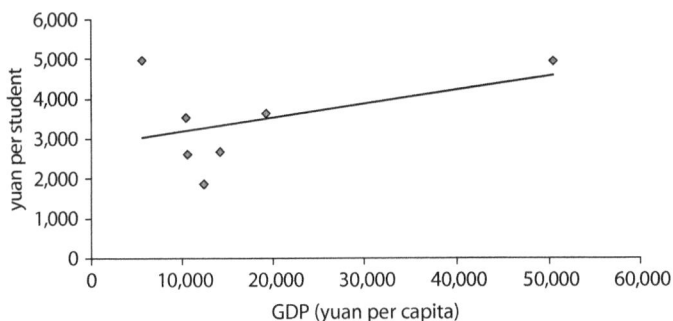

Sources: Guangdong Education Finance Bureau 2004–07; author's elaborations; see table 6A.2.12 in this chapter.

Figure 6.34   Relationship between GDP Per Capita in 2004 and Percentage Increase in Spending Per Student

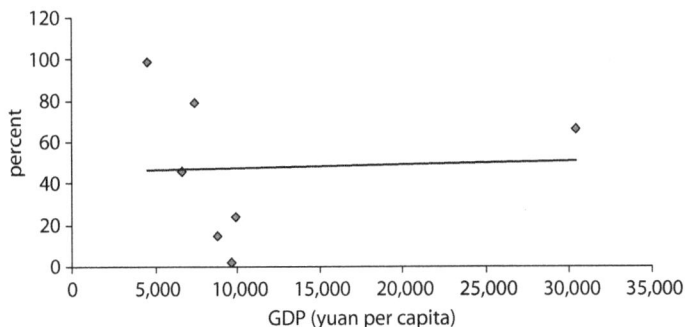

Sources: Guangdong Education Finance Bureau 2004–07; author's elaborations; see table 6A.2.12 in this chapter.

Figure 6.35   Relationship between GDP Per Capita in 2004 and Percentage Increase in Budgetary Revenues Per Student

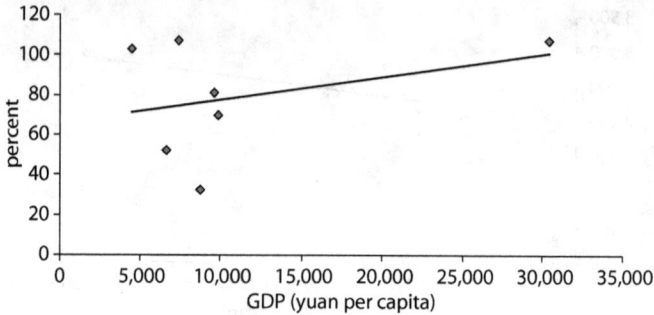

Sources: Guangdong Education Finance Bureau 2004–07; author's elaborations; see table 6A.2.12 in this chapter.

Figure 6.36   Decrease in Miscellaneous Fees, Fee Gap, and Change in Rural Enrollment in Junior Secondary, Yuan Per Student

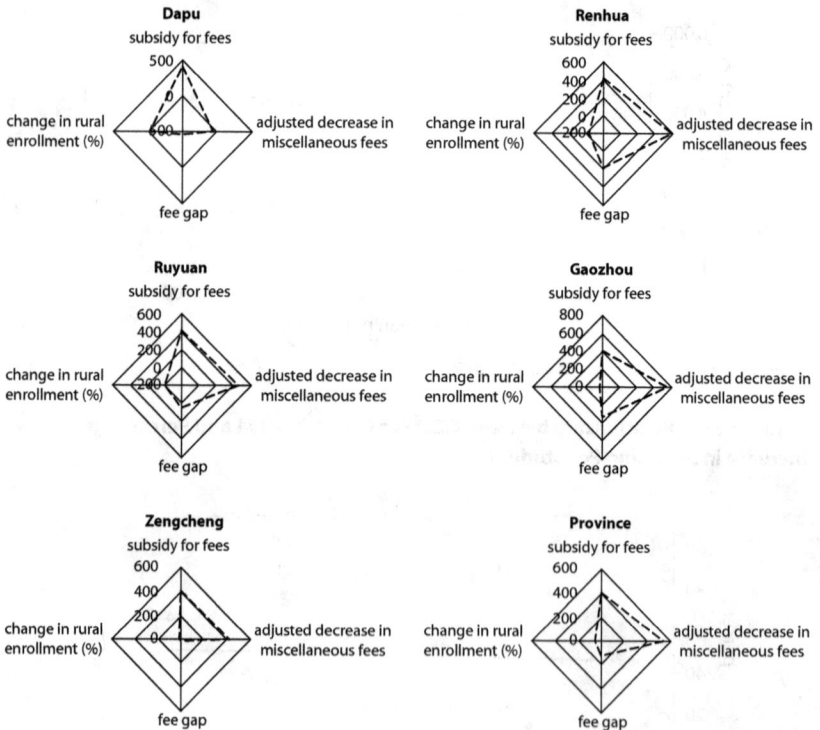

Sources: Guangdong Education Finance Bureau 2004–07; author's elaborations; see table 6A.2.12 in this chapter.
Note: The fee gap has been calculated as the difference between the subsidy for fees and the decrease in miscellaneous fees (of table 6A.2.12 in this chapter) adjusted for the share of rural student population to work on the same denominator.

Over 50 percent of the FCE scheme still comprises the subsidy for fees, but the share of other subsidies increased in 2007. The data confirm that in 2007, over 50 percent of the new scheme still went into subsidies in replacement of miscellaneous fees,[6] followed by textbooks and maintenance subsidies and, last, subsidies for needy students (figure 6.37). The proportion of subsidies other than in replacement of miscellaneous fees increased in 2007 relative to 2006, largely because of increased coverage and standards for textbooks and the 2007 one-time maintenance and renovation subsidy. Interestingly, we see that while the textbook subsidies in both level and proportion were quite similar across counties because of a generally synchronized move toward full coverage of rural students at a higher yearly standard, there is much more variation in subsidies for needy students and maintenance, with both tending to be higher in proportion and level in the counties located in mountainous regions. These trends are fairly similar across primary and junior secondary education.

The rationale behind the coverage of the subsidy for needy students is unclear. For the subsidy for needy students, the variation is due in large part to the different coverage across counties, with counties like Renhua able to cover about 30 percent of their rural student populations with the provincial subsidy, and others like Deqing only able to cover about 2 percent of their rural populations (and 12 percent of their boarding populations). In truth, beyond the small standard value (see above), one may wonder what is the exact rationale behind these figures, as Deqing turns out to have been as poor as Renhua according to 2007 GDP data and had an even higher boarding population (13 percent versus 7 percent).

Figure 6.37   Allocation of the FCE Scheme across the Different Subsidies in the County Sample (Primary Education), 2007

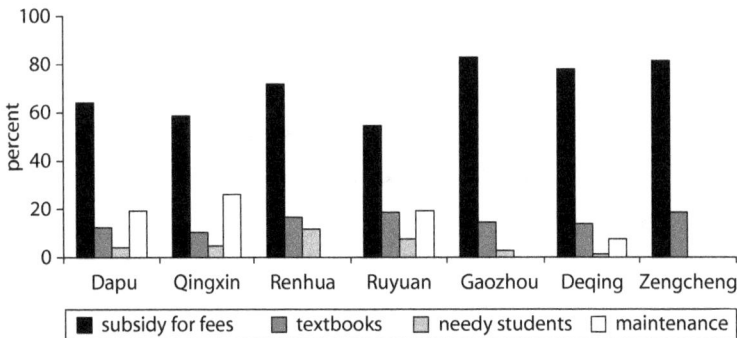

Sources: Guangdong Education Finance Bureau 2004–07; author's elaborations; see table 6A.2.13 in this chapter.

Apparently, subsidies were granted to students of families with net per capita income below 1,500 yuan. It is not clear if this was the case in all counties.

In spite of a successful renovation effort, O&M policies were not always consistent, and amount per student varied a lot across counties. For maintenance subsidies, the rationale behind the different amounts allocated in 2007 was to replace all seriously dilapidated buildings in 2007, and that seems to have happened according to the almost total disappearance of buildings in seriously dilapidated status by 2007 (see figure 6.38)—though not entirely due to the 2007 subsidy, since some counties had already spent funds on dilapidated buildings in 2004, 2005, and 2006. While the provincial data do not show all details, the county data also show some cosharing across levels in Dapu and Qingxin (with between 25 percent and 32 percent of maintenance expenditure financed by the county as matching contributions), and in Ruyuan and Gaozhou (where a coshared scheme between the central government and the province, with some minor county contribution in Ruyuan, seems to have been in place). This variation suggests different and possibly inconsistent practices. Additionally, as above for urban and rural areas, O&M per student was very different across counties, without a clear apparent logic (figure 6.39). These findings suggest that there is an urgent need for a more structured and systematic maintenance plan within the new scheme that ensures that all school buildings and facilities are properly maintained.

Figure 6.38   Ratio of Dilapidated Primary School Buildings in the County Sample, 2004 and 2007

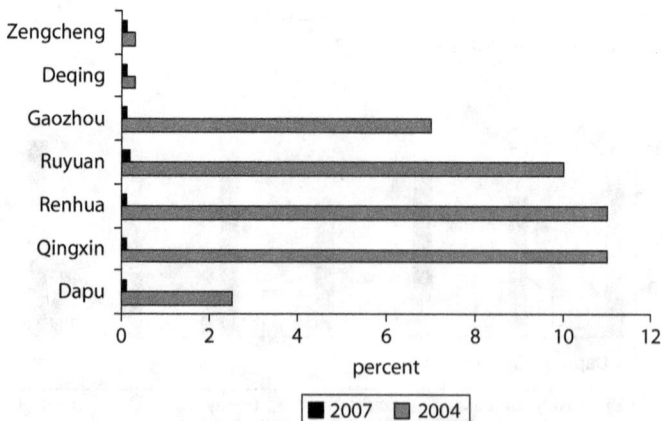

Sources: Guangdong Education Finance Bureau 2004–07; author's elaborations.

Figure 6.39   O&M by Student for Guangdong and in the County Sample, 2007

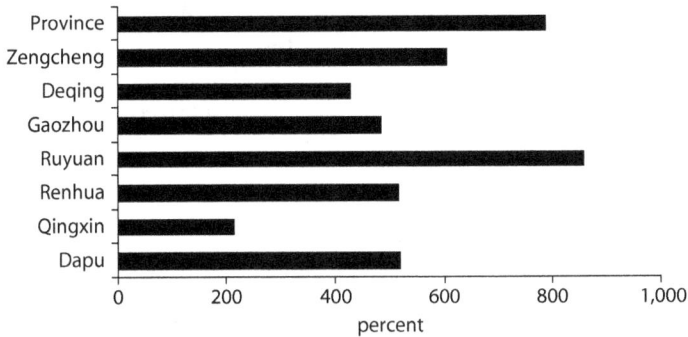

Sources: Guangdong Education Finance Bureau, 2004–07; author's elaborations.

Conclusions and Policy Implications

This section reviews the main findings of the analysis while putting forward some policy recommendations on how to address remaining challenges.

Summary

Some critical findings stand out from the analysis.

Guangdong has put renewed emphasis on compulsory education over the past decade or so, following the broader trend in compulsory education reforms in China; clearly, educational attainment has been increasing in a significant way. Access to compulsory education has improved across generations, with about 91 percent of the 25–35 age cohort attaining at least junior secondary education, versus only about 80 percent of the 25–55 age cohort. While there is still about 9 percent of the 25–35 age cohort with primary or less, this ratio has also been further reduced in the current school-age population (15–20). Primary completion and access to junior secondary have, therefore, significantly increased, shifting most of the challenge to completion of junior secondary and access to senior secondary and above. Importantly, there is evidence of continuous increases in primary completion and access to junior secondary education in rural areas (when comparing results across different generations).

At the same time, public compulsory education spending, overall and in rural areas, has increased, and all rural students were exempted from miscellaneous fees in 2007 as part of the new FCE scheme, as confirmed in provincial and county financial tables. As also confirmed by the financial information, subsidies in replacement of miscellaneous fees and for textbooks were extended to the whole rural population in 2007, and a significant and timely effort to refurbish dilapidated school buildings was undertaken in the same year. The new FCE reform has therefore been implemented and reached its intended beneficiaries. The expenditure burden on rural households has significantly decreased, which may have contributed to increased enrollment and permanency in school attendance. Importantly, in spite of the decrease in fees, overall spending per student in compulsory education increased from 2004 to 2007 in both rural and disadvantaged areas, fueled by increased public budgetary revenues, providing potential, therefore, for improved quality.

While this is a positive story, many challenges remain. Education challenges remain very acute in rural areas, where differences with urban areas are still significant, although decreasing, for completion of primary education and access to junior secondary, and highly significant for completion of and access to senior secondary and above. There are also noticeable gaps among households of different income quintiles and geographic areas of different GDP per capita, with most of the gap concentrated between the very wealthiest and the others. Finally, gaps in educational quality cannot be fully appreciated without comparable assessment of learning outcomes, but gaps in completion rates and other intermediate outcomes such as books and infrastructure quality per student also indicate strong quality gaps.

While there may be several reasons for the persistent outcome gaps, gaps in spending per student and a still-too-limited effect of the new FCE scheme are certainly part of the explanation. In particular, the evidence shows rather clearly that, in spite of increasing spending in rural and disadvantaged areas, gaps in compulsory education spending per student increased between urban-rural and advantaged-disadvantaged areas during 2004–07; in other words, spending increased faster in urban and wealthy areas. This is due to the small relative size of the FCE scheme, whose main subsidy—the one in replacement of miscellaneous fees—would not even make up for the school fees collected in 2004 in rural areas. Other reasons explaining the growing spending gap are the different local fiscal capacities and lack of sufficient financial prioritization of rural areas within each geographic area (county or city or district). This increasing gap is worrisome. It makes it difficult to close the quality gap (illustrated, for instance, by books and O&M per student or salary allowances needed to attract more qualified staff in rural and disadvantaged areas) and the educational attainment gap (in particular, in junior secondary education). Urgent action would, therefore, need to be taken to start reducing this spending gap, while providing adequate incentives for more effective use and management of education spending. Guangdong has room both to increase public compulsory education spending and to improve further the way this spending is used, allocated, and managed, to a large extent just by building on the new FCE scheme.

Main Policy Implications

Key findings and remaining challenges suggest a number of policy recommendations, reviewed below.

A first policy implication of the above analysis is that the province needs to put more emphasis on measuring and monitoring multiple dimensions of education performance, with particular focus on gaps across groups to identify where the equity challenges really are, and on a developing learning outcome diagnostic. The current diagnostics are still very much focused on the school-age population, on average indicators or at most disaggregations across geographic areas, and on standard enrollment and transition rates, providing, therefore, only part of a more complex picture. For completion of a thorough diagnostic, it will be important to (1) look at the education performance of both the workforce and the school-age population across urban-rural areas, socioeconomic strata, and geographic areas; and (2) to consider a wider array of indicators, including dropout rates across and survival rates to different schooling grades and standardized learning outcome indicators. Beyond more effective use of national testing, Guangdong should also consider participating in international assessments of learning outcomes, such as TIMSS and PISA, which would provide useful international benchmarking.

Action then needs to be taken to help address the identified outcome gaps, and policies on education spending are one of the central policies to do so. While making rural compulsory education free, the new scheme has put increasing pressure on rural and disadvantaged areas in the provision of compulsory education.

A second policy recommendation is, therefore, to increase over time the subsidy in replacement of miscellaneous fees to help close the gap. Clearly, the current minimum standards of 288 yuan and 408 yuan per student for rural areas are very low, as they do not even make up for the lost fees in very poor counties. The province is well aware of this and of the increasing pressure on rural schools, and standards have been set at 350 yuan and 550 yuan per student in 2009. This measure goes in the right direction, but, as demonstrated by the simple simulations shown in figures 6.40 and 6.41, it will not be enough to make a substantial difference.[7] In fact, our

Figure 6.40   Primary Urban-Rural Spending Gaps under Different Scenarios

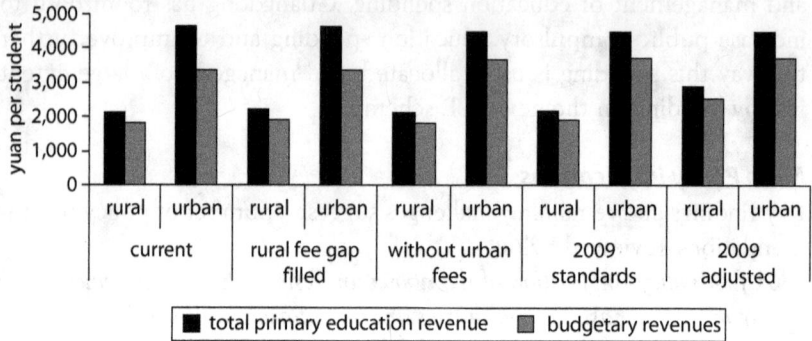

Sources: Guangdong Education Finance Bureau 2004–07; and author's elaborations.

Figure 6.41   Junior Secondary Urban-Rural Spending Gaps under Different Scenarios

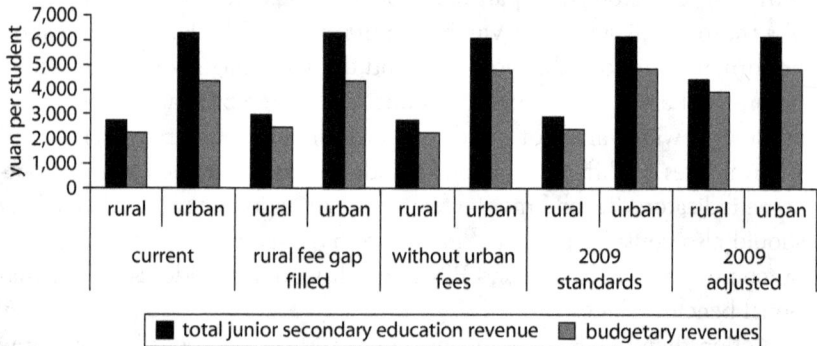

Sources: Guangdong Education Finance Bureau 2004–07; and author's elaborations.

analysis shows that about 390 yuan and 580 yuan per student would be the minimum needed to fill the rural fee gap (that is, to make up for the average rural fees collected in 2004 at 2007 prices), and even that would only just marginally help close the gap (see figures). From 2008 onward, the province also decided to eliminate all fees on urban students in a move to make compulsory education free for everybody. While commendable from a social perspective, this measure will only marginally help to close the gap. This is all the more true as subsidies have been set a bit higher in urban areas (326 and 466 yuan per student) to reflect higher lost fees, and (although not factored in the figures) the more visible urban sector may be better able to negotiate counteracting increases in budgetary revenues. Applying the same increased standards (350 and 550 yuan per student) for both urban and rural areas in 2009 would also not really help. What really would start to make a difference is a substantial rise in the minimum subsidies to rural areas to levels that would be enough to, say, grant the provincial average in teacher salary allowances per student (the basic salary is already very similar between urban and rural areas) and reach the urban standard in O&M per student (so-called adjusted 2009 standards in the figures). This points to the need for much more drastic increases in the rural subsidy based on solid justification, leading us to discuss elements of an improved funding formula.

A third policy implication is the need for an improved funding formula for the subsidy in replacement of miscellaneous fees. The high and increasing spending gaps between urban and rural areas in the province clearly point to the need for differentiating urban and rural standards in replacement of miscellaneous fees to make sure rural schools can satisfy basic needs. As the province is currently doing, it is important to continue working with minimum and predictable subsidies per student that limit the scope for lengthy negotiations and provide strong incentives for efficient behavior. This way, the issue is not about changing the subsidy per student approach, but rather about getting a better grasp on what the subsidy "needs to buy" in rural areas and adjusting the current minimum subsidy accordingly over the short to medium run. If the subsidy in replacement of miscellaneous fees needs to allow rural schools to cover acceptable teachers' costs[8] and O&M such as basic school supplies, utilities, and simple classroom maintenance,[9] it would make sense to fix minimum acceptable standards for both (set at the provincial average or, more likely, other standard costs) and review the overall amount of the subsidy.

There are some useful examples of funding formulas across the world that could be used as a reference for Guangdong to fund rural schools. Some countries like El Salvador and Honduras in Central America transfer periodically to rural schools a fixed amount composed of (1) the salary (and social security) for each teacher, and (2) the operation and maintenance expenditure of the school (calculated per school or per student; see box 6.1). This a useful way of packaging and transferring funds to cover basic school needs, which can help small rural schools overcome some of their financial constraints; but allocation of salary funds by teachers or schools may not be generally efficiency enhancing.

An alternative, used for instance in Chile and Nicaragua, consists of calculating a global amount (block grant), obtained by multiplying the

Box 6.1

Examples of Funding Formulas in Central America

Earmarked Grants to Rural Schools

Honduras

1. $215 monthly per teacher + social security contributions (11 percent of salary)
2. $100 annually per school for teaching materials
3. $65 annually per school for maintenance
4. $1,000 annually per school for the Education Improvement Plan.

El Salvador

1. $418 monthly per teacher + social security contributions (14 percent of salary)
2. $35 annually per school for teaching materials and maintenance
3. Additional grants of varying amounts for quality improvements, teacher training, nutrition, and so forth.

Block Grants Per Student for All Schools

Nicaragua

A school with less than 500 students receives a monthly grant of $1,845, which is obtained by multiplying 450 (attending students) by $4.1, which is obtained by adding the following:

1. $3.5 for minimum costs (reflecting teacher salaries)
2. $0.3 for O&M costs
3. 10 percent equity adjustment (for location and school size).

Source: Di Gropello 2006a.

number of attending students per school by a cost per student. The cost per student is composed of (1) a minimum cost per student, which includes salary costs for teaching and administrative staff; (2) the O&M expenditure per student; and (3) an equity adjustment (that is, an additional amount proportional to school size and location). In this second model, more aligned to the one used in Guangdong, one basic subsidy per student is used across urban-rural and advantaged-disadvantaged areas, but adjustments are made to take into account the school size and location of the area or school, so that smaller rural schools, for instance, would receive more funds. In Chile, for example, rural schools would receive a supplement to take into account their higher O&M costs and the higher salary allowances needed to attract qualified teachers to these schools. In the case of Guangdong, given the current high inequity between urban and rural areas, per-student supplements for rural areas and schools would need to be quite high to make sure their initial disadvantage diminishes in time and acceptable O&M and teacher salaries are achieved. The total subsidy per student for rural areas (basic subsidy plus supplement) would ultimately need to reflect minimum acceptable standards of teachers' and O&M costs in schools in rural areas. It is important to point out that relating the subsidies to minimum standards of service delivery also has the potential to reinforce efficient behavior by increasing the accountability of counties to the provincial level for the delivery of a basic-quality package in rural areas and by providing incentives to keep delivery costs low.

Financing shares are the right tool to take care of socioeconomic differences, but they may need to be realigned and simplified. An open question is if additional socioeconomic or location criteria, such as measures of GDP per capita and regional location, should be used to determine the subsidy amount. The analysis on the—admittedly very small—county and city sample suggests that this would not really be advisable because the relationship between spending per student and counties or cities of different GDP per capita and region is less marked and linear than the urban-rural one (possibly suggesting also a lack of prioritization given to rural areas within a county or city). However, fiscal capacity remains an issue, and the relationship between spending and GDP per capita generally became tighter during 2004–07, which suggests that it makes sense to continue using socioeconomic, fiscal capacity, and regional location criteria to determine the financing shares of the subsidy. Wealthy counties and cities can, indeed, finance the whole subsidy, while poorer areas cannot.

Two specific recommendations here would, however, be (1) to make sure to regularly review the GDP and fiscal capacity levels of Guangdong counties, districts, and cities, as the analysis has shown there have already been large changes in relative status between 2004 and 2007 for some counties without a corresponding change in financing shares; and (2) to reassess the logic behind the financing shares themselves (10 percent, 40 percent, 80 percent, 100 percent), because the analysis has shown that the difference is really between the top counties and cities and the rest (in terms of both spending per student and outcomes). This may justify a simpler framework, where, pushed to the extreme, a very limited number of counties and cities would pay the whole amount, and all others would receive a 100 percent provincial subsidy.

A fourth policy recommendation of the analysis is that there is strong justification for a systematic, predictable, and well-articulated maintenance scheme. The analysis has shown that regular O&M per student is much lower in rural areas—while they typically experience a stronger pace of dilapidation of school buildings—and is fairly different across counties without an apparent logic (with policies for financing it also fairly different). These findings provide strong justification for the more structured, systematic, and predictable longer-term maintenance plan proposed for the rural areas and already implemented by the province in 2008. One question is how this new plan would be best articulated with the subsidy in replacement of miscellaneous fees, which also covers some operation and maintenance. We argue that these two subsidies could, in principle, be seen as complementary, with the subsidy in replacement of fees covering just the basic O&M (supplies, utilities, minor classroom maintenance) and the separate maintenance subsidy feeding into a longer-term fund that would be used for more in-depth refurbishing and renovation of the infrastructure when the time comes. The articulation between these two subsidies may need to be further reviewed to make sure their different purposes and mechanisms are well understood and implemented. Finally, the proposed 50-50 coshared county-provincial scheme (with a 100 percent county- and city-financed scheme in the PRD) would seem to be a generally acceptable solution to ensure rational infrastructure decisions and cost sustainability.

A fifth recommendation is the need for a further review and rationalization of the textbook and needy-student subsidies. As above, care will need to be taken to articulate well the subsidy in replacement of fees and the textbook subsidy—which was extended to almost all compulsory education students in 2008—to make sure they are complementary (and if it is justifiable at all to keep them separate, now that they have the same coverage). It is still an open question how to ensure that the current textbook gap is filled between urban and rural areas, as the textbook scheme has been extended to urban areas. An option would be to factor in a one-time supplement in the subsidy in replacement of fees to rural areas to allow them to fill this gap.

Further, the targeting of the subsidy for needy students may need to be reviewed. The 2008 increase in the subsidy for 20 percent of needy students in special difficulty—to include supplements of 500 yuan in primary and 750 yuan in junior secondary—is welcome, as it will help address the still significant private education expenditure burden faced by poor rural households. Coverage of needy students, however, still seems to be quite low and, more important, does not seem to respond to very clear poverty logic when comparing beneficiary groups across counties and cities. The targeting of the subsidy may need to be reviewed to ensure that it is at least as equitably allocated as possible.

The data suggest that wealthy areas have some room to have the new scheme benefit migrants, but further analysis is needed. We did not have the opportunity to explore how the new FCE scheme could apply to migrants because of lack of data allowing us to disentangle them from the rest of the student population. Clearly, a further discussion would be needed to identify how this scheme could also benefit the students of families who do not have permanent residence in the areas where they work and their children go to school. The data honestly suggest that the urban and wealthier areas of Guangdong should not have too many problems absorbing and having at least some of the migrants benefit from the new scheme, given their high and increasing spending per student. In particular, having at least the migrants who come from within the province to these areas benefit from the scheme would seem to be both an affordable situation and a rather fair way to rebalance the unequal spending across areas. We see, for instance, that the suppression of all urban fees (including for migrants) and replacement by the city's own revenues in Zengcheng, the wealthy city included in our sample, would only bring its ratio of primary education per student to GDP per capita to about 6.5 percent—even lower than the already low provincial ratio—suggesting that there is room for maneuver.[10] Clearly, however, an exact quantification of the financial costs involved in covering the migrants from outside the province (many of whom may not even be currently enrolled in the public system) would need to be made and related to local fiscal capacity. If financial costs are prohibitive, some innovative solution—such as a system of vouchers cofinanced by the sending and recipient provinces and maybe even the central government—could be envisaged.

Finally, it will be important to consider the relationship among the priority, amount, and allocation of the new scheme and the broader intergovernmental fiscal transfers. While beyond the scope of this chapter, the main intention of which was to analyze the working of the new RCE scheme, the province would also be well advised to review the integration of the new scheme within its broader intergovernmental fiscal system to make sure the scheme's rationale and purpose within the broader system are clear. They are to provide complementary or additional funds for school operation in poor and rural areas; to minimize the risk of crowding-out of the regular budget for education civil servants' salaries; and to verify the possibility of also more equitably allocating the general transfers for civil servants' salaries across areas—and to do all this with the final purpose of helping decrease spending gaps. By simplifying and coordinating transfers earmarked specifically for education, a well-integrated RCE scheme also has the potential to simplify the working of the overall intergovernmental fiscal transfer system in the province.

Overall, all these measures to improve transfers for compulsory education will also need to be accompanied by improved management practices at all levels to make sure funds always reach their intended beneficiaries and to be done in the most efficient way possible. The move toward giving more responsibilities in budget management to schools is a positive one: the schools generally have better knowledge of where and what the needs are and are accountable to their communities, and it is also consistent with the use of block grants per student. This move will need to be accompanied by coaching and training in financial management and procurement.

Annex 6.1: Outcome Indicators in Guangdong Province

Table 6A.1.1   Primary Indicators by Area (City), 2006

City	GDP per capita (yuan)	Primary enrollment rate (%)	Transition to junior secondary education (%)	Rate of graduates of junior secondary education to graduates of primary education (%)
Guangzhou	63,100	99.9	93.3	79.7
Shenzhen	69,450	100.0	84.1	58.2
Zhuhai	52,185	100.0	97.7	82.9
Shantou	14,872	99.5	96.4	71.9
Foshan	50,232	100.0	96.6	87.6
Shaoguan	13,690	97.7	99.4	105.5
Heyuan	9,495	99.9	100.0	88.1
Meizhou	8,478	100.0	100.0	96.5
Huizhou	25,043	100.0	99.4	74.0
Shanwei	8,832	98.9	97.1	68.7
Dongguan	39,468	100.0	83.9	57.3
Zhongshan	42,058	99.9	95.6	85.3
Jiangmen	22,936	100.0	98.4	89.5
Yangjiang	14,581	99.1	99.7	92.6
Zhanjiang	11,505	99.9	97.6	86.8
Maoming	15,689	99.8	100.0	77.1
Zhaoqing	13,991	100.0	99.3	91.3
Qingyuan	11,991	99.7	99.2	95.1

(continued)

Table 6A.1.1   Primary Indicators by Area (City), 2006 *(continued)*

City	GDP per capita (yuan)	Primary enrollment rate (%)	Transition to junior secondary education (%)	Rate of graduates of junior secondary education to graduates of primary education (%)
Chaozhou	13,060	98.6	100.0	89.7
Jieyang	8,657	99.9	95.3	71.3
Yunfu	10,431	100.0	99.9	91.3

Sources: Guangdong Bureau of Statistics 2008; author's elaborations.

Table 6A.1.2   Education Distribution across Rural and Urban Areas, 2005 and 2007

15–20 age range

Education	2005 (%)			2007 (%)		
	Rural	Urban	Total	Rural	Urban	Total
None	0.05	0	0.04	0.15	0	0.13
Primary	9.39	10.42	9.57	6.45	4.11	6.06
Junior secondary	61.59	41.20	58.00	57.59	39.07	54.54
Senior secondary	18.14	35.88	21.26	25.14	42.42	27.99
Technical	8.16	6.48	7.86	7.77	8.74	7.93
University	2.67	6.02	3.26	2.89	5.66	3.35
Total	100	100	100	100	100	100

25–35 age range

Education	2005 (%)			2007 (%)		
	Rural	Urban	Total	Rural	Urban	Total
None	1.38	0	0.93	1.45	0.12	1.04
Primary	14.43	1.15	10.11	11.23	1.15	8.18
Junior secondary	61.25	14.47	46.04	62.71	12.89	47.63
Senior secondary	13.54	24.45	17.09	12.68	21.40	15.32
Technical	5.86	18.71	10.04	6.54	15.42	9.23
University	3.54	41.22	15.78	5.39	49.02	18.59
Total	100	100	100	100	100	100

25–55 age range

Education	2005 (%)			2007 (%)		
	Rural	Urban	Total	Rural	Urban	Total
None	4.36	0.30	2.95	4.01	0.17	2.70
Primary	27.25	3.67	19.08	24.29	3.17	17.07
Junior secondary	50.50	21.93	40.60	52.49	18.89	41.00
Senior secondary	13.80	33.21	20.53	13.79	32.62	20.23
Technical	2.54	11.59	5.67	3.03	10.19	5.48
University	1.55	29.30	11.17	2.38	34.95	13.52
Total	100	100	100	100	100	100

Sources: Guangdong Bureau of Statistics 2005, 2007.

Table 6A.1.3   Education Distribution across Income Quintiles and Rural and Urban Areas, 2007

proportion of population ages 25–35 attaining each level

Education	Rural				
	Q1	Q2	Q3	Q4	Q5
None	4.04	1.44	0.63	0.47	0.96
Primary	19.14	11.78	11.69	7.78	5.11
Junior secondary	61.73	68.75	66.60	64.15	47.92
Senior secondary	10.78	11.54	11.90	11.56	19.17
Technical	1.89	4.33	5.85	8.96	12.78
University	2.43	2.16	3.34	7.08	14.06
Total	100	100	100	100	100

Education	Urban				
	Q1	Q2	Q3	Q4	Q5
None	0.63	0	0	0	0
Primary	3.77	0.60	1.38	0.57	0
Junior secondary	27.67	13.17	11.72	5.75	6.50
Senior secondary	37.74	23.95	20.00	17.82	12.00
Technical	13.21	22.75	22.07	10.34	10.00
University	16.98	39.52	44.83	65.52	71.50
Total	100	100	100	100	100

Education	Total				
	Q1	Q2	Q3	Q4	Q5
None	0.71	0.68	0.96	2.34	0.72
Primary	7.09	9.40	11.90	7.21	3.61
Junior secondary	53.72	65.26	57.40	28.46	18.55
Senior secondary	15.60	11.58	11.41	15.01	28.19
Technical	11.52	5.99	5.47	7.99	18.31
University	11.35	7.08	12.86	38.99	30.60
Total	100	100	100	100	100

Sources: Guangdong Bureau of Statistics 2005, 2007.

Table 6A.1.4   Education Distribution across Regions or Cities, 2007

proportion of population ages 25–35 attaining each level

Region or city	GDP per capita (yuan)	Education					
		None	Primary	Junior secondary	Senior secondary	Technical	University
Meizhou	8,478	0	3.23	50.23	16.59	11.06	18.89
Jieyang	8,657	3.57	27.86	49.29	9.29	5.71	4.29
Shanwei	8,832	8.33	39.29	36.90	5.95	4.76	4.76
Heyuan	9,495	0	4.71	71.18	8.24	7.06	8.82

(continued)

Table 6A.1.4   Education Distribution across Regions or Cities, 2007 *(continued)*
proportion of population ages 25–35 attaining each level

Region or city	GDP per capita (yuan)	None	Primary	Junior secondary	Senior secondary	Technical	University
Yunfu	10,431	0	3.66	84.15	8.54	3.66	0
Zhanjiang	11,505	0.91	9.09	47.27	16.82	13.18	12.73
Qingyuan	11,991	1.19	12.50	57.74	13.10	5.36	10.12
Chaozhou	13,060	3.95	3.95	60.53	10.53	7.89	13.16
Shaoguan	13,690	3.15	14.17	39.37	18.90	11.81	12.60
Zhaoqing	13,991	0.52	5.21	57.29	18.23	5.73	13.02
Yangjiang	14,581	0	11.24	64.04	11.24	5.62	7.87
Shantou	14,872	0	7.92	52.48	14.85	8.91	15.84
Maoming	15,689	2.09	10.47	62.83	9.95	6.28	8.38
Jiangmen	22,936	1.08	4.30	29.03	34.41	13.98	17.20
Huizhou	25,043	0	7.82	53.91	12.76	10.29	15.23
Dongguan	39,468	0	0	0	23.81	7.14	69.05
Zhongshan	42,058	1.22	7.32	42.68	30.49	6.10	12.20
Foshan	50,232	0	0.93	25.93	14.81	16.67	41.67
Zhuhai	52,185	0	1.64	19.67	21.31	6.56	50.82
Guangzhou	63,100	0	1.19	28.96	16.72	12.84	40.30
Shenzhen	69,450	0	0	3.92	23.53	13.73	58.82

Source: Guangdong Bureau of Statistics 2008.

Annex 6.2: Spending Indicators in Guangdong Province

Table 6A.2.5   Primary Education Expenditure Trends and Patterns across Rural and Urban Areas
yuan

Rural

Expenditure and uses of funds	2004 Per student	2004 %	2004 (2007 yuan) Per student	2004 (2007 yuan) %	2007 Per student	2007 %
Total primary education expenditure	1,592	100.0	1,719	100.0	2,098	100.0
Operational expenditure	1,497	94.0	1,617	94.0	2,063	98.3
Salaries and welfare expenses	920	57.8	994	57.8	1,418	67.6
Basic salaries	460	28.9	497	28.9	633	30.2
Other[a]	460	28.9	497	28.9	785	37.4
O&M	514	32.3	555	32.3	601	28.6
Equipment	63	4.0	68	4.0	44	2.1
Capital expenditure	95	6.0	103	6.0	35	1.7

(continued)

Table 6A.2.5   Primary Education Expenditure Trends and Patterns across Rural and Urban Areas *(continued)*

yuan

Urban

Expenditure and uses of funds	2004		2004 (2007 yuan)		2007	
	Per student	%	Per student	%	Per student	%
Total primary education expenditure	3,144	100.0	3,395	100.0	4,510	100.0
Operational expenditure	2,906	92.4	3,138	92.4	4,413	97.8
Salaries and welfare expenses	1,907	60.7	2,059	60.7	3,071	68.1
Basic salaries	514	16.3	555	16.3	753	16.7
Other[a]	1,393	44.3	1,504	44.3	2,318	51.4
O&M	802	25.5	866	25.5	1,191	26.4
Equipment	197	6.3	213	6.3	151	3.3
Capital expenditure	239	7.6	258	7.6	97	2.2

Sources: Guangdong Education Finance Bureau 2004–07; author's elaborations.
a. Includes subsidy, social security, other salaries, and employee welfare.

Table 6A.2.6   Lower Secondary Education Expenditure Trends and Patterns across Rural and Urban Areas

yuan

Rural

Expenditure and uses of funds	2004		2004 (2007 yuan)		2007	
	Per student	%	Per student	%	Per student	%
Total junior secondary education expenditure	2,249	100.0	2,429	100.0	2,736	100.0
Operational expenditure	2,102	93.5	2,270	93.5	2,687	98.2
Salaries and welfare expenses	1,190	52.9	1,285	52.9	1,628	59.5
Basic salaries	607	27.0	656	27.0	754	27.6
Other[a]	583	25.9	630	25.9	874	31.9
O&M	799	35.5	863	35.5	989	36.1
Equipment	113	5.0	122	5.0	70	2.6
Capital expenditure	146	6.5	158	6.5	49	1.8

(continued)

Table 6A.2.6   Lower Secondary Education Expenditure Trends and Patterns across Rural and Urban Areas *(continued)*

yuan

Urban

Expenditure and uses of funds	2004		2004 (2007 yuan)		2007	
	Per student	%	Per student	%	Per student	%
Total junior secondary education expenditure	3,458	100.0	3,734	100.0	6,144	100.0
Operational expenditure	3,155	91.2	3,407	91.2	5,877	95.7
Salaries and welfare expenses	1,857	53.7	2,005	53.7	3,700	60.2
Basic salaries	653	18.9	705	18.9	978	15.9
Other[a]	1,204	34.8	1,300	34.8	2,722	44.3
O&M	1,075	31.1	1,161	31.1	1,942	31.6
Equipment	223	6.4	241	6.4	235	3.8
Capital expenditure	302	8.7	326	8.7	267	4.3

Sources: Guangdong Education Finance Bureau 2004–07; author's elaborations.

Table 6A.2.7   Primary Education Expenditure Sources across Rural and Urban Areas

yuan

Rural

Sources of funds	2004		2004 (2007 yuan)		2007	
	Per student	%	Per student	%	Per student	%
Total primary education revenue	1,674	100.0	1,808	100.0	2,126	100.0
In budget[a]	1,054	63.0	1,138	63.0	1,826	85.9
Education appendix[b]	61	3.6	66	3.6	51	2.4
Tuition and miscellaneous fees	362	21.6	391	21.6	0	0
Capital revenues	75	4.5	81	4.5	28	1.3
Other[c]	122	7.3	132	7.3	221	10.4

(continued)

Table 6A.2.7   Primary Education Expenditure Sources across Rural and Urban Areas *(continued)*
yuan

Urban

Sources of funds	2004		2004 (2007 yuan)		2007	
	Per student	%	Per student	%	Per student	%
Total primary education revenue	3,096	100.0	3,344	100.0	4,653	100.0
In budget[a]	1,888	61.0	2,039	61.0	3,348	72.0
Education appendix[b]	192	6.2	207	6.2	326	7.0
Tuition and miscellaneous fees	544	17.6	587	17.6	516	11.1
Capital revenues	208	6.7	225	6.7	79	1.7
Other[c]	264	8.5	285	8.5	384	8.3

Sources: Guangdong Education Finance Bureau 2004–07; author's elaborations.
a. Includes mostly fund allocation on operating expenses.
b. Includes urban, rural, and local appendixes.
c. Includes mostly other school income and donations.

Table 6A.2.8   Junior Secondary Education Expenditure Sources across Rural and Urban Areas
yuan

Rural

Sources of funds	2004		2004 (2007 yuan)		2007	
	Per student	%	Per student	%	Per student	%
Total junior secondary education revenue	2,268	100.0	2,449	100.0	2,759	100.0
In budget[a]	1,366	60.2	1,475	60.2	2,256	81.8
Education appendix[b]	71	3.1	77	3.1	95	3.4
Tuition and miscellaneous fees	536	23.6	579	23.6	0	0
Capital revenues	74	3.3	80	3.3	39	1.4
Other[c]	221	9.7	239	9.7	369	13.4

(continued)

Table 6A.2.8   Junior Secondary Education Expenditure Sources across Rural and Urban Areas *(continued)*

yuan

Urban

Sources of funds	2004 Per student	%	2004 (2007 yuan) Per student	%	2007 Per student	%
Total junior secondary education revenue	3,552	100.0	3,836	100.0	6,283	100.0
In budget[a]	2,064	58.1	2,229	58.1	4,319	68.7
Education appendix[b]	251	7.1	271	7.1	361	5.7
Tuition and miscellaneous fees	656	18.5	708	18.5	693	11.0
Capital revenues	258	7.3	279	7.3	232	3.7
Other[c]	323	9.1	349	9.1	678	10.8

Sources: Guangdong Education Finance Bureau 2004–07; author's elaborations.

a. Includes mostly fund allocation on operating expenses.

b. Includes urban, rural, and local appendixes.

c. Includes mostly other school income and donations.

Table 6A.2.9 Composition of the New FCE Scheme and TEOS, Average Subsidies, and Distribution by Institutional Source, 2006
2006 yuan

Subsidies	Average annual standard subsidy	Average total subsidy	Average subsidy per student	Average subsidy per rural student	Distribution (%)		
					Central	Provincial	County or City
Miscellaneous fees—two exemptions							
Primary	260	71,338,280	7	10	0	n.a.	n.a.
Lower secondary	360	41,826,060	9	13	0	n.a.	n.a.
Percentage of FCE/TEOS	n.a.	5	n.a.	n.a.	n.a.	n.a.	n.a.
Miscellaneous fees—new scheme							
Primary	288	1,127,847,312	106	162	0	72	28
Lower secondary	408	757,389,372	159	230	0	70	30
Percentage of FCE/TEOS	n.a.	86	n.a.	n.a.	n.a.	n.a.	n.a.
Textbooks							
Primary	60	43,348,680	4	6	0	100	0
Lower secondary	140	43,082,060	9	13	0	100	0
Percentage of FCE/TEOS	n.a.	4	n.a.	n.a.	n.a.	n.a.	n.a.
Needy students							
Primary	100	72,240,000	7	10	0	100	0
Lower secondary	100	30,780,000	6	9	0	100	0
Percentage of FCE/TEOS	n.a.	5	n.a.	n.a.	n.a.	n.a.	n.a.

Sources: Guangdong Education Finance Bureau 2004–07; author's elaborations.
Note: n.a. = not applicable; FCE = free compulsory education; TEOS = two exemptions, one subsidy.

Table 6A.2.10 Composition of the New FCE Scheme and TEOS, Average Subsidies and Distribution by Institutional Source, 2007
2007 yuan

	Average annual standard subsidy	Average total subsidy	Average subsidy per student	Average subsidy per rural student	Distribution (%)		
					Central	Provincial	County or City
Miscellaneous fees							
Primary	288	2,001,036,960	189	288	12	57	31
Lower secondary	408	1,345,433,448	283	408	11	56	33
Percentage of FCE/TEOS	n.a.	55	n.a.	n.a.	n.a.	n.a.	n.a.
Textbooks[a]							
Primary	Spring 60; fall 100	369,076,590	35	53	0	100	0
Lower secondary	Spring 140; fall 180	318,327,820	67	95	0	100	0
Percentage of FCE/TEOS	n.a.	11	n.a.	n.a.	n.a.	n.a.	n.a.
Needy students							
Primary	Spring 100; fall 200	108,360,000	10	16	0	100	0
Lower secondary	Spring 100; fall 200	46,160,000	10	14	0	100	0
Percentage of FCE/TEOS	n.a.	3	n.a.	n.a.	n.a.	n.a.	n.a.
Maintenance[b]							
Primary	n.a.	1,351,310,000	130	190	0	100	0
Lower secondary	n.a.	556,130,000	120	170	1	99	0
Percentage of FCE/TEOS	n.a.	31	n.a.	n.a.	n.a.	n.a.	n.a.

Sources: Guangdong Education Finance Bureau 2004–07; author's elaborations.

Note: n.a. = not applicable; FCE = free compulsory education; TEOS = two exemptions, one subsidy.

a. Estimates; final data yet not available.

b. Includes a one-time expenditure on renovation and refurbishing of dilapidated buildings in the non–Pearl River Delta region.

Table 6A.2.11 **Spending and Revenue Sources for Primary Education in the Seven County/City Sample**
2007 yuan, per student

Counties	GDP per capita		Spending			Budget revenues			Miscellaneous fees			Other private funds		
	2004	2007	2000	2004	2007	2000	2004	2007	2000	2004	2007	2000	2004	2007
Mountainous areas														
Dapu	4,505	5,448	1,240	2,777	2,863	775	2,302	2,583	162	260	105	139	175	152
Qingxin	6,678	14,098	1,012	1,462	1,739	490	961	1,497	260	437	150	52	32	90
Renhua	7,406	19,212	1,382	2,204	3,342	911	2,039	2,692	258	373	91	82	22	217
Ruyuan	8,786	10,393	1,290	2,450	2,881	857	1,943	2,521	277	407	160	109	73	200
West wing														
Gaozhou city	9,669	12,354	798	1,167	1,365	402	690	1,174	280	442	41	20	48	129
Deqing	9,940	10,613	1,203	1,481	1,850	683	1,028	1,757	312	327	66	106	79	23
Pearl River Delta														
Zengcheng city	30,382	50,443	1,675	2,547	4,165	933	1,698	3,211	348	361	51	37	338	548
Province	21,471	32,895[a]	—	2,284	2,854	—	1,441	2,303	—	458	162	—	184	272

Sources: Guangdong Education Finance Bureau 2000, 2004–07; author's elaborations.
Note: — = not available.

Table 6A.2.12 Spending and Revenue Sources for Junior Secondary Education in the Seven County/City Sample
2007 yuan, per student

Counties	GDP per capita 2004	GDP per capita 2007	Spending 2000	Spending 2004	Spending 2007	Budget revenues 2000	Budget revenues 2004	Budget revenues 2007	Miscellaneous fees 2000	Miscellaneous fees 2004	Miscellaneous fees 2007	Other private funds 2000	Other private funds 2004	Other private funds 2007
Mountainous areas														
Dapu	4,505	5,448	1,412	2,504	4,986	852	1,874	3,806	195	368	412	160	244	674
Qingxin	6,678	14,098	1,076	1,834	2,681	622	1,222	1,858	343	473	278	116	124	375
Renhua	7,406	19,212	1,638	2,031	3,634	1,003	1,274	2,637	279	631	153	132	71	304
Ruyuan	8,786	10,393	1,660	3,055	3,517	999	2,249	2,985	323	609	256	128	134	277
West wing														
Gaozhou city	9,669	12,354	1,488	1,826	1,865	601	850	1,537	342	676	70	323	313	255
Deqing	9,940	10,613	1,475	2,122	2,626	761	1,236	2,096	435	493	282	127	25	36
Pearl River Delta														
Zengcheng city	30,382	50,443	2,033	2,972	4,941	1,075	1,981	2,895	419	550	278	127	542	988
Province	21,471	32,895	—	3,063	3,985	—	1,841	3,012	—	641	254	—	293	482

Sources: Guangdong Education Finance Bureau 2000, 2004–07; author's elaborations.
Note: Numbers in italics are estimated. — = not available.

Table 6A.2.13 Amount and Allocation of the Free Compulsory Education Scheme across the Seven County Sample

yuan per student

Counties in sample	Subsidy for fees		Subsidy for textbooks		Subsidy for needy students		Subsidy for renovation/ refurbishing		Financing shares
	2006	2007	2006	2007	2006	2007	2006	2007	2007
Dapu	n.a.	n.a.	n.a.	n.a.	n.a.	n.a.	n.a.	n.a.	100% province except maintenance (M)
Primary	288	288	12	56	19	19	155	85	M: 68% province; 32% county
Junior secondary	408	408	18	99	19	19	1363	911	M: 95% province; 5% county
% of each subsidy (primary)	60.8	64.3	2.5	12.5	4.0	4.2	32.7	19.0	n.a.
% of each subsidy (junior secondary)	22.6	28.4	1.0	6.9	1.1	1.3	75.4	63.4	n.a.
Qingxin	n.a.	n.a.	n.a.	n.a.	n.a.	n.a.	n.a.	n.a.	100% province except fees (F) and maintenance
Primary	288	288	10	50	17	25	27	128	F: 80% province; 20% central government; M: 76% province; 24% county
Junior secondary	408	408	19	90	14	21	64	392	F: 80% province; 20% central government M: 74% province; 26% county
% of each subsidy (primary)	84.2	58.7	2.9	10.2	5.0	5.1	7.9	26.1	n.a.
% of each subsidy (junior secondary)	80.8	44.8	3.8	9.9	2.8	2.3	12.7	43.0	n.a.
Renhua	n.a.	n.a.	n.a.	n.a.	n.a.	n.a.	n.a.	n.a.	100% province except fees
Primary	185	288	25	68	32	47	0	0	F: 80% province; 8% central government; 12% county

Junior secondary	293	408	36	112	23	34	0	0	F: 80% province; 8% central government; 12% county
% of each subsidy (primary)	76.4	71.5	10.3	16.9	13.2	11.7	n.a.	n.a.	n.a.
% of each subsidy (junior secondary)	83.2	73.6	10.2	20.2	6.5	6.1	n.a.	n.a.	n.a.
Ruyuan	n.a.	n.a.	n.a.	n.a.	n.a.	n.a.	n.a.	n.a.	100% province except maintenance
Primary	288	288	100	100	39	39	0	103	M: 73% central; 22% province; 5% county
Junior secondary	408	408	180	180	32	32	0	209	M: 57% central; 35% province; 8% county
% of each subsidy (primary)	67.4	54.3	23.4	18.9	9.1	7.4	n.a.	19.4	n.a.
% of each subsidy (junior secondary)	65.8	49.2	29.0	21.7	5.2	3.9	n.a.	25.2	n.a.
Gaozhou	n.a.	n.a.	n.a.	n.a.	n.a.	n.a.	n.a.	n.a.	100% provinces except fees
Primary	144	288	0	50	7	10	0	0	F: 80% province; 20% county
Junior secondary	204	408	0	90	4	6	0	0	F: 80% province; 20% county
% of each subsidy (primary)	95.4	82.8	0	14.4	4.6	2.9	n.a.	n.a.	n.a.
% of each subsidy (junior secondary)	98.1	81.0	0	17.9	1.9	1.2	n.a.	n.a.	n.a.
Deqing	n.a.	n.a.	n.a.	n.a.	n.a.	n.a.	n.a.	n.a.	100% provinces except fees and maintenance

(continued)

Table 6A.2.13 Amount and Allocation of the Free Compulsory Education Scheme across the Seven County Sample *(continued)*
yuan per student

Counties in sample	Subsidy for fees		Subsidy for textbooks		Subsidy for needy students		Subsidy for renovation/ refurbishing		Financing shares
	2006	2007	2006	2007	2006	2007	2006	2007	2007
Primary	144	288	3	50	2	4	0	29	F: 80% province; 20% county M: 100% central
Junior secondary	204	408	8	90	3	5	0	0	F: 80% province; 20% county
% of each subsidy (primary)	96.6	77.6	2.0	13.5	1.3	1.1	n.a.	7.8	
% of each subsidy (junior secondary)	94.9	81.1	3.7	17.9	1.4	1.0	n.a.	n.a.	
Zengcheng	n.a.	n.a.	n.a.	n.a.	n.a.	n.a.	n.a.	n.a.	100% county/city except fees
Primary	168	336	5	78	0	0	0	0	F: 8% province; 92% city
Junior secondary	240	480	7	155	11	27	0	0	F: 8% province; 92% city
% of each subsidy (primary)	97.1	81.2	2.9	18.8	n.a.	n.a.	n.a.	n.a.	
% of each subsidy (junior secondary)	93.0	72.5	2.7	23.4	4.3	4.1	n.a.	n.a.	

Sources: Guangdong Education Finance Bureau 2004–07; author's elaborations.
Note: n.a. = not applicable.

Notes

1. Also see Guangdong Education Finance Bureau (2007) for a description of the new scheme.

2. This is where the de facto subsidy is the result of the extended new scheme applied in the fall and the targeted new scheme applied since the spring (and then merged into the extended new scheme).

3. Although, strictly speaking, counties also add additional funds toward textbooks and needy students (as they do in replacement of lost fees), which, however, are not part of the new scheme or the TEOS (but are recorded in total revenues and expenditures).

4. Dapu turns out to be quite an exception for that educational level, given its proactive policy of resource mobilization in its small urban areas (making up for lost rural fees), its emphasis on maintenance, and its clearly decreasing rural and total enrollment in junior secondary (while Zengcheng is increasing in both).

5. Note that all amounts in table 6A.2.13 are presented with relationship to rural students to make them comparable—although we know that subsidies for needy students and maintenance are not necessarily only for rural areas (however, probably they are to a large extent). Similarly, these amounts do not generally reflect the full yearly standards, as they take into account the actual coverage of the subsidies in terms of rural population (such as in the case of textbooks, where only from fall 2007 were all rural students covered by the new subsidy and before that only a small portion of them with a lower subsidy, and for needy students, where only a limited portion of students is covered with an increasing subsidy in time). This brings down the yearly standards to reflect actual coverage and phasing of the subsidies.

6. As per the law, 100 percent was financed by the province or central government in the poorest counties (at least as per 2004 data) and 80 percent in the other poor ones (while Zengcheng financed practically all of it).

7. These are, admittedly, very simplified simulations, which use the 2007 revenue data as their basis, since full 2008 data were not yet available at the time of the analysis.

8. Costs include salary allowances and bonuses for permanent teachers and substitute teachers.

9. All items used to be, to the extent possible, covered by the old miscellaneous fees.

10. This is making the assumption that all migrants are already enrolled in the public urban system.

References

Di Gropello, Emanuela. 2006a. "A Comparative Analysis of School-Based Management in Central America." Working Paper, World Bank, Washington, DC.

———, ed. 2006b. *Meeting the Challenges of Secondary Education in Latin America and East Asia.* Washington, DC: World Bank.

Guangdong Bureau of Statistics. Various years. "Rural and Urban Household Survey Data." Unpublished.

———. 2005. "Rural and Urban Household Survey Data." Unpublished.

———. 2007. "Rural and Urban Household Survey Data." Unpublished.

———. 2008. *Guangdong Statistical Yearbook 2008.* Beijing: China Statistics Press.

Guangdong Education Finance Bureau. 2004–07. Provincial and County Financial Tables, 2004–07. Unpublished data set.

———. 2007. "Report on Implementation Status of Reforming Fund Guarantee Scheme for Rural Compulsory Education in Guangdong." Unpublished.

UNESCO (United Nations Educational, Scientific, and Cultural Organization) Institute of Statistics. 2006. *Global Education Digest: Comparing Education Statistics across the World.* Montreal, Canada: UNESCO Institute of Statistics.

World Bank. 2008. "China—Rural Compulsory Education Finance Reform," Vol. 1. Chapter 3 ("Impact of the Reform on Provincial and County Finance—A Case Study of Gansu," by Emanuela di Gropello), Report, World Bank, Washington, DC.

CHAPTER 7

Skills Development in Guangdong Province

Guangdong continues as an engine of growth for China and a force for economic reforms. With a population of 93 million in 2006, the province accounts for 12.4 percent of national gross domestic product (GDP). The Pearl River Economic Development Zone is the province's economic hub. From its early agricultural origins, it has benefited richly from China's reforms and rapid industrialization. From 1978 to 2005, the share of labor employed in the primary sector, mainly agriculture, fell from 77 percent to 62 percent, and the share of labor working in urban areas in state-owned enterprises fell from 99 percent to 47 percent, as employment in the

This chapter was written by Arvil Van Adams, former senior advisor for social protection of the World Bank, now retired. He has been engaged in China in different projects and studies for two decades working on employment and training issues. The author is indebted to Liping Xiao and Yingjie Han for working with the Guangdong Department of Finance, Department of Education, and Department of Human Resources and Social Security to gather background information for analysis. As part of this study, Colin Xu assisted in analyzing the World Bank's 2006 Investment Climate Assessment survey for China. The city data used in this chapter come from the 2007 *Guangdong Statistical Yearbook* and are reported in annex 7.1. Dewen Wang and Yue Qu of the Chinese Academy of Social Sciences analyzed the Guangdong rural and urban household surveys for this study. The results are reported in annex 7.2. The analysis was carried out as part of the overall study led by Xiaoqing Yu. The author gratefully acknowledges the contribution and collaboration of the Guangdong authority.

nonstate sector grew. The economy today is based on manufacturing and exports. Its GDP in 2006 was 2.6 trillion yuan, among the highest in the nation, with year-to-year growth in real terms of 14.4 percent. Its exports account for 31 percent of the nation's total.

This growth has been fed by an abundant supply of rural surplus labor, but competition for this labor is increasing. Gains in agricultural productivity nationally have helped create a large pool of surplus labor on farms that is supporting growth and industrialization through rural to urban migration. Migrants have come from within the province's own rural areas, but also from other provinces, providing an estimated additional 16 million to 21 million temporary residents. These migrants have filled jobs in construction and labor-intensive assembly operations producing electronics, garments, toys, and shoes. Conditions are changing, however, as the flow of rural labor has begun to tighten. Other regions like the Yangtze River Delta are attracting migrants with higher wages and better working conditions. A labor shortage began to emerge in 2004, with estimates indicating that Guangdong needed an additional 2 million workers.

The rapid growth of the economy has created wealth, but failed to close the income gap between rural and urban areas. Since 1978, China's reforms and subsequent growth have lifted over 400 million out of poverty. In 2006, Guangdong's per capita income exceeded $3,500, making it one of China's six provinces and municipalities to reach this level. This growth, however, has come with greater inequality, as the per capita income of urban areas is 2.9 times that of rural areas. The gap is large by international standards, but lower than that in other regions. In western China, the income ratio is above 4.0. When adjustments are made for purchasing power, the ratio falls, but is still well above international norms. Differences in household characteristics explain nearly half of the gap, with education accounting for 25–30 percent of the gap (Sicular et al. 2006).

Like other areas in China with rapid growth, Guangdong's economy is beginning to face new challenges. Wages, long kept low by the flow of surplus labor from rural areas, including from within Guangdong itself, have begun to rise, with wages in manufacturing and services outpacing those in agriculture. Economic pressures are introducing changes in the structure of employment and reducing the importance of older, labor-intensive industries using large quantities of unskilled labor. Recent appreciation of the yuan against the U.S. dollar is, in turn, increasing competitive pressures on exports. In response, the mix of industries has begun to shift. The share of heavy industries in gross industrial output grew from 47.1 percent in

2000 to 61.6 percent in 2006. The output of high-technology industries in 2006 was 4.7 times that in 2000. Despite the global economic
downturn of 2008, Guangdong has seen continued growth in its high-
technology sector.

Employment is growing in urban areas and in the nonstate sector. Large
numbers of adult workers will feel the effects of economic restructuring
and changes brought about by economic pressures and the growing global
financial crisis. In 2006, some 52.5 million workers were employed in the
province, with large numbers moving to urban areas and employment in
the nonstate sector. The fastest growing segments since 2000 were in the
urban private sector, which grew by 251 percent, and among the urban
self-employed, whose numbers expanded by 120 percent. These segments accounted for 17 percent of total employment in 2006, nearly
matching urban state-owned enterprises and collectives that accounted
for 18 percent of total employment. Employment in the rural sector, representing 6 out of 10 workers, many in agriculture, showed an increase of
only 11 percent from the year 2000.

The changes taking place anticipate a workforce that has a higher level
of skills than those used by older, labor-intensive industries. Among the
leading new industries are electronic information, electrical and special
purpose equipment, petroleum, and chemicals. These industries together
accounted for 50.6 percent of industrial output in 2006. As part of the
eleventh five-year plan, the province expects to become a regional financial center and logistics hub in southern China, while further developing
itself as a center for international business travel and shopping. These
structural changes in the economy present important implications by
increasing the demand for skilled workers to support the growth of new
knowledge-based industries and sustain the competitiveness of traditional
manufacturing. Evidence of skill bias in the demand for labor is found in
rising returns to education, as observed in a number of recent studies.[1]

Preparing for structural changes in the economy is important to sustaining social harmony. Guangdong faces growing social pressures as its
economy changes. The global financial crisis that emerged in late 2008
threatened exports and related employment in Guangdong and produced
worker protests. As older industries decline and new industries emerge,
jobs and income may be lost by workers as factories are downsized.
Structural changes bring benefits and costs to workers, but not always
in the same proportions. New industries can bring higher earnings, but
those who lose their jobs may not be the same as those who qualify for
employment in growing sectors. Policies that realign the cost and benefits

of structural change can promote labor mobility and improve market effi-ciency, productivity, and social harmony. Providing temporary income assistance to job losers, information about new employment, and access to the skills required by job openings can reduce workers' resistance to lost jobs and promote a smoother, more harmonious transition to new employment (Betcherman, Olivas, and Dar 2004).

Governments play an important role in managing the cost of structural change. In most countries of the Organisation for Economic Co-operation and Development (OECD), governments play a central role in protecting workers facing job changes, allocating 1 to 2 percent of GDP for programs that protect incomes and facilitate change. Where job growth is active, helping displaced workers search for new employment is a low-cost, effec-tive measure promoting labor mobility and change in the economy. Counseling, instruction in how to search for work, job matching, and placement services (as offered by labor departments and some nonstate agencies) provide low-cost options for helping workers find first jobs or look for new jobs. Retraining workers is effective where displaced workers lack the requisite skills for the jobs available. Engaging employers in the design and delivery of training works better than school-based programs alone, but the latter can work, too, where schools contract directly with employers to deliver training that meets the employers' standards.

Preparing for Change

Workers' skills and education are an important constraint on growth, as viewed by employers. The World Bank's Investment Climate Assessment (ICA) survey was conducted in China in three waves from 2002 to 2004, covering 120 cities and 12,400 firms (World Bank 2006). Nine cities in Guangdong with a total of 900 firms were included in the survey and have been analyzed as part of this chapter. Guangdong was among five southeastern provinces ranked as having the best investment climate in China. Fourteen factors were ranked as potential constraints to growth. Among the factors in Guangdong, workers' skills and education were ranked as either the first or the second most important constraint to growth by one-third of the firms surveyed. Only access to dependable electrical power exceeded this in importance, as shown in figure 7.1. Nationally, access to finance was ranked as the most important constraint to growth, followed by worker skills and education. Improvements in workers' skills are a high priority as seen by employers.[2]

Investments in education and training are crucial to support Guangdong's shift to a more knowledge-intensive economy. China is close to achieving

Figure 7.1   Items Ranked as First- or Second-Most Important Constraint to Growth by ICA Firms

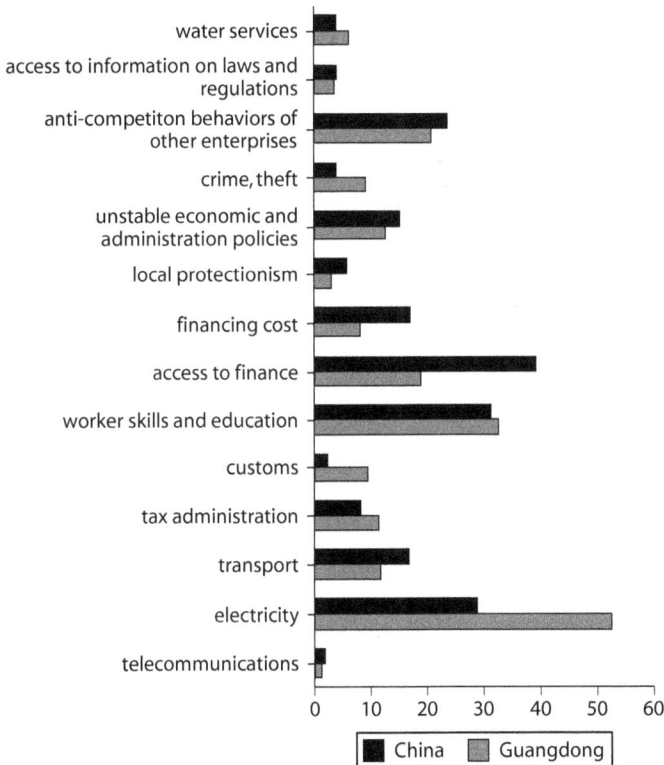

Source: World Bank 2006.

universal compulsory education of nine years, although issues of quality remain. More attention is being given to post–basic education covering secondary and higher education. The nation's eleventh five-year plan calls for expansion of enrollments in vocational secondary education, with improvements in quality and teaching and improvements in the quality of higher education. Guangdong is following this plan and has virtually achieved universal compulsory education of nine years. Six out of 10 youth who complete nine years of schooling progress to senior secondary schools. Enrollment in senior secondary schools has grown by 40 percent since 2000, from 5.42 million to 7.58 million in 2006, while higher-education enrollments in the province have nearly tripled to 1 million. Local government spending per student doubled from 2000 to 2006, shown in figure 7.2, with spending as a share of government's total budget increasing from 13.4 percent to 15.4 percent over this period. Guangdong is making a commitment to expand the education and training of the population.

Figure 7.2   Local Government Spending on Education Per Student, 2000–06

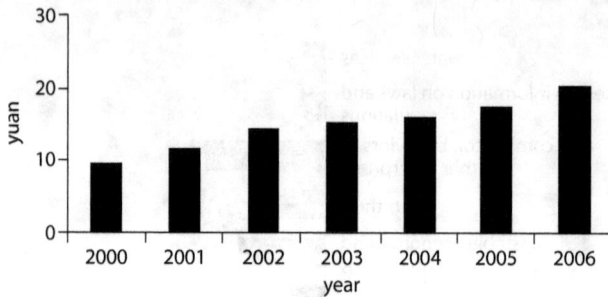

Source: Guangdong Statistical Yearbook 2007.

Students are given choices when pursuing a secondary education. For students completing nine years of basic education, the decision is whether to enter the workforce or continue onward to secondary education. For many youths in rural areas, rather than continue their education, the decision is made to migrate to urban areas for employment. As an option for further education, secondary education is split into general, vocational, and technical schools, with the first two under the direction of the Department of Education and the third under the Department of Human Resources and Social Security. Many secondary technical schools, known as skilled worker schools, were formerly administered by other economic departments before their transfer to the Department of Human Resources and Social Security. State-owned enterprises played an important role in running these schools, but in the interest of focusing on their core business, reforms led to their divestiture of this responsibility. Consolidation reduced the number of technical schools from 717 in 1995 to 202 in 2006, with average enrollments per school increasing.

Enrollments in vocational and technical education are expanding in comparison with regular secondary education. Reflecting the demand for skills, enrollments in vocational and technical schools are now expanding at a faster pace than enrollments in general secondary education. From 2000 to 2006, vocational and technical enrollments grew by 55 percent and 158 percent, respectively, while the increase in general secondary education trailed at 35 percent. Strong job growth has underpinned the demand for vocational and technical education and plans for its expansion. Overall, enrollment in vocational and technical schools is 15.7 percent of secondary enrollment, with vocational school enrollments outnumbering those in technical education two to one.

The demand for advanced skills is also driving an expansion of higher education. The shift of the economy toward more knowledge-intensive industries is increasing the demand for advanced skills provided by higher education. Higher education includes a mix of institutions covering universities, colleges (including technical colleges and senior vocational training colleges), and adult colleges. Several of the senior secondary technical and vocational schools also deliver two years of postsecondary education and, thus, have a 3+2 structure. Enrollments in higher education have surged since 2000, increasing from under 300 thousand to over 1 million in 2006. As in other industrializing countries, vocational and technical education content in the first two years of higher education is expanding. The expansion of secondary and higher education is consistent with an economy that is becoming more knowledge-based.

The economic benefits associated with education and training are evident from rural and urban household surveys in Guangdong and are driving demand for schooling. Estimates of private economic returns to schooling from the household surveys in China cited above provide evidence of growing demand for skills. There is evidence of this demand in Guangdong, as observed in new estimates of the returns to education and training from rural and urban household surveys conducted in 2005 and 2007.[3] Estimates are produced for a representative sample of just over 2,000 rural residents 16 years of age and older who had been away from home six months or more in the survey period and are therefore considered migrants. The rural sample of migrants is compared with estimates from a representative sample of some 3,000 urban residents 16 years of age and older in the same survey periods (see table 7A.2.15 in annex 7.2). Both samples demonstrate positive and statistically significant returns to schooling with the returns rising by level of schooling. The returns to education are higher for urban residents than rural migrants, reflecting possible differences in the quality of rural and urban schools, but also possible labor market segmentation in the jobs available to rural migrants in urban areas.

Earnings are higher for those who attend vocational and technical secondary schools and for rural migrants who participate in vocational training. The education regression coefficients estimated in table 7A.2.15 of annex 7.2 for rural and urban samples reflect the percentage difference in annual earnings between those in a schooling category and those in the omitted group with some primary or no schooling. Eight out of 10 rural migrants in the sample have only a junior secondary education. Their earnings are 10 percent higher than those with some primary or no schooling. For the roughly 10 percent of rural migrants who have a general secondary education, earnings are nearly 14 percent higher than for those who have only primary or no schooling, but for the 7.5 percent of rural migrants who have a secondary vocational or technical education, the earnings differential rises to 31 percent. For urban residents there are positive earnings differences for both general secondary and vocational and technical secondary education, but the difference still favors vocational and technical education.[4] Rural migrants were asked if they had participated in a vocational training program. Less than one-third in the sample reported this training, but those who did showed a 4 percent gain in annual earnings in the merged samples.

For those enrolling in secondary and higher education, there are issues of quality and relevance to be addressed. Quality turns out to be an important determinant of demand. Schools that meet a higher standard of quality are called key schools, and fees are higher in these schools. The Asian Development Bank in a 2006 study of Guangdong highlighted teachers and teaching quality as an issue in secondary schools. Courses in vocational and technical schools were expected to balance theory and practice in roughly a 60:40 ratio, with the ratio for practice rising as the student progressed in the program. In key schools, only 30–40 percent of teachers had industrial experience for guiding practice, and in other schools the percentage was lower. The problem was compounded by inadequate facilities and outdated equipment in even some of the key schools. Curricula were also dated and no longer relevant to industry using modern technologies. Management of schools in a market economy was also found to require strengthening and updating. When combined, quality and relevance are important issues affecting vocational and technical secondary schools.

Meeting these education challenges may be more difficult in rural areas. Rural areas tend to be weaker in fiscal terms than urban areas. As a consequence, government expenditures per capita are lower in cities with large rural populations. Guangdong is divided into 21 cities. This is shown in figure 7.3 below by regressing per capita spending by local governments on the share of a city's population in urban areas. The relationship of the two measures is statistically significant. To the extent lower government spending translates into lower spending on education in rural areas, as it likely would unless these areas gave a higher priority to spending on education, the pattern points to an issue that stands in the way of reducing the urban-rural income gap. The data in figure 7.3 are taken from the 2007 *Guangdong Statistical Yearbook*. They exclude government spending in Shenzhen, which is higher than that in other cities due to spending in the industrial zone.

Figure 7.3   Lower Per Capita Government Spending in Cities with Large Rural Populations

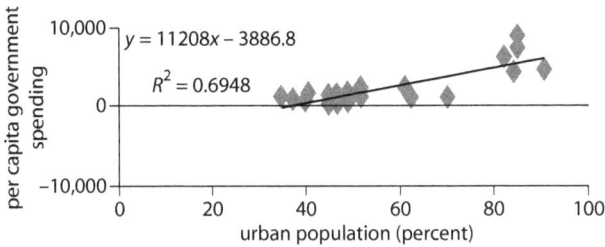

$$y = 11208x - 3886.8$$

$$R^2 = 0.6948$$

Source: Guangdong Statistical Yearbook 2007.

Living in a rural area lowers the chances of attending a secondary school, but does not appear to alter the quality of the school or access to vocational schooling. In the 21 cities that constitute Guangdong province, 9 percent of the population attends either a regular or a vocational secondary school. Figure 7.4 shows this percentage rising with the share of a city's population in urban areas. Rural residents are less likely to attend a secondary school, with this relationship statistically significant. Schools in rural areas are slightly larger in size, but this is not correlated with quality as measured by student-to-teacher ratios, which range from 17.9 in Chaozhou to 29.3 in Guangzhou. The share of vocational enrollment is also not correlated with the share of a city's population in urban areas.

Other dimensions of quality in education may be captured by patterns of spending on education in rural and urban areas. Efforts to assemble these data have proven difficult. Ideally, spending on education should be accessible by school, with the possibility for comparing spending per student among counties and cities. This would also allow for comparison of spending on educational inputs for instruction, textbooks, equipment, and facilities between urban and rural areas as an indicator of education quality. While aggregate government spending per capita is higher in urban areas, as shown above in figure 7.3, questions remain about spending for education in urban and rural areas. Steps need to be taken to capture spending on education by school for further analysis of differences in spending between urban and rural areas.

The urban-rural income gap can be reduced by increasing the number of youth in rural areas who continue on to a secondary education. The reasons behind lower secondary enrollments in rural areas include such factors as the cost of school fees for low-income families, distance to

Figure 7.4   Rise in Share of the Population Enrolled in a Secondary School with Rise in Urban Share of a City's Population

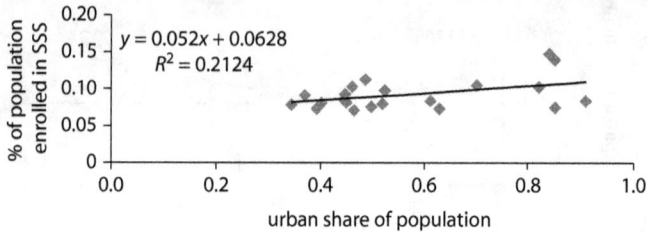

Source: *Guangdong Statistical Yearbook 2007.*

schools, and the potential earnings gains for migrants to urban areas who complete nine years of schooling. The *Dibao* poverty program pays school fees for youths from low-income families, but the size and coverage of the subsidy may or may not be sufficient to cover the direct and indirect costs of schooling for those in rural areas. It may not offset the attraction of earnings for those who migrate to urban areas. This issue merits further study to understand the level of fees paid by the *Dibao* program, as compared with the opportunity costs of a secondary education for rural migrants. These costs include the direct cost of secondary schooling, as well as the indirect cost in the form of forgone earnings from migration and work in urban areas.

Without more emphasis on retaining rural youth in secondary education, rural residents will fall further behind in incomes as Guangdong's economy becomes more knowledge-intensive. In 2006, migrant workers from rural areas accounted for one-quarter of the working population in Guangdong (*Guangdong Statistical Yearbook 2007*). Eight out of 10 migrants were under 30 years of age. Young men outnumbered young women and accounted for 59 percent of migrants. The majority of migrants were temporary, generally returning to their area of origin after three to five years, but as *hukou* reforms took hold, more migrants were likely to remain in Guangdong, along with their limited educations. Eight out of 10 migrants had nine years of schooling or less, with 70 percent having completed nine years of schooling. Only 1 out of 10 had completed a senior secondary education and another 7.5 percent a secondary specialized school, with 2.5 percent having some junior college or more. Two-thirds of migrants had not taken any professional training. Nearly half worked in assembly operations in manufacturing. This population will be disproportionately affected by the structural changes taking place in the province.

Offsetting the attraction of migration is one way to encourage more rural youth to continue on to a secondary education. In Latin America, conditional cash transfers are found to be a cost-effective instrument for encouraging young people to remain in school. Cash transfers are made to families of the poor on the condition they keep their children enrolled in school. These programs have been successful in countries like Brazil, Honduras, Jamaica, and Mexico (Bourguignon, Ferreira, and Liete 2003; Rawlings and Rubio 2003). As an illustration, the *Progresa* program in Mexico has increased transitions to secondary school by nearly 20 percent, with educational attainment increasing by two-thirds of a year (Skoufias 2001). In Indonesia, scholarships given to 6.5 million children during the East Asia crisis as part of a social safety-net program helped reduce lower secondary school dropouts by 24 percent. The *Dibao* program could easily target rural poor families and provide a direct subsidy to households to offset the forgone earnings from migration, in return for youth continuing to secondary schools.

Offering more options for vocational and technical education appeals to students with different learning interests and provides another means to retain more rural youth in secondary education. Expanding access to vocational and technical education can expand secondary enrollments. The attraction of vocational content in the curriculum can lead some youths to remain in school longer than they might have with only the choice of an academic curriculum. This, of course, may come at a higher unit cost than general secondary education, where equipment for practical studies is provided. Allowing students to prepare for their chosen careers in upper secondary school provides for greater choice and increases the share of young people who choose to stay in school when they are past the compulsory schooling age. Evidence of this comes from studies in OECD countries reporting that a 10 percent increase in the share of upper secondary students in vocational and prevocational programs is associated with a 2.6 percent increase in the secondary school graduation rate and a 1.9 percent increase in the proportion of 15- to 19-year-olds in school (Bishop and Mane 2005).

Other countries have set targets for the share of students enrolled in vocational and technical education, but the share of enrollments shows no statistical relationship with the successful integration of youth into employment. China has called for the enrollment of 50 percent of secondary students in vocational secondary education. Guangdong is some distance from this target, with 15.7 percent enrolled in vocational and technical education. Figure 7.5 plots the youth-to-adult unemployment

Figure 7.5   Youth-to-Adult Unemployment Ratio and Percentage of Senior Secondary Vocational Enrollment in OECD Countries, 2005

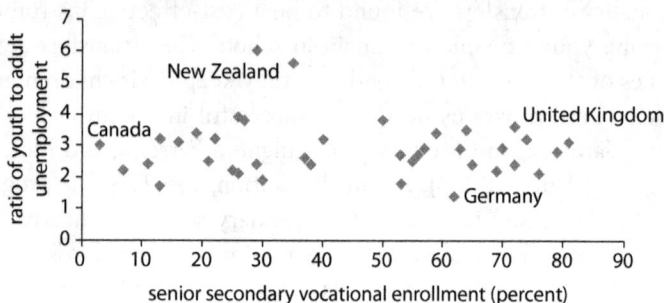

Source: United Nations.

ratio against the share of youth in vocational secondary education in a number of OECD countries. Youth unemployment rates are typically two to three times those of adult rates. While providing an incentive to stay in school, an increase in the share of secondary enrollments in vocational and technical education shows no correlation with the subsequent integration of youth into the labor market as reflected by the ratio of youth-to-adult unemployment rates. Countries like Germany have enrolled nearly 65 percent of students in vocational secondary schools and kept the ratio of youth-to-adult unemployment near 1, but a country like the United Kingdom, with a similar share enrolled in vocational schools, shows no benefit, with a ratio of youth-to-adult unemployment that is over 3.

Nonstate providers offer an opportunity to expand education and training opportunities without substantial cost to the state. In 2005, there were 123 private vocational senior secondary schools in Guangdong. These schools enrolled 80,171 students, with the average school size about half that of public vocational secondary schools. Estimates from the Asian Development Bank in 2006 indicated that private vocational and technical schools represented approximately 7 percent of vocational and technical enrollments in Guangdong (Asian Development Bank 2006, 42–44). Less than 10 percent of schools owned their own facilities. They adhere to standards set by the Department of Human Resources and Social Security and are given up to three years to comply with standards and become registered. If they fail, they are closed. Their quality is said to be variable and, on average, lower than that of state schools. While China's education policy supports private schools like these, in practice there is little government support available.

Employers are another source of financing and provision of skills that can reduce demands on state provision. The World Bank in its 2006 ICA survey documented the role of employers in training in China and Guangdong.[5] Firms were asked by the survey if they trained their employees. Nine out of ten firms in Guangdong provided some training to their workers, a figure slightly higher than the national figure. The percentage of firms training in China was high in comparison with other countries in East Asia. As a region, East Asia in 2005 had the highest share of firms training, with 60 percent. The share, for example, falls to under 20 percent in the Middle East and North Africa (Hong 2005). About half of the training financed by employers is delivered by external providers, often on-site in the enterprise, but also outside in institutional settings. Employers may further provide their own training in the enterprise using their own skilled workers.

Enterprises, however, cannot be depended upon to provide all the training needed in the economy. Not all firms will train, and among those that do, not all workers will be trained. Firms that train are likely to be larger in size, engaged in exporting, and investors in research and development. Large firms with 150 or more workers are three times more likely to train than smaller firms with less than 10 workers. Figure 7.6 illustrates the relationship between firm size, measured by employment, and the likelihood of workers being trained. The proportion of workers trained in each firm also increases with firm size. This pattern is evident in other countries with ICA surveys. Firms are also more likely to train when they have an educated workforce. This is correlated with the firm's use of more advanced technology (see figure 7.7). Viewed from another perspective, part of the benefit of expanding secondary education comes in the form of the additional access these

Figure 7.6   Large Firms in Guangdong More Likely to Train than Smaller Firms

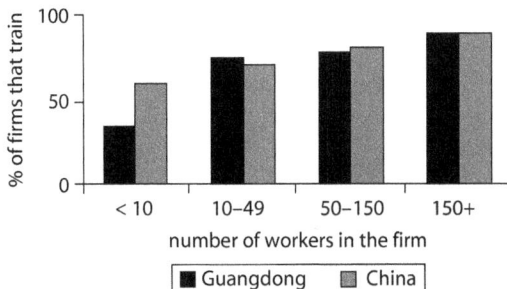

Figure 7.7   Firms with an Educated Workforce More Likely to Train

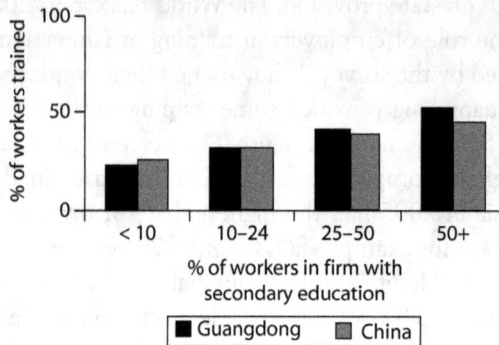

Source: World Bank 2006.

workers will have to enterprise training. The same pattern applies to those with a higher education and is confirmed by household surveys.

For rural migrants, additional years of schooling increase the chance of participating in a postschool training program, leading to higher earnings. As reported above, one out of three rural migrants has participated in a training program providing work skills. Using the Guangdong rural household surveys in 2005 and 2007, estimates of the likelihood of participating in a postschool training program are provided by years of schooling for household heads who are away from home six months or more and are likely to be migrants. These estimates, shown in table 7A.2.14 of annex 7.2, indicate that a junior secondary education, when compared with a primary education or less, does not increase the chances for participating in work skills training; but a general secondary education raises the likelihood of training by nearly 36 percent, and a secondary technical education increases this likelihood by 78 percent—higher, even, than a university education.[6] In general, an additional year of schooling raises the chances for training by 9 percent when the likelihood of training is regressed on a continuous measure of years of schooling. These results are statistically significant. Keeping rural youth in school for secondary education increases their chances for acquiring additional work skills. As reported, the earnings of those with training are, on average, 4 percent higher than the earnings of those without training.

Meeting the Challenge for Skills Development

Guangdong faces a series of interrelated challenges to meeting the rapidly changing skill needs of its economy. The challenges begin with how to govern a community of skills providers that encompasses state and non-state providers to ensure that national and local objectives for a skilled workforce are met. The Ministry of Education is only one of many providers in this community. A second challenge is how to finance this diverse provider system and ensure its efficient operation, including getting the most from public expenditure on skills development. A third challenge, related to this, is how to broaden the role played by the non-state sector in the financing and provision of skills in partnership with the state sector, while promoting quality and providing protection against consumer abuses. A fourth challenge is how to build and strengthen market institutions that promote quality and enable a diverse provider community and consumers to produce the skills needed by the economy. A final challenge at the school and training-center level is how to deliver high-quality skills relevant to market needs in a cost-effective manner.

Governance

Coordination of the diverse provider community for skills development requires a strong governance framework. The Department of Education and the Department of Human Resources and Social Security play a central role in preparing youths for employment with secondary education. They are joined by other technical ministries and a small, but growing, number of private schools in the delivery of education and training. Once a youth leaves school and enters the world of work, the ways by which skills can be acquired become more diverse. Employers play an important role in providing apprenticeships and structured work experience, but also in financing short-term training for upgrading of the workforce. The short-term training may be provided within the firm by the employer's skilled workers or by financing training by public or private training institutions. Governments play an important role in providing a policy framework that guides the functioning of these diverse providers of skills. Faced with this diversity, governments in countries like Australia, Chile, Singapore, and South Africa have created coordination bodies.

Governance frameworks include national and regional training authorities run by governing boards that include public and private members, with roles and responsibilities defined in legislation and decrees. The duties and powers of these authorities vary, but all have the overarching objective of creating a more coherent policy and operations framework for providers and consumers of education and training whose purpose is helping a workforce prepare for employment. The option exists for

Guangdong to establish its own provincial training authority and give it oversight and advisory responsibilities, and possibly implementation responsibilities for some activities. The powers accorded these bodies in other countries include providing advice to policy makers, as in the case of the National Skills Authority in South Africa serving the Minister of Labour, but also having actual authority for implementation of policies and delivery of training services, as in the case of the National Industrial Training Service (SENAI) in Brazil.

Training authorities serve as an umbrella for other market institutions that improve the operation of training markets. Training authorities are established with a board of governors. The membership varies in number, with members representing government, employers, and sometimes community and worker organizations. The board meets on a regular basis to establish policies and set strategic direction for skills development and to monitor and guide activities. It is supported by a permanent staff and director carrying out the designated functions of the authority. The authority may function at the provincial level, but also establish subprovincial bodies at the city or sector level to bring activities closer to local markets. The functions performed vary and may include such activities as development of training strategies, review and coordination of government budget allocations for skills development, monitoring of labor market developments and trends, maintenance of a quality assurance framework covering accreditation and certification systems, operation of training funds, regulation of nonstate provision, and monitoring and evaluation.

Creating a provincial training authority would address the growing fragmentation in the provision of skills and lead to a more strategic use of public expenditure. A provincial training authority includes representatives from provincial government agencies responsible for education, training, and human resources development; employers representing state-owned and private enterprises and key sectors of the economy; and community leaders. The last might, for example, include representatives of rural migrants. The powers and duties of the body would be defined by provincial leaders in bylaws, but focus on development of a provincial skills strategy; review and coordination of spending by provincial government agencies on skills development; oversight of a quality assurance framework to ensure the quality and relevance of training offered by public and private providers; and monitoring and evaluation of outcomes relative to performance targets and use of this analysis in provincial planning, policy development, and budgeting for skills development.

Financing

Changing how skills are financed is a powerful tool to get better results from public expenditure. While mobilizing more financing for skills development is a concern of governments, how money is spent can be even more important to meeting an economy's objectives for skills development. Spending in many cases focuses on inputs to education and training, starting with the number of classrooms built or refurbished, equipment bought, instructors hired, and classes offered. Budgets are created based on plans for these inputs. Yet buying the inputs does not guarantee marketable skills will be produced. Incentives need to be put in place to encourage public and private providers to deliver education and training of good quality that is responsive to market demand. For private providers of education and training, the incentives are already in place, since consumers who pay for services are not expected to continue enrolling in programs that do not produce results in employment and earnings. The same type of incentives can be put in place for public providers by financing them in ways that hold them accountable for good performance.

Shifting to performance-based budgeting (PBB) that holds public education and trainers accountable for results would change the incentives for their performance. The incentives faced by private providers of education and training can be replicated for public providers. PBB has been used in countries like India, Indonesia, and the United States to shift the focus of public service delivery away from budgeting for inputs to budgeting for outcomes. The objective of PBB is to make the budget process more policy oriented by presenting information on the intended policy objectives, the methods to be used, and their cost. Rather than combining inputs and their cost in a budget, PBB calls for agreement first on the results to be achieved—for example, the share of students who can pass national certification exams for the program, the share of students who can find work using their skills in a given period of time, or even targets such as raising the percentage of program completers. These results are called key performance indicators, and the budgeting process focuses on strategies to achieve these objectives and the activities to produce the results.

The key to PBB is holding those who deliver public services accountable for results. This is what "changing the incentives" for performance means. No longer is it sufficient to purchase the inputs and deliver the education or training program. Success is judged by whether key performance outcomes are achieved. Good performance can be encouraged by either positive or negative reinforcement. Applying this approach requires merit-based personnel systems. Managers may be rewarded for meeting agreed-upon performance goals or sanctioned for failing to meet them. Sanctions come in the form of lower salary increases, fewer promotions, or even reassignments where failure persists. At the same time, managers and teachers must be given the tools with which to succeed. This includes adequate training and operating resources to accomplish the agreed-upon task and achieve the key performance indicators. Some countries with PBB experience include Australia, Chile, Colombia, France, the Russian Federation, the United Kingdom, and the United States.[7]

Chile has been on the cutting edge of performance-based budgeting for many years, having started by introducing performance indicators in 1993 and a system of program evaluation in 1997. PBB represents a general approach to public management and is not specific to skills development, but it can be readily adapted to public delivery of education and skills. In Chile today, every program identifies its clients, outputs, performance indicators, and goals with evaluations linked to the budget cycle. In a report given to the World Bank in October 2008, a representative of the Ministry of Finance offered some lessons from Chile's experience with PBB.[8] Budget reforms have taken place gradually, shaped by the capacity of agencies. Strengthening capacity for program evaluation is essential to make PBB work. Evaluations can be kept simple with desk studies and reviews of program logical frameworks. Monitoring systems need to be established with performance indicators that initially focus on processes before moving to outputs and outcomes. A range of financial incentives is provided to encourage good performance. Chile's Budget Office has played an important role in guiding the budget reform.

Using public finance and competition can also promote better outcomes for skills development. Rather than financing schools and training institutes for services delivered, governments can elect to provide financing to the end user, the trainee, usually in the form of a voucher, and allow the user to shop for services. The rationale is that the user is better equipped to make decisions on the choice of providers and services needed by the market. By placing purchasing power in the user's hands, competition by service providers is expected to provide the user with more choices at a lower cost. Spending may be restricted to certain providers and classes of services and targeted to those meeting eligibility criteria, such as youths, displaced workers, rural migrants, or households in poverty. Some countries using vouchers for education and training services are Australia, Canada, Chile, Denmark, France, Germany, the United Kingdom, and the United States.[9] China has its own version, as found in the "Sunshine Program," which provides rural migrants with support for training and personal expenses, but without promoting competition for delivery of the training services.

Vouchers have been used to encourage further education for youths and young adults. In the United Kingdom, if you are 16–18 years of age and have left or are about to leave compulsory schooling, you may apply through the Learning and Skills Council for an Education Maintenance Allowance of up to $45 per week to cover books, tuition, travel, or anything useful to continue learning. For those 19 and over who are studying for their first full level 2 or level 3 qualifications, Adult Learning Grants are available, paying a similar amount. These voucher programs have increased the numbers of youth engaged in learning. In Australia, Work Skills Vouchers worth $2,000 are available from the Department of Education, Employment, and Workplace Relations to those 25 years of age or over who lack a year 12 or equivalent qualification. The voucher may be used at accredited institutions for the cost of basic education, vocational level 2 courses, and accredited literacy and numeracy courses. Similarly, vouchers for $330 per year are available for the first two years of an apprenticeship program in an area of high demand. Critics of these vouchers in Australia argue the shift to demand-side financing has failed to offset the concurrent reduction in financing for training institutions.

There are preconditions that enable vouchers to meet their objectives. First, the approach is based on the assumption that the user has adequate information about the service to be bought—for example, on differences among providers in cost and quality. This may be difficult to satisfy in the case of training where the service is heterogeneous and quality is difficult for the individual user to ascertain. Second, there has to be an adequate number of providers to promote competition. Where government is the only provider, this condition is unlikely to be met. Certain markets, like rural areas, may not be sufficiently attractive to sustain enough providers to promote competition. Collusion among providers on services offered and prices cannot be allowed. Governments can mitigate these risks by providing information about services to consumers, establishing accreditation systems, and using bidding competitions to establish market prices for services. The potential scale of the market created by the purchasing power of the vouchers may attract new entrants and providers. In the end, when both state and nonstate providers are eligible for receipt of vouchers, competition is enhanced.

Training funds are an intermediate step to vouchers, using financing and competition to promote better outcomes for skills development. Training funds are a popular financing tool used by countries to encourage more enterprises to train, but also to buy training services competitively on the open market from public and private providers for target groups (Dar, Canagarajah, and Murphy 2003). Malaysia and Singapore are two countries that offer examples of well-run training funds. Financing for funds often comes from a tax on employer payrolls of 1–2 percent; from a government's budget provided by general taxation; and, in some countries, from donors and financing agencies like the World Bank. The fund in turn buys training services for target groups, using competitive procedures or levy-grant arrangements where it disburses funds to enterprises to carry out approved training programs. In Brazil, employer tax proceeds flow directly to a national training service administered by employers (SENAI). In South Africa, 27 Sector Education and Training Authorities administer a levy-grant scheme providing employers with financing for training.

The fund offers a convenient vehicle for consolidating government spending on training and administering resources in a strategic manner. A fund is administered by a governing board that includes employer representatives, thus linking decisions on spending to the demand side of the market and improving the relevance of the training purchased. The fund and its technical staff are often in a better position than individuals to sort out good from bad training, by virtue of seeing providers and their services on a frequent basis. The scale of a fund's activities also places it in a better competitive position than individuals to purchase training services and hold the provider accountable for quality and relevance. A fund could be useful in Guangdong to focus government training initiatives on, say, rural migrants. Where financed by payroll taxes, the fund ensures a more equitable distribution of training costs among enterprises, avoiding the "free-rider" problem by all eligible firms paying their share of training costs. These funds are more often used for in-service training rather than pre-service training, but they can support both.

Nonstate Provision

Few countries can afford to meet all the skill needs of a modern economy with public expenditure only. By opening the market to nonstate providers, pressure on the state as a provider of skills is reduced and private capital mobilized in building education and training capacity. In Guangdong, nonstate providers of both education and training are relatively underdeveloped. The Asian Development Bank estimate from

2006 indicated 7 percent of training capacity in secondary education is privately owned. The evidence available describing this capacity highlights its responsiveness to market demand, but raises questions about its quality. Experience in many countries suggests that nonstate providers of training tend to focus on short-term training programs, programs that require modest capital for entry allowing easy exit, and locations in urban areas where industry tends to locate, leaving rural areas underserved. These programs fill a useful niche in the market for training, but are unlikely to meet all the needs for training and replace the role of the state.

Steps can be taken by government to promote expansion of nonstate capacity. These steps start with a clear set of regulations that do not discriminate against private providers in favor of state provision. The regulation of private providers of education and training by the state is done with the intent of protecting consumers from exploitation and abuse. Licensing, for example, is an instrument of the state to apply minimum standards for carrying out private training activities in return for the legal right to offer these services. Care should be taken to ensure that requirements for licensing are reasonable and relevant to protecting the consumer and do not unreasonably act as a barrier to entry for providers. Costly regulations, rather than having a clear business rationale, can be used as a tool to prevent new providers from entering a market. This restricts competition, raises prices, and reduces incentives for innovation. Thailand provided an example of this some years ago when it placed a cap on fees that could be charged by private providers, with the result that providers of more costly advanced skills were screened out of the market.

Public information on performance and abuses can serve as a low-cost means for regulation of private education and training. Information on accreditation, for example, can help consumers sort good from bad training, both public and private. Unlike licensing, which establishes a minimum set of standards for providers, accreditation establishes a higher standard for quality and relevance that is met voluntarily by providers. Both public and private providers can become accredited. Consumers can use information on accredited training organizations to identify good training. Public financing and support for training, like that offered by the *Dibao* program, can be restricted to accredited providers, therefore becoming an incentive for providers to meet accreditation standards. Accrediting can be done by the state, by international bodies, by industry groups, and by voluntary associations of providers. The United Kingdom offers an example of an international accreditation body in APMG-Australasia, which has offices in Australia. A regional accreditation body, the New

South Wales Vocational Education and Training Accreditation Board, also provides services in Australia.

Opening access to public financing for private education and training creates a level playing field for public and private provision and encourages competition. As described above, countries with training funds have used these funds to promote competition by making public and private providers eligible for financing. The case of the National Service of Training and Employment in Chile is an example. It offers training fellowships for low-income groups and procures these services from public and private providers. The competition helps improve quality and secure services at competitive prices. The source of funding ensures a market for private providers who wish to enter the competition. Another example of this practice is found in the Industrial Vocational Training Board of the island state of Mauritius. The earlier example of vouchers also provides a potential market for private providers of education and training. Assurances of the market and its size can reduce the risk to investment for private providers of education and training.

Market Institutions

Market institutions help guide the decisions made by all participants in labor markets. Institutions that produce and disseminate labor market information help households make decisions about what jobs to pursue and qualifications to acquire, while also helping employers set wages that match demand with supply and choose cost-effective ways to produce their products and services. This information helps schools and training centers determine what fields of study to offer and competencies to develop. Other institutions set competency standards and test and certify that trainees meet these standards. Setting competency standards helps guide curriculum development, determine what equipment is to be purchased for workshops, assess the potential productivity of a worker, and measure the effectiveness of education and training programs. Still other institutions license and accredit education and training organizations, providing information to market participants about the quality of services offered. Regulators protect consumers and reduce risk in the market. Research organizations monitor and analyze labor market trends and evaluate the effectiveness of education and training programs as a guide for policy development.

Without effective market institutions performing these functions, Guangdong may suffer bottlenecks in the delivery of skills, with these bottlenecks acting as a constraint to growth. Without adequate information, essential skills may not be produced in sufficient quantities and quality to meet market demand. Other skills may be produced when no longer needed, leading to unemployment for those with these skills. The problem of matching demand with supply may go beyond adjusting the supply. Wages may be set at levels that discourage sufficient private investment in education and training, leading the state to subsidize the cost of investment in skills to ensure adequate supplies of qualified labor for the economy. Households may not be able to sort good from bad training, leading to wastage of private and public resources. Labor markets work best, therefore, when market institutions provide the information needed by all participants to guide their activities.

Governments play a critical role in developing and maintaining market institutions. While private employment services are emerging in Guangdong to match skilled labor with demand, and employers are directly contracting with training organizations to produce the labor and skills needed, not all workers are served by these institutions. The labor exchanges operated by the Department of Human Resources and Social Security play a critical role in serving those left out, often those who are unskilled and in small rural markets that are unprofitable for private employment services to serve. Not all labor market information is profitable to produce and disseminate, and thus, governments play a critical role in assuring its availability to all. Large corporations in the field of information technology are helping set competency standards for training—Cisco and Microsoft, for example—but in many fields no widely accepted standard-setting bodies exist as a guide to training organizations. Similarly, no widely accepted system is in place for assessing and certifying competencies to help in hiring, setting wages, and identifying good-quality training. Self-regulation may work in some cases, but governments are an essential part of market regulation. Governments also have a strong interest in monitoring and evaluating market outcomes as a guide to policy development that is evidence-based.

The need for building and strengthening market institutions by government is often overlooked, and this may be the case in Guangdong. The private sector will underinvest in this activity because of its public-goods nature. A nascent training market and its institutions have begun to emerge in China and Guangdong. These market institutions that provide labor market information, a qualifications framework and instruments for quality assurance of the education and training offered, and capacity for the testing and certification of skills and accreditation need to be carefully studied and evaluated. Many schools and training centers have begun to track graduates and assess their employment and earnings. This helps schools determine the relevance of the education and training they offer. Missing amidst these initiatives is a world-class institution with capacity to monitor labor market developments, highlight the effectiveness of education and training policy initiatives, and use this information as an empirical basis to guide policy development for the province. Guangdong would benefit from giving more attention to strengthening its market institutions.

A provincial qualifications authority, operating independently or under the direction of a provincial training authority, holds promise for improving the quality and relevance of education and training. Countries like Ireland, New Zealand, and the United Kingdom have introduced national qualifications authorities for this purpose. These authorities play a role in defining qualifications, setting competency standards, and testing individuals and certifying skills. These are functions now performed by the Department of Human Resources and Social Security. By government providing these services, employers are able to identify workers with relevant skills, and individuals can sort among education and training institutions with successful records in helping students meet certification requirements. These authorities may play a second role in assessing past learning and qualifications, regardless of the provider of skills, enabling individuals to qualify for further education or training. This improves articulation and mobility between education and training institutions. While the benefits of this are substantial, the cost of establishing and maintaining this second role can be considerable. Countries like South Africa have encountered considerable difficulty in implementing such a system (Young 2005).

School Reforms

The weaknesses noted earlier in vocational and technical education affecting the quality and relevance of skills produced require additional investment and reforms at the school level. School-based reforms join other reforms involving governance, financing, the role of the nonstate sector, and development of market institutions to influence how successful the province is in adjusting the skills of its workforce to the structural changes taking place in the economy. With support from the World Bank, the province is currently piloting school-based reforms in three technical schools: the Guangdong Urban Construction Secondary and Tertiary Technical School, the Guangdong Light Industry Secondary and Tertiary Technical School, and the Yangjiang Secondary and Tertiary Technical

School. The three schools offer a 3+2 structure combining senior secondary education and the first two years of postsecondary education. Located in urban areas in the province, the three schools each enroll large numbers of students from rural areas.

The pilot project will be monitored for lessons to guide the reform of technical and vocational schools in Guangdong and other provinces. The project interventions address issues affecting the quality and relevance of the skills training offered by the three schools. It supports initiatives to strengthen the link between schools and employers, covering short-term attachments to industry for instructors, internships for students, and advisory committees. It promotes innovation by introducing a modular, competency-based training (CBT) curriculum with competency standards defined in consultation with industry. Instructors will be trained to use the CBT curriculum, and a new assessment system will be developed to test and certify the competencies acquired by students. School management will also be strengthened. Along with these interventions, the project supports the upgrading of school facilities and equipment. The project is a pilot and includes actions to capture and disseminate lessons from the experience.

The introduction of the modular CBT curriculum shifts attention away from inputs to outcomes of the education and promotes greater accountability by schools and training centers. Outcomes are defined in terms of competencies established with advice from industry and schools, and training centers are measured by their success in helping students attain these competencies. The modularity of the curriculum provides a more flexible training system aiding lifelong learning. The curriculum accommodates new entrants to the labor market and workers seeking to upgrade their skills. It provides just-in-time training, allowing workers the flexibility to enter training and acquire skills required by new technologies and changing labor market requirements. With a focus on competencies set in cooperation with industry, the curriculum offers improvements in the quality and relevance of training and greater accountability for results. As more experience is gained with CBT, the program can be adapted to allow flexible entry of students into training and flexible exit once competencies have been achieved.

Care has to be given to balancing hardware and software in school reforms. Pressures exist for school systems to invest in new infrastructure, but a balance needs to be struck between the need for facilities and equipment for education and the need for software that allows schools to deliver the education and training required by industry. This software includes curriculum, textbooks and instructional materials, and trained instructors with industry experience. Good school management is also required. The importance of software is emphasized by what other countries like Argentina, Australia, Mexico, the Republic of Korea, and Singapore are doing to change the learning environment from one that is teacher-centered to one that is learner-centered. Changing the student's role in the classroom can help the student become proficient in problem solving, teamwork, and communications, skills that are actively sought by industry. School reforms with these features provide for a more accountable school system, producing the skills needed in a competitive global economy. The construction and equipping of classrooms alone is not enough to produce skilled workers.

Guangdong province can benefit from broad-based reforms of vocational and technical education and training that go beyond school-based reforms. Ensuring the success of schools requires schools and training centers linked with industry, well-equipped facilities, motivated and well-trained instructors, relevant curricula and a pedagogy that is learner centered, equipping of students to become lifelong learners, and the use of assessment tools to improve instruction in the classroom. Guangdong's ability to make the shift to a knowledge-based economy, however, will require more than this. How it addresses the other challenges identified in this chapter is important. Integration of the diverse provider system, the use of financing incentives to promote good outcomes, and an expanded role for the nonstate sector need to be part of the reforms for skills development. Amidst the challenges, the development of market institutions promises an especially high payoff to building an effective market for skills development. This role is unlikely to be filled by the nonstate sector.

Annex 7.1: Tables

Table 7A.1.1 Schools, Students, and Teachers in Guangdong Province by Level of School, 2000–07

Levels of schools	2007			2006			2005		
	Schools	Students	Teachers	Schools	Students	Teachers	Schools	Students	Teachers
Primary	19,891	10,176,170	414,470	20,512	10,569,906	407,584	21,228	10,670,304	403,824
Junior secondary	3,297	4,829,437	238,399	3,327	4,758,296	228,956	3,301	4,627,044	221,224
Senior secondary	1,805	3,089,900	140,209	1,808	2,823,068	130,768	1,813	2,528,077	130,113
General	1,019	1,724,319	103,445	1,005	1,634,639	95,581	981	1,489,863	86,079
Vocational	595	907,581	36,764	612	808,429	35,187	641	710,162	33,734
Technical	191	458,000	n.a.	191	380,000	n.a.	191	328,052	10,300
Tertiary (general and vocational)	128	1,119,655	73,283	124	1,008,577	66,577	122	874,686	61,528

Levels of schools	2004			2003			2002		
	Schools	Students	Teachers	Schools	Students	Teachers	Schools	Students	Teachers
Primary	21,944	10,496,221	396,487	22,792	10,253,706	389,262	23,314	9,796,069	379,755
Junior secondary	3,243	4,495,533	213,640	3,181	4,321,843	205,399	3,150	4,158,610	197,746
Senior secondary	1,868	2,248,544	118,624	1,868	2,007,052	74,990	2,017	1,795,802	90,715
General	998	1,313,116	75,330	995	1,137,234	66,190	1,012	984,104	57,475
Vocational	684	655,428	33,794	717	630,818	33,700	361	228,460	14,328
Technical	186	280,000	9,500	156	239,000	8,800	186	200,000	n.a.
Tertiary (general and vocational)	124	726,866	53,984	111	587,779	47,451	108	467,807	40,687

(continued)

Table 7A.1.1 Schools, Students, and Teachers in Guangdong Province by Level of School, 2000–07 *(continued)*

Levels of schools	2001			2000		
	Schools	Students	Teachers	Schools	Students	Teachers
Primary	23,611	9,529,844	371,283	24,202	9,299,314	364,118
Junior secondary	3,081	4,063,792	189,674	3,017	3,881,614	184,661
Senior secondary	2,089	1,629,868	85,230	2,093	1,525,555	87,954
General	1,000	842,763	50,124	947	725,276	43,941
Vocational	375	213,351	14,167	960	655,657	37,213
Technical	186	166,716	n.a.	186	144,622	6,800
Tertiary (general and vocational)	102	381,926	29,103	93	299,475	25,905

Source: Guangdong Statistical Yearbook 2007.
Note: n.a. = not available.

Table 7A.1.2   Features of Senior Vocational Schools in Guangdong Province, 2005

	Public	Private	Total
Schools	641	123	764
Enrolled students	710,200	80,171	790,371
Full-time teachers	33,700	3,632	37,332
Student-teacher ratio	21.1	22.1	21.2
Students per school	1,108	652	1,035

Source: Guangdong Statistical Yearbook 2007.

Table 7A.1.3   Urban Population, Local Government Expenditures, and Per Capita GDP by City for Guangdong Province, 2006

Cities	Urban population (percent)	Local government expenditure (100 million yuan)	Per capita GDP
Chaozhou	63	27.14	20,535
Dongguan	85	147.90	39,468
Foshan	91	175.40	50,232
Guangzhou	82	506.79	67,407
Heyuan	40	45.85	22,578
Huizhou	61	66.03	34,519
Jiangmen	49	63.40	31,750
Jieyang	45	40.35	16,240
Maoming	37	56.59	26,197
Meizhou	47	59.20	22,120
Qingyuan	34	49.55	21,919
Shantou	70	59.93	14,976
Shanwei	52	24.44	14,285
Shaoguan	46	48.22	25,326
Shenzhen	100	571.42	69,450
Yangjiang	44	28.29	20,571
Yunfu	50	28.27	20,149
Zhanjiang	39	69.88	30,580
Zhaoqing	45	48.94	31,232
Zhongshan	84	64.36	42,058
Zhuhai	85	70.49	52,185

Source: Guangdong Statistical Yearbook 2007.

Table 7A.1.4   Average Annual Wage of Fully Employed Staff and Workers by Economic Sector, 2003 and 2006

Economic sector	2003 (yuan)	2006 (yuan)	Ratio of 2006 to 2003
Farming, forestry	8,997	11,185	1.243
Mining, quarrying	12,961	26,724	2.062
Manufacture	15,763	19,785	1.255
Electric, gas, water	28,574	37,518	1.313
Construction	14,608	19,462	1.332
Transport	25,936	34,995	1.349
IT, computer services	42,966	53,121	1.236
Wholesale, retail	18,296	26,339	1.440
Hotels, catering	14,778	18,560	1.256
Finance	33,426	55,508	1.661
Real estate	22,312	26,286	1.178
Leasing, business services	21,306	26,209	1.230
Scientific research	32,963	46,587	1.413
Environment	16,257	20,367	1.253
Resident services	17,832	22,454	1.259
Education	20,449	26,706	1.306
Health care, social work	25,157	33,319	1.324
Sports, recreation	25,901	35,846	1.384
Public administration	25,642	35,142	1.370

Source: Guangdong Statistical Yearbook 2007.
Note: IT = information technology.

Table 7A.1.5   Local Government Spending on Education in Guangdong Province, 2000–06

Year	Local government expenditures (100 million yuan)	Education expenditures (100 million yuan)	Education expenditures (%)	Yuan per student
2000	1,069.86	144.75	13.5	9.64
2001	1,321.33	180.28	13.6	11.56
2002	1,521.08	233.12	15.3	14.40
2003	1,695.63	265.25	15.6	15.45
2004	1,852.95	287.95	15.5	16.03
2005	2,289.07	329.21	14.4	17.60
2006	2,553.34	392.62	15.4	20.49

Source: Guangdong Statistical Yearbook 2007.

Table 7A.1.6 Schools, Enrollment, and Full-Time Teachers by Type of School and City, 2006

City	Population (10,000 persons)	General secondary schools				Vocational secondary schools			
		Number of secondary schools	Enrollment	FT teachers	Pupil-teacher ratio	Number of secondary schools	Enrollment	FT teachers	Pupil-teacher ratio
Chaozhou	251.71	123	195,810	9,257	21.2	16	11,125	623	17.9
Dongguan	168.31	154	214,638	10,953	19.6	23	32,498	1,679	19.4
Foshan	358.06	175	319,735	18,553	17.2	37	52,178	2,856	18.3
Guangzhou	760.72	456	567,619	33,602	16.9	122	216,555	7,392	29.3
Heyuan	341.25	191	228,558	12,878	17.7	12	14,318	412	34.8
Huizhou	306.41	194	257,051	13,315	19.3	33	44,922	1,456	30.9
Jiangmen	387.34	258	278,126	16,209	17.2	44	55,054	2,566	21.5
Jieyang	623.95	262	460,937	18,427	25.0	16	15,421	841	18.3
Maoming	701.59	312	603,234	27,945	21.6	37	49,564	2,039	24.3
Meizhou	500.94	265	388,435	21,181	18.3	44	34,837	1,710	20.4
Qingyuan	398.03	201	273,173	14,941	18.3	14	21,775	904	24.1
Shantou	495.35	239	393,470	17,572	22.4	21	24,088	1,160	20.8
Shanwei	323.23	156	234,883	10,048	23.4	11	9,131	446	20.5
Shaoguan	320.32	190	218,369	12,839	17.0	26	41,294	1,737	23.8
Shenzhen	200.89	260	256,630	15,678	16.4	13	24,599	1,234	19.9
Yangjiang	267.73	103	188,213	9,030	20.8	12	10,692	896	11.9
Yunfu	266.82	113	201,196	10,334	19.5	14	12,998	714	18.2
Zhanjiang	736.52	346	622,795	25,270	24.6	65	49,142	2,364	20.8
Zhongshan	142.26	97	135,314	7,479	18.1	16	25,828	1,468	17.6
Zhaoqing	404.65	179	270,588	14,239	19.0	29	48,952	2,042	24.0
Zhuhai	92.63	58	84,161	4,787	17.6	7	13,458	645	20.9

Source: Guangdong Statistical Yearbook 2007.

Table 7A.1.7   Employees Training by Firm Size in Guangdong Province, 2006

	Guangdong (%)	China (%)
Percentage of firms training		
< 10	33	61
10–49	78	71
50–150	80	84
150+	92	93
Percentage of employees trained		
< 10	33	61
10–49	32	28
50–150	29	35
150+	46	44
Percentage of firms training in IT		
< 10	33	61
10–49	43	40
50–150	48	52
150+	70	68

Source: Author's calculations using Investment Climate Assessment survey (World Bank 2006).
Note: IT = information technology.

Table 7A.1.8   Firms Training by Export Status in Guangdong Province, 2006

	Guangdong (%)	China (%)
Export status and training by firms		
Has no direct exports	87	83
Has direct exports	90	93
Percentage of employees trained by export status		
Has no direct exports	36	35
Has direct exports	44	45
Export status and training by firms for IT		
Has no direct exports	52	52
Has direct exports	68	73

Source: Author's calculations using Investment Climate Assessment survey (World Bank 2006).
Note: IT = information technology.

Table 7A.1.9   Training by Firms by Share of Employees with a High School Education in Guangdong Province, 2006

	Guangdong (%)	China (%)
Firms training		
Percentage of employees with HS education		
< 10	77	71
10–25	82	80
25–50	86	88
50+	95	92
Employees trained		
Percentage of employees with HS education		
< 10	22	24
10–25	30	30
25–50	39	37
50+	51	46
Firms training in IT		
Percentage of employees with HS education		
< 10	54	41
10–25	54	48
25–50	62	59
50+	71	60

Source: Author's calculations using Investment Climate Assessment survey (World Bank 2006).

Table 7A.1.10   Training by Firms by Share of Employees with a University Education in Guangdong Province, 2006

	Guangdong (%)	China (%)
Percentage of employees with university education		
0	52	58
< 10	84	82
10–24	91	90
25–50	97	95
50+	100	94

Source: Author's calculations using Investment Climate Assessment survey (World Bank 2006).

Table 7A.1.11   Ranking of Most Severe Constraints to Growth by World Bank Investment Climate Assessment Survey, 2006

Constraint to growth	Ranking as most severe constraint to growth (%)		
	Guangdong	China	Difference
Telecommunications	0.2	0.6	−0.4
Electricity	37.5	18.3	19.3
Transport	5.6	7.7	−2.2
Tax administration	4.0	3.7	0.3
Customs	3.4	0.8	2.6
Worker skills and education	15.5	14.4	1.1
Access to finance	10.3	26.0	−15.6
Financing cost	1.5	4.3	−2.8
Local protectionism	1.1	2.3	−1.2
Unstable economic and administration policies	5.4	6.9	−1.4
Crime, theft	3.4	1.4	2.0
Anticompetition behaviors of other enterprises	10.2	11.8	−1.6
Access to information on laws and regulations	0.8	0.9	−0.1
Water services	1.0	1.0	0.1

Constraint to growth	Ranking as second-most severe constraint to growth (%)		
	Guangdong	China	Difference
Telecommunications	0.9	1.0	−0.1
Electricity	14.9	10.6	4.3
Transport	6.2	8.7	−2.6
Tax administration	7.4	4.6	2.8
Customs	6.0	1.4	4.7
Worker skills and education	17.1	17.0	0.1
Access to finance	8.4	13.0	−4.7
Financing cost	6.8	12.7	−5.9
Local protectionism	1.7	3.2	−1.5
Unstable economic and administration policies	7.1	8.2	−1.0
Crime, theft	5.7	2.3	3.3
Anticompetition behaviors of other enterprises	10.3	11.7	−1.3
Access to information on laws and regulations	2.7	2.8	−0.1
Water services	4.9	2.9	2.0

(continued)

Table 7A.1.11   Ranking of Most Severe Constraints to Growth by World Bank Investment Climate Assessment Survey, 2006 *(continued)*

Constraint to growth	Ranking as first- or second-most important constraint to growth(%)		
	Guangdong	*China*	*Difference*
Telecommunications	1.1	1.6	−0.5
Electricity	52.4	28.8	23.6
Transport	11.7	16.5	−4.8
Tax administration	11.4	8.3	3.1
Customs	9.4	2.2	7.3
Worker skills and education	32.6	31.4	1.3
Access to finance	18.7	39.0	−20.3
Financing cost	8.2	17.0	−8.7
Local protectionism	2.9	5.6	−2.7
Unstable economic and administration policies	12.6	15.1	−2.5
Crime, theft	9.1	3.7	5.4
Anticompetition behaviors of other enterprises	20.5	23.5	−3.0
Access to information on laws and regulations	3.5	3.7	−0.2
Water services	5.9	3.8	2.1

Source: Author's calculations using Investment Climate Assessment survey (World Bank 2006).

Table 7A.1.12   Characteristics of Migrant Labor in Guangdong Province, 2006

Migrants	Percent distribution	
	2003	*2006*
Ages 16–30	80.2	80.2
Education		
Illiteracy or semi-illiteracy	0.3	0.1
Primary	10.0	9.7
Junior high school	72.9	70.2
Senior high school	9.5	10.0
Taken professional training	18.7	31.8
Migrant labor as share of total labor	25.2	27.0

Source: Guangdong Statistical Yearbook 2007.

Annex 7.2: Rural and Urban Household Surveys

Table 7A.2.13   Summary Statistics for Key Variables

Key variables	Rural		Urban	
	2005	2007	2005	2007
Mean of annual income (yuan)	9,663.29	10,718.64	21,575.59	26,840.96
Mean of annual income (in log)	9.08	9.20	9.56	9.77
Mean of age (year)	25.63	26.73	44.19	43.92
Mean of experience (year)	10.10	11.06	25.91	25.37
Married (percent)				
Yes	—	—	85.47	87.71
No	—	—	14.53	12.29
Sex (percent)				
Male	59.76	59.13	50.58	51.23
Female	40.24	40.87	49.42	48.77
Education (percent)				
None	0.20	0.09	1.25	0.94
Primary	9.69	9.01	6.47	6.14
Junior secondary	71.29	70.53	22.74	20.12
Senior secondary	10.23	9.95	29.00	29.35
Technical	6.36	7.56	12.37	10.72
University	2.24	2.86	28.17	32.74
Participating in training or not				
Yes	32.44	31.35	—	—
No	67.56	68.65	—	—

Source: Survey Office of the National Bureau of Statistics in Guangdong.
Note: — = not available.

Table 7A.2.14   Probit Estimates of the Likelihood of Participation in Training in Guangdong (Merged Sample from the 2005 and 2007 Rural Household Surveys)

	Rural migrants (participating in training = 1)	
Education		
Years of schooling	—	0.0938***
	—	(10.51)
Junior secondary	0.0466	—
	(0.62)	—
Senior secondary	0.3573***	—
	(3.78)	—
Technical secondary	0.7849***	—
	(7.61)	—
University	0.6626***	—
	(4.69)	—
Age	−0.0071**	−0.0061**
	(−2.32)	(−2.01)
Male	0.1945***	0.1730***
	(4.47)	(4.02)
Year 2007	−0.0366	−0.0384
	(−0.89)	(−0.93)
Cons	−0.5331***	−1.3075***
	(−4.79)	(−10.9)
Pseudo R^2	0.0305	0.0281
Obs	4144	4144

Source: Survey Office of the National Bureau of Statistics in Guangdong.

Note: — = not available. z-statistics in parenthesis.

*** denotes statistical significance at the 1 percent level, ** at the 5 percent level, and * at the 10 percent level.

Table 7A.2.15   Wage Regressions

Annual income (in log)	Rural			Urban		
	2005	2007	Merged	2005	2007	Merged
Education						
Junior secondary	0.1115***	0.0800***	0.0977***	0.1738***	0.2643***	0.2142***
	(3.66)	(2.85)	(4.74)	(3.08)	(3.4)	(4.75)
Senior secondary	0.1705***	0.0964***	0.1366***	0.4766***	0.3823***	0.4691***
	(4.29)	(2.65)	(5.09)	(8.08)	(4.83)	(10.12)
Technical	0.3628***	0.2538***	0.3081***	0.8648***	0.5913***	0.7909***
	(7.46)	(6.03)	(9.68)	(13.32)	(6.91)	(15.54)
University	0.6545***	0.4999***	0.5649***	1.1234***	0.8194***	1.0421***
	(9.89)	(9.05)	(13.35)	(18.00)	(9.97)	(21.4)
Experience	0.0164***	0.0127***	0.0144***	0.0393***	0.0411***	0.0295***
	(4.53)	(4.39)	(6.4)	(11.65)	(8.52)	(11.57)
Experience squared	-0.0003***	-0.0002***	-0.0003***	-0.0002***	-0.0007***	-0.0001**
	(-2.79)	(-3.03)	(-4.16)	(-3.18)	(-6.78)	(-2.34)
Married	—	—	—	0.1986***	0.1496***	0.2187***
				(4.47)	(3.39)	(6.85)
Male	0.0906***	0.0761***	0.0829***	0.1772***	0.3163***	0.2217***
	(4.95)	(4.7)	(6.83)	(6.98)	(13.76)	(12.56)
Participation in training	0.0312*	0.0543***	0.0416***	—	—	—
	(1.66)	(3.19)	(3.29)			
Year 2007	—	—	0.1079***	—	—	0.2001***
			(9.55)			(7.83)
Cons	9.2489***	9.0193***	9.1538***	7.3548***	8.6613***	7.6140***
	(26.34)	(29.93)	(41.43)	(69.62)	(42.68)	(83.68)
Adj R²	0.1305	0.1029	0.1396	0.5338	0.4905	0.5363
Obs	2013	2131	4144	3614	2756	6370

Source: Survey Office of the National Bureau of Statistics in Guangdong.

Note: — = not available. z-statistics in parenthesis. The model controls the dummy variables of industry and region. Education is a dummy variable and the education level of primary or less is omitted.

*** denotes statistical significance at the 1 percent level, ** at the 5 percent level, and * at the 10 percent level.

Notes

1. See, for example, Yang (2005), Heckman and Li (2004), and Liu (2007).

2. Cities contained in the Guangdong sample included Dongguan, Foshan, Guangzhou, Huizhou, Jiangmen, Maoming, Shantou, Shenzhen, and Zhuhai.

3. Earnings functions are estimated for this chapter using household surveys conducted in Guangdong in 2005 and 2007, with surveys for rural and urban residents. Annual earnings in natural log form are regressed on years of schooling completed, years of experience, years of experience squared, a dichotomous measure of vocational training (for rural residents only), and controls for gender and marital status. Estimates are provided for each survey period and the combined survey years. The latter provides a more robust measure of the returns to education and assumes there are no differences in these returns for the two survey periods. See table 7A.2.15 in annex 7.2.

4. The earnings differences provide an estimate of the benefits realized by the student in higher annual earnings, but do not include other benefits to society that may arise from education. In making investment decisions, the higher returns to vocational and technical secondary education need to be offset against the higher unit cost of this education, ranging from two to four times that of a general secondary education due to smaller class sizes and the higher cost of workshops.

5. These are statistics produced by the author from the China Investment Climate Survey 2006 for this chapter. The ICA survey is described in World Bank (2006) in the references, but none of the data used here are from this publication. They are the author's own calculations prepared with the assistance of Xu Colin (DECRG).

6. These are probit estimates controlling for age and gender, as found in table 7A.2.14 in annex 7.2. The dependent variable is a zero-one variable, with one representing those with training and zero without. The dependent variable is regressed first on a categorical measure of schooling and then on a continuous measure of years of schooling. The coefficients of the education variables are interpreted as the probability of participating in a training program for work skills.

7. For a review of PBB and lessons from the experiences of governments around the world explaining what works under what circumstances, see Robinson (2007).

8. Theo Thomas, "Performance Management—The Chilean Experience," posted to the International Monetary Fund's Public Financial Management Blog, December 1, 2008, http://blog-pfm.imf.org/pfmblog/2008/12/performance-man.html#more.

9. See, for example, Bruttel (2005), Gasskov (2000), West et al. (2000), Finkelstein and Grubb (2000), and Carnoy and McEwan (2001).

References

Asian Development Bank. 2006. "Greatly Promoting TVET in Guangdong Province During the 11th Five-Year Period." Unpublished paper, Manila.

Betcherman, Gordon, Karina Olivas, and Amit Dar. 2004. "Impacts of Active Labor Market Programs: New Evidence from Evaluations with Particular Attention to Developing and Transitional Countries." Social Protection Discussion Paper 402, Human Development Network, World Bank, Washington, DC.

Bishop, John H., and Ferran Mane. 2005. "Economic Returns to Vocational Courses in U.S. High Schools." In *Vocationalisation of Secondary Education Revisited*, ed. Jon Lauglo and Rupert Maclean, 329–62. Netherlands: Springer.

Bourguignon, Francois, Francisco H. G. Ferreira, and Phillippe G. Liete. 2003. "Conditional Cash Transfers and Child Labor: Micro-simulating Brazil's Bolsa Escola Program." *World Bank Economic Review* 17 (2): 229–54.

Bruttel, Oliver. 2005. "Delivering Active Labour Market Policy through Vouchers: Experiences with Training Vouchers in Germany." *International Review of Administrative Sciences* 71 (3): 391–404.

Carnoy, Martin, and Patrick J. McEwan. 2001. "Privatization through Vouchers in Developing Countries: The Cases of Chile and Colombia." In *Privatizing Education: Can the Marketplace Deliver Choice, Efficiency, Equity, and Social Cohesion?* ed. Henry M. Levin, 151–77. Cambridge, MA: Westview Press.

Dar, Amit, Sudharshan Canagarajah, and Paud Murphy. 2003. "Training Levies: Rationale and Evidence from Evaluations." Unpublished paper, World Bank, Washington, DC.

Finkelstein, Neal D., and W. Norton Grubb. 2000. "Making Sense of Education and Training Markets: Lessons from England." *American Educational Research Journal* 37 (3): 601–31.

Gasskov, Vladamir. 2000. *Managing Vocational Training Systems*. Geneva: International Labour Organization.

Guangdong Statistical Yearbook 2007. 2007. Beijing: China Statistics Press.

Heckman, James J., and Xuesong Li. 2004. "Selection Bias, Comparative Advantage and Heterogeneous Returns to Education: Evidence from China in 2000." *Pacific Economic Review* 9 (3): 155–71.

Hong, Tan. 2005. "In-Service Skills Upgrading and Training Policy: Global and Regional Perspectives." Paper presented at the Middle East and North Africa Job Creation and Skills Development Conference, Cairo, December 4–6.

Liu, Zhiqiang. 2007. "The External Returns to Education: Evidence from Chinese Cities." *Journal of Urban Economics* 61 (3): 542–64.

Rawlings, Laura B., and Gloria Rubio. 2003. "Evaluating the Impact of Conditional Cash Transfer Programs: Lessons from Latin America." Policy Research Working Paper 3119, World Bank, Washington, DC.

Robinson, Marc, ed. 2007. *Performance Budgeting: Linking Funding and Results.* England: Palgrave Macmillan.

Sicular, Terry, Ximing Yue, Bjorn Gustafsson, and Shi Li. 2006. "The Urban-Rural Income and Inequality in China." Research Paper 2006/135, World Institute for Development Economics Research, United Nations University, Helsinki.

Skoufias, Emmanuel. 2001. "Conditional Cash Transfers and Their Impact on Child Work and Schooling: Evidence from the PROGRESA Program in Mexico." *Economia* 2 (1): 45–86.

United Nations Statistics Division, Department of Economic Affairs. http:\\unstats.un.org/unsd/mdg/SeriesDetail.aspx?seid=672.

West, Anne, Jo Sparkers, Todor Balabanov, and Sarah Elson-Rogers. 2000. *Demand-Side Financing: A Focus on Vouchers in Post-Compulsory Education and Training: Discussion and Case Studies.* European Centre for the Development of Vocational Training (CEDEFOP) dossier. Thessaloniki, Greece: CEDEFOP.

World Bank. 2006. "China Governance, Investment Climate, and Harmonious Society: Competitiveness Enhancements for 120 Cities in China." Report 37759-CN, Poverty Reduction and Economic Management Unit, East Asia and Pacific Region, World Bank, Washington, DC.

Yang, Dennis. 2005. "Wages and Returns to Education in Chinese Cities." Unpublished paper, Department of Economics, Virginia Polytechnic Institute and State University, Blacksburg, VA.

Young, Michael. 2005. "National Qualifications Frameworks: Their Feasibility for Effective Implementation in Developing Countries." Unpublished paper, International Labour Organization, Geneva.

CHAPTER 8

Reducing Regional Disparities in Health Services in Guangdong Province: Challenges and Options

Located on the southern coast of China, Guangdong is one of the most developed provinces in China. Backed by its remarkable economic growth, the health sector in Guangdong has seen considerable progress in the past decade. Government health spending has increased steadily every year, with a growth rate of 31.3 percent in 2006. (The consumer

---

This chapter was written by Zhang Shuo, health specialist of the World Bank Beijing Office, with the guidance and advice of John Langenbrunner, lead health economist and human development sector coordinator of the World Bank Beijing Office. Qu Yue, postdoctoral student of the Chinese Academy of Social Sciences, provided support for data analysis and the formulation of tables and figures. The work was carried out under the technical guidance and general supervision of Xiaoqing Yu and Chunlin Zhang, who are the task team leader and co-task team leader of this Analytical and Advisory Activities study.

This chapter benefited from many forms of collaboration with the Guangdong government. First, the authors are grateful for the close collaboration with the team from the Development Research Center of the Guangdong government, led by Li Huiwu and Ding Xiaolun. Second, the team benefited greatly from insights and guidance gained in discussions and consultations with the various departments of the Guangdong government, including Zhang Yiyu, Chen Zhusheng, and others from the provincial health bureau; Zhong Kai from the provincial finance bureau; Zhang Yi from the Guangdong party school; Ms. Tan and colleague from the provincial Bureau of Civil Affairs; and colleagues from the Bureau of Labor and Social Protection. The team is thankful to the various departments of the government

(footnote continued on next page)

price index of Guangdong was 1.8 percent in 2006.) Total government health spending in 2006 accounted for 2.64 percent of total government expenditure, higher than the national average of 1.8 percent. Health insurance schemes—the New Rural Cooperative Medical Scheme (NRCMS), the Medical Assistance scheme, and the new Urban Resident Basic Medical Insurance scheme—have been rolled out rapidly. The insurance coverage and funding for NRCMS have increased remarkably over the past few years, and the NRCMS enrollment rate exceeded 90 percent in 2009. The health service delivery system is also being strengthened. As one of the government's development priorities, the urban community health care system has grown considerably: in 2008 the number of community health centers increased 10.4 percent. The government has also begun an upgrade of rural health services in the lagging areas—providing direct provincial fiscal transfer to support township health centers and village clinics—the frontier of China's three-tiered rural health service network. Overall, the residents in Guangdong appear to have a better health status than the nation overall. The province's maternal mortality rate and infant mortality rate in 2006 were 17.58 per 100,000 and 0.698 percent, respectively—both significantly better than the national averages of 47.8 per 100,000 and 1.9 percent, respectively (Guangdong Provincial Health Bureau 2007).

Despite all this remarkable progress, Guangdong is facing significant challenges in its health sector, such as increased health issues among the large migrant populations, rising health expenditure, and the fragmented health insurance system. Among these main issues, significant regional disparity in health status and service access is the one of major concerns. The Chinese government has in the past years shifted its policy focus from emphasizing only economic development to emphasizing balanced development and the building of a "harmonious society." Reducing the imbalance and inequality in all areas, including health, has been viewed as one of the important measures to achieve this overall objective. It is

for their support in data collection. Finally, the team is indebted to the local governments of Qingxin and Luyuan for their hospitality and thoughtful arrangements during the field visits.

The author is particularly thankful to Li Shuyuan and his colleagues in the World Bank Project Management Office of the Finance Department of Guangdong province and Lin Ying from the party's research center for their overall coordination of and arrangements for all activities leading to the development of this chapter, including substantial dialogues and consultations with various departments, field visits to the counties, and data collection.

Special thanks go to Magnus Lindelow, who peer-reviewed the chapter and provided invaluable comments and suggestions for the final revision.

certainly at the top of the Guangdong government's agenda, given the considerable regional disparities in the province.

This chapter is based on a policy study of the World Bank's joint Analytical Advisory Activities and study with the Guangdong government on Reducing Inequality and Promoting Lagging Region Development in Guangdong Province. The chapter first reviews the situation in Guangdong with regard to inequality and regional disparities in health status and health services. It then analyzes and recommends options for tackling the challenges from three specific perspectives: resource mobilization, health insurance and strategic purchasing, and health service delivery. Specific recommendations are provided in terms of policy options the government can consider in the next steps forward. China is in the process of undertaking an unprecedented large-scale reform of its national health system with the ultimate goal of achieving universal coverage for basic health services. Quite a few new programs and new policy frameworks are being developed and initiated. This chapter was developed within this broader context.

The Challenge of Inequality and Regional Disparities

Based on geographic location and economic development situation, the 21 municipalities in Guangdong are normally divided into four regions: the Pearl River Delta (PRD) region; the northern mountainous area; and the eastern and western areas, or "wings," of the PRD. We combine the two wings into one region in this chapter, as they have similar social and economic situations. As shown in figure 8.1, the three regions differ considerably in terms of their economic prosperity: the per capita gross domestic product (GDP) of Shenzhen (the highest) is more than 3.5 times that of Shanwei (the lowest).

Disparity in Health Status
The ultimate goal of the health system is to improve the population's health and to provide financial protections when large health expenditures occur. As mentioned earlier, Guangdong leads the country overall in terms of the main health status indicators; in 2006, the maternal mortality rate and infant mortality rate were 17.58 per 100,000 and 0.698 percent, respectively—both significantly better than the national averages of 47.8 per 100,000 and 1.9 percent, respectively. However, this doesn't mean every person in the province enjoyed the same good health. A look at the infant mortality rate of 21 municipalities as well as the three regions reveals that the disparity across the municipalities and the regions in 2007 was clearly substantial (figure 8.2): the worst-performing municipality

Figure 8.1   Per Capita GDP by Region, 2006

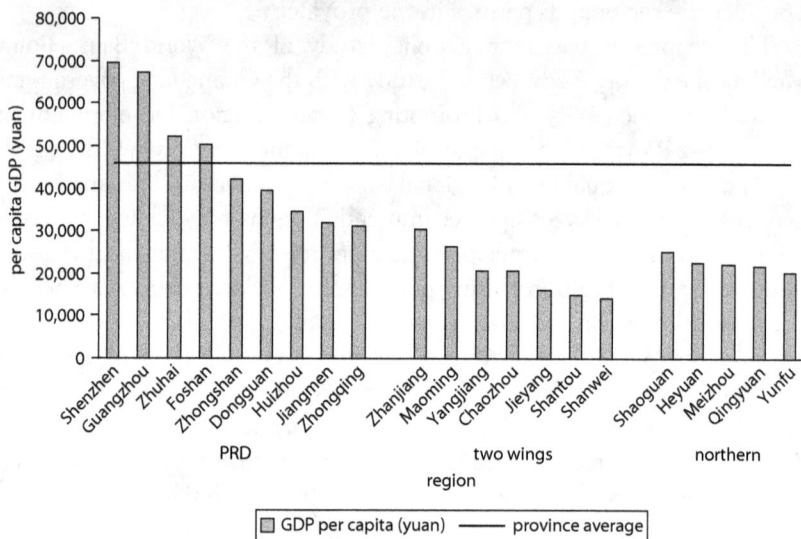

Source: Guangdong Health Bureau 2008.

Figure 8.2   Infant Mortality Rate, 2007

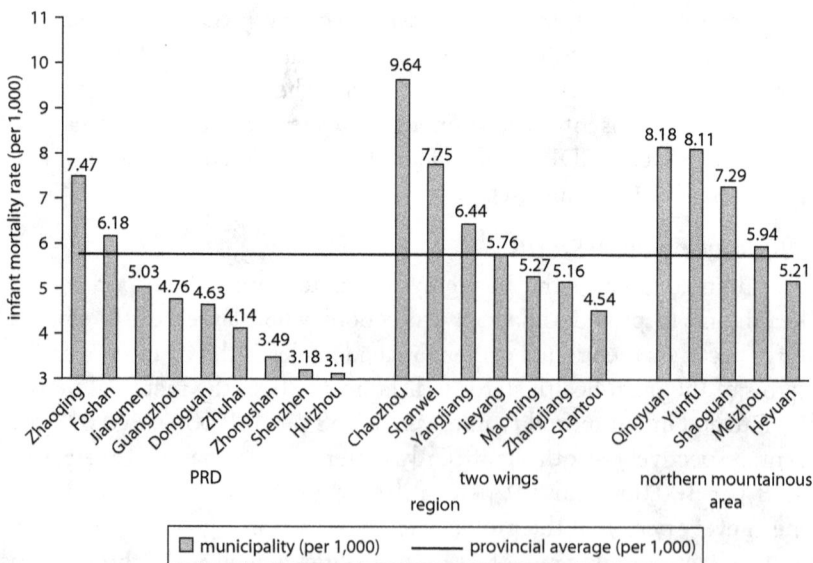

Source: Guangdong Statistics Bureau 2007.

had an infant mortality rate that was three times that of the best-perform-ing city, and the infant mortality rate of the PRD area was much lower than that of the other two areas. The same level of disparity also existed for the mortality rate of children under five years of age.[1]

The change in the disparities over the years was also examined in order to get a sense of the trend. The absolute value of the difference of infant mortality between the PRD and the northern mountainous area seems to have been decreasing from 2000 to 2007, as seen in figure 8.3. However, the infant mortality rate of the northern mountainous area as a ratio remained 1.5–1.8 times as high as that of the PRD region.

Disparity was also evident in general sanitation and hygiene. Figure 8.4 shows access to safe drinking water across different regions in 2007. In 2005, over 70 percent of the residents in the PRD area had access to tap water, whereas in the two lagging areas, only about 30 percent of the residents had access to tap water. The provincial average was 48.5 percent in 2006—the sixth lowest in the country and lower than the national average of 61.1 percent. The same situation applied to hygienic toilet coverage in Guangdong. Coverage in 2006 was 43.8 percent—again lower than the national average of 55 percent—and ranked as the eighth lowest in the country. The significant disparity among the municipali-ties contributed to this unexpectedly low ranking of Guangdong in the country.

Figure 8.3   Changes in Infant Mortality Rates, 2000–07

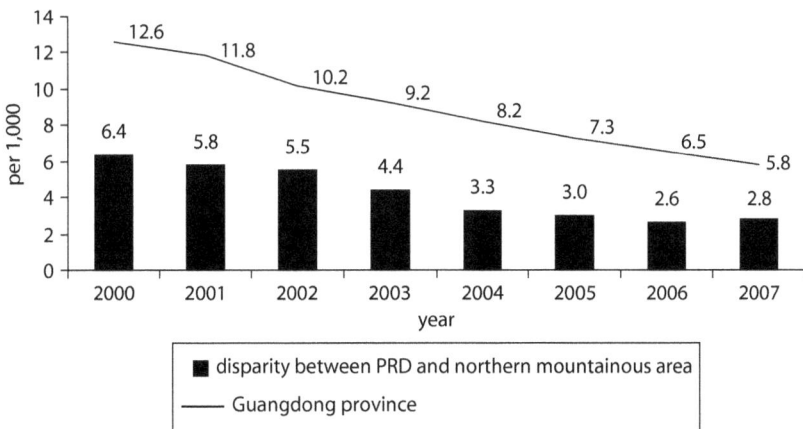

Source: Guangdong Provincial Health Bureau.

Figure 8.4   Access to Safe Drinking Water, 2007

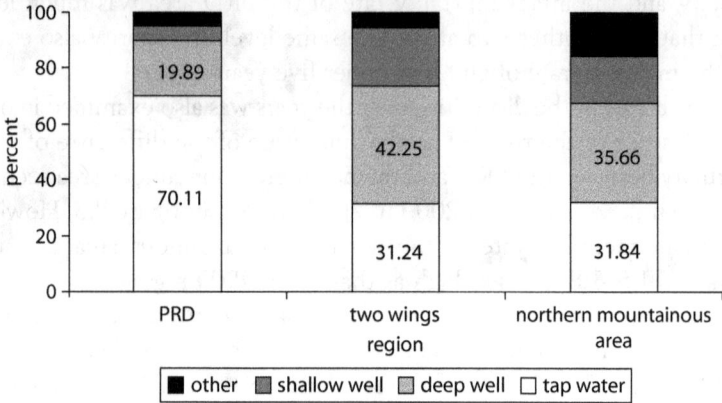

Source: Guangdong Department of Household Survey, National Bureau of Statistics 2007.

Service Utilization and Cost of Services

How about the utilization of health services—have people in different areas been getting the same amount of services, on average? Utilization of the three most common services—hospital delivery of babies, outpatient visits, and hospitalization—was analyzed. Overall, the hospital delivery rate of Guangdong in 2006 was among the highest in the nation (88.4 percent), with a provincial average close to 92 percent, but lower than that in Zhejiang province (99.4 percent), one of the most developed provinces in China (figure 8.5). Most of the cities in the PRD area, except for Zhuhai,[2] had reached a rate of almost 100 percent, whereas in the two wings and the northern mountainous area, 10–20 percent of the population still had their babies delivered out of the hospital setting.

Compared with hospital delivery rates, the difference in utilization of outpatient and inpatient service, as shown in figures 8.6 and 8.7, was much more substantial in 2007 among different regions and different municipalities. The city with the highest volume of outpatient visits had six times more volume than the city with the lowest volume, and the volume of inpatient services was five times higher. The service utilization in the PRD area was significantly higher than that in the other two regions for both outpatient and inpatient services.

Why did the people in lagging areas use considerably fewer health services than the people in developed areas? Were people in the lagging areas healthier than those in the developed areas? The Guangdong data from the third national health survey in 2003 do not support this. The data show that the percentage of people who had been ill in the two

Figure 8.5   Hospital Delivery Rates, 2007

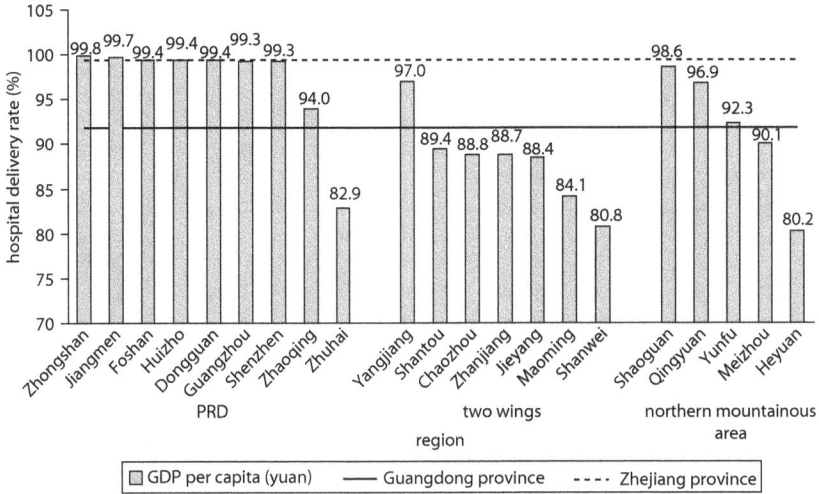

Source: Guangdong Provincial Health Bureau 2007.

Figure 8.6   Outpatient Visits Per Capita, 2007

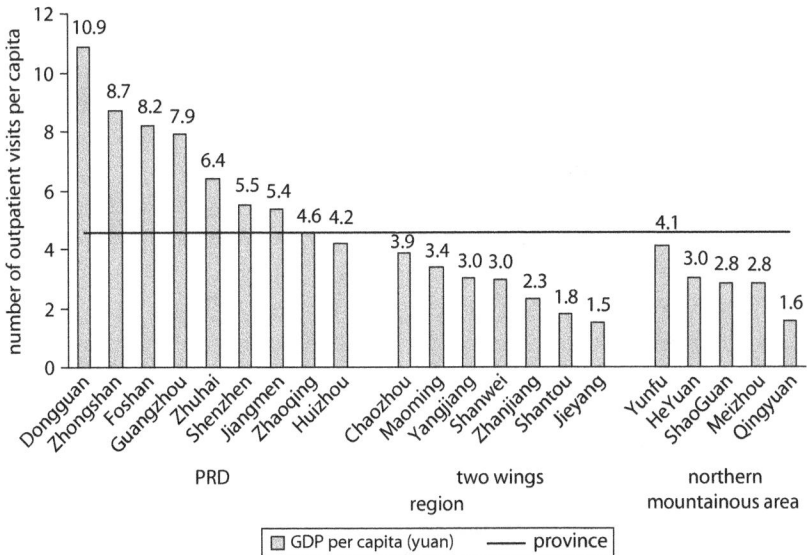

Source: Guangdong Provincial Health Bureau 2007.

Figure 8.7   Inpatient Services Per Capita, 2007

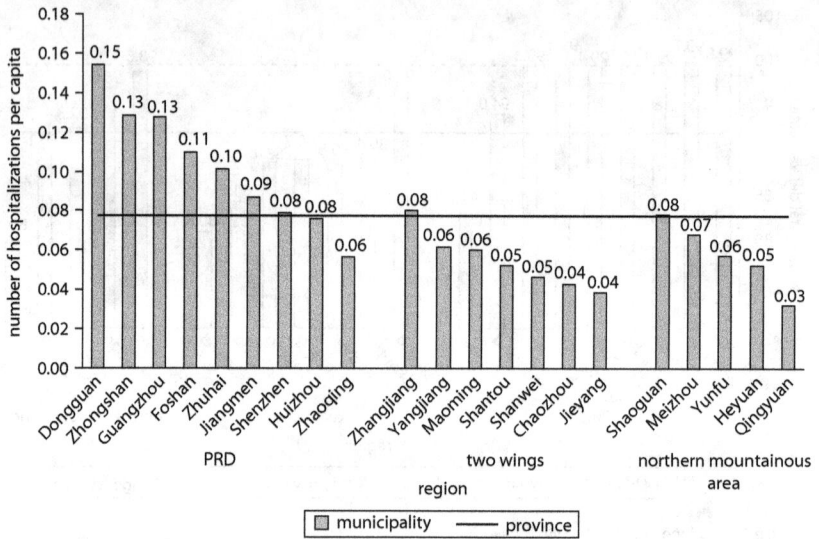

Source: Guangdong Provincial Health Bureau 2007.

weeks prior to the survey was higher in the rural areas than in urban areas (Guangdong Provincial Health Bureau 2005).

While many factors could contribute to people's decision on whether to seek health services, the cost of care and the ability to pay would be of particular importance. The same household survey in 2003 showed that economic difficulty was the reason for not going to the hospital for child delivery; while it might have cost more than 1,000 yuan to have a normal delivery in a township health center in 2003, it cost only about 200 yuan if the baby was delivered at home (Guangdong Provincial Center for Health Statistics and Information 2005). The 2007 Guangdong household survey showed that an urban resident spent an average of 716 yuan on health services in 2007—3.5 times the amount a rural resident spent. The data for rural areas also show that the higher the income, the more was spent on health care. As figure 8.8 shows, the higher income group in rural areas spent much more on health care than the lower income group.[3]

Another important factor affecting service utilization is insurance coverage. The municipalities in the Pearl River Delta—Dongguan, Foshan, Guangzhou, Zhongshan, and Zhuhai—appear to have higher insurance premiums than the others. As will be shown in figure 8.15, the average per capita NRCMS revenue was 60–70 yuan in 2007 for most cities,

Figure 8.8   Average Per Capita Health Expenditure by Income Quintile and Urban-Rural Difference, 2007

yuan

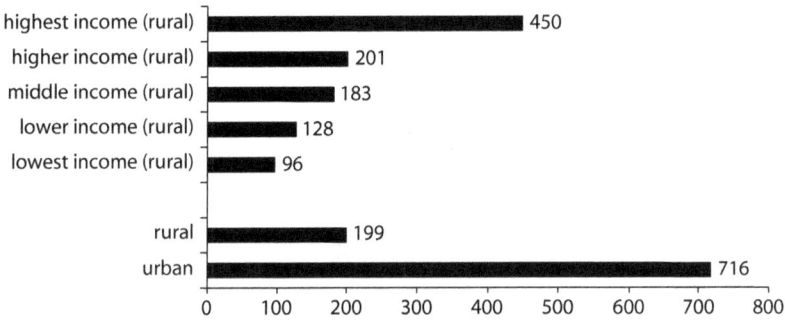

Source: Guangdong Department of Household Survey, National Bureau of Statistics 2007.

whereas it was over 200 yuan for Dongguan and Foshan. Generally, higher insurance premiums imply higher reimbursement rates and better financial protections for the insured, which in turn tend to push up the utilization of services.

Gap in Capacity for Provision of Health Services

Another important factor affecting health outcomes and service utilization is the availability and quality of services when people need them. In poor and remote areas, there is often a shortage of essential resources for health services, such as qualified staff, drugs, or necessary equipment. This undoubtedly influences the use and quality of the services. An initial review by the study shows a significant regional gap in the capacity for service delivery across the province.

First, there is clearly regional disparity in the infrastructure of rural health facilities. The township health centers (THCs) in the PRD area obviously have more beds, bigger facilities, and better medical equipment than those in the less developed areas. While the difference should not come as a surprise, the magnitude is significant (table 8.1).

Second, there is also clearly regional disparity in the density of the supply of health professionals among different municipalities and regions in Guangdong province. Overall, Guangdong has 1.4 physicians per 1,000 people—lower than the density of 2.0 per 1,000 in Zhejiang province, one of the most developed provinces in China (figure 8.9). Moreover, out of the 21 municipalities in Guangdong province, 8 have lower physician

Table 8.1   Disparities in Facility Infrastructure of THCs

Region	Number of beds per 1,000 rural population	Average business area (m²)	Number of pieces of medical equipment valued at over 10,000 yuan
PRD	2.44	5,951	36
Two wings and northern mountainous area	0.79	1,969	8

Source: Guangdong provincial research report for this study, forthcoming.

Figure 8.9   Physician Density across Municipalities and Regions, 2007

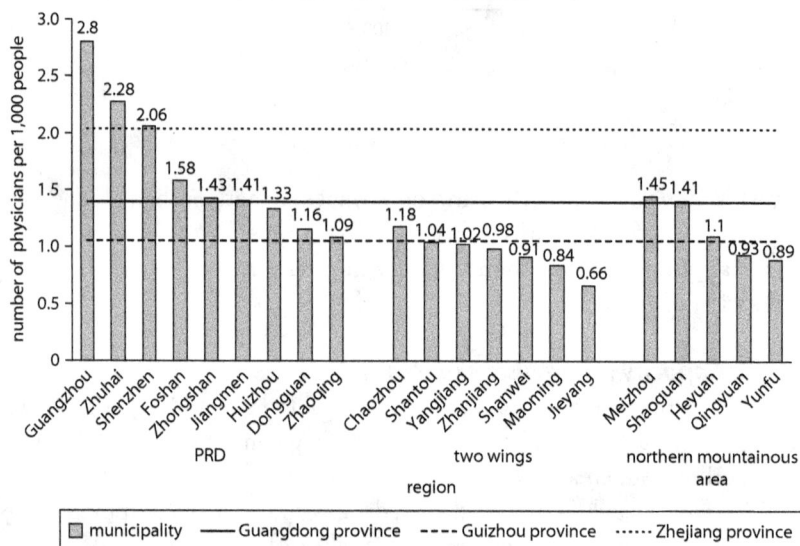

Sources: China Health Statistical Yearbook 2007. Ministry of Health; China Publisher of China's Concord Medical University 2008 and Guangdong Health Statistical Yearbook 2007; Guangdong Health Bureau, Huacheng Publisher 2008.

density than the mountainous neighboring province of Guizhou—one of the least developed provinces in China—and the majority of these 8 municipalities are in the east and west wing areas.

The density is lower, and more important, the quality of the health professionals in the less developed areas is also inadequate. In Guangdong, only about one-third of the health workers in THCs are accredited as physicians or physician assistants, a required qualification for being able to prescribe drugs. As can be seen from figure 8.10, only 10–20 percent of all the health workers in the lagging areas (non-PRD

Figure 8.10   Quality of Health Workers across Municipalities and Regions, 2007

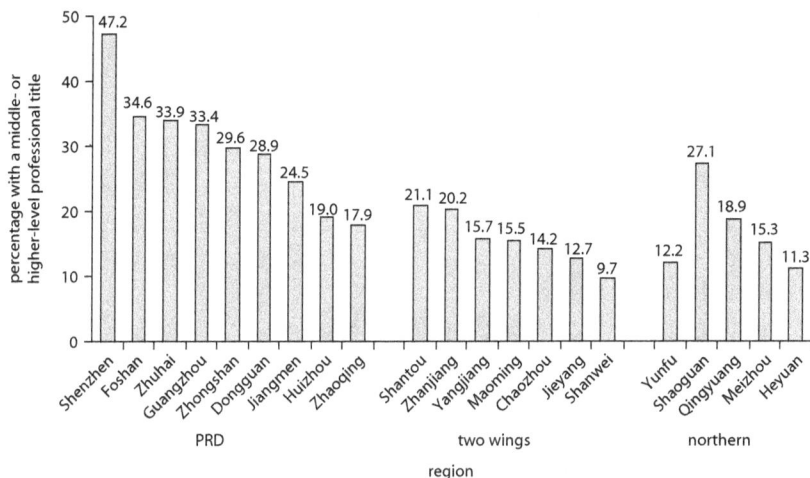

Source: Guangdong Health Statistics Yearbook 2007; Guangdong Health Bureau.

areas) have a middle-or higher-level professional title. The majority have only primary qualifications.

Summary

The challenges Guangdong is facing are clearly substantial, based on the above review. First, there are not only regional disparities in Guangdong with regard to health status, sanitation and hygienic conditions, health service utilization, health service provision capacity, and people's ability to pay for the services; the disparities are also significant in their magnitude.

Second, these significant disparities have disappointed people's expectations of Guangdong as the frontrunner of social and economic development in the country. Compared with Zhejiang province, another developed province in China, Guangdong has fallen behind on many indicators. Moreover, the indicators of some lagging areas are even lower than those in Guizhou, one of the least developed provinces in China.

Steps have been taken in Guangdong under the broad context of the Chinese government's health sector reforms since 2003—notably, the New Rural Cooperative Medical Scheme, the Medical Assistance scheme, the new Urban Resident Basic Medical Insurance scheme, and increased investment in lower-level health facilities. The government has been making efforts to address the inequality in health outcomes and improve access to health services.

Guangdong has planned to invest one billion yuan each year to renovate 100 township health centers. Another significant initiative of the Guangdong government is to provide direct provincial fiscal transfer to support THCs and village clinics. Since 2007, the provincial government has been providing 10,000 yuan per village to subsidize the services of a village doctor and 12,000 yuan for staff for the township health centers (the staff number is decided based on 10 staff per 100,000 population covered). Those are all important steps in the right direction and have generated initial impact.

Aiming at finding possible causes for the disparity and exploring possible ways of reducing it, the chapter will next examine current practices in the three major areas including health financing (resources mobilization and allocation), health protection, and service delivery. Recommendations for reducing the regional disparity, including international best practices and domestic reform initiatives, will be provided, and possible options for improvement will be summarized.

Resource Mobilization and Allocation

The first area to be examined is financial input to the health service. Health financing typically comes from three main resources: individual out-of-pocket payment, social insurance schemes, and government health spending (Gottret and Schieber 2006, 4); in Guangdong, collective economy has also contributed to the health financing pool. For example, some affluent townships provide subsidies to their residents to pay for better insurance coverage. In the context of lagging areas, first, the local residents' ability to pay is obviously low, and financing services through user charges is clearly restrained by what the local population can afford—this has been proved by the survey data shown in figure 8.8. Second, due to the inability to pay, the families in the lagging areas, especially the poor ones, are more prone to the devastating consequences of health shock. They usually have to sell their assets or fall into deep debt to pay for health services, which calls for increased financial protection to prevent them from impoverishment. Third, government health spending usually comes from different levels of government, including the central, provincial, municipal, and county levels. The central government has significantly increased its spending on health; however, the main responsibilities still fall on the shoulders of the local government. How much the local government can put into health is closely linked with its local economic development. In lagging areas, the local government's health spending is constrained by its ability to generate adequate revenues.

Government Health Funding

The chapter will now examine two of the three resources for health financing. This section will focus on the financial input from the government, especially on the intergovernmental fiscal transfer, and the question of how to improve the effectiveness of the health insurance programs will be examined in the next section on social protection. The chapter will not look at the central government input, as central fiscal transfer targets the poor and less developed provinces, and what Guangdong has received from the central government is relatively minimal.

Overall, total health expenditures represented 3.17 percent of the total GDP of Guangdong in 2006, which was lower than the national average of 4.67 percent. The Guangdong government's health spending has been increasing steadily in the past several years. Total government health spending in 2006 accounted for 2.64 percent of total government expenditure—higher than the national average of 1.8 percent, but lower than the health spending of Zhejiang province, which was 3.54 percent (Zhejiang Health Bureau 2006). Also in 2006, 16.8 percent of the total health expenditure of Guangdong was from government input; 38.1 percent was from social insurance, enterprises, and other public resources; and 45.1 percent was from individual out-of-pocket payment. Out-of-pocket payment was lower than the national average, which was over 52 percent, and about the same as out-of-pocket payment in Fujian (45.5 percent) and Tianjing (45.6 percent); apparently, Guangdong's residents paid relatively less out of pocket for their health services than residents of some of the other provinces. This was largely attributable to the higher contribution of social insurance, enterprises, or, in the case of Guangdong, the collective economy—the percentage out of total health expenditure was 29.9 percent in 2006 for the whole country, whereas it was 38.1 percent for Guangdong.

Although 45.1 percent was lower than the national average for out-of-pocket payment, it was significantly higher than the average in upper-middle-income countries, which was 36.3 percent in 2002 (Gottret and Schieber 2006, 41). The relative higher percentage of out-of-pocket expenditure deserves the special attention of the provincial government of Guangdong, because the higher the share of out-of-pocket expenditure is to total health expenditure, the larger is the share of the population who find health care services unaffordable, and thus are left out. The possible options to reduce the share of out-of-pocket expenditure are to increase the share of government input or increase the share of health insurance out of total health expenditure, or both. As a matter of fact, the Guangdong government's health spending has been relatively lower (in percentage, not in real value) than that of Fujian and Tianjing, and lower than the national average in recent years (as seen in table 8.2). Therefore, there seems to be room for the Guangdong government to increase its share of total health expenditure.

Coming to local government, in 2006 the municipal governments in the lagging areas seemed to have devoted higher percentages of their government expenditure to health than did the developed areas (figure 8.11). The percentages for the majority of the cities in the PRD area were lower than the provincial average of 4 percent. The health spending of the local government should have included the portion of the provincial general fiscal transfer that had been spent on health, plus the local government's own spending on health.

When one looks at the data on per capita health spending across regions, a different trend is observed (figure 8.12). The per capita health spending in the PRD region in 2006 was much higher than in the two wings and the northern mountainous area. For instance, Shenzhen, one of the richest cities in the province, spent only 3.7 percent of its total government expenditure on health, but per capita health spending amounted to 247 yuan, the highest among all municipalities; whereas in Shanwei, one of the poorest cities in Guangdong, per capita government health spending was only 19 yuan.

It is notable that the poorer cities tend to have lower per capita government spending on health, but they have spent quite a large share of government budget on health. In this sense, there is not much room for the poor cities to increase health spending so as to catch up with the

Table 8.2   Government Health Spending as a Percentage of Total Health Expenditure

	2001	2002	2003	2004	2005	2006
China	16.0	15.7	17.0	17.0	17.9	18.1
Guangdong province	21.7	20.8	17.3	17.1	15.3	16.8
Tianjing province	17.2	16.6	19.2	18.8	16.9	19.4
Fujian province	18.6	18.3	20.6	20.7	23.4	20.8

Sources: China National Health Accounts report 2007, China National Health Economics Institute and Guangdong Provincial Health Account (internal data).

Figure 8.11   Government Health Spending as a Percentage of Total Government Expenditure, 2006

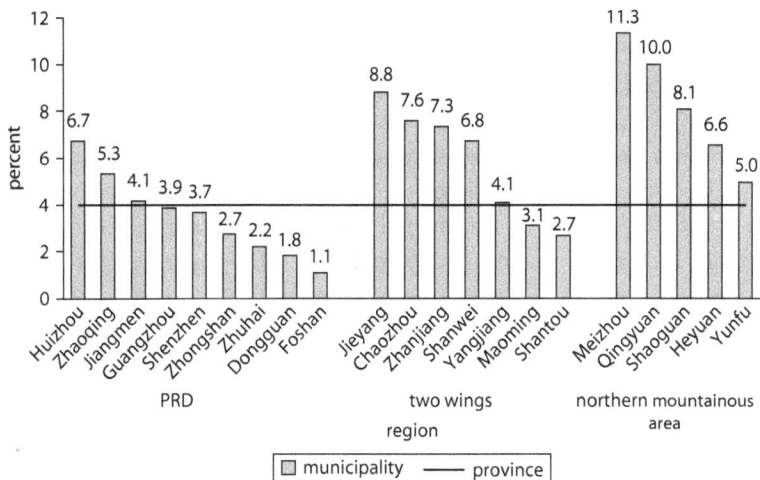

Sources: Guangdong Health Statistical Yearbook 2007; Guangdong Provincial Health Bureau; Guangdong Statistical Yearbook 2007; Guangdong Statistics Bureau.

Figure 8.12   Per Capita Government Health Spending, 2006
(based on the number of residents)

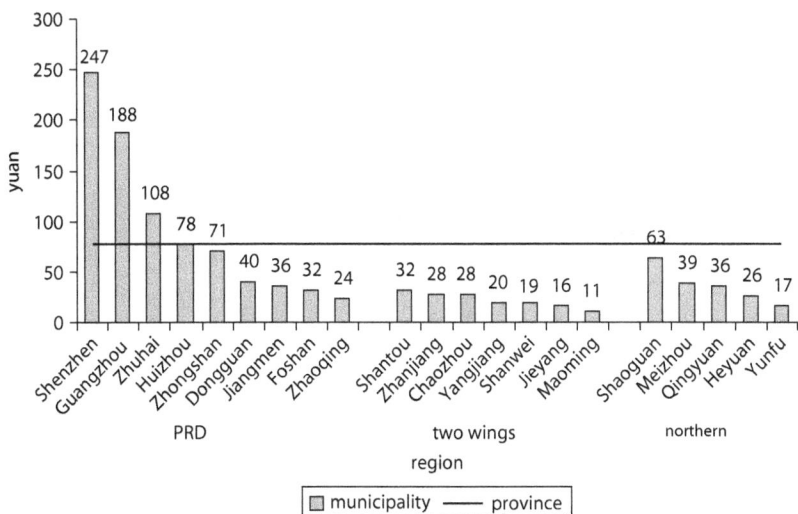

Source: Guangdong Health Statistical Yearbook 2007; Guangdong Provincial Health Bureau.

rich areas. To reduce the regional disparities, the intergovernmental fiscal transfers on health are of great significance.

The relationship is clearly disproportionate between health needs and the resources available among the municipalities (figure 8.13). While cities like Chaozhou, Qingyuan, and Shanwei have worse health indicators (such as infant mortality) than Guangzhou or Shenzhen, they have much less government spending on health available. These inequalities reveal that although the poorer cities and counties receive fiscal transfers from higher levels, the current intergovernmental fiscal transfer hasn't broken the link between local governments' fiscal capacity and their spending on health.

Intergovernmental Fiscal Transfer

In the lagging areas, local government's possible input to health is constrained by the undeveloped local economy and poor government revenue. In this context, the intergovernmental transfer needs to play an important role in redistributing income and promoting balanced development. The preliminary review for the study showed that the intergovernmental fiscal transfer in Guangdong didn't break the link between the local economy and government health spending. Unfortunately, as the Guangdong government is currently in the process of developing provincial health accounts, data on the fiscal transfer between the province and lower levels are not accessible.

Figure 8.13   Where Need Is Greater, Resources Are Less

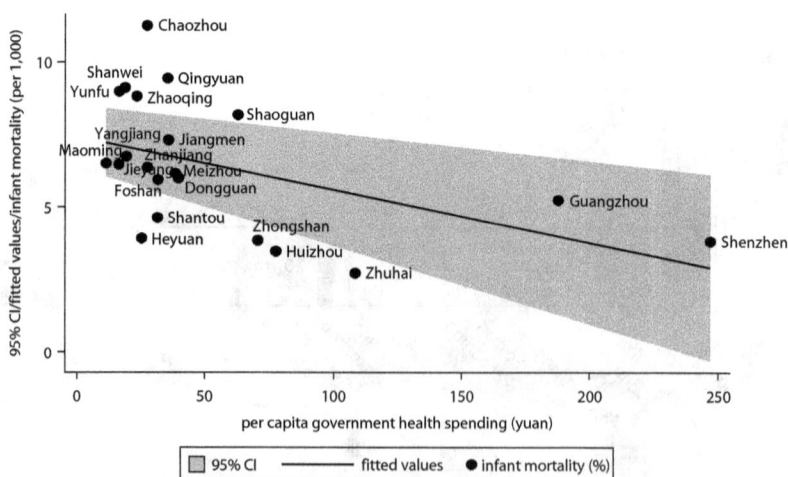

Sources: Guangdong Health Statistical Yearbook 2007; Guangdong Provincial health Bureau; Guangdong Statistical Yearbook 2007; Guangdong Statistics Bureau.

The chapter next tries to examine the current arrangement of inter-governmental fiscal transfer based on the limited data that are available. There are basically two major types of intergovernmental fiscal transfer in Guangdong. One is the earmarked transfer, such as the government sub-sidy for the NRCMS, for immunization, for tuberculosis control services, and so forth. Those funds are appropriated with clear allocation criteria and defined tasks. Another is the general transfer or base transfer. This transfer is a lump-sum subsidy provided to the lower-level government for such purposes as tax rebates, quota subsidies, wage increases, pensions, and so forth. The local government has discretion to decide how to allocate the funds. In short, government spending on health could be from these two types of transfers—a transfer earmarked for health and the allocation of a portion of the general transfer to health.

With respect to how much funding is available for health, it is impor-tant to know how the amount of the fiscal transfer is decided. The gen-eral transfer is determined by a formula that has been evolving over the years (table 8.3). Overall, the signal sent by the formula is clear: the provincial fiscal transfer is directly linked with the economic develop-ment of the counties and their ability to generate tax revenue. There is no indicator of social sector development in the formula. As the government has shifted its policy focus from emphasizing economic development only to emphasizing balanced development and the building of a "harmo-nious society," this policy change should be reflected in the government's fiscal transfer policies.

Table 8.3   Criteria for General Provincial Fiscal Transfer

Years	Government fiscal transfer
2000	Based on the headcounts on the government staff list
2001–03	Based on the total amount of fiscal transfer of the base year, with 8–10 percent increase every year afterward; poverty-stricken counties enjoy a slightly higher increase rate
2004–09	*Incentivized fiscal transfer policy* is linked with county's economic growth: the higher the growth, the more the fiscal transfer.
	Indicator of economic growth is the comprehensive fiscal growth rate (CFGR), calculated as local fiscal revenue + growth rate of tax revenue remitted to central government + growth rate of tax revenue remitted to provincial and municipal government.
	In 2004–07, if CFGR ≥ 18 percent, the county will get additional transfer as reward.
	In 2008–09, if CFGR ≥ 16 percent, the county will get additional transfer as reward.

Source: Guangdong Financial Bureau 2008.

Summary and Recommendations

The following is a summary of the above analysis and steps that might be taken to mobilize resources to support health services in lagging areas:

- Health financing in lagging areas is constrained by people's ability to pay, as well as local government's capacity to generate revenue. In the long run, economic development is the fundamental solution to reducing the regional disparity. In the short run, the solution is income redistribution and more equalized health financing. Short-term solutions in the health sector most commonly take two approaches. One is for the government to redistribute revenue through taxation and disproportionate spending on health care to subsidize lower-income households and regions. The other is for the health insurance schemes to collect revenue in the form of contributions and spend it on health care—again, disproportionately—to subsidize higher-risk and lower-income individuals.

- Considerable room exists for Guangdong's government to equalize further its health financing system. There is room for the government to increase its share of health spending out of total health expenditures. Government spending as a percentage of total health expenditure in Guangdong is low compared with spending at the national level, or in other provinces such as Fujian and Tianjing. Guangdong also spends a lower percentage of its overall government expenditure on health than Zhejiang, another rich province in China. Guangdong has steadily increased its spending on health in the past years. However, the momentum should be kept up, especially in light of the forthcoming implementation of national health system reform.

- The government could examine its current practice with respect to intergovernmental fiscal transfer. The current practice may have weakened the link between the local government's available revenue and its spending on health, but it clearly didn't break it. The lagging areas with the worst health indicators, which need enhanced input, have in fact had many fewer resources available to spend on health. An improved system should be formulated to achieve a much higher degree of equalization.

- A number of measures aimed at reducing the inequality in health services could be considered by the government to improve the efficiency and equity of current and future increased government spending on health:

○ *Better sectoral targeting toward social sector development.* Revise the formula of general fiscal transfer. In addition to linking with economic development, the formula should link the general fiscal transfer with social sector development as well—for example, through reduction of out-of-pocket health expenditure, expansion of social insurance coverage, and so forth. This will provide a fiscal incentive and send a clear signal to local governments, encouraging them to spend more on social sector development.

○ *Better geographic targeting toward the lagging areas.* Increase the fiscal transfer to the lagging areas, especially the poorest. This could be done by giving the poor area a higher weight or rate in the formula. Given the rural and urban difference, another way is to increase resource allocation to the rural areas.

○ *Better targeting of the services that are closer to the poor.* Given that tertiary hospitals are predominantly used by the wealthy and urban populations, the government may want to consider reallocating some of its budget to the primary and secondary facilities (Yazbeck 2009), such as village clinics and township health centers. The same rationale applies to preventive health care and public health services.

Improvement of the Efficiency and Equity of Health Protection Schemes

Health protection (insurance) is an important tool of health financing. It mobilizes resources and pools the health risks of its enrollees. It transfers the unpredictable risk of large expenses into predictable, small, and regular contributions for insurance premiums. Insurance can equalize the health risks of high-risk and low-risk groups. The bigger the pool, the lower the cost and the higher the efficiency. Another function of insurance is to provide risk protection when enrollees get sick. In the context of lagging areas, the residents are more vulnerable to the financial risks of rising medical costs. They are, therefore, in greater need of financial protections.

There are four major health insurance programs in China: the New Rural Cooperative Medical Scheme (NRCMS), the Medical Assistance (MA) scheme, the new Urban Resident Basic Medical Insurance (URBMI) scheme, and the Urban Employee Basic Medical Insurance (UEBMI) scheme. All four health insurance schemes in Guangdong province have been developing rapidly. By 2007, the UEBMI had enrolled 58 percent of all qualified workers with an average per capita contribution of 2,000 yuan. The URBMI pilot has also started in some cities and is being rapidly rolled out to all the cities; in 2009, it covered about 60 percent of the target population. By 2007, the NRCMS program had been rolled out into all the villages, and 84 percent of the rural population had enrolled. The provincial contribution to NRCMS increased from 10 yuan to 35 yuan per person in 2007 and increased again to 61 yuan in 2008. The total NRCMS contribution per person reached 100–120 yuan in 2009 in underdeveloped areas and over 200 yuan in developed regions.

While rapid progress has been made, Guangdong is increasingly facing challenges to its health insurance system. In line with the subject of this book, this chapter will specifically examine the challenges to equity and efficiency.

Challenge of Inequity

The challenge of inequity is evident from the experience of the NRCMS program—the major health insurance system in rural areas. There has been a consistent increase in enrollment in this program in Guangdong since 2002. The enrollment rate in 2007 was 83.8 percent, close to the enrollment rate of the nation, which was 87 percent by the end of 2007. Meanwhile, the geographic inequity in coverage has also been consistent since the program's launch in 2003 (figure 8.14). The enrollment rate

Figure 8.14   Enrollment Rate for NRCMS

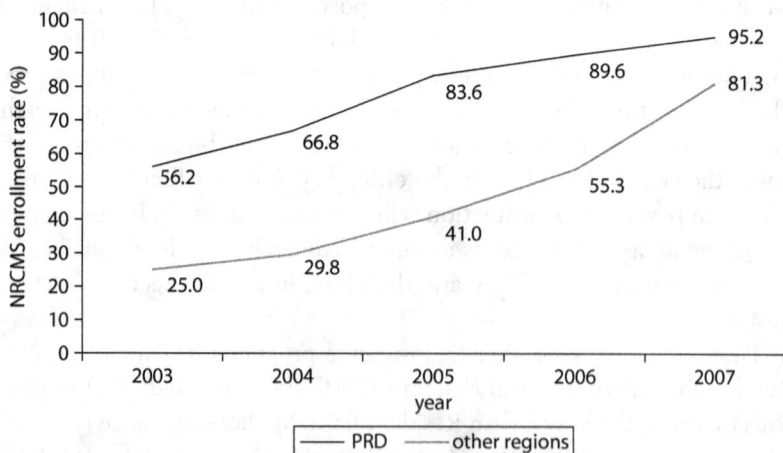

Source: Unpublished data provided to the author by the Guangdong Provincial Health Bureau.

for the PRD area has been significantly higher than in the other regions. Even though the lagging areas were catching up quickly in 2007, the enrollment rate overall was only about half that of the PRD area. While the residents in the lagging areas were in greater need of financial protection from high medical expenses, many of them are still not in the program.

The inequity is evident not only in the breadth of the coverage, but also in the depth of the coverage (figure 8.15). In 2007, the per capita NRCMS contribution reached 200 yuan per person in the rich cities, whereas in the underdeveloped areas, it was about 62 yuan, with 35 yuan coming from provincial subsidies. As a result, the enrollees from the rich cities enjoyed more financial protection from the NRCMS—the real reimbursement rate (after considering deductibles, copayments, ceilings, exemptions, and so forth) for inpatient care was about 46 percent. However, the residents from the lagging areas endured a much higher out-of-pocket payment—only about 28 percent of their inpatient care expenses were reimbursed by NRCMS.

What can be done to address this disparity? Clearly, due to fiscal incapacity, the local governments of poor counties will not be able to raise substantially their contributions to the NRCMS. Two options might be considered. One obvious option would be to raise significantly the

Figure 8.15   Regional Disparity in Per Capita NRCMS Contributions, 2007

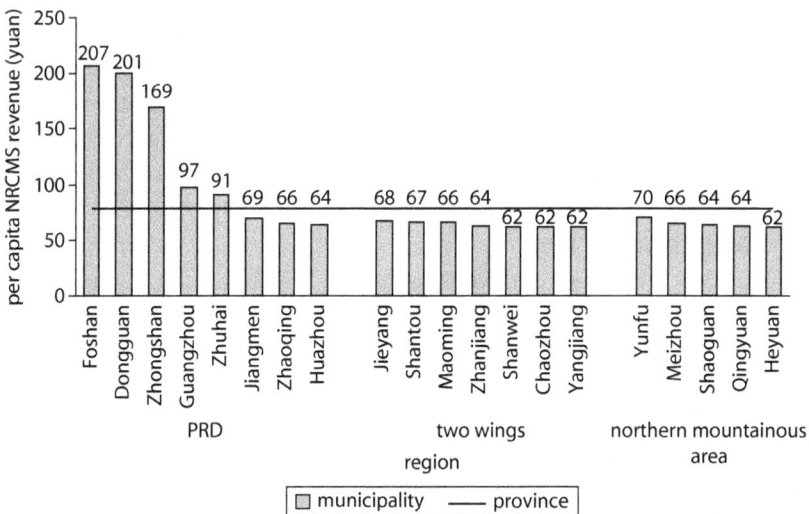

Source: Guangdong Provincial Health Bureau.

provincial government's subsidy to the poor counties to help these counties raise the total revenue of the NRCMS. This will, however, require large subsidies from the provincial government and may call for an increase in the tax rate by the government to generate revenue. In the previous section, we suggested that a feasible way to reduce geographic inequity would be through solidarity, which means the rich help the poor. This leads to the second option: the NRCMS pooling at a higher level.

Currently, the NRCMS is pooled at the county level. Figure 8.16 illustrates what might happen if the NRCMS were pooled at the municipal level or even the provincial level. Figure 8.16, panel a, shows a relatively rich county, with a combined contribution in excess of the provincial average set at 200 yuan. The county in figure 8.16, panel b, is poorer; its total contribution falls short of the average budget of 200 yuan. If the contributions of both counties are pooled together at a higher level, then the surplus from the rich county can offset, at least in large part, the shortfall of the poor county, while at the same time the two counties can enjoy the same or nearly the same coverage from the NRCMS.

The higher-level pooling not only increases equity through cross-subsidization and unified coverage, but can also increase efficiency and lower administrative costs through scale of economy and improved leverage for contracting and purchasing. It also has a positive impact on portability and increased labor mobility. Both are important merits, given the large number of migrant workers in Guangdong. The national government has already called for higher-level pooling and unification of different health insurance schemes in its national health system reform plan and has set them as goals to be reached by 2020. As the "experimental field of reform for China," Guangdong should consider increasing its insurance pooling level from its current county level to municipal or even provincial level. As the first step, at least the pilot could be conducted in certain areas.

Challenge of Inefficiency

Still in the early stages of development, the health insurance schemes are facing the challenge of inefficiency on a number of fronts. First of all, the funds are fragmented. The three insurance schemes plus MA are managed by three different departments with very limited coordination and information sharing. This fragmentation results in diseconomies of scale, decreases the size of risk pooling, and increases inequity across the schemes (the average per capita contribution is 2,000 yuan for UEBMI, whereas it is only 110 yuan for NRCMS). Second, awareness of cost containment is rising, but the providers are still largely paid by fee for service. Third, the

Figure 8.16   Illustration of Higher-Level Pooling of the NRCMS

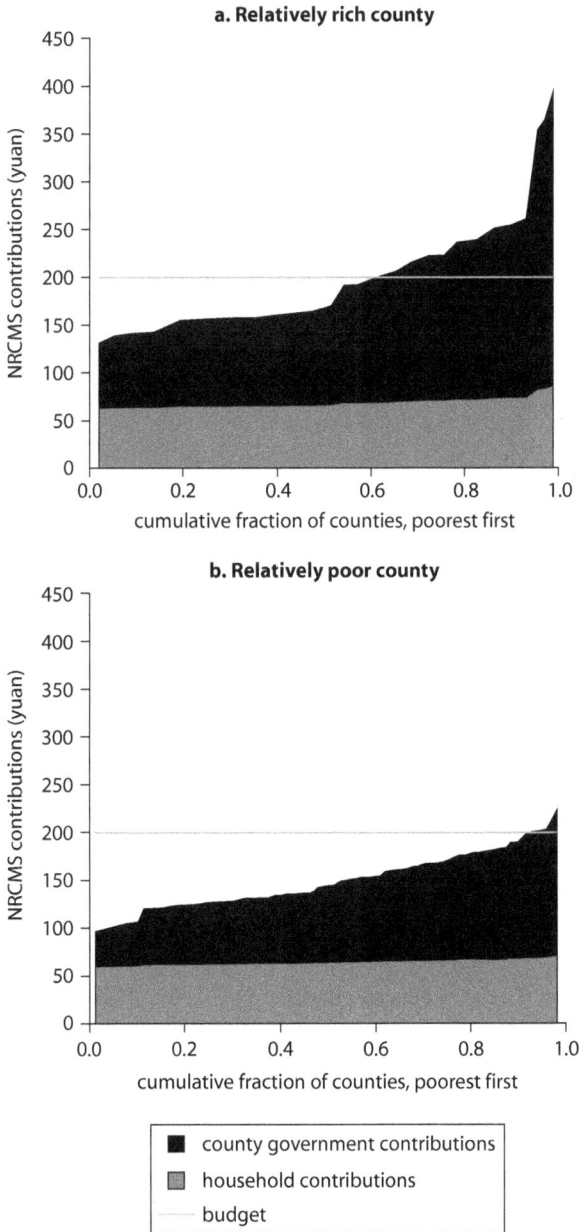

a. Relatively rich county

b. Relatively poor county

■ county government contributions
▨ household contributions
⋯ budget

Source: Wagstaff et al. 2009.

real reimbursement remains low (30 percent, about the same as the national level), even though Guangdong has high per capita revenue relative to the nation. While the enrollees still pay a large portion of their health expenses out of pocket, there are considerable savings of insurance funds in both urban and rural schemes (figure 8.17). The variety presented in figure 8.17 is significant: there is one municipality (Fushan) whose accumulated savings in 2007 was seven times its total contribution collection of the same year; at the same time, another one (Yangjiang) is running under a deficit. The great variation in the fund savings could be attributed to many factors (lack of management capacity, excessive caution to avoid deficits, and so forth). However, there is clearly a need for a better-designed program and a better-designed benefit package.

The majority of the challenges are rooted in the original design and institutional arrangement of the programs and are a problem for the whole nation, not just Guangdong. For example, an individual savings account was designed at the very beginning of the UEBMI scheme to pay for outpatient services for the people insured. The funds in the savings account belong to the individual and are not pooled to cross-subsidize the enrollees. The funds in the saving accounts can be carried over to the next year if not fully used in the current year. It is estimated that a large portion of the current savings in the UEBMI scheme come from the unused funds of individual accounts. Another issue of great concern is the portability of health insurance. Guangdong has a large population of migrant workers, the pooling at county level, and the unportability of the insurance inevitably

Figure 8.17   Accumulated Savings of NRCMS Revenue, 2007

accumulated savings /revenue

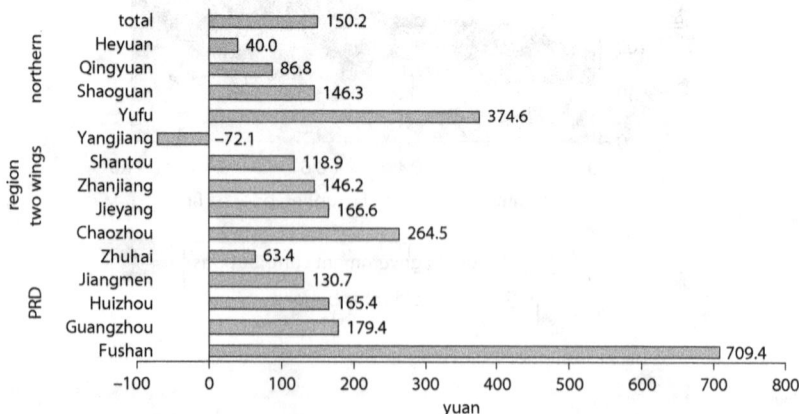

Source: Unpublished data provided by the Guangdong Social Security Bureau.

constrain the mobility of the laborers, which has a negative impact on employment and economic growth.

Government concern over such issues of inefficiency have led to a variety of reforms and pilots taking place in many other provinces to improve the insurance programs. Pilots and explorations have also been seen in Guangdong in recent years. For example, Shunde has started a pilot using capitation to pay service providers; Zhuhai has integrated the URBMI with the NRCMS. Given Guangdong's role as the "experimental field of reform for China," however, and the challenges it is facing in this important area, much more needs to be done to improve the equity and efficiency of the insurance programs in the province.

Medical Assistance Program

MA is a special program in the health safety net of China. It is a very important institutional arrangement in the context of reducing regional disparity and protecting the poor and the vulnerable. In 2003, along with the establishment of NRCMS, MA was set up to protect the poor and vulnerable population. The aim of this program is to provide financial assistance with medical expenses and NRCMS contributions to specific vulnerable populations. The MA budget is financed mostly by central, provincial, and county governments. The target populations for the MA scheme are the poor and disadvantaged groups (typically *Tekun*, *Wubao*, and *Dibao*) and the households who suffer large and potentially impoverishing medical expenses. MA is managed by the Ministry of Civil Affairs at the central level and the Bureau of Civil Affairs at the local levels. According to data from the Ministry of Health, the average assistance provided by MA in rural areas was 420 yuan per claim in 2007.

Guangdong quickly set up the MA program in all its counties. There are two parallel MA programs in Guangdong. One is managed by the Bureau of Civil Affairs, and the funding is mainly from two resources: the county government input (14 percent of the provincial subsistence standard) and the social welfare lottery (2 percent of the total proceeds). In addition, the provincial government provides earmarked fiscal transfer to the less developed areas (20 million yuan in 2007). The other program is managed by the Bureau of Health and gets its budget from the government.

MA data could not be obtained from the provincial Bureau of Civil Affairs, but the data from the central Ministry of Civil Affairs and the data collected in the field investigation suggest that the MA program in Guangdong is facing significant challenges. The first challenge seems to be the low level of financial assistance the MA program has provided to its beneficiaries in Guangdong compared with those in other provinces (figure 8.18). In 2007, the MA program in Guangdong provided on average 200 yuan per person to its beneficiaries in need, ranked as the fifth lowest in the country. This was also very low in comparison with catastrophic health expenditures.

The second challenge is that the MA program funds in Guangdong seem to be seriously underdisbursed. The data for overall disbursement of the province as well as for the local governments were not provided, but table 8.4 shows the data collected from one of the poverty-stricken

Figure 8.18   Per Capita MA Assistance across Provinces, 2007

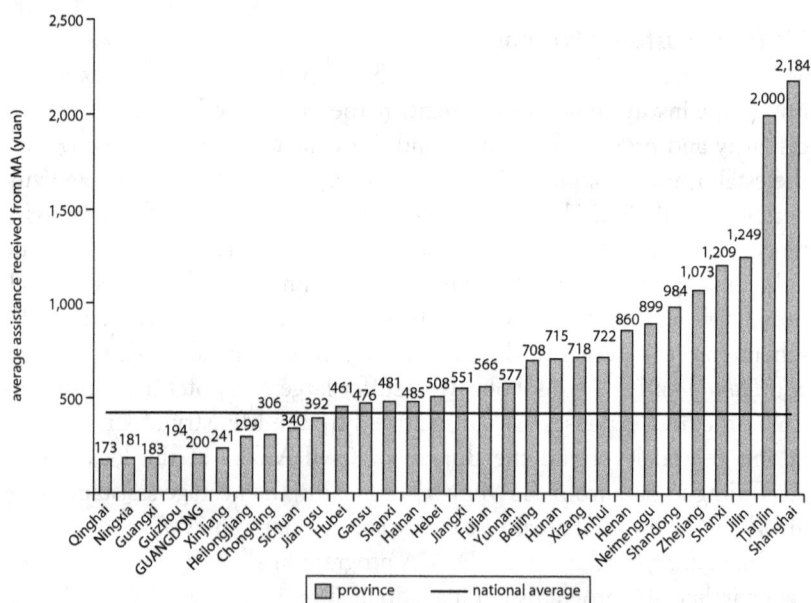

Source: Ministry of Civil Affairs 2007.

Table 8.4   MA Program Disbursement for a Poverty-Stricken County

Year	Beneficiaries	Persons subsidized	Revenue (10,000 yuan)	Expenditures (10,000 yuan)	Surplus (10,000 yuan)
2003	9,677	1,310	151.0	30.0	121.0
2004	117,248	54	158.6	13.5	145.1
2005	20,785	145	145.1	5.3	139.8
2006	21,421	1,680	199.8	50.0	149.8
2007	27,213	119	236.8	20.0	216.8

Source: Provided by the county government.

counties we visited. Clearly, the majority of the funding was left unused. This could be partially due to the extra caution the program managers have exercised in fear of running into deficit. On the other hand, this also implies the need for a better-designed scheme and an improved benefit package. One obvious question to ask is whether there is a monitoring and evaluation system to monitor the implementation of the program, as clearly the issue of underdisbursement has existed for years.

The third challenge is building the capacity of the management teams for the MA program. MA is a relatively new responsibility for the Bureau of Civil Affairs. The traditional skill mix in the bureau did not include the skills specifically desired for MA management, such as actuarial skills or knowledge of the health system, medical science, and provider payment.

Fourth, is it efficient and necessary to retain two parallel MA programs in the province that are managed by different bureaus? Actually, for the MA program per se, questions have already been raised about whether there is a need to have a stand-alone MA program that is managed by a separate ministry. If one considers that the beneficiaries of the MA program include only a special group of enrollees of health insurance, the program could be easily pooled with and managed under the health insurance scheme. The MA beneficiaries could enjoy the same benefits within the insurance scheme, with premiums and copayments waived and extra reimbursement available when catastrophic health expenditures occur.

Summary and Recommendations

The following are the key observations and recommendations for enhancing the health insurance schemes:

- Health insurance is an important tool for health financing. It mobilizes health resources and pools the health risks of its enrollees. Health insurance provides financial protection to its enrollees when health expenditures occur. In the context of lagging areas, health protection programs are more important: the poor residents are more vulnerable to the financial risks of rising medical costs and are therefore in greater need of financial protection.

- Guangdong is facing challenges in terms of geographic inequity in insurance coverage and levels of benefits. One possible solution is to increase substantially the fiscal transfer by provincial government to the lagging areas. This, however, will require a substantial increase of government revenues—by imposing taxes on the rich and the more developed areas.

- Another option is solidarity on higher-level pooling and cross-subsidization. Higher-level pooling not only increases equity through cross-subsidization and unified coverage, but also can increase efficiency and lower the administrative costs. Solidarity, however, will likely encounter resistance, given that in Guangdong, the rich counties are largely backed up by collective economy or private business and may not be willing to cross-subsidize the poor counties. The national government health reform plan, however, has called for higher-level pooling and unification of the different health insurance schemes and has set them as goals of the reform. As the "experimental field of reform for China," Guangdong may consider higher-level pooling for its health insurance schemes, or at least conduct a pilot program in certain areas.

- There is a clear need to improve continuously the management and governance of the insurance schemes and the MA scheme. Addressing that need will include a better actuarial modeling for the programs and an improved design of the benefit package, including, for example, outpatient risk pooling, portability of benefits for migrant workers, and more effective use of insurance funds. Even without further government spending, the residents in Guangdong can benefit substantially through merely increasing the efficiency of current health spending and health insurance schemes.

- Controlling escalating medical costs is crucial for any sustainable insurance scheme. Shifting from fee-for-service to prospective provider payment systems and using service purchasing and contracting are strongly recommended.

- The implementation of pilots and reforms needs to be closely monitored and evaluated, so that any issues that emerge can be solved quickly, and any lessons learned can be disseminated.

There have been good reform initiatives in Guangdong and in other provinces in China that could provide lessons and models of best practice for reform in Guangdong. For example, Chongqing, Jiangsu, Sichuan, and Zhejiang have started piloting unified administration, greater pooling, and integration of different schemes. The MA model in the Yubei district of Chongqing described in box 8.1 is something to which Guangdong could refer in reforming its own MA scheme.

Box 8.1

MA Pilot in the Yubei District of Chongqing Municipality

Yubei is a district of Chongqing with a rural population accounting for 67 percent of its total population. Since the establishment of the MA program in 2005, Yubei has been pragmatic and innovative in institutional development, and the Yubei model has become the national model for best practice in MA implementation.

The Yubei model's success stems from several characteristics.

First, Yubei expanded its coverage from the most vulnerable (*Dibao, Wubao,* and *Youfu*) to the near poor and non-MA beneficiaries through provisional assistance. The total beneficiaries identified comprised around 20,000 persons in rural areas, accounting for 3 percent of the total rural population, and around 30,000 persons in urban areas, accounting for 9 percent.

Second, Yubei established a multisource financing mechanism. The funds are from government at different levels (including central, municipal, and district); proceeds of the welfare lottery; and social donations. In particular, the municipal government's input has increased steadily and substantially.

Third, different from most MA programs in the country, Yubei's model provides a much wider range of financial assistance. It pays for individual NRCMS contributions and, in some cases, for deductibles and copayments for beneficiaries. It also covers outpatient services, especially those relating to noncommunicable diseases. Among *Wubao* beneficiaries, people with severe disabilities as well as elderly people who are over 80 years of age can be reimbursed for their outpatient services up to 300 yuan per year. For the rest of MA beneficiaries, out-of-pocket (OOP) outpatient expenses can be reimbursed 50 percent, with a ceiling of 30 yuan per year. Inpatient services are also covered: if total inpatient care expenditure is over 1,000 yuan, after reimbursement by NRCMS, 100 percent of OOP expenditure is reimbursed by MA. If total inpatient care expenditure is between

(continued)

Box 8.1 (*continued*)

1,000 and 3,000 yuan, after reimbursement by NRCMS, 60 percent of OOP expenditure is reimbursed by MA. In addition, 20 percent of the total MA funds are kept separately as a fund for provisional medical assistance for the poor population who otherwise are not qualified as MA beneficiaries; their inpatient care can be reimbursed at 80 percent of the standard described earlier.

Fourth, the Yubei model has additional charity medical assistance, funded with 20 percent of charitable contributions received by the District Charities Association. Beneficiaries still facing large health expenditures after all types of MA have been used can apply for further reimbursement from charity medical assistance.

Finally, the Yubei model allows health service providers to be reimbursed on site. The MA management information system has been built into the existing NRCMS management information system. All MA beneficiaries are entered into the system upon being identified by the Bureau of Civil Affairs as MA beneficiaries. When it is time to pay at the service site, the system translates the total service expenditure into three parts: NRCMS reimbursement, MA reimbursement, and OOP expenditure. The MA beneficiaries need only pay the OOP portion on site.

Strengthening of Health Services Delivery Capacity in the Lagging Areas

Health service providers are an important component of a health system. The capacity of the service delivery system is critical in determining whether a resident can access and receive good-quality health services. The following will examine the existing gaps and propose suggestions for supply-side strengthening.

Identifying the Gaps

The accessibility of health services in the lagging areas is often hampered by the unavailability of health facilities or the shortage of essential resources, including necessary equipment, drugs, and qualified health staff. The preliminary review and the field visit in Guangdong indicated that there are significant gaps on the supply side in the rural and less developed areas in Guangdong.

First, there is a gap in the financing of services at the lower level. The health facilities obtain their income mainly from three resources: the government, health insurance, and user charges. As discussed in the prior section, the real reimbursement rate of NRCMS is about 30 percent in the lagging areas, and in most places, NRCMS covers inpatient care only. That means the insurance scheme can only cover about 30 percent of the inpatient service expenses of the insured population. In terms of the government input, among the several township health centers we visited in the lagging areas of Guangdong, the majority received no financial input from the county government, or only a small amount of input occasionally on capital investment as of 2007. There was one THC that received funding from the county government to cover 80 percent of the basic salaries of staff. Clearly, in the lagging areas of Guangdong, the THCs are mainly relying on user charges to generate revenue. While the ability of the local population to pay is constrained in lagging areas, most of the THCs are struggling to maintain services.

Second, in this situation, the THC has no funds to invest in the renovation of the facility or the procurement of necessary equipment, let alone upgrading or expansions. As shown in table 8.1, there is clearly a significant gap in infrastructure and equipment in the THCs in the lagging areas. As a matter of fact, 7 out of 981 townships in Guangdong have no THC, and 380 THCs don't meet the minimum requirement of total construction area according to the national THC construction standard. In addition, 632 villages in the lagging areas have no village clinics.

Third, there is a significant gap in human resources in the lagging areas in terms of both quantity and quality (figures 8.9, 8.10, and 8.19). Physician density in the lagging areas is lower than the provincial average, and some of the municipalities even have lower physician density than the mountainous neighboring province of Guizhou. Over half of the health workers in the THCs have educations equivalent only to secondary technical school. Out of a total of 1,600 village doctors in Guangdong, 44 percent have never received formal medical training, and only 5 percent have received training at junior college.

Guangdong's Latest Policy Initiatives to Address Supply-Side Inequality

A series of important steps have been taken by the Guangdong government to address the supply gaps in the lagging areas. First, the government has increased its investment in local-level health facilities. In its "10-Year Primary Care Development Plan" of 2003, the provincial government proposed investing 150 million yuan each year to be used in the renovation of and equipment procurement for THCs. One significant initiative of the Guangdong government is to provide direct provincial

Figure 8.19   Education of the Village Doctors of Guangdong

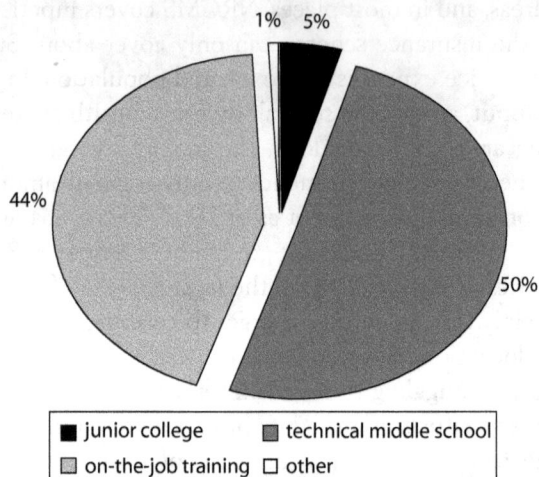

Source: Guangdong Provincial Health Statistics Yearbook 2006; Guangdong Provincial Health Bureau.

fiscal transfer to support THCs and village clinics. Since 2007, the provincial government has provided 10,000 yuan per village to subsidize the services of a village doctor, and 12,000 yuan per 10 staff members for the THCs (staff number is decided based on 10 staff members per 100,000 population covered). Two government documents were issued in April 2008 on the "Management of the Village Health Facility" and the "Management of the Township Health Center." The tasks and functions of the respective health facilities were clearly defined in these two documents.

One issue that particularly concerns the government is how to attract and retain qualified health staff for the rural and remote areas. This supply gap is of particular importance, but at the same time, it is very hard to address. The government has taken several measures to tackle this issue, for example, providing direct financial subsidies to the health workers working in the poor and remote areas. Selective recruitment, a widely used strategy in China, was also adopted by Guangdong. Although these measures have made a somewhat positive impact, the problem remains unsolved.

What Government Can Do to Address the Gaps in Service Delivery

As discussed, health facilities in the lagging areas face the challenge of financing gaps. As they struggle to survive, there is no scope for them to upgrade their infrastructure, to strengthen their service capacity, to provide training for their staff, or to recruit more qualified doctors or nurses. What can government do to address this financing gap and to ensure the availability of basic health services in the underserved areas?

Health services can be financed by the government through demand-side subsidy or supply-side subsidy. Purchasing health services or investing in health insurances such as NRCMS and MA constitutes demand-side financing, as it subsidizes residents and patients. Furnishing health service providers with direct resources, such as budget for salaries, facility construction, and equipment, is supply-side financing. There are several ways in which the government can provide financial support:

- *Demand-side financing.* One approach to demand-side financing would be to expand the breadth and depth of the insurance coverage, with more people covered, more services included, and a substantial portion of medical expenses reimbursed. The expanded health insurance would bring more income to the health facilities through increased service utilization. Although government is clearly moving in this direction, there is still a long way to go, given that the current reimbursement rate is only 30 percent.

- *Service purchasing.* The government can link its financial input with the services it would like to deliver to its citizens, such as public health services like tuberculosis control, immunization, maternal and child services, noncommunicable disease control, and so forth. The financial input can be provided on the basis of capitation. For example, health providers can obtain an average of 15 yuan per resident in the catchment areas of their health facilities for the public health services they provide. What is important for this approach is that the financial input be closely linked with the service delivered; thus, a performance evaluation mechanism needs to be developed and put into place. The Guangdong government's initiative to provide 10,000 yuan per village to subsidize the services of a village doctor and 12,000 yuan per 10 staff members for the THCs (with the number of staff based on 10 staff members per 100,000 population covered) is a good step in this direction. It is not very clear, however, whether this financial input is linked with the performance and service delivered by the providers. The policy would have more impact if it could be linked with performance.

- *Supply-side financing.* With well-functioning demand-side financing, the costs of services delivered by service providers are fully recovered by payments from users, who are covered by various financing programs. This includes costs of fixed assets such as buildings, equipment, and so forth, as well as the true market costs of health workers. As a result, health service providers are able to finance their own investments and pay market-level compensation to their staffs. However, when demand-side financing is not functioning well and health services are underpriced in relation to real costs, health service providers have a hard time raising funds to finance investments, especially in poor areas. This seems to be the case in Guangdong—although the rapidly expanding NRCMS and other insurance schemes have resulted in increased service utilization, health care providers still cannot be fully covered by the payment of insurance. While continuing to subsidize health insurance, the government might consider investing in the necessary capital investment in the short run (two to three years) to ensure the adequate service capability of the providers in the lagging areas. A fund for capital investment of health facilities in lagging areas could be established for the renovation or reconstruction of health facilities, as well as for the purchase of basic equipment. The national State Bond Program has set a good example.

A large number of strategies have been applied domestically and internationally to address the human resource shortage in rural and remote areas. The most widely used approaches can be grouped into three categories: financial incentives and nonfinancial incentives, compulsory or regulatory policy, and selection and education policies.

- *Financial incentives and nonfinancial incentives.* Almost all countries offer extra monetary compensation to health workers working in rural areas, such as higher salaries, bonuses, extra subsidies, hardship allowances, and so forth. In some countries, with bonuses and subsidies, the salaries of rural health workers can be 1.5 to 2 times higher than those of urban health workers so as to make working in rural areas sufficiently attractive. In some provinces in China, rural health professionals get extra hardship allowances and slightly higher salaries, but together they can hardly compare with the incomes of health professionals practicing in urban settings. In addition to monetary compensation, indirect financial incentives are used—for example, scholarships, health insurance, and pensions. The provision of pensions and health insurance to health professionals in THCs as well as to village doctors has been implemented in some provinces of China. It is usually very hard to define how big the financial incentive should be to make it attractive, and they might in some cases become very expensive. Nonfinancial incentives are often offered as well to provide a more comprehensive package. Nonfinancial incentives mostly address the issues of satisfaction and career development and can take many forms, including opportunities for training, opportunities for professional development, recognition from peers and society, or access to professional networks, as well as housing and the education of children.

- *Compulsory or regulatory policy.* The government can use its tool of regulation to fill the service gap in rural and remote areas. The most common practice is to require health professionals to work one or several years in a rural setting or a certain geographic area. Typically, compulsory services are linked with punishment if the commitment of service is not met. For example, in Japan, newly qualified physicians must either practice in rural settings or pay back tuition that has been financed by the government. In some provinces of China, the government requires health professionals from urban hospitals to work in rural areas for at least half a year to a year before they can be promoted to a higher professional level. While compulsory service may seem appealing and feasible in many countries, it is not a silver bullet. International experience shows that compulsory service is effective in reducing rural vacancies in the short term, but the impact on long-term retention is less effective. Many of the graduates leave the rural area after they complete the required period.

- *Selection and education policies.* Evidence from many countries shows that health professionals raised in rural areas are more likely to work and stay in rural areas (World Bank). Similarly, students with a commitment to work in rural areas also tend to choose and stay in the rural areas. Therefore, some medical or nursing schools recruit students from rural areas and provide tuition exemptions or reductions for those students on the condition that they commit to work in the rural areas after graduation. This approach is widely used in many countries, including Australia, Indonesia, and the United States. Many provinces in China have also adopted this policy for years.

Many countries, rich and poor, face the challenge of recruiting and retaining health professionals to work in rural and lagging areas (box 8.2).

Box 8.2

Practice on Retention of Rural Health Workers

Direct financial incentives, such as rural bonuses and hardship allowances, offer monetary compensation for rural employment. Nearly every country with rural shortages has used them, including Australia, Canada, Indonesia, South Africa, Thailand, the United States, Vietnam, Zambia, and Zimbabwe, among others. With the bonuses, rural doctors' and nurses' salaries can be 1.5 to 2 times higher than those of their urban counterparts. For example, South Africa implemented the Rural Allowance and the Scarce Skills Allowance, which increased rural health workers' salaries by 8–22 percent. A rigorous evaluation of the policy suggested that it had a positive impact on retention—28–35 percent of health workers who received these allowances believed it affected their career plans for the next year. Another key finding of the study was that the health workers still ranked career opportunities, job satisfaction, and the opportunity for postgraduate education along with financial benefits as the top priorities when choosing where to work. This suggests a potentially more effective strategy, which is to combine financial incentives with policies addressing these nonfinancial priorities.

Several countries have developed rural incentive packages that combine career, work, family, and lifestyle incentives. In remote areas of Zambia, clinics provided staff transport, group performance incentive schemes, salary bonuses, and renovations of clinics and housing (including installation of solar electricity). A study revealed that 67 percent of existing health workers had been retained, but many problems still needed to be addressed, including road improvements and access to amenities.

Different countries have adopted different approaches to address the issue. As the empirical data show, there are many factors affecting their choice of whether to work in the lagging areas. The factors range from income, health insurance, job satisfaction, career development, or working environment to job opportunities for the spouse and education for the children. To solve this complex problem would require developing a comprehensive recruitment and retention strategy. While an individual policy (such as financial incentives or compulsory services) can be helpful, international experience suggests a more comprehensive and coordinated strategy, with multipronged measures (Lindelow).

Summary and Recommendations
The findings and recommendations regarding health service gaps in lagging geographic areas can be summarized as follows:

- In the context of lagging areas, although the NRCMS has improved the service utilization of low-level health facilities, they still can barely survive by generating revenues through user charges. This situation calls for the government to assume responsibility for ensuring adequate service supply in the lagging areas. The government's support can be provided through different approaches, including direct supply-side subsidy and demand-side financing. The latest government policy initiatives of Guangdong are good first steps.

- In the long run, with the expansion of health protection schemes and purchasing of services by government, service utilization in the lagging areas will increase. The costs of services delivered by service providers will be fully covered by payments of the users.

- In the short run, however, the government may need to consider providing financial support on capital investment to the lower-level health facilities, such as township health centers. A fund for capital investment could be established for this purpose. The national State Bond Program would be a good example.

- In any case, the first thing the government should consider is to conduct a problem assessment. The health bureau may need to do a stock-taking investigation to learn what and where the gaps are in terms of qualified staff, necessary equipment, and the required skill mixture. It will also be important to develop monitoring indicators to track the availability of critical services and to develop maps showing the distribution of the service gaps. The data on what factors affect the choice of health professionals on whether to work in rural areas would also need to be collected so that the set of policies on recruitment and retention can be developed based on those factors.

- A wide range of strategies has been implemented in many countries to address human resource shortages in lagging areas. International experience suggests that applying individual measures has limited effectiveness. The recommended approach to attracting and retaining health professionals in rural areas is through a coordinated set of measures, which could be any combination of measures including financial incentives, nonfinancial incentives, compulsory service, and recruitment from rural areas.

• There is, nevertheless, also a need to enhance the organization and management of health services, such as performance-based evaluation, quality assurance of health services, and integrated management of THCs and village clinics.

Issues Needing Further Attention and Suggestions for Further Study

When this chapter was developed, some of the important data, such as data on provincial health accounts, intergovernmental transfers, the MA program, and the financing of public health, were either unavailable or inaccessible. The lack of data inevitably limited the scope and depth of the chapter. Nevertheless, obtaining knowledge of the areas with inadequate data is important for the government in formulating its policy framework, and thus these areas deserve continued attention once the data become available. The following studies are therefore suggested for the province to consider conducting in the future:

• *A study on health expenditure and government fiscal transfer on health,* based on ongoing efforts to establish a total provincial health account for Guangdong. The analysis in the present study of government health expenditure and intergovernmental fiscal transfer was based on the limited data provided. Given the poor fiscal capacity of the government in the lagging areas, one would have to rely on intergovernmental fiscal transfer to address regional disparities and inequity. This warrants a close look at government health spending at different levels and at intergovernmental fiscal transfer.

• *A study on health service utilization patterns.* This study found significant disparities in service utilization across cities, but due to the lack of data, it could not go any further in examining people's service-seeking behaviors or the type of providers they used in different regions of the province. Data from the fourth National Health Services Household Survey, conducted in June 2008, are to be available in 2009. This is the perfect time to do a study on health service utilization patterns in different regions of the province.

- *An in-depth study on the management of the health insurance programs,* including UEBMI, NRCMS, and the MA program. A great deal of funding under the insurance schemes is currently available but dormant. In addition, the benefit package, the design of the scheme (such as the family savings account of UEBMI), and the portability issue for the migrant workers all deserve careful review and evaluation.

- *An in-depth study on rural health staffing in the lagging areas,* which may involve work to (1) identify gaps in health staffing in terms of quality, quantity, skill mixture, and so forth; (2) summarize and evaluate experiences and practices, successful or unsuccessful, in recruitment and retention of health workers in rural areas; and (3) survey health workers and medical graduates on their needs, on the reasons they are unwilling to work in rural settings or lagging areas, and on what incentives or policies may attract them to work in rural areas or stay there. This would provide a basis for the government to formulate a comprehensive and coordinated approach to recruiting and retaining qualified health professionals for rural areas.

- *A study on the public health system in Guangdong.* Due to time constraints, the authors of this study were not able to collect sufficient data to support an in-depth analysis of issues in the public health domain. This area is, nevertheless, very important. The provincial health account, which is currently under development, should be a good resource for data on public health financing. It is, however, not very clear whether the provincial health account will provide aggregated and disaggregated data on public health.

- *A study on disparities within regions or municipalities.* This chapter focused almost exclusively on disparities and inequities among municipalities across three main regions of Quangdong—the PRD, the two wings, and the northern mountainous area. Disparities within regions or municipalities could be another important dimension to examine and a focus for a future study.

Notes

1. The data on infant mortality and under-five mortality were provided to the author by the Guangdong government. The data were collected through its regular statistics reporting system.

2. Zhuhai is the only city in the Pearl River Delta area that had a lower hospital delivery rate than the provincial average. Though relatively developed and a frontrunner in health services, Zhuhai has adopted a different monitoring and registration system that has resulted in lower hospital delivery rates.

3. In addition to more use of health services, some other factors, including price of services, types of providers, and utilization patterns, could also contribute to the difference in out-of-pocket health expenditure. For example, an urban health facility where urban residents tend to go for health services charges a higher price for treating the same health condition than a rural facility charges.

References

China Ministry of Health. 2008. *China Health Statistical Yearbook 2007*. China's Concord Medical University.

China National Health Economics Institute. China National Health Accounts Report. 2007.

Gottret P., and G. Schieber. 2006. *Health Financing Revisited*. Washington, DC: World Bank.

Guangdong Health Bureau. 2008. *Guangdong Health Statistical Yearbook 2007*. Huacheng Publisher.

Guangdong Provincial Center for Health Statistics and Information. 2005.

Guangdong Provincial Center for Health Statistics and Information. 2005. 2003 Guangdong Health Service Household Survey Report. Huangchen Publisher.

Guangdong Provincial Health Bureau. 2005. Third National Health Service Survey of Guangdong Province. Huacheng Publisher, June.

Guangdong Provincial Health Bureau. 2006. *Guangdong Provincial Health Statistics Yearbook 2006*. Huangchen Publisher.

Guangdong Statistics Bureau. 2007. *Guangdong Statistical Yearbook 2007*. China Statistics Press.

Guangdong Statistics Bureau. The Household Survey of Guangdong Province.

Lindelow, Magnus. Geographic Imbalance in the Health Workforce in China. Working Paper, World Bank, Washington, DC.

Wagstaff, A., M. Lindelow, S. Y. Wang, and S. Zhang. 2009. *Reforming Rural China's Health System*. Washington, DC: World Bank.

World Bank. Approaches to Reduce Health Workers Shortages In Remote Areas: A Global Review of Recruitment and Retention Policies. Working Paper, World Bank, Washington, DC.

Yazbeck, Abdo S. 2009. *Attacking Inequality in the Health Sector*. Washington, DC: World Bank.

Index

Boxes, figures, notes, and tables are denoted by *b*, *f*, *n*, and *t* following page numbers.

free compulsory education (FCE). *See* education
free-rider problems, 280
Fujian
  finance, access to, 136
  health spending in, 316, 320
  out-of-pocket payments in, 315

G

Gansu province, mutual societies in, 170
Gaozhou county
  education spending in, 228, 230
  O&M policies in, 234
gender differences
  in educational attainment, 202
  in labor markets, 109–10, 270
general transfer subsidies, 319
Germany, youth-to-adult unemployment ratio in, 272
Gini coefficients, 66, 66*b*, 67*f*, 67–68, 76*n*3, 105*b*
global warming, 184*b*
governance
  of *Dibao* system, 97–98, 100
  of RCCs, 151–52
government spending, per capita, 268–69, 269*f*, 290*t*
greenhouse gas emissions, 183
gross domestic product (GDP)
  Dibao system and, 88, 93
  educational attainment and, 200, 202*f*
  education expenditure and, 204, 205*t*, 209, 225, 227–28*f*, 230, 231–32*f*, 241
  employment and, 113, 264
  of Guangdong, 45, 46–48*f*, 47, 70, 79, 127, 173, 261–62, 289*t*, 305, 306*f*
  health expenditures and, 315
  of Pearl River Delta, 127
  property taxes and, 190*b*
  provincial per capita, 224, 224*f*
Guangdong
  Bureau of Statistics, 102*n*3, 138
  Dibao system, 79–102. *See also Dibao* system
  education, 193–260. *See also* education
  financial sector, 127–72. *See also* financial sector development
  health care, 303–42. *See also* health services

labor and employment, 103–25. *See also* labor markets
land policy, 173–92. *See also* land policy
Light Industry Secondary and Tertiary Technical School, 284
Postal Savings, 147*b*
poverty, 47–65. *See also* poverty
Provincial Committee, xviii, xix, xxiii
Provincial Government, xviii, xix
skills development, 261–301. *See also* skills development
Survey Department, 48*b*
Urban Construction Secondary and Tertiary Technical School, 284
Guangdong Statistical Yearbook, 76*n*1, 268
Guangzhou, health indicators in, 318
guaranteed minimum income (GMI), 101
Guizhou province
  health services in, 313
  physical density in, 312, 333

H

hardship allowances, 338*b*
"harmonious society," 304, 319
"hazardous financial regions," 135*b*
headcount indexes for poverty measurement, 54*b*, 54–55, 55*t*, 58, 74
Health Ministry (PRC), 327
health services, 303–42
  delivery capacity, 314, 332–40
    gap identification in, 332–33, 339
    service delivery, gaps in, 334–38, 339
    summary and recommendations for, 339–40
    supply-side inequality, policy initiatives for, 333–34, 339
  demand-side financing in, 335–36, 339
  future research needs, 340–41
  government spending on, 314–18, 316*t*, 317*f*, 320–21, 340
  health protection schemes, 314, 321–32
    inefficiency challenge, 324–27, 326*f*, 330
    inequality challenge, 322–24, 323*f*, 329–30
    Medical Assistance program, 327–29, 328*f*, 328*t*, 330–31, 331–32*b*
    recommendations for, 329–32
  inequality and regional disparities, 305–14

www.ingramcontent.com/pod-product-compliance
Lightning Source LLC
Chambersburg PA
CBHW071830270326
41929CB00013B/1946